LABOR LAW AND BUSINESS CHANGE

Recent Titles from Quorum Books

Retail Marketing Strategy: Planning, Implementation, and Control
A. Coskun Samli

Venturing Abroad: Innovation by U.S. Multinationals
Frank Clayton Schuller

Microcomputers, Corporate Planning, and Decision Support Systems
The WEFA Group, David J. Gianturco and Nariman Behravesh, editors

The Investment Side of Corporate Cash Management
Robert T. March

A Practical Approach to International Operations
Michael Gendron

Exceptional Entrepreneurial Women: Strategies for Success
Russel R. Taylor

Collective Bargaining and Impasse Resolution in the Public Sector
David A. Dilts and William J. Walsh

New Directions in MIS Management: A Guide for the 1990s
Robert J. Thierauf

The Labor Lawyer's Guide to the Rights and Responsibilities of Employee Whistleblowers
Stephen M. Kohn and Michael D. Kohn

Strategic Organization Planning: Downsizing for Survival
David C. Dougherty

Joint Venture Partner Selection: Strategies for Developed Countries
J. Michael Geringer

Sustainable Corporate Growth: A Model and Management Planning Tool
John J. Clark, Thomas C. Chiang, and Gerard T. Olson

Competitive Freedom Versus National Security Regulation
Manley Rutherford Irwin

LABOR LAW AND BUSINESS CHANGE

Theoretical and Transactional Perspectives

Edited by
SAMUEL ESTREICHER
and
DANIEL G. COLLINS

Q

QUORUM BOOKS
New York • Westport, Connecticut • London

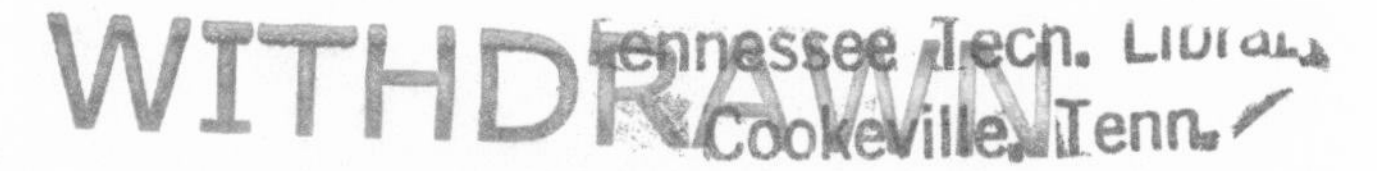

Library of Congress Cataloging-in-Publication Data

Labor law and business change : theoretical and transactional
perspectives / edited by Samuel Estreicher and Daniel G. Collins.
p. cm.
Bibliography: p.
Includes index.
ISBN 0-89930-199-1 (lib. bdg. : alk. paper)
1. Industrial management—Employee participation—Law and
legislation—United States. 2. Trade-unions—Law and legislation—
United States. 3. Labor laws and legislation—United States.
4. Industrial relations—United States. 5. Business enterprises—
United States. 6. Organizational change—United States.
I. Estreicher, Samuel. II. Collins, Daniel G.
KF3369.L28 1988
344.73'0189—dc19
[347.304189] 88-12401

British Library Cataloguing in Publication Data is available.

Library of Congress Catalog Card Number: 88-12401
ISBN: 0-89930-199-1

First published in 1988 by Quorum Books

Greenwood Press, Inc.
88 Post Road West, Westport, Connecticut 06881

Printed in the United States of America

The paper used in this book complies with the
Permanent Paper Standard issued by the National
Information Standards Organization (Z39.48-1984).

10 9 8 7 6 5 4 3 2 1

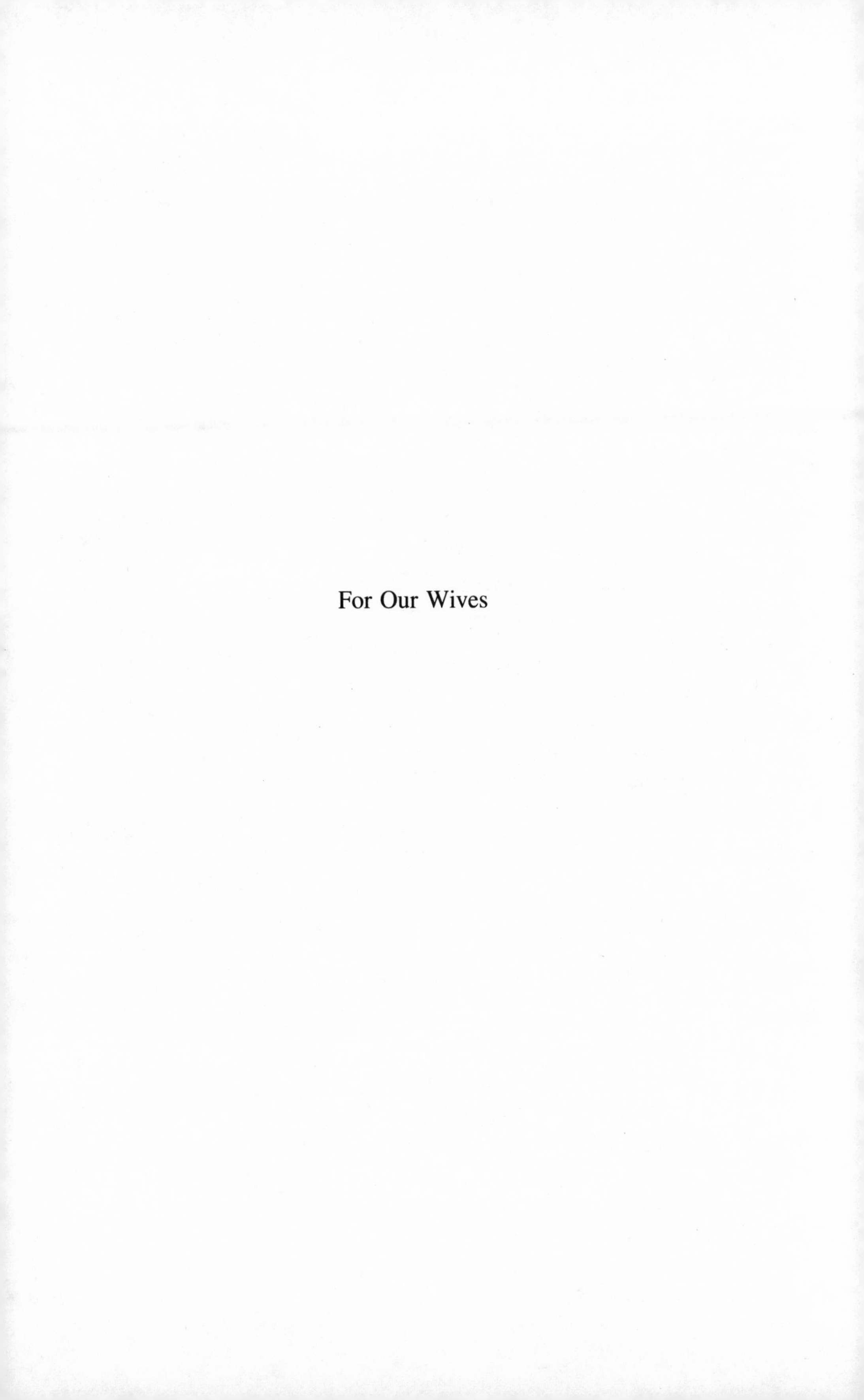

For Our Wives

CONTENTS

PREFACE

This book evolved from the 1984 ''Workshop on Labor Law and Business Change'' at New York University School in which we and many of the other chapter authors participated. That workshop was made possible by financial assistance from the Law School, for which Dean Norman Redlich and Director of Continuing Legal Education Loula Barkas were responsible.

The chapter authors acknowledge their appreciation for research and other assistance at the beginning of their chapters. In the preparation of the book as a whole, we wish to express our appreciation for research assistance to Richard Epstein, Felice Farber, Bob Haroche, Jonathan Mothner, and Eileen Shields, all J.D. graduates of New York University. We are particularly indebted to Jeanetta Ross not only for typing the manuscript but also for her patient, unstinting assistance in every aspect of the book's preparation. The book would never have materialized but for her dedication. We also wish to thank Michele Jennings for her assistance in typing the Index and Bibliography, as well as our wives and children for their forbearance.

LABOR LAW
AND
BUSINESS CHANGE

INTRODUCTION

Not too long ago, collective bargaining was a fairly stable, predictable matter of administering contracts and gearing up for periodic crises at contract renewal time. Organizing drives would often involve pitched battles, but once recognition rights were obtained, labor and management worked out a set of mutual accommodations. Organized labor, enjoying relative institutional security, would endeavor to organize all of the competitors in the product market to ensure the security of negotiated improvements. Management, having made its peace with labor, would install human resources specialists to facilitate contract administration and would absorb increased labor costs either through capital improvements or price increases. The sphere for collective bargaining was clearly defined: Labor would seek improvements in wages and working conditions, while management would pursue its entrepreneurial objectives without direct restraint from the labor contract or the collective-bargaining agent. This scenario was, after all, the goal of the National Labor Relations and Railway Labor Acts—"industrial peace" brought about by a routinization of labor conflict in place of the industrial warfare that marked much of the nineteenth and early twentieth centuries.[1]

Each day the newspaper articles suggest, however, that we are entering a new era of industrial relations in this country. Labor's representative share of American employment has steadily declined from a high of 35 percent of the nonagricultural work force in 1945 to 19 percent as of 1984 (a drop in union density in the private sector that becomes even more dramatic if labor's gains in the public sector are excluded).[2] Management opposition to unionism even in heretofore organized sectors of our economy has intensified, with the emergence of vibrant nonunion firms in previous union strongholds, such as construction, coal, and transportation,[3] and an ever-increasing willingness to "take" strikes by hiring permanent replacements and ultimately withdrawing recognition.[4] Collective bargaining is moving away from what Samuel Gompers, founding president of the American Federation of Labor, termed the governing ideology of the American working class—the insistent demand for "more," for ever-escalating wages and benefit packages.[5] "Concessionary bargaining"—scaling back negotiated improvements—is increasingly the theme at contract renewal time.[6] Management's commitment to multiemployer bargaining units—a principal means by which union scales have been insulated from competition—is on the wane. The incidence of assets sales and corporate takeovers has tended further to erode the stability of bargaining relationships. And the ability of companies to secure relief from collective-bargaining agreements through reorganization under Chapter 11 of the Bankruptcy Code has undermined the sanctity of the labor contract.

Unions have had to adjust to this new bargaining environment by tolerating arrangements such as "two-tier" wage structures,[7] and more flexible job classifications,[8] and by refashioning their objectives to embrace contractual guarantees of job security,[9] stock rights,[10] participation in management and labor representation on the board[11]—in exchange for concessions. They have also had to move away from an exclusively bilateral focus on the signatory employer to make provision for the eventuality of shifts in corporate control: by seeking to negotiate restrictions on, or attempt to enjoin, sales to firms unwilling to assume the labor contract; by meeting and attempting to reach agreement with prospective purchasers; by insisting upon the right to reopen contracts in the event of takeover bids and the right to match or top such bids[12]; and by dealing directly with hostile bidders and even, in some cases, by successfully pressing for changes in corporate management as the price for support of incumbent officers and wage concessions.[13]

These new developments derive from a number of sources. Management's willingness to take on organized labor is certainly attributable in part to the fact that the nation's presidency for over a decade has been in relatively sympathetic hands, as reflected in the administration's prompt dismissal of striking air traffic controllers and its appointments to the National Labor Relations Board. But the underlying causes seem more fundamental and enduring: deregulation of the basic transportation industries; an ever-growing internationalization of product market competition in the basic manufacturing industries; volatility in the market for corporate control with its accompanying emphasis on short-term improvements in stock prices in order to stave off corporate raiders; and a shift in employment patterns away from traditional blue-collar jobs to service, knowledge-based occupations, historically infertile terrain for unions.

Whatever the causes, what appears to be a structural revamping of labor-management relations in the United States will require changes in the body of legal rules and practical considerations that practitioners will need to master in order to represent properly their respective clients. An exclusive preoccupation with the details of the National Labor Relations and Railway Labor Acts will no longer suffice. Labor lawyers and personnel specialists not only need a working knowledge of these laws and other federal and state workplace regulations, such as the Employee Retirement Income Security Act (ERISA) and the common law of "wrongful discharge," but also need to keep abreast of corporation law and developments in other countries that may be harbingers for the United States. They also need to be able to think in transactional terms—to be masters of the interplay of legal rules and practical constraints in the context of particular transactions, whether plant closings, assets or stock sales, corporate restructuring, technological overhaul, or corporate reorganization.

This book attempts to meet the challenge posed by these changes in the practice of labor law and industrial relations by offering a comprehensive treatment of business change in the context of the federal labor laws.

Part I of this book considers in detail those aspects of the federal labor laws that are likely to be of critical importance to business change decisions: the sphere of compulsory bargaining, information sharing, successorship obligations, arbitration of business change disputes, and ERISA. In addition, a chapter is devoted to corporate law considerations, including legal restraints on the seating of union representatives on boards of directors. The opening chapter of Part I presents an overview, on the whole rather optimistic, of the role of collective bargaining in the current "era of economic restructuring." The final chapter of Part I compares the American labor law's treatment of business change with that of certain Western European countries and Japan, taking up in some detail the foreign law treatment of "worker participation" in management, an institutional approach that has begun to emerge as a key union demand in concessionary bargaining in the United States. All of the chapters in Part I have been written by law professors (or, in one instance, a former academic) who are specialists in this area and who have attempted, if not total impartiality, at least to place their subjects in a theoretical perspective.

Part II of this book offers transactional presentations by leading labor and management lawyers. In these chapters, the authors not only offer an analysis of the applicable law but also suggest practical approaches to dealing with that law in a manner that furthers the objectives of their respective clients. The transactions treated are plant closings, relocations, and transfers of unit work; sales of assets, mergers, and acquisitions; automation and technological change; employee stock option plans and pension plan financing; and Chapter 11 reorganization.

NOTES

1. For a critique from a left-wing perspective, see Stone, "The Post-War Paradigm in American Labor Law," 90 Yale L.J. 1509 (1981); Klare, "Judicial Deradicalization of the Wagner Act and the Origins of Modern Legal Consciousness, 1937–1941," 62 Minn. L. Rev. 265 (1978).

2. See T. Kochan, H. Katz & R. McKersie, The Transformation of American Industrial Relations 31 (Fig. 2.1) (1986); R. Freeman & J. Medoff, What Do Unions Do?

222 (Fig. 13–1) (1984); Adams, "Changing Employment Patterns of Organized Workers," 108 Monthly Lab. Rev. Feb. 1985, at 25–31 & Table 1.

3. See T. Kochan, H. Katz & R. McKersie, supra note 2, at 49–50.

4. See R. Freeman & J. Medoff, supra note 2, at 239–40; Estreicher, "Strikers and Replacements," 3 Lab. Lawy. 897 (1987); Weiler, "Striking a New Balance: Freedom of Contract and the Prospects for Union Representation," 98 Harv. L. Rev. 351 (1984); Weiler, "Promises to Keep: Securing Workers' Rights to Self-Organization under the NLRA," 96 Harv. L. Rev. 1769 (1983).

5. See S. Perlman, A Theory of the Labor Movement (1928); S. Gompers, Seventy Years of Life and Labor: An Autobiography 130 (N. Salvatore ed. 1984).

6. See generally Barbash, "Do We Really Want Labor on the Ropes?," Harv. Bus. Rev., July-Aug. 1985, at 10 ff.

7. Two-tier pay scales present considerable problems for unions in terms of their ability to maintain solidarity and for managements in terms of employee morale and job commitment. See Wessel, "Split Personality: Two-Tier Pay Spreads, but the Pioneer Firms Encounter Problems," Wall St. J., Oct. 14, 1985, at 1, col. 1; Brown, "American Air's Flight-Attendant Accord Will End 2–Tier Wage Carrier Pioneered," Wall St. J., Dec. 24, 1987, at 2, col. 1.

8. See, e.g., Holusha, "A New Spirit at U.S. Auto Plants," N.Y. Times, Dec. 29, 1987, at D1, col. 1.

9. See, e.g., "U.A.W. Proposed Ford Guarantee Jobs in New Pact," N.Y. Times, Sept. 9, 1987, at A16, col. 3; "A Demanding Year for Labor: In Most Industries, It Faces Fierce Fights to Win Job Security," Bus. Week, Jan. 11, 1988, at 34.

10. See Majerus, "Workers Have a Right to a Share of Profits," Harv. Bus. Rev. Sept.–Oct. 1984, at 42 ff.

11. See T. Kochan, H. Katz & R. McKersie, supra note 2, at 146–205; T. Kochan, H. Katz & N. Mower, Worker Participation and American Unions: Threat or Opportunity? (1984); McKersie, "Union Involvement in Entrepreneurial Decisions of Business," in Challenges and Choices Facing American Labor 149–66 (T. Kochan ed. 1985). For the Eastern Air experience, see "Eastern Air Union Head Is Nominated a Director," Wall St. J., Mar. 2, 1984, at 35, col. 5; "Eastern Air's Borman Badly Underestimated Obduracy of Old Foe," Wall St. J., Feb. 25, 1986, at 1, col. 1; Salpukas, "The Maneuvering at Eastern Air," N.Y. Times, Dec. 24, 1987, at D2, col. 1.

12. See Salpukas, "Labor Pact Could Foil United Bids," N.Y. Times, Nov. 24, 1987, at 1, col. 6.

13. See Salpukas, "Pan Am, in a Union Deal, Ousts 2 Top Executives," N.Y. Times, Jan. 22, 1988, at A1, col. 2; Salpukas, "Western to be Sold by Allegis, "N.Y. Times, Oct. 28, 1987, at D1, col. 6; Stevenson, "United's Pilots Pick Acquisition Chief," N.Y. Times, Aug. 14, 1987, at D1, col. 4.

PART I
THEORETICAL PERSPECTIVES

1

THE POTENTIAL OF COLLECTIVE BARGAINING IN AN ERA OF ECONOMIC RESTRUCTURING

Lewis B. Kaden

Editors' Note. Mr. Kaden regards the assumptions of the New Deal labor law structure as being sorely tested by economic change and "assaulted by both business and labor, as well as by scholars on the far left and the far right." He looks carefully at the reformist critique, which would maintain the essentially procedural nature of that law while enhancing union bargaining power, and at the rejectionist view of the critical legal studies movement. The alternative to collective bargaining, the author cautions, is governmental "standard setting." Kaden concludes, though, that our system of collective bargaining is far from moribund, but instead has demonstrated remarkable vitality in coping with deregulation in the airline industry and the new competitive forces confronting the steel, rail, and auto industries.

Fifty years after the Wagner Act,[1] the United States may be on the verge of a new era in labor-management relations. Changes in the economy are forcing a new look at the interaction between unions and employers at all levels and are compelling a sweeping review of the laws and regulations affecting industrial relations.

The future is likely to be marked by new forms of employee or union participation on the shop floor and in the corporate boardroom; by new patterns of cooperation, giving unions more of a stake in the success of the enterprise in exchange for reductions in fixed costs and increased flexibility for employers; and by a reduced reliance on unions' traditional economic weapons, including strikes. As a result of these changes in their relationship with employers, some unions have had to acquire new expertise in corporate finance, law, and international economics to cope with the new economic order.

For the most part, these dramatic changes affect employers and unions in industries with mature relationships, where the union's role has been accepted over a long period of time but competitive changes in the enterprise and in the economy have forced labor and management to alter their relationship. In other sectors, the traditional adversarial model prevails—unions seek to organize the work force, to bargain over the terms of labor contracts, and to protect their status, while employers are increasingly prepared to use aggressive antiunion tactics against them. Here, legal reforms are needed to maintain a balance in the relationship and protect the values that have framed labor-management relations since 1937.

The structure of American labor relations now faces more thoroughgoing criticism than at any other time in the past half century. The assumptions and values which shape the system have been assaulted by both business and labor, as well as by scholars on both the far left and the far right. The labor movement itself often seems hesitant, unsure of its own role and defensive about its declining membership and the low repute in which unions as institutions are held (according to surveys of public opinion). In this climate, managers are emboldened to make full use of antiunion tactics, either to defeat union organizing efforts or to fight back against strikes.

Without doubt, the forces of economic change are sufficient to test any institutional process. The manufacturing sector in the United States, long the source of our economic strength, may account for the same 20 percent of gross product at the end of the century as it does today,[2] but these goods will be produced with five million fewer workers. From 1981 to 1986, 10.8 million workers were displaced as a result of plant closings, business failures, automation, and other restructuring.[3]

In the private economy, the labor movement has not had much success in organizing the rapidly expanding service sectors.[4] Although the work force in services includes many women and minorities, groups naturally inclined to support unions, the pace of organizing them continues to lag. Overall, the pressures of international competition, technological change, and new demands for worker participation add to the strains on the established order of industrial relations.

It is time for a fresh examination of the assumptions underlying the labor law, the extent to which its promise has been matched by experience, the validity of its principles today, and the capacity of the legal process to respond to the challenges of the future.

THE WAGNER ACT: VALUES AND PREMISES

Both the premises and the values incorporated in the Wagner Act are evident from the findings set forth in Section 1:

The denial by employers of the right of employees to organize and the refusal by employers to accept the procedure of collective bargaining lead to strikes and other forms of industrial strife or unrest. . . . [T]he inequality of bargaining power between employees who do not possess full freedom of association or actual liberty of contract and employers . . . substantially burdens . . . commerce and tends to aggravate recurrent business depressions, by depressing wage rates and the purchasing power of wage earners in industry and by preventing the stabilization of competitive wage rates and working conditions within and between industries.[5]

Although these words were undoubtedly chosen with an eye to the certain constitutional challenge the draftsmen foresaw, they betray with remarkable clarity the values as well as the solutions established by the new legal order in 1935:

1. The primacy of industrial peace and, more specifically, the idea that the industrial stability necessary for sustained economic growth requires public regulation of the decision-making process between labor and management.[6]

2. The principle that the marketplace is an inadequate determinant of the wage bargain, since individual employees lack the power to deal effectively with their employers. Thus, government needs to create, nurture, and protect a countervailing force more nearly to achieve equality in bargaining power.[7] A corollary of this premise was the belief that government intervention to reduce inequality would have a positive economic effect in two specific ways: By increasing wages (the share of income going to labor), the law would help increase purchasing power or demand; and by standardizing wage rates and working conditions, it would shift economic competition to other factors.[8]

3. The principle that the solution to these two threats to the economic order—unequal bargaining power and industrial strife—should be found not in public determination of the substantive terms of employment, but rather through public intervention to ensure freedom of association and a collective rather than individual liberty of contract.[9] By assuring the procedural right to organize and bargain collectively, Congress intended to achieve the substantive goal of increasing labor's share. The determinant of collective liberty of contract was the principle of majority rule. Unlike the European practice, in which several unions each represent their supporters,[10] in the United States the majority representative was granted the sole and exclusive right to deal with the employer concerning the terms and conditions of employment.[11] In this peculiarly American solution to the dilemma of how to correct unequal bargaining power without succumbing to governmental wage determination lay the seeds of continuing tension, which have been reflected in over fifty years of judicial and administrative experience of applying the Wagner Act.

The idea of increasing purchasing power by redressing unequal bargaining power is hardly nonsubstantive. But that substantive—indeed, radical—objective was to be realized entirely by procedural means. The Wagner Act was not neutral on the value of organization and bargaining. Its theory was that enforcement of these procedural guarantees would, in turn, generate enough countervailing force to change the market-based outcome of the bargains struck between employees and their employers. At the same time, the legislators' traditional regard for economic liberty of contract and the protection of private property impelled them to stop there, and to leave the collective forces of capital and labor "free" to make their own bargain.

Of course, as unions, managers, and judges immediately perceived, substantive outcomes were inevitably influenced by procedural rules. The National Labor Relations Board (NLRB or Board) and the courts were soon wrestling with a range of disputes under the new law whose resolution would necessarily affect the balance of power. Was a sit-down or other partial strike protected?[12] Could an employer continue operations during a strike by assigning supervisors to do the work of strikers?[13] Could he hire replacements?[14] If so, could he assure these replacements the opportunity for continued employment after the strike was over?[15] What rights did an employer have to campaign against a union during a representational election?[16] What limits should apply to an employer's ability to implement changes in benefits or conditions while he was bargaining over a new contract?[17] Conversely, what limits should there be on a union's capacity to use its economic leverage during the bargaining period?[18] Should either party be limited in the subjects pressed across the bargaining table?[19] To what extent is the "good faith" of a negotiator to be judged by an objective appraisal of the positions taken in bargaining?[20]

The new statute did not clearly answer these questions, or many others of similar import. Nor did the purposes or values of the legal system established by the Wagner Act, the original enactment of the NLRA, provide certain guidance. Instead, the Act created conflicts between competing goals which the Board and the courts were obliged to sort out, and the resolution of these tensions materially affected the results reached in collective bargaining.

Among the crucial and distinctive features of the labor law, one emerged as much by judicial innovation as by congressional intention—the development of grievance arbitration as a virtually universal method for interpreting and applying the terms of a collective-bargaining agreement during its term, and the availability of judicial power to compel resort to this system of private enforcement.

Although the labor movement opposed Section 301 of the Taft-Hartley Act,[21] which provided federal jurisdiction to enforce labor contracts, the unions came to see benefits in this access to the judicial process for compelling employers to follow the contractual machinery for grievance determination. In 1960, in three cases involving the United Steelworkers,[22] the Supreme Court gave a wholesale, unqualified endorsement of the virtues of grievance arbitration, its broad jurisdiction, and the narrow scope for subsequent judicial review. The extension of these principles to permit specific enforcement of the union's promise not to strike over an arbitrable grievance—a narrow exception to the legislative prohibition against labor injunctions to stop strikers[23]—completed the blend of private ordering and the legal process intended to promote economic stability. Bargaining between management and labor was expected to be a continuous process, but it was to be carried on in different forms at different times. The framework envisioned periodic battles over basic benefits and conditions, with the pressure for decisions driven by the potential of a strike or lockout and, in the interim, the availability of impartial arbitration, a system of private judges to apply the contractual provisions and resolve the tensions and ambiguities which naturally arise in industrial life.

The framers of this system of industrial relations were motivated by the perceived economic effects—growth and stability—of taking wage determination out of the marketplace. After fifty years, there remains little doubt that unionism does increase wages for both organized and unorganized workers. The monopoly wage effect is real.[24] But Senator Wagner probably underestimated the extent to which his work would change the way in which rules were established in the workplace and alter the nature and extent of workers' participation in the process of making those rules. The statute did not introduce rules to the industrial relationship. Every organization has to have rules governing its internal affairs, and corporations had rules long before there were unions. But the law changed the method by which these policies were designed and adopted. It substituted joint determination by managers and workers, acting through their majority representative, for the employer's unilateral control over the decisions. And it established in the grievance procedures a private system for adjudicating compliance with the rules. This form of worker participation became an important and independent objective of the system.

To be sure, the law did not purport to create a worker democracy. Workers participate in selecting their representatives, and the law, at least since 1959, safeguards up to a point their right to democratic procedures in the internal governance of the labor organization.[25] But the statute also circumscribes the subject matter for joint rule making, and court decisions on the scope of bargaining have made the distinction important. Workers' representatives may participate by right only in the design of rules governing mandatory conditions, and they do this through a kind of stylized combat.[26] Indeed, the adversarial metaphor of battle and warfare is a significant feature of our system of industrial relations. An important question in the current debate over the labor law is whether this "regulated conflict" between countervailing forces over a circumscribed territory meets the demands of a modern economy in which markets are global, international competition is intense, automation is changing the content of work as well as the number of jobs, and flexible production and continuous change in requisite skills are the watchwords of the day.

CRITICS AND COMMENTATORS

Until recently, commentary on the system of labor law and industrial relations was dominated by scholars who shared a commitment to the pluralistic values underlying the process they helped to shape. Archibald Cox, John Dunlop, David Feller,[27] and others had participated in the development of the labor law, and their writings influenced the court's effort to fill the statutory gaps, suggesting how to resolve the conflicts raised in the cases in a manner that wove disparate threads into a whole cloth. As often as not their arguments nudged the courts, including the United States Supreme Court, in directions supporting the principles of pluralism—the idea that economic growth required industrial stability as well as fair treatment for employees, and that these values would best be served by promoting union organization, supporting a vigorous exercise of collective bargaining, having the courts rigorously enforce the employer's promise to use contractual grievance procedures, and otherwise limiting the judicial influence over labor relations. In a series of important decisions, the Supreme Court protected union organizational activities against employers' claims to control their property[28]; broadened the scope of bargaining[29]; created not only jurisdiction over suits on collective agreements but also new uniform federal rules of decision comprising a national common law of labor relations[30]; and enshrined the breadth and security of grievance arbitration.[31]

The industrial pluralists argued that for the individual worker, the "system of law" in the workplace was worth the price of admission, including the dues paid to his union, the risk of lost income (or even a lost job) if the union called a strike, and the obligation to be bound by the majority's view of the workers' goals and ambitions. For management, there was the advantage of stability during the terms of a contract, the limits imposed on employee aspirations, and the opportunity to ensure compliance with management's objectives throughout the organization.

Pluralist ideology not only dominated labor law scholarship, but also influenced debates over reform of the laws when the balance of countervailing power seemed in jeopardy. Thus, Taft-Hartley introduced regulation of unfair practices by unions, including limitations on secondary boycotts,[32] and Landrum-Griffin regulated internal union procedures in order to promote democratic process and to curb corruption among union officials.[33] More recently, reform proposals have emphasized corrections to protect union organizing campaigns against the tactics of aggressive employers willing to stop unionism by firing union supporters or, if a union gains representative status, refusing to compromise or agree on the terms of a labor contract.[34]

Professor Paul Weiler, among others, has argued that the Board's slow process and inadequate remedial power have left workers unprotected against the anti-union employer.[35] He attributes the dramatic decline in union membership in substantial part to the tactics adopted by management during union election campaigns and to the ineffectiveness of the Board and the courts in controlling coercive management practices.[36] Rejecting the more modest reforms proposed by others, including accelerated regulatory proceedings or stiffer penalties,[37] Weiler argues instead for wholesale elimination of protracted union election campaigns in favor of instant elections, modeled after the Canadian experience, to curb the effect of discriminatory discharges on the union's electoral success.[38]

Professor Weiler would also amend the labor law to permit a union to proceed to bargaining without certification once a majority of the workers in the bargaining unit has indicated support for the union by signing authorization cards.[39] Even when the union successfully gains recognition or certification as a bargaining agent, experience indicates that the fledging union representative has a difficult time achieving an initial collective-bargaining agreement.[40] Professor Weiler criticizes many of the rules and decisions which reflect the weight attached to employers' interest in freedom of contract. In his view, in an effort to protect this property interest, the courts and the Board have made it too difficult for a union to bargain with the recalcitrant employer.[41] Weiler would, therefore, qualify the rule allowing an employer to replace strikers[42] and relax the prohibition against secondary pressure.[43] In addition, when an employer has refused to bargain in good faith, he would in some circumstances provide recourse to compulsory arbitration of open issues, with the arbitrator authorized to decide the terms of the initial labor agreement.[44]

Industrial pluralists, including reformers like Weiler, continue to argue that the institution of collective bargaining is worthy of support because it is the only practical alternative to governmental direction of the terms and conditions of employment. In the last few years, however, a group of scholars linked to the critical legal studies movement has launched a sweeping attack on the fundamental structure of the labor laws, addressed both to the basic statutory scheme and to the way in which the courts have interpreted it. The precept of critical legal studies is the notion that legal doctrine must have normative drive—that neutrality is a sham and that rules and decisions necessarily serve ideological goals. These writers see the labor laws as obstacles blocking workers from greater political and economic power, and from the enhancement of working life in terms of both material rewards and participation in directing the enterprise.

Professor Roberto Unger, an intellectual leader of the critical legal studies movement, views "the paradox of procedural justice"[45] as the crucial problem with labor law doctrine. The bargaining process works only if the parties are truly committed to it; if the government's role in enforcing the duty to bargain in good faith is limited to "a show of compliance . . . , the duty loses its force."[46] But if the government is more ambitious and tries to test the fairness of proposals, it is drawn into "something perilously close to the substantive regulation of labor conditions that the whole mechanism of countervailing power is designed to avoid."[47] And this route is closed by Congress' rejection in Section 8(d) of the Taft-Hartley Act of the Board's authority to specify the content of bargaining positions.[48]

A related problem is the conflict between managerial discretion to direct the enterprise and the workers' interest in a continuing process of joint determination. Unger focuses on the longstanding controversy concerning retained rights—whether the collective-bargaining agreement incorporates limited concessions to jointly determined rules, or whether there exists a continuing duty during the contract term to negotiate or arbitrate matters not set forth in the written agreement.[49] Unger concludes that these tensions between the goals of countervailing power and freedom of contract doom the system of collective bargaining and justify more radical political action.[50]

Others develop similar arguments. Katherine Stone finds the structure built by the industrial pluralists, including the promise of jointly determined rules developed through collective bargaining and neutral adjudication of disputes by impartial arbitrators, a system designed to place the stamp of democratic legitimacy—the ''illusion of [worker] consent''—on the continued exercise of employer domination over the workplace.[51] According to Professor Stone, as a result of collective bargaining, the employee is asked to share the blame for unpleasant decisions, such as automation and other techniques of job displacement, and the illusory form of democracy created by the labor law involves consent by the workers to their own subjugation.[52] Stone thus offers a thoroughgoing objection to the very features of the process of industrial relations applauded by the pluralists—the substitution of arbitration for strikes over midterm disputes, the virtual elimination of wildcat walkouts, and the principle of exclusive recognition.[53] Regarding the Wagner Act as an effort by those in power to ''channel employee discontent,''[54] Professor Stone, like Professor Unger, finds the core problem to reside in the ultimate conflict between private property and political democracy.[55] If more equal distribution of the benefits of society is desirable, ''either to improve wages, hours and working conditions or to affirm workers' dignity,''[56] the legal system must be changed to alter private ownership or, at the least, to subject resolution of issues involving labor conditions to the political process. Stone would thus have the government—presumably the Congress rather than the courts—more directly involved in the determination of wages, benefits, and worker protections.[57]

Although he directs his fire more toward the courts for abandoning what he sees as the radical improvements for workers intended by Congress in the Wagner Act, Professor Karl Klare's conclusions are similar to those reached by Unger and Stone.[58] In his view, the labor law system created over the past half century has ''served as a vehicle for the preservation of capitalism and the alienated social relationships that constitute it.''[59] Indeed, Professor Klare sees the decisions strengthening the institutional interests of unions as ultimately harming the interests of individual employees, ''particularly in an industrial world in which it is debatable whether the institutional interests of labor unions are entirely congruent with the needs and interests of working people.''[60] He believes that the courts have emasculated the statutory potential for a regime of worker co-ownership with capital. Decisions giving employers the right to hire permanent strike replacements, barring sit-down strikes, denying the right to press non-mandatory subjects to impasse, and transforming grievance arbitration into a system for maintaining the enterprise, including the availability of antistrike injunctions, have, in Klare's view, cut the heart out of the Wagner Act's revolutionary promise.[61]

Conservatives like Professor Charles Fried,[62] currently the Solicitor General of the United States, and Professor Richard Epstein[63] have also mounted a sweeping criticism of the institution of collective bargaining as established over the past fifty years. Fried and Epstein start with the values established by the Congress in the Wagner Act and, in particular, stress that the statute is not neutral, but rather promotes unionism by requiring employers to deal exclusively with the majority representative and by prohibiting employers from lending support to labor organizations. Epstein questions the efficiency of this interference with the market,[64] and Fried poses doubts about the continuing viability of the adversarial framework.[65] He sees in statutory protections of minimum standards—the Fair Labor Standards Act (FLSA), the Occupational Safety and Health Act (OSHA), and ERISA—and in the prohibitions against discrimination a recognition of the rights of individual workers separate and apart from their interest in union organization or collective bargaining.[66] As the law goes beyond assurances of minimum income, safe working conditions, and freedom from discrimination to impose limits on employers' ability to dismiss workers, Fried wonders if the collective relationship has continuing significance, or if it serves only to impose a needless rigidity on the relationship between managers and individual workers.[67] He notes that narrow job classifications, uniform treatment of employees within classifications, and statutory restrictions in Section 8(a) (2) on employer support for methods of participation or cooperation established outside the collective-bargaining relationship all serve to limit the capacity of workers and employers alike to adapt the workplace to a fast-changing economy.[68] Fried argues further that whatever the justification for giving unions monopoly control over the work force to increase wage rates in the 1930s, today's global marketplace demands more flexible responses to competition. With technology forcing a breakdown in the sharp distinctions between managers and workers, Fried challenges the contemporary relevance of the goals and values underlying the system of industrial relations created by the Wagner Act.[69]

RESTRUCTURING THE AMERICAN ECONOMY: THE NEW CHALLENGES FOR COLLECTIVE BARGAINING

During the last ten years, a series of court decisions and regulatory orders have restricted the scope of collective bargaining over decisions involving corporate restructuring, including decisions to close plants, shut down part of a business, relocate production, or subcontract work.[70] When these orders were issued, most employers praised the recognition of managerial prerogatives and property rights, and they hailed the decisions as a necessary curb on union power.

In the same period, employers have aggressively resisted union organizational efforts, taking advantage of the slow process and limited remedies available under the law—the same features Professor Weiler has linked to the decline in union membership. President Ford vetoed legislative reforms of labor law in 1976, and management resistance blocked reform legislation proposed by President Carter the following year.[71]

Many employers cheered these judicial and legislative developments, but their rejoicing may have been premature. The only practical alternative to a vigorous collective-bargaining process as the means of ordering industrial relations is increased standard setting by government. Both the labor movement and individual employees have responded to the restrictions imposed on organization and collective bargaining under federal law by pressing for broader protections in state courts and legislatures.

For the unorganized workers, this effort initially produced judicial limitations on an employer's ability to dismiss at-will employees. More than half the states have circumscribed the traditional doctrine of employment-at-will, introducing limits on the ability to discharge an employee who protests employer misconduct and in some cases even implying contractual limits on discharge except for cause.[72] Substantial litigation costs and large damage recoveries have marked these developments in employment law. More recently, judicial expansion of employee rights has prompted legislative action in the states. On July 1, 1987, Montana became the first state to protect all nonunion employees against discharge except for good cause, a protection commonly afforded unionized workers through the grievance procedures in a labor contract.[73] Grievance arbitration is generally faster and cheaper and offers more limited remedies against unjust dismissals than litigation. Nonunion employers are discovering that the judicial process can be far more time-consuming and expensive, with juries often granting large damage awards to employees whom they perceive to be victims of unfair treatment.[74] In fact, Montana employers ultimately supported statutory restrictions on their right to dismiss in exchange for limits on damages and incentives for employees to use binding arbitration.[75]

In the organized sector of the economy, the labor movement turned away in the early 1980s from an unsympathetic Labor Board, federal judiciary, and Congress to the more promising forum provided in state capitals. From 1981 to 1985, fourteen states adopted right-to-know laws requiring employers to inform workers about exposure to hazardous chemicals, after a federal analogue to this proposal had been blocked by the White House.[76] Twenty-two states have given workers statutory protection against lie detector tests,[77] and, in 1987 alone, six states have enacted restrictions on mandatory drug testing.[78] The Maine legislature enacted a statute requiring advance notice and minimum severance payments to workers who lose their jobs as a result of a plant closing.[79] The Supreme Court recently rejected an argument that the Maine statute was preempted by federal labor law.[80] Other states have raised the minimum wage above the federal level, and there is active consideration in several state legislatures of bills requiring minimum health insurance for all employees.

After the Democrats regained control of the Senate in 1986, Congress has been more receptive to labor's legislative agenda, giving serious consideration to federal laws raising the minimum wage, providing advance notice of plant closings, protecting health benefits for retirees against the effects of bankruptcy, and legislating minimum health insurance for all workers.[81] These legislative proposals all reflect an inclination to regulate the substantive terms of employment—a development which goes well beyond the antidiscrimination principles or the minimum wage and hour, safety, and retirement standards which characterized the substantive aspects of labor and employment law before 1980. Most of these recent proposals have been opposed by the Reagan administration and are still pending in Congress. But employers are now directing their criticism at the "hidden tax" imposed by these new employment laws, and some may be taking a fresh look at the potential of collective bargaining as an alternative to government substantive regulation.[82]

At the same time, dramatic changes in the economy are imposing new pressures on the collective-bargaining process. Corporate restructuring, mergers, bankruptcies, automation, deregulation, and foreign competition all present new, unfamiliar challenges to participants in collective bargaining. Notwithstanding the legal limits on bargaining obligations and the assessment of some critics that the labor movement has become an obstacle to economic change, the capacity of collective bargaining to meet the new economic demands has been striking. Some examples:

1. Deregulation of airline fares and routes has brought dramatic new forms of competition to the airline industry. Although there has been conflict between unions and employers, and some notable failures, many carriers have been able to reduce labor costs by 20 to 30 percent. The new contracts lower wages, increase hours of work, and revise work rules, generally in exchange for significant profit sharing, stock ownership, and new forms of participative management, including seats on the board of directors and special committees to share information.[83]

At Eastern, Western, and Frontier, these concession bargains were not sufficient ultimately to prevent a sale of the company to another airline.[84] At TWA, pioneering agreements with the pilots and machinists enabled Carl Icahn to defeat Texas Air and take control of the company. The Icahn agreements—an unusual combination of labor and commercial contracts—demonstrated the new framework for bargaining, covering not only wages and work rules but also stock plans, investment and capital spending requirements, business strategy, restrictions on Icahn's ability to dispose of TWA assets, and extensive information sharing.[85] At Pan Am, four of the five labor organizations have joined in a union coalition and are actively soliciting outside investors and potential acquirors.[86] United's pilots have actually mounted a buy-out bid of their own.[87] Their bid is still pending, but, together with pressure from a large shareholder who initiated a proxy contest, the pilots' effort prompted the Allegis board to change management and alter the company's long-term strategy by selling hotel and car rental companies only recently acquired.[88]

2. The Railroad Brotherhoods—until recently the model of traditional unionists holding on to work rules and benefit standards designed long ago—made sizable concessions in pay and benefits in exchange for stock ownership in Conrail[89] and played a crucial role in the government's program to return the railroad to

private ownership. The rail unions also agreed to concessions which enabled state government agencies to take over responsibility for commuter lines previously operated by the bankrupt Penn Central and later by Conrail. At the present time, the Railroad Brotherhoods are one of the bidders for the Southern Pacific, which must be separated from the Santa Fe as a result of a regulatory order disapproving the merger of these two lines.[90]

3. The United Steelworkers (USWA) has worked through a painful decade when United States steel production has been shrinking steadily, the number of steelworkers has been reduced from 380,000 to 168,000, and the industry has sustained losses exceeding $12 billion. In 1986, the industry also shifted from industry-wide bargaining to separate negotiations with each major producer, and two large companies, Wheeling-Pittsburgh and LTV, filed for reorganization under the bankruptcy law.[91] At the same time, repeated efforts by labor and management to involve the government in efforts to restore competitiveness to domestic steel producers have been unavailing.[92]

These dramatic changes in the steel industry have strained to the limit the capacities of the union and employers alike. Wages have not increased, even in nominal terms, since 1978; the shrinking base of production and employment has left some companies with pension plans supporting three or four retirees on the production of one active steelworker; and underfunded pension plans and retiree health programs add up to billions of dollars of liabilities, blocking the competitiveness of companies and contributing to the bankruptcies of LTV and Wheeling-Pittsburgh as well as several smaller companies.[93] (In the economy as a whole, accounting for future retiree health liability, as the Financial Accounting Standards Board has proposed, would have reduced the earnings of the Fortune 500 by from 30 to 60 percent in 1986.)[94] The steel industry accounts for 80 percent of the pension liabilities assumed by the Pension Benefit Guaranty Corporation (PBGC), the governmental retirement insurance program established by Congress in 1974.[95] Excess capacity worldwide threatens to exact more painful downsizing in domestic steel production. Foreign steel makers have reduced capacity as well, but their adjustment is eased by huge government subsidies.

Although these pressures are intense, and strikes stopped steel production at both USX and Wheeling-Pittsburgh, the bargaining process has met the challenge of these harsh circumstances. Wages and work rules have been restructured, contributing substantially to the recent though modest revival of steel profits. Negotiated benefits have eased the adjustment of workers and communities to plant closings, bankruptcies, and buy-outs. Profit-sharing and stock ownership plans have given the remaining workers a greater stake in the future and have contributed to productivity gains—the first distributions of profits to steelworkers, based on 1987 performance, are expected early in 1988.[96] Numerous experiments in cooperation and participation are under way between the USWA and the steel producers. For example, at the LTV-Sumituomo electrogalvanizing plant in Cleveland, a special agreement has eliminated work classifications and introduced top-to-bottom participation by all employees in designing and implementing business plans. In 1987, LTV and the Steelworkers agreed to joint efforts to extend this model to other facilities—local union and management committees volunteered to have their units take part in this program. At several companies, top-level labor-management review committees bring union leaders together with senior managers to discuss strategic decisions affecting the business.

4. The United Autoworkers (UAW) and the major auto manufacturers have concentrated their bargaining on new forms of employment (rather than job) security, and developing training programs to adjust skills to the changing production techniques in the industry.[97] At the same time, fixed wage gains have been modest, with more compensation shifting to performance-based formulas.[98] The UAW negotiated special rules for the General Motors–Toyota joint venture in Fremont, California, eliminating many job classifications to increase flexibility and enhance participation by the workers in a team approach to production.[99] Chrysler symbolically emphasized its partnership with the UAW when it added Douglas Fraser to the board of directors as part of the rescue program which included government bond guarantees as well as labor concessions.[100]

These experiments in new patterns of bargaining and new forms of cooperation between management and labor are tentative and fragile. It is much too early to judge them. Each success or hopeful development can be matched with an example of an aggressive employer harassing union organizers, discharging labor supporters, or blocking a collective-bargaining agreement by refusing to engage in meaningful negotiations. Each can be matched as well by an example of a trade union's refusing to depart from outdated, rigid rules and classifications that inhibit competitiveness.

Notwithstanding this reality, the evidence is growing that the institution of collective bargaining is far from moribund as its critics have charged. Rather, it is alive and well, demonstrating that when it is exercised by skilled hands, the bargaining process has the capacity to devise innovative solutions to difficult problems and to adapt the relationship between capital and labor to the complex demands of a new economic order. Some of the features of this emerging landscape include:

An emphasis on cooperation rather than conflict and a reduction in the number and duration of strikes.

A substitution of performance-based compensation for fixed costs, with the performance of the enterprise the key measurement. Profit- or gain-sharing and stock ownership plans are the established means to reward management when the enterprise performs well, and they are becoming more common for rank-and-file workers. The unions' historic concern about arbitrary exercise of management's power, and the political difficulty caused by variations in compensation among workers doing similar jobs, make labor reluctant to embrace incentives based on individual rather than firm or unit performance.

An increasing willingness to relax rigid rules or classifications in order to facilitate flexible production techniques and accommodate automation and new technology, in exchange for negotiated procedures for employee involvement in the production decisions and negotiated programs to enhance employment security.

A recognition of the modern need for smarter, better educated workers whose skills are constantly changing to match the demands of new technology.

A broad appreciation that labor and management need to cooperate not only in structuring their own relationship but also in the effort to enlist government participation in the development of strategies to increase competitiveness, coupled with a recognition that when government does assume its appropriate role, it is likely to insist on better management, more capital investment, and more productive labor, each of which is necessary to the success of an enterprise in the global marketplace. Government's proper role is to ease the adjustment of individuals and communities to a changing economy, in part through training and placement programs, and to ensure open markets and a level playing field for U.S. firms and foreign competitors.

In identifying these features, I do not intend to suggest that the model of labor-management cooperation is a substitute for the adversary relationship which underlies the labor laws and established practice in the United States. In fact, the adversary nature of bargaining remains the source of its creative force and its capacity to solve complex problems. Real partnerships among management, labor, and government are necessary to promote economic growth and competitiveness. But these partnerships also mean real conflicts. The secret is not to find ways to paper over adversarial interests, but to develop the means, the skills, and the techniques to resolve them effectively. Robert Kuttner has repeatedly and aptly reminded us that the goal is not to increase competitiveness by driving down standards of living or to increase production by imposing austerity and sacrifice on workers of modest means.[101] Rather, the path to American economic success has to be the development of a system in which our products become competitive while we maintain the highest standard of living in the world. There are surely times when wage and benefit concessions are necessary to restore the competitive balance, but the objective ought to be higher wages, higher profits, and sustained economic growth. The fact that real wages for manufacturing workers have not changed since 1972 ought not to be a source of satisfaction. Instead, the goal of public policy, as well as labor's and management's interest, ought to be to build more world-class market success stories while keeping our promise of a job, personal dignity, and a decent standard of living for every American.

In labor-management relationships that are still developing, economic conflict—including the possibility of strikes—remains the lever by which labor can realize the promise inherent in the law to ensure fair standards of benefits and conditions, and to replace arbitrary action with fair procedures. To keep these promises requires attention to the law reform agenda, ensuring that organization of workers and bargaining opportunities cannot be thwarted by an employer because the legal process is too slow to react or the penalty is too slight to deter unlawful conduct. Professor Weiler has provided a useful guide to the debate which should now take place over the specific reforms needed to restore balance to the process.

The distinctive contribution of American labor law and industrial experience is that there need not be a choice between adversarial relationships on one hand and cooperation or partnership on the other. When practiced by experts, collective bargaining retains the potential envisioned by its framers. It offers the best means to promote economic growth in a complex industrial society while ensuring fair treatment for workers and avoiding governmental control over the terms and conditions of employment. That objective remains the best accommodation of the employer's interest in private property, the workers' justifiable demand for economic fairness and participation, and the nation's interest in growth and stability.

NOTES

1. National Labor Relations Act of 1935, ch. 372, 49 Stat. 449, codified as amended at 29 U.S.C. §§ 151–169 (1982 & Supp. III 1985).
2. See U.S. Dept. of Commerce, Statistical Abstract of the United States 723 (1987) (figure as of 1985).
3. See Novack, "Hidden Taxes," Forbes, Sept. 21, 1987, at 37.
4. See R. Marshall, Unheard Voices: Labor and Economic Policy in a Competitive World, 136 (1987).
5. 29 U.S.C. § 151 (1982).
6. See id.
7. See American Ship Bldg. Co. v. NLRB, 380 U.S. 300, 316–17 (1965).
8. See 29 U.S.C. § 151.
9. See H.K. Porter Co. v. NLRB, 397 U.S. 99, 103 (1970).
10. See Bok, "Reflections on the Distinctive Character of American Labor Law," 84 Harv. L. Rev. 1394, 1397 (1971).
11. See 29 U.S.C. § 159(a).
12. See NLRB v. Fansteel Metallurgical Corp., 306 U.S. 240 (1939).
13. Cf. American Broadcasting Companies, Inc. v. Writers Guild of America, West, 437 U.S. 411 (1978); Florida Power & Light Co. v. IBEW Local 641, 417 U.S. 790 (1974).
14. See NLRB v. Mackay Radio & Tel. Co., 304 U.S. 333 (1938).
15. See id.
16. See id.
17. See NLRB v. Crompton-Highland Mills, Inc., 337 U.S. 217 (1949) (upholding NLRB decision that the employer's improvement of wages and benefits during negotiations with the union, without having previously proposed such improvement to the union, was an unfair labor practice).
18. See NLRB v. Insurance Agents' Int'l Union, 361 U.S. 477 (1960).
19. See NLRB v. Wooster Div. of Borg-Warner Corp., 356 U.S. 342, 349 (1958) (permissive subjects may not be insisted upon to impasse).
20. See White v. NLRB, 255 F.2d 564 (5th Cir. 1958) (disapproving Board decision to judge "good faith" by terms of bargaining proposal).
21. Labor Management Relations Act of 1947, ch. 120, 61 Stat. 136, codified as amended at 29 U.S.C. §§ 141–197 (1982 & Supp. III 1985).
22. United Steelworkers of America v. Enterprise Wheel & Car Corp., 363 U.S.

593 (1960); United Steelworkers of America v. Warrior & Gulf Navigation Co., 363 U.S. 574 (1960); United Steelworkers of America v. American Mfg. Co., 363 U.S. 564 (1960).

23. See 29 U.S.C. § 104 (1982).

24. See Klare, ''Judicial Deradicalization of the Wagner Act and the Origins of Modern Legal Consciousness, 1937–1941,'' 62 Minn. L. Rev. 265, 267 (1978).

25. Labor-Management Reporting and Disclosure Act of 1959, tit. I, § 101, Pub. L. 86–257, 73 Stat. 522 [codified at 29 U.S.C. § 411 (1982)].

26. See *Borg-Warner Corp.*, 356 U.S. at 349.

27. See, e.g., J. Dunlop, Dispute Resolution: Negotiation and Consensus Building (1984); D. Bok & J. Dunlop, Labor and the American Community (1970); Cox, ''Rights under a Labor Agreement,'' 69 Harv. L. Rev. 601 (1956); Feller, ''A General Theory of the Collective Bargaining Agreement,'' 61 Calif. L. Rev. 663 (1973).

28. See Republic Aviation Corp. v. NLRB, 324 U.S. 793 (1945).

29. See *Borg-Warner Corp.*, 356 U.S. at 342.

30. See Textile Workers Union of America v. Lincoln Mills, 353 U.S. 448 (1957).

31. See cases cited in note 22 supra.

32. See 29 U.S.C. § 158.

33. See generally 29 U.S.C. §§ 401–531.

34. See, e.g., Comment, ''Union Busters and Front Line Supervisors: Restricting and Regulating the Use of Supervisory Employees by Management Consultants during Union Representation Campaigns,'' 135 U. Pa. L. Rev. 453, 465 n.65, 492–93 (1987) (need to control firing of union organizers); Weiler, ''Striking a New Balance: Freedom of Contract and the Prospects for Union Representation,'' 98 Harv. L. Rev. 351 (1984).

35. Weiler, ''Promises to Keep: Securing Workers' Rights to Self-Organization under the NLRA,'' 96 Harv. L. Rev. 1769 (1983).

36. See id. at 1769, 1773–74.

37. See id. at 1798, 1790–91.

38. See id. at 1804–22.

39. See id. at 1805.

40. See id. at 1805.

41. See Weiler, supra note 34, at 357–63.

42. See id. at 420 n.220.

43. See id.

44. See id.

45. Unger, ''The Critical Legal Studies Movement,'' 96 Harv. L. Rev. 563, 630 (1983).

46. Id.

47. Id.

48. Id. at 631.

49. Id.

50. Id. at 631–32.

51. Stone, ''The Post-War Paradigm in American Labor Law,'' 90 Yale L.J. 1509, 1566 (1981).

52. Id. at 1575.

53. Id. at 1575–76.

54. Id. at 1577.

55. Id. at 1579–80.

56. Id. at 1580.

57. Id.

58. Klare, supra note 24.

59. Id. at 339.

60. Id. at 336.

61. Id. at 293–336.

62. See Fried, ''Individual and Collective Rights in Work Relations: Reflections on the Current State of Labor Law and Its Prospects,'' 51 U. Chi. L. Rev. 1012, 1023–24 (1984).

63. See Epstein, ''A Common Law for Labor Relations: A Critique of the New Deal Labor Legislation,'' 92 Yale L.J. 1357, 1396–97 (1983).

64. See id. at 1396–98.

65. Fried, supra note 62, at 1037–39.

66. Id. at 1028.

67. See id. at 1037–39.

68. See id.

69. See id.

70. See, e.g., First National Maintenance Corp. v. NLRB, 452 U.S. 666 (1981) (decision to shut down facility or close part of business not subject to mandatory bargaining); Garwood–Detroit Truck Equip., 274 N.L.R.B. 113 (1985) (Decision to subcontract work not subject of mandatory bargaining); Otis Elevator Co., 269 N.L.R.B. 891 (1984) (decision to relocate not subject of mandatory bargaining).

71. See generally B. Townley, Labor Law Reform in U. S. Industrial Relations (1986); Cohen, ''How Congress Disposed of What Carter Proposed,'' 10 Nat'l J. 1689 (Oct. 21, 1978).

72. See Novosel v. Nationwide Ins. Co., 721 F.2d 894, 896 & n.4 (3d Cir. 1983).

73. See Novack, supra note 3.

74. See, e.g., McKinney v. National Dairy Council, 491 F. Supp. 1108 (D. Mass 1980) (Damage award of $ 94,080 for wrongful discharge); Maddaloni v. Western Mass. Bus Lines, Inc., 396 Mass. 877, 438 N.E.2D. 351 (1982) (award of $61,000).

75. See, Novack, supra note 3.

76. See id.

77. See id.

78. See id.

79. Act effective March 28, 1980, ch. 663, § 157, codified as amended at Me. Rev. Stat. Ann. tit. 26, § 625-B (West Supp. 1987).

80. See Fort Halifax Packing Co. v. Coyne, 107 S. Ct. 2211 (1987).

81. See generally Novack, supra note 3.

82. See id.

83. See generally Noble, ''Labor Takes a Chair in the Board Room,'' N.Y. Times, Mar. 9, 1986, § 4, at 4, col. 3 [hereinafter ''Labor Chair in Board Room''].

84. See Vartan, ''Market Place: More Airline Mergers Seen,'' N.Y. Times, Sept. 11, 1986, at D8, col. 3 (Western); Salpukas, ''People Express Sale Talks Reported,'' N.Y. Times, July 3, 1986, at D1, col. 3 (Eastern and Frontier).

85. See Salpukas, ''Pan Am's Unions Offer Wage Cuts for Security,'' N.Y. Times, Feb. 2, 1987, at D1, col. 1 [hereinafter ''Pan Am's Unions''].

86. See Salpukas, ''Pan Am Pilots at the Controls,'' N.Y. Times, Dec. 3, 1987, at D2, col. 1; see also Salpukas, ''Pan Am's Unions,'' supra note 85.

87. See Stevenson, ''United's Pilots Pick Acquisition Chief,'' N.Y. Times, Aug. 14, 1987, at D1, col. 4.

88. See Salpukas, ''Western to Be Sold by Allegis,'' N.Y. Times, Oct. 28, 1987, at D1, col. 6.

89. See ''Labor Chair in Board Room,'' supra note 83.

90. See Stevenson, ''Henley Lifts Stake in Santa Fe to 14%,'' N.Y. Times, Oct. 29, 1987, at D5, col. 1.

91. See Raskin, ''The Steelworkers: Limping at 50,'' N.Y. Times, June 15, 1986, § 3, at 1, col. 2; Hicks, ''Who Has to Keep a Troubled Company's Pension Promises?,'' N.Y. Times, Oct. 11, 1987, § 4, at 5, col. 1 [hereinafter ''Pension Promises'']; Cowes, ''Pension Funds Weather the Market Collapse,'' N.Y. Times, Nov. 1, 1987, § 3, at 12, col. 1 [hereinafter ''Market Collapse''].

92. See Greenhouse, ''LTV Problems Stir Concerns on Survival of Steel Industry,'' N.Y. Times, July 28, 1986, at A1, col. 2.

93. See ''Pension Promises,'' supra note 91; ''Market Collapse,'' supra note 91.

94. See ''Retirees' Health Care Could Shock Firms; Study Says Planned Regulations Could Cause Big Economic Woes,'' L.A. Times, Nov. 12, 1987, pt. 1, at 2, col. 4.

95. See Skrzycki, ''Investment Fund for Steelworkers' Pension Proposed,'' Wash. Post, Oct. 23, 1987, at D3.

96. See Noble, ''Steel Union Locals Back USX Pact,'' N.Y. Times, Jan. 19, 1987, at D1, col. 3.

97. Holusha, ''Auto Job Guarantees Sought,'' N.Y. Times, July 7, 1987, at D1, col. 3.

98. Cf. id. (discussing low wage gains).

99. See Gould, ''Watch for a Historic Auto Pact,'' N.Y. Times, July 27, 1987, at A19, col. 1.

100. See ''Detroit Strikes Back,'' N.Y. Times, Sept. 14, 1980, § 6, at 28, col. 1 (magazine).

101. Kuttner, ''Austerity or Collaboration,'' unpublished paper given at Industrial Cooperation Council Symposium on the Future of Business, Labor and Government Relations, New York City (Nov. 18–19, 1987).

2

THE SCOPE OF THE DUTY TO BARGAIN CONCERNING BUSINESS TRANSFORMATIONS

Michael C. Harper

Editors' Note. Professor Harper notes that the term "wages, hours and other conditions of employment" which delimits the scope of the duty to bargain is defined neither by the statutory text nor the legislative history. Yet, important legal consequences, including the ability to use economic force, flow from whether a topic is or is not characterized a "mandatory" subject of bargaining. The author maintains that there has been a failure by the Board and the Supreme Court to provide a coherent approach for determining which business change decisions are bargainable. He maintains that a "product market" principle best defines the scope of mandatory bargaining and hence the arena for permissible use of collective economic action. Under that principle, bargaining is not required over decisions concerning the price, quality or identity of, or market for, the firm's goods or services, but decisions such as plant relocations which are essentially attempts at reducing costs must be bargained and may be subjected to strike pressure. The author proceeds to explore the implications of the "product market" principle for union demands for stock rights and labor directors in exchange for wage concessions.

THE IMPORTANCE OF DEFINING THE SCOPE OF THE DUTY TO BARGAIN

This chapter focuses on the extent to which an employer does or should have an obligation to bargain with an exclusive representative of its employees over significant business decisions that will affect the jobs of these employees. In order to analyze this problem intelligently, however, one must understand clearly the legal consequences of classifying a topic within the scope of obligatory bargaining. Without such an understanding, it is impossible to render a judgment on the suitability of requiring bargaining over a topic with any assurance that the judgment accords with the policies and purposes of the labor legislation on which the bargaining obligation rests. The National Labor Relations Act (NLRA or Act), of course, requires employers and exclusive bargaining representatives to "confer in good faith with respect to wages, hours, and other terms and conditions of employment."[1] But a moment's reflection should convince any good lawyer that these words alone cannot define the scope of obligatory bargaining. Although "hours" is sufficiently clear; "wages" could be not only as narrow as cash "on the barrel head," but also as broad as any policy or practice by an employer that employees might view as compensation for their work. Similarly, "terms or conditions" of employment might mean only the working conditions at the plant or office site, but it might also mean any terms and conditions that an employer must meet before the employees are willing to work.

Furthermore, the legislative history of the NLRA does not provide any meaningful instruction about the meaning of this critical, but elastic phrase. Justice Stewart tried to read the history of the Taft-Hartley Act to impose a narrow interpretation on the phrase,[2] but he could find no particular meaning, and more recent Supreme Court majorities,[3] as well as numerous commentators,[4] have found only a congressional intent to give broad discretion to the NLRB.

Determining how that discretion should be exercised requires an appreciation of the consequences of defining a topic to be encompassed by the phrase and thus within the scope of mandatory bargaining. Five such consequences should be noted. The most obvious and probably least controversial consequence is that placing a topic within the mandatory scope means that the NLRB will require the party who would control the topic unilaterally absent bargaining obligations to bargain about decisions concerning the topic with a sincere desire to reach an agreement. The "controlling" party—who on decisions to transfer a business is, of course, almost always the employer—need not make any particular concessions on the topic to the "noncontrolling" party, but must discuss and explore alternatives thoroughly, with an authentic interest in reaching some mutually acceptable compromise. Failure to do so is an illegal action, an unfair labor practice under the NLRA, and the Board will remedy it not only by ordering further bargaining, but also in some cases by ordering the undoing of any action taken without adequate bargaining.[5]

Second, and perhaps more important, the Board will permit the party who, absent bargaining would not control a decision that requires bargaining, to use economic leverage to attempt to compel the controlling party to compromise. This economic leverage can be exerted by refusing to reach an agreement on other mandatory bargaining topics unless the other party compromises on the disputed topic. The leverage can also be exerted by some commonly employed means of industrial coercion, such as strikes or lockouts. In a somewhat controversial decision almost thirty years ago, the Supreme Court in *NLRB v. Wooster Div. of Borg-Warner Corp.*[6] held that employers, and by implication unions, may not use economic leverage to compel the other party to compromise on topics about which the other party is not required to bargain. Since this decision, the definition of mandatory bargaining topics thus has determined not only the topics over which the Board will compel bargaining, but also the topics over which the Board will permit noncontrolling parties to attempt to compel compromise.[7]

The third notable consequence of including a topic within the mandatory scope derives from the Board's general and judicially approved policy of offering more protection to employees striking in protest of unfair labor practices than to employees striking merely over economic issues. The Board requires employers to reinstate unfair labor practice strikers, but not economic strikers, to their former positions even if this requires the discharge of permanent replacements.[8] This distinction means that when an employer refuses to bargain in good faith on a mandatory topic of bargaining, the employees not only may invoke the legal assistance of the Board, but also may engage in collective and coercive action themselves with the assurance that they will be able to reclaim their jobs after the action.[9]

Fourth, the Act prohibits either party without the consent of the other party from modifying collectively bargained agreements until their expiration dates.[10] In *Allied Chemical Workers v. Pittsburgh Plate Glass Co.*,[11] the Court held that the prohibition attaches only to modifications concerning mandatory topics of bargaining.

The fifth and final consequence of defining a topic to be within the mandatory scope to be noted was also established by a Supreme Court decision, or at least by a broad interpretation of it. In *NLRB v. Katz,*[12] the Court held that even a party generally willing to negotiate in good faith on a topic commits an unfair labor practice if it implements a change concerning a topic without first bargaining to impasse with the other party over that change. The *Katz* Court, of course, made it clear that the rule against unilateral action that it announced applies only to mandatory topics of bargaining.[13]

Although all five of these legal consequences of classifying a particular topic to be within the mandatory scope seem clearly significant, they all may not be of equal importance in determining what makes a particular topic appropriate for compulsory bargaining. One reason this is true is that some of the legal rules concerning the consequences of making a topic mandatory might be adjusted for certain decisions without removing an entire class of topics from obligatory bargaining. As elaborated below, this is certainly true for the rule against unilateral changes of mandatory topics before bargaining to impasse. The law, for instance, could qualify this rule when an employer claims a compelling emergency without deciding that a particular topic is generally unsuitable for compulsory bargaining.

One legal consequence of classifying a topic within the mandatory scope that will not and should not be adjusted without an amendment to the statute is the authorization of coercive action by the noncontrolling party to compel the controlling party to compromise its decision making about that topic. Everyone who has studied American labor-management negotiations must appreciate that it is the parties' own economic power, rather than the Board's regulatory authority, that makes collective bargaining work in those critical situations where the parties perceive their interests to conflict fundamentally. Defining the scope of mandatory bargaining therefore requires a consideration of what types of decisions we want made unilaterally by one controlling party and what types of decisions may properly be influenced by the use of coercive economic power by the other party.

We must consider which decisions concerning substantial business transformations we want to be influenced by the exercise of collective and coercive employee economic power. We cannot determine whether a topic should be within the mandatory scope simply by judging whether the noncontrolling party can offer adequate concessions to induce the controlling party to compromise its desired decisions on that topic. One may believe that a controlling party, say, a supposedly "misguided" employer "blind to its own interests," might be enlightened by being forced to listen to the other party's concessions. Ordinarily, however, legal coercion is not necessary to compel one party to consider concessions that would be forthcoming from the other side. More fundamentally, such a focus on the likelihood of concessions slights the importance of economic coercion to the collective-bargaining process. Given the fact that the NLRA and the labor-management relations system that it supports clearly contemplate use of economic power as "part and parcel of the process of collective bargaining,"[14] we cannot avoid asking why the use of collective economic power appropriately influences decision making on some topics, but does not appropriately influence it on others.[15]

Furthermore, we should be able to arrive at one coherent definition of the scope of mandatory bargaining that addresses at least all decisions concerning business transformations, not several mutually contradictory answers that allow decision makers to arrive ad hoc at different definitions of mandatory bargaining that depend primarily on individual value judgments. In order that collective bargaining operate effectively, the law defining the scope of mandatory bargaining must be rationalized, so that it might be respected, and it must be stable, so that it might be predictable.

FAILURES OF THE COURT AND BOARD IN DEFINING THE SCOPE OF THE DUTY

Unfortunately, neither the Court nor the Board thus far has offered a comprehensive definition of the scope of mandatory bargaining that explains why any particular decision concerning the future course of businesses should not be influenced by the collective-bargaining process. In order to illustrate how the

Court and the Board have failed to do so and to explain the somewhat incoherent law that they have nonetheless made, we will next examine what are at present probably the three most important precedents concerning bargaining about business transformations: one relatively old Supreme Court decision, one relatively new Supreme Court decision, and a recent Board decision.

Recall, first, the more than twenty-year-old Supreme Court decision in *Fibreboard Paper Products Corp. v. NLRB*,[16] which holds an employer's decision to subcontract bargaining unit work to be a mandatory topic for bargaining. The majority opinion[17] offers no coherent approach to the question of whether our national labor policy supports subjecting certain business decisions to the potential influence of collective employee action. The Court does defend the "appropriateness" of collective bargaining over Fibreboard's subcontracting, but it does so primarily by stressing that Fibreboard's decision turned on labor cost savings from subcontracting that presumably could have been superseded by employee concessions.[18] The appropriateness of forcing *employer* concessions is not thereby addressed.

By noting that Fibreboard did not contemplate any capital investment,[19] the opinion could be read to suggest that the coercive influence of collective action on capital investment decisions is less appropriate than the coercion of other business decisions with a similar impact on employees. While this differential treatment of capital allocation decisions may have some superficial appeal, it ignores the fact that any restrictions on an employer's unilateral control over the allocation of resources, including labor-cost saving measures such as the subcontracting involved in that case, can limit the money available for capital investment. Economic analysis thus indicates that the distinction between capital investment decisions and labor-cost measures is not fully coherent.

Justice Stewart's *Fibreboard* concurrence directly expresses a view that employees ought not to have the power to compel the compromise of business transformation decisions that "lie at the core of entrepreneurial control."[20] But the opinion offers no principle by which to define either what is at this "core" or how close to its center collective employee action can probe.

The Supreme Court's more recent consideration of the appropriateness of mandatory bargaining over business change decisions that threaten employees' job security contrasts sharply with the majority opinion in *Fibreboard*. In *First National Maintenance Corp. v. NLRB (FNM)*[21] the Court held that an employer did not have to bargain about a decision to terminate its maintenance and cleaning services to a particular nursing home. The *FNM* majority opinion not only purports to remove an entire category of decisions from mandatory bargaining, but also its reasoning threatens further to restrict bargaining.

The opinion claims to determine whether mandatory bargaining over business termination decisions serves the "neutral purposes of the Act" by balancing the benefit of bargaining "for labor-management relations" against the burden placed by bargaining "on the conduct of the business."[22] The opinion's analysis, however, quickly distills to balancing the interest of employees in bargaining against the interest of management in escaping a bargaining obligation. Given the strong interest of employees in job security on one side and the strong interest of employers in business efficiency on the other, such a balance cannot be struck without the imposition of the values of the balancers. Indeed, it certainly is not difficult to discern that the justices in the *FNM* majority place extra weight on management's side of the scale.

Most importantly, when considering the costs of making bargaining compulsory, the majority notes that employees through coercive action may disrupt an employer's decision making over mandatory topics; but the opinion's discussion of the possible benefits of collective bargaining addresses only whether employees need an opportunity to offer concessions, not whether they need an opportunity to extract concessions.[23] Even the facts of *FNM* suggest the significance of the failure to consider the potential for achieving a collective-bargaining compromise through employer as well as employee concessions. FNM operated maintenance and cleaning services at many other sites that the union at least theoretically could have picketed. If it represented the employees at those sites or if it could have convinced truckers to refuse to make deliveries, it perhaps could have shut down the sites. Whereas picketing to force the employer to compromise on a nonmandatory topic presumably would have constituted an unfair labor practice, a contrary ruling in *FNM* making bargaining mandatory might have enabled the terminated FNM employees to protect their jobs through such economic pressure.

The *FNM* majority also demonstrates its relatively low evaluation of the job security interests of employees by the manner in which it acknowledges that employers must, in any event, bargain about the effects on employees of decisions to terminate operations.[24] This acknowledgement, it should in turn be noted here, was an important part of the decision because it means that unions may resort to economic coercion to extract concessions from employers on such matters as severance pay and hiring priorities at other plants. The *FNM* majority, however, also claimed that the opportunity to bargain over the effects of the decision to terminate would give the union ample opportunity to offer concessions and suggestions that could affect the decision to close,[25] even though the opinion seems to permit the employer to enter into obligations with third parties to make the termination decision final before notifying the union. Nevertheless, when the *FNM* majority considers the impact of the termination decision on management flexibility[26] it ignores the impact that effects bargaining already has on this flexibility. The Court thus seems to weigh the marginal benefit of decision bargaining against the total burden of all bargaining, including that which the Justices plainly intend to require.

Even the Court's treatment of the impact of bargaining on management flexibility reflects a special solicitude for management prerogatives. Sometimes bargaining, whether over the effects of a decision to terminate operations or the decision itself, could result in the compromise of confidentiality or timeliness essential to management's response to a major emergency. Often it would not, however. As the facts of *FNM* itself illustrate, there may even be no third party with whom the employer needs to deal quickly and with confidentiality before termination. More importantly, excluding all termination of operations decisions from the mandatory scope of bargaining seems to authorize an employer to reject without bargaining union proposals during contract negotiations to protect employees from shutdowns that the employer has not even yet considered. If confidentiality and delay in face of a true emergency, rather than the general protection of management power, were the Court's real concern, the Court could have simply announced that the rule against unilateral changes in mandatory topics of bargaining should be relaxed when employers make major business decisions in response to emergencies.

The *FNM* majority tried to limit its holding, both in a footnote that distinguishes "other types of management decisions, such as plant relocation, sales, other kinds of subcontracting, automation, etc."[27] and in a closing paragraph that even suggests that not all economically motivated decisions to shut down part of a business fall outside of the mandatory scope.[28]

Three years later, however, the Board decided to read *FNM* expansively to exclude any employer decision about "the nature or direction of the business" from the sphere of mandatory bargaining. In *Otis Elevator Co.*[29] a four-member Board, sitting together and dividing into three opinions, held that United Technologies, Otis Elevator's parent company, could without bargaining consolidate Otis' inefficient and duplicative research and development operations in New Jersey with its research and development facility in Connecticut.

The lead opinion of Chairperson Dotson and Member Hunter established doctrine that has controlled Board cases for the past several years. Since the *Otis* decision, the Board has not required an employer to bargain over any decision to transform the operation of its business, whether it be through work transfer[30] or a plant relocation[31] or consolidation[32] or even—notwithstanding *Fibreboard*—through subcontracting,[33] so long as the employer can show it was in any significant way motivated by something other than a desire to reduce the formal compensation of its unionized employees.[34]

Otis ostensibly avoids balancing management's interest in not bargaining versus the interest of employees in bargaining by focusing on the motivation of the employer for wishing to make a business change, rather than on the effects or potential of bargaining.[35] The doctrine, however, seems as incoherent and arbitrary as any that has been applied in this area. It is incoherent for the same reason the capital investment-labor cost distinction is: Virtually any employee demand that an employer compromise its business plans is a demand that the employer reallocate resources to satisfy labor and thus effectively increase its labor costs. For instance, the union's demand in *Otis* to keep the New Jersey facility open could have been satisfied by the company's absorption of the additional costs of that facility as a special job security expenditure. Any employer resistance to such a demand is motivated at least in significant part by a desire to reduce the costs that labor wishes to impose. The *Otis* doctrine seems arbitrary because it rejects collective bargaining for no apparent reason beyond the distaste of particular Board members for compromising management decision-making flexibility. The doctrine is not built on an analysis of why some employer decisions should not be subject to the influence of collective employee action.

Neither of the two concurring opinions on decision bargaining in *Otis* has been influential, and, given the departure of both authors from the Board, it is doubtful that either will be. In any event, each is inadequate.

Member Zimmerman's concurrence also avoided the *FNM* balancing approach by focusing on employer motivation. Zimmerman concluded that employers must bargain only about business decisions that are motivated by a concern with overall enterprise costs, including but not limited to labor costs.[36] This position cannot be faulted as merely an arbitrary assertion of Zimmerman's attitudes toward collective bargaining because he can relate his standard to the likelihood that employee concessions will influence the employer. The position nevertheless has two previously discussed problems. First, as just noted, an employer's resistance to any employee effort to influence its decision making almost always ultimately derives from a concern about costs of some nature. Second, Zimmerman's analysis shares, with the other Supreme Court and Board opinions discussed, the underlying assumption that collective bargaining can only compromise business decisions by yielding employee, rather than employer, concessions.

The opinion of Member Diaz-Dennis combines the *FNM* majority's balancing approach with the Dotson-Hunter motivational analysis. She concludes that business decisions that do not "focus" on the employment relationship, but nonetheless directly affect employment are not mandatory subjects of bargaining unless: (1) they are motivated to some extent by a factor over which the union has control, primarily formal labor costs, and (2) the benefit to labor-management relations of mandatory bargaining would outweigh the burden placed on management.[37]

Member Dennis' test could define mandatory bargaining even more narrowly than does the lead *Otis* opinion because it requires topics to clear the second balancing hurdle as well as the employer motivational hurdle. However, Member Dennis dissented from what has perhaps been the Board's most restrictive application of *Otis* in *Garwood-Detroit Truck Equipment*.[38] In that case, the Board upheld an employer's unilateral decision to subcontract truck equipment service work, even though "labor costs were one component of the overhead costs" the employer "intended to reduce by the subcontracting."[39] For Dotson and Hunter, the fact that the employer was also attempting to eliminate other overhead costs meant that the decision could be made without bargaining. For Dennis, however, the importance of labor costs made the decision amenable to collective bargaining.

As noted above, however much they are open to criticism, these *Otis Elevator Co.* opinions at present frame employers' obligations to bargain concerning business transformations. An employer can avoid bargaining on any decision entailing the elimination of bargaining unit work that it can show was substantially based on some factor other than direct labor costs.[40] Inasmuch as a party does not violate the NLRA by effecting a unilateral change on a nonmandatory topic, even a work preservation clause in a collective-bargaining agreement will not subject an employer to a statutory, as opposed to a contractual, remedy if jobs are eliminated for some legitimate reason other than labor compensation levels.[41]

Under present Board doctrine, employers generally need to be more concerned about an obligation to bargain about the effects of a business transformation decision than about bargaining over the decision itself. As noted, the *First National Maintenance* Court approved the Board's insistence that employers bargain on such items as employee severance benefits and reemployment and representational rights at other facilities.[42] In accord with the *FNM* Court's assertion that effects bargaining is to take place "in a meaningful manner and at a meaningful time"[43] the Board has now clarified that the employer must notify the union of an impending elimination of jobs "at a time when the union retain[s] at least a measure of bargaining power."[44] Pretermination notice is excused only when "justified by emergency circumstances."[45]

As a practical matter, however, employers are not likely to be concerned about the remedial bite of any effects bargaining, pretermination notice rule.[46] An employer confronting a strong union that might block a business transfer after receiving early notice need not fear that the Board would order a return to the status quo ante as a remedy for untimely effects bargaining. The Board generally has imposed only limited back-pay liability and bargaining orders on employers who have failed to discharge effects bargaining obligations.[47]

A COHERENT AND PRINCIPLED DEFINITION OF THE SCOPE OF MANDATORY BARGAINING

This might be the end of the story for now,[48] but times change, and the world may once again become more interesting. With an eye to this future, the Board and the courts do not have to choose between making all decisions that could affect employees mandatory and an unprincipled balancing of employer and employee interests that eventually can devolve into a position like that which now commands a majority of the Board. I have elsewhere suggested a coherent principle that defines a limited set of employer decisions that our national labor policy does not demand be subject to collective employee bargaining power, and that our general social and political ideology suggests should be insulated from such pressures, notwithstanding their possible effects on employees.[49] This principle holds that any decision determining what products are created and sold, in what quantities, for which markets, and at what prices should not be subject to the influence of collective and coercive employee economic power. Any decision that need not determine such product market policies if adequate resources are reallocated to the needs of employees, however, should be subject to the influence of the collective action of employees.

This principle is based on two important policy considerations, one central to the NLRA and one central to the organization of our society and not compromised by the Act. A fundamental tenet of the Act is the authorization of collective employee action to attempt to influence the share of resources of a business enterprise that are allocated to the needs of labor. The Act assists employees not by giving priority to any particular set of needs, but by protecting whatever economic power that the employees can aggregate to satisfy their own preferences as they perceive them. A statute that establishes a system of free contracting between employers and collectivities of employees should not be read to authorize an agency or the courts to determine how or at what level employees can ask to be compensated by a different allocation of company resources.

While the Act thus contemplates the use of collective employee power to influence the level and form of the allocation of resources to meet employee needs, it does not seem in any way to compromise the means by which our society makes decisions about the goods and services that are made available for its consumption. In the public sector, of course, those decisions are made by managers under the supervision of elected officials, who presumably want to be responsive to citizens as voters. In the private sector, those decisions are made by managers under the supervision of shareholder representatives, who presumably seek to be responsive to citizens as consumers. Private companies, of course, attempt to modify the desires of consumers, just as politicians attempt to modify the desires of voters; however, product market manipulations should be addressed by public representatives through regulatory legislation, not by employees through collective bargaining.

The product market principle is thus cogent as well as coherent. Collective bargaining should be concerned with the division of economic resources between capital and labor, not the allocation of products to consumers. Any increase in the relative labor costs of one business of course affects distributional efficiencies in the economy by increasing the relative price of that business' products. This much indirect distortion of product markets must be accepted if the NLRA is to offer any protection to collective bargaining. Direct distortion of product markets, however, need not be accepted and protected.

The principle is also relatively predictable and easy to apply. It utilizes no elastic and unpredictable balancing tests. Nor does it require any uncertain inquiry into the motives or purposes of employers in reaching decisions.

Moreover, the principle can draw relatively sharp lines around mandatory bargaining without excluding entire categories of cases. For instance, the principle would exclude some, but not all, partial closing decisions. It distinguishes a case like *FNM*, in which an employer decided no longer to offer services to a particular customer, from a case like *Bob's Big Boy Restaurants*,[50] in which the pre–*Otis Elevator* Board held that a restaurant chain had to bargain about a decision to eliminate its own shrimp processing operations and provide its customers instead with shrimp processed by an independent contracting company. As the Board in *Bob's Big Boy* noted, the employees' demand that their employer's fish processing operations be continued could have been met by a reallocation of company resources to new processing machines without changing the shrimp product offered to the market. Employees should have as much authority to bargain about the reallocation of resources to machines that will protect their jobs as they have to bargain about the wage levels of their jobs.[51]

Other business transformation decisions also can be analyzed under the product market principle, without either uncertain balancing and motivational judgments or arbitrary categorizations. Most plant relocation decisions should be bargainable because most do not directly concern marketing. For instance, while the management of United Technologies might have intended to improve Otis Elevator's product by consolidating their research and development operations, there was no evidence in the case to suggest that the old research and development plant could not have been modernized by sufficient reallocation of resources to achieve the same result. Similarly, most subcontracting decisions should be bargainable because most concern only the transfer of production from one employer to another. In *Garwood-Detroit Truck Equipment*,[52] for instance, the subcontracting did not change the product offered to the market, for the employer continued to provide for service and mounting under a subcontract's aegis.[53]

A NEW FRONTIER FOR BARGAINING

The product market principle also can at least help illuminate questions concerning an employer's obligation to bargain about perhaps the most intriguing proposals to transform business operations: proposals to grant employees ownership or participation in the management of the enterprise. There is little law on bargaining obligations concerning such proposals, no doubt in part because these proposals generally have been pressed in recent concession bargaining for which the scope of the objects of legitimate union coercive power has not required definition.

Proposals to increase the control and investment of employees in the enterprises for which they labor can be divided into four categories for consideration of bargaining obligations: representation on boards of directors or other high corporate policy-making committees; participation in collective decision making about plant operations; ownership and control of the voting rights of corporate stock; and rights to timely notice of planned liquidation and to the opportunity to purchase corporate assets before the implementation of such plans.

The first category—employee representation on corporate boards—has of course achieved particular prominence in this present era of economic transformation and dislocation. One might argue that proposals to place at least union officials on corporate boards ought not to be even permissible, let alone mandatory, bargaining items because union representation on corporate boards would lead inevitably to the violation of some law. Some have suggested that placing a union official on a corporate board (1) could eventuate in a violation of federal antitrust laws, especially Section 8 of the Clayton Act, which proscribes interlocking directorates between competitive corporations[54]; (2) could constitute employer interference with the union's autonomy in violation of Section 8(a) (2) of the NLRA[55]; or (3) could result in the union board member violating either his corporate fiduciary duty or his duty of fair representation to unit employees under the NLRA or his fiduciary duty to union members under Section 501 of the Landrum-Griffin Act.[56]

All of these problems of potential illegality are surmountable. First, notwithstanding the refusal of the Department of Justice to approve United Auto Workers representation on the board of American Motors as well as that of Chrysler,[57] it seems an unwarranted expansion of the Clayton Act to prohibit corporate efforts to expand worker input into corporate decision making. Any antitrust problems should at least be avoidable by not choosing national union officials to represent employees on boards of competing corporations.[58]

Surmounting the other two problems might be somewhat more difficult. Problems of fiduciary responsibility might be overcome by specifying in a corporation's articles that individuals may be elected to the board of directors to serve employee rather than shareholder interests. Such specification should avoid placing the union representative in the position of having to violate one or another fiduciary duty, and also should dispel any suggestion that the union board member might act as an agent of corporate influence in the union. However, some voting equity shareholders might still object that the applicable state corporate law protects their expectations that only shareholder interests will be represented on corporate boards.

In any event, it should not suffice simply to disclose in a proxy statement to shareholders that the union candidates that they are asked to elect to the board will represent employees.[59] Even after a fully informed open vote, shareholders who object to having any director represent employees can cite the presumption of corporate law that directors are to represent shareholders. Since some shareholders may have invested with this presumption in mind, if it is reversible at all without legislative action, the presumption should be overcome only by the procedures and majorities required by the articles of incorporation and state corporate law to redefine the rights of shareholders.[60]

No matter how potential conflict of interest and Section 8(a) (2)[61] problems are avoided, employers should not be obligated to bargain about union proposals to place any employee representative in any high corporate post, including a seat on the board, that has responsibility for making decisions that are themselves outside the mandatory scope of bargaining, whether these decisions be the selection of an employer's collective-bargaining team[62] or the definition of a product line. Decisions that should not be influenced by collective employee power ought not to be influenced by an employee whose decision-making influence has been secured through the exercise of such power. This seems true even if the employee's influence on such decisions is limited to his or her power to persuade after consultation and does not include a voting right. Employers who wish to secure wage concessions by offering unions board representation can do so through voluntary negotiation without treating board representation as a mandatory topic over which unions can exert economic pressure.

Of course, this analysis does not preclude mandatory bargaining over proposals fitting in the second category listed above—proposals to make more democratic decision making about production operations. Although management might resist, or indeed advance, such proposals for reasons other than a desire to reduce labor costs as narrowly conceived by the *Otis Elevator* Board, even the present NLRB might view employee-participation proposals as appropriate for bargaining because they primarily concern labor costs and labor relations.

Proposals to blur lines between supervisors and other employees must, in any event, also be tested against the commands of Section 8(a)(2). Employer-proposed schemes that establish committees of employee representatives merely to offer advice or present grievances to management can violate these commands because the committees may be considered labor organizations dominated or supported by the employer. As the Supreme Court has recognized, even employee advisory committees that do not actually negotiate come within the definition of "labor organizations" covered by Section 8(a)(2).[63] Nevertheless, the NLRB, which generally has interpreted Section 8(a)(2) as more restrictive of labor-management cooperation schemes than have the courts,[64] has held that schemes that provide some job enrichment benefit to all employees and not simply to representatives,[65] or schemes that give some employees direct administrative authority,[66] do not establish "labor organizations" and therefore cannot violate Section 8(a)(2). Moreover, labor-management cooperation schemes should be legal if proposed or voluntarily agreed to by an incumbent, independent union representative. Such committees should be able to be established when a union is willing to waive its statutory right to resist them without being subject to an employer's bargaining pressure.[67]

The third category of worker-control proposals—measures to facilitate employee ownership in the enterprise that employs them—requires a somewhat different analysis. Requests of unions, as well as managements, that employees who are represented be compensated by a particular negotiable instrument of value should not be outside the scope of mandatory bargaining simply because the instrument happens to be stock in the employees' company. As the Board recognized thirty years ago in a decision holding that a company must bargain about a plan to subsidize its employees' purchase of the company's own stock, shares of company stock are as much "emoluments of value" as rights in pension or insurance plans.[68]

Control by employees of common stock in the corporation that employs them, however, may have much different implications than the control of rights in pension or insurance plans, if enough voting stock is controlled to enable the employees to influence corporate decision making. Should unions be able to insist that management bargain about a proposal to place employees in a collective role of controlling shareholders in the company, perhaps through the creation of an Employee Stock Ownership Plan (ESOP) with pass-through voting rights?[69] The issue may seem fanciful because management cannot commit incumbent shareholders either to the dilution of their equity through the authorization of new stock or to the sale of the incumbents' own stock. There are, however, several realistic scenarios for union bargainers proposing employee control of management through ownership: the employees' company might be a wholly or primarily owned subsidiary of a larger corporation with whose management the union could bargain; the employees already might be majority owners in the enterprise, again perhaps through an ESOP *without* pass-through of voting rights; or incumbent stockholders might otherwise have authorized management to issue sufficient new voting stock and to take other steps necessary to pass control to the employees.[70] At least, the employees could negotiate with management to solicit shareholders' proxies to obtain such authorization, just as they could negotiate for the solicitation of proxies to place employee representatives on the board of directors.

A strong argument can be made that employees ought not to be able to use collective economic leverage to compel management to bargain about facilitating employee control of the enterprise through stock ownership because such control would enable employees to use collective power to achieve full control over matters that ought not themselves be topics of mandatory bargaining. Achieving control of a board of directors through stock ownership, however, is fundamentally different from achieving direct employee representation on the board of directors. Control of a large block of common voting stock would enable employees to achieve control of the corporation as stockholders, rather than as employees. The difference is of more than formal importance. Control over the destiny of a corporation, as any equity market analyst knows, is part of the wealth of the corporation. When employees seek to secure that wealth, they seek to obtain a particular form of compensation and a particular allocation of corporate resources.

Making the collective employee purchase of a corporation's equity a mandatory topic nonetheless presents a close issue in my mind. Employees may seek to control the destiny of their corporation not simply to secure the best return on their investment capital, but also to provide the best security for their human capital. Collectively bargained employee ownership of enterprises therefore is somewhat in tension with the present social policy in favor of consumer control of product market decisions. On balance, however, I would favor making employee purchases of controlling equity interests mandatory, even without special legislation, because the board of directors' mandate to represent the interest of shareholders as such would remain formally unchanged; the representatives of employee stockholders would have to be much more sensitive than union officials to consumer demand in the product market.

The present Board probably would reject this position, perhaps by stressing that decisions about corporate control are at the very center of entrepreneurial prerogative and are only tangentially concerned with labor costs as narrowly conceived. It might be more difficult, however, to place outside the mandatory scope topics within the fourth category listed above—employee rights to have notice of planned liquidation and an opportunity to buy assets prior to liquidation. Bargaining over such rights can be viewed as bargaining only over the effects of management decisions to curtail operations in some manner, for granting employees the rights would not restrict management's authority to dispose of assets. Put differently, management decisions to leave a particular product market would not be directly restrained.

Nevertheless, the present Board would be likely to consider this fourth category to be outside the mandatory scope as well. A management's decision to sell corporate assets to one rather than another buyer can itself be viewed as an entrepreneurial decision, not at all motivated by labor-cost considerations. Furthermore, requiring employers to consider employee purchase offers before finalizing the alternative disposition of assets in at least some cases could lead to the delay or compromise of confidentiality that the *FNM* Court, as well as the *Otis Elevator* Board, seemed to view as intolerable corporate burdens.

As suggested above, the tone as well as the analysis of the most recent decisions on obligations to bargain about corporate transformations certainly does not promise an interesting or brave new world of collective bargaining. But the law as well as the economic reality defining the perimeters of bargaining could change rapidly. I, for one, believe that at present the law is only pausing temporarily before it proceeds to develop further doctrine granting American workers a stronger voice in the decision making that determines their future. If so, it would be well during this pause to consider how we might in some coherent manner determine for which decisions that voice should be heard through mandatory bargaining and the collective and sometimes coercive economic action that it entails.

NOTES

1. 29 U.S.C. § 158(d).

2. Fibreboard Paper Prods. Corp. v. NLRB, 379 U.S. 203, 220–21 (1964) (Stewart, J., concurring).

3. See First National Maintenance Corp. v. NLRB, 452 U.S. 666, 675 (1981); Ford Motor Corp. v. NLRB, 441 U.S. 488, 495–96 (1979).

4. See e.g., Oldham, "Organized Labor, the Environment, and the Taft-Hartley Act," 71 Mich. L. Rev. 935, 984–85 (1973); Rabin, "The Decline and Fall of Fibreboard," N.Y.U. 24th Ann. Conf. on Lab. 237, 243 (1972).

5. See e.g., Fibreboard Paper Prods. Corp. v. NLRB, 379 U.S. at 203, 215–16; Kronenberger d.b.a. American Needle & Novelty Co., 206 N.L.R.B. 534 (1973).

After confronting some judicial hesitation to enforce orders to restore discontinued operations, see, e.g., NLRB v. R & H Masonry Supply, 627 F.2d 1013 (9th Cir. 1980); NLRB v. Townhouse T.V., Inc., 531 F.2d 826, 831 (7th Cir. 1976), the Board now holds that it will not enter such orders when they are "unduly burdensome" to employers, i.e., when "they would require capital investment resources, or impose substantial, continuing losses.'' Woodline Motor Freight, 278 N.L.R.B. No. 152 (1986). See also, e.g., Hood Industries, Inc., 273 N.L.R.B. 1587 (1985); Purolator Armored, Inc., 268 N.L.R.B. 1268 (1984).

6. NLRB v. Wooster Div. of Borg-Warner Corp., 356 U.S. 342 (1958).

7. The *Borg-Warner* Court held that the Board properly decided that the employer—the noncontrolling party in the case—could not condition its willingness to sign an agreement on the union's compromise on topics the NLRA had assigned to the union's unilateral control. Id. at 349. Justice Harlan argued in his dissent that, although the Board need not have compelled the union to bargain over one of the company's proposals, it should have permitted the company to use its own economic leverage to force the union to compromise. Id. at 353–54.

The *Borg-Warner* decision has proved controversial because many distinguished commentators have worried that it authorizes the Board and the courts, rather than the parties, to decide which bargaining topics are sufficiently important to warrant the use of economic leverage. See, e.g., H. Wellington, Labor and the Legal Process 63–90 (1968); Cox, ''Labor Decisions of the Supreme Court at the October Term, 1957,'' 44 Va. L. Rev. 1057, 1083–86 (1958); St. Antoine, ''Legal Barriers to Worker Participation in Management Decision Making,'' 58 Tul. L. Rev. 1301, 1304–07 (1984).

8. See Mastro Plastics Corp. v. NLRB, 350 U.S. 270, 288–89 (1956); NLRB v. Dubo Mfg. Co., 353 F.2d 157, 161 (6th Cir. 1965).

9. This should be true unless the union has waived the employees' statutory protection by agreeing not to strike in protest of unilateral changes that do not repudiate or undermine the collective-bargaining relationship. See Harper, ''Union Waiver of Employee Rights under the NLRA,'' pts. 1&2, 4 Indus. Rel. L.J. 335, 364–68 (1981). This essay discusses, inter alia, Mastro Plastics Corp. v. NLRB, 350 U.S. at 270 (suggesting a presumption against the coverage of unfair labor practice strikes by no-strike clauses) and Dow Chemical Co. v. NLRB, 636 F.2d 1352 (3rd Cir. 1981) (suggesting that the presumption need not apply to minor Section 8(a) (5) violations not threatening to the bargaining relationship).

10. 29 U.S.C. § 158 (d).

11. Allied Chemical Workers v. Pittsburgh Plate Glass Co., 404 U.S. 157, 185–88 (1971).

12. NLRB v. Katz 369 U.S. 736 (1962).

13. Id. at 742–43.

14. NLRB v. Insurance Agents' International Union, 361 U.S. 477, 495 (1960).

15. Proposals to require ''notice and consultation'' on some topics on which economic pressure cannot be asserted thus must be made to Congress rather than the Board or the courts. Those who advance such proposals should explain why compulsory consultation with a union unable to use its economic power is likely to influence a management that would otherwise avoid giving the union a chance to offer concessions.

16. Fibreboard Paper Products Corp. v. NLRB, 379 U.S. 203 (1964).

17. Id. at 211.

18. Id. at 214.

19. Id. at 213.

20. Id. at 217, 223.

21. 452 U.S. at 666.

22. Id. at 679–81.

23. Id. at 681–83.

24. Id. at 681.

25. Id. at 682.

26. Id. at 682–83.

27. Id. at 686 n.22.

28. Id. at 687–88.

29. Otis Elevator Co., 269 N.L.R.B. 891 (1984).

30. See Hawthorn Mellody, Inc., 275 N.L.R.B. 339 (1985).

31. See Metropolitan Teletronics, 279 N.L.R.B. No. 134 (1986); Inland Steel Container Co., 275 N.L.R.B. 929 (1985).

32. See Bostrom Div., UOP Inc., 272 N.L.R.B. 999 (1984).

33. See Garwood–Detroit Truck Equipment, Inc., 274 N.L.R.B. 113 (1985); Ausable Communications, Inc., 273 N.L.R.B. 1410 (1985); Fraser Shipyards, Inc., 272 N.L.R.B. 496 (1984).

34. In cases in which the employer could not pass this test, the Board has ordered bargaining. See Griffith-Hope Co., 275 N.L.R.B. 487 (1985); Pennsylvania Energy Corp., 274 N.L.R.B. 1153 (1985); Nurimco, Inc., 274 N.L.R.B. 764 (1985); Clinton's Ditch Cooperative Co., 274 N.L.R.B. 728 (1985).

35. The Board has frequently quoted language from the Dotson-Hunter opinion in *Otis*, 269 N.L.R.B. at 892: ''[T]he critical factor to a determination whether the decision is subject to mandatory bargaining is the essence of the decision itself, i.e., whether it turns upon a change in the nature or direction of the business, or turns upon labor costs; *not* its effect on employees nor a union's ability to offer alternatives'' (Emphasis in original).

36. Id. at 900–901.

37. Id. at 895, 897.

38. 274 N.L.R.B. 113 (1985).

39. Id. at 115.

40. See Brown Co., 278 N.L.R.B. No. 113 (1986) (finding that the decision in question was made ''for the sole purpose of escaping from its wage obligations under the existing collective bargaining contract'').

41. Cf. Allied Chemical Workers v. Pittsburgh Plate Glass Co., 404 U.S. at 185–88.

42. 452 U.S. at 681–682.

43. Id. at 682.

44. See, e.g., Metropolitan Teletronics, 279 N.L.R.B. No. 134, 122 L.R.R.M. 1107, 1109–10 (1986).

45. Id., 122 L.R.R.M. at 1109.

46. On effects bargaining, see generally Kohler, ''Distinctions without Differences: Effects Bargaining in Light of *First National Maintenance*,'' 5 Indus. Rel. L.J. 402 (1983).

47. See Metropolitan Teletronics, 279 N.L.R.B. No. 134, 122 L.R.R.M. at 1111; Garwood-Detroit Truck Equipment, Inc., 274 N.L.R.B. 113 (1985).

48. There is no evidence in the circuit court reception of the *FNM* case that these courts will be anxious either to develop limitations on the *FNM* holding or to reject the Board's own present expansive reading of that case. See, e.g., Local 2179, United Steelworkers of America v. NLRB, 822 F.2d 559 (5th Cir. 1987); NLRB v. Master Slack, 773 F.2d 77, 84 (6th Cir. 1985); Weather Tamer, Inc. v. NLRB, 676 F.2d 483

(11th Cir. 1982); NLRB v. Robin American Corp., 667 F.2d 1170 (5th Cir. 1982).

49. See Harper, "Leveling the Road from *Borg-Warner* to *First National Maintenance*: The Scope of Mandatory Bargaining," 68 Va. L. Rev. 1447 (1982).

50. Bob's Big Boy Restaurants, 264 N.L.R.B. 1369 (1982).

51. The original response of some previous members of the Board to the *FNM* decision was consistent with the product market principle. In addition to *Bob's Big Boy*, in another 1982 decision, Whitehead Brothers Co., 263 N.L.R.B. 895 (1982), the Board adopted an administrative law judge's decision that required a company to bargain about a decision to subcontract all of its truck deliveries. The administrative law judge distinguished *FNM* by stressing that the trucking company continued to provide its customers with the exact same services. Id. at 898. Furthermore, in a memorandum issued a few months after *FNM* was decided, then General Counsel Lubbers distinguished decisions like that in *FNM* to terminate part of a business, from decisions like subcontracting or plant relocation or consolidation or automation that do not change or reduce the goods produced, but merely the location or method of production. See "Bargaining about Business Changes; What Would Be Beneficial for Labor-Management Relations?," (BNA) Labor Relations Yearbook—1981, at 315; 4 (CCH) Lab. L. Rep.¶ 9271 (Ad. Mem. of General Counsel, Nov. 30, 1981).

52. 274 N.L.R.B. 113 (1985).

53. For a discussion of the rare plant relocation, subcontracting, and automation decisions that should *not* be subject to mandatory bargaining, see Harper, supra note 49, at 1473–77.

54. See, e.g., Note, "Labor Unions in the Boardroom: An Antitrust Dilemma," 92 Yale L.J. 106 (1982).

55. See, e.g., McCormick, "Union Representatives as Corporate Directors: The Challenge to the Adversarial Model of Labor Relations," 15 U. Mich. J.L. Ref. 219, 246 (1982).

56. See, e.g., Note, "An Economic and Legal Analysis of Union Representation on Corporate Boards of Directors," 130 U. of Pa. L. Rev. 919, 920–22 (1982). See also Olson, "Union Experiences with Worker Ownership: Legal and Practical Issues Raised by ESOPs, TRASOPs, Stock Purchases and Co-operatives," 1982 Wis. L. Rev. 729, 796–801.

57. See Yale Note, supra note 54, at 117 n.43; "Interlocking Directorates–Union Representation," 5 (CCH) Trade Reg. Rep., para. 50,425, at 55,967 (Feb. 26, 1981).

58. See Yale Note, supra note 54, at 125–26.

59. Apparently, Chrysler shareholders were so advised before electing Douglas Fraser to their board. See Fraser, "Worker Participation in Corporate Government: The U.A.W.–Chrysler Experience," 58 Chi.-Kent L. Rev. 949, 955–56 (1981).

60. See, e.g., General Corporation Law of Delaware § 242.

61. The NLRB, in any event, has held that at least minority representation by unions on boards of directors of corporations in which the union is not financially involved does not in itself constitute a Section 8(a)(2) violation. Compare, e.g., Anchorage Community Hospital, Inc., 225 N.L.R.B. 575 (1976) with Centerville Clinics, Inc., 181 N.L.R.B. 135 (1970).

62. Union coercion of an employer's choice of collective-bargaining representatives is, of course, proscribed by Section 8(b) (1) (A).

63. In NLRB v. Cabot Carbon Co., 360 U.S. 203 (1959), the Court held that any

organization that seeks to "deal with" an employer is within the statutory definition contained in Section 2(5), 29 U.S.C. 152(5), regardless of whether actual bargaining occurs.

64. See, e.g., Hertzka & Knowles v. NLRB, 503 F.2d 625 (9th Cir. 1974), cert. denied, 423 U.S. 875 (1975); Chicago Rawhide Manufacturing Co. v. NLRB, 221 F.2d 165 (7th Cir. 1955). See generally Note, "Collective Bargaining as an Industrial System: An Argument against Judicial Revision of Section 8(a) (2) of the National Labor Relations Act," 96 Harv. L. Rev. 1662 (1983).

65. General Foods Corp., 231 N.L.R.B. 1232 (1979).

66. John Ascuaga's Nugget, 230 N.L.R.B. 275 (1977); Mercy Memorial Hosp. Corp., 231 N.L.R.B. 1108, 1121 (1977). Of course, the employees risk losing the protection of the Act if the authority of these committees is broad. See NLRB v. Yeshiva University, 444 U.S. 672 (1980). Employees who are given significant discretionary authority to "formulate and effectuate management policies" on behalf of a firm's ownership are considered managerial and thus outside the Act's protection. See NLRB v. Bell Aerospace Co., 416 U.S. 267, 288 (1974). However, employees who are given rights to participate in the firm's decision-making in their own behalf should continue to be protected because the firm's ownership need not be concerned about the priorities of these employees being influenced by union activities. See also Note, "Collective Authority and Technical Expertise: Reexamining the Managerial Employee Exclusion," 56 N.Y.U.L. Rev. 694, 730–38 (1981) (suggesting a somewhat different multifactor distinction of managerial employees).

67. On the other hand, inasmuch as employers have no statutory rights, through Section 8(a)(2) or any other provision, to be free of employee advisory committees, employers cannot claim that they should be free of bargaining pressure when rejecting union-proposed committees. Nothing in the holding or logic of *Borg-Warner* prevents the same topics from being mandatory bargaining subjects for one party and not for another. For instance, the union in *Borg-Warner* surely could have insisted on a recognition clause confirming its certification. Cf. Harper, supra note 49, at 1478 and n.116 (example of why topics must be defined precisely to determine whether bargaining is mandatory). When employee statutory rights that are waivable by collective-bargaining agents are implicated, an asymmetrical scope of bargaining thus may be appropriate. See generally Harper, supra note 9, at 335–89, 680–704 (discussing union control over employee rights).

68. Richfield Oil Corp., 110 N.L.R.B. 356 (1954), enf'd, 231 F.2d 717 (D.C. Cir.), cert. denied, 351 U.S. 909 (1956).

69. See Olsen, supra note 56, at 783–88.

70. See id. at 742–69 for examples.

3
INFORMATION-SHARING OBLIGATIONS
John D. Feerick

Editors' Note. Dean Feerick observes that an employer's duty to share information with the bargaining representative turns, with some exceptions, on the relevance the information has for mandatory subjects of collective bargaining. Directly related information is presumptively disclosable; however, to obtain indirectly related information, a union must affirmatively demonstrate relevance. Thus, for example, before a union challenging "double-breasting" may obtain information concerning a company's nonunion operations, it must furnish a basis for believing that, in fact, there is a single entity under the NLRA. As to financial information, mere unwillingness to pay triggers no disclosure requirement, whereas a declared inability to pay does. Confidentiality concerns, whether privacy interests of employees or company trade secrets, may also limit disclosure. In the author's view, the NLRB's narrow view of what constitutes mandatory bargaining subjects, in the context of business change decisions, has deprived unions of access to information having an "enormous impact on unit work."

The author wishes to acknowledge the extensive drafting and research assistance of Fred Glass, of the New York Bar, and to express to him his deepest gratitude. This article reports developments as of September 1987.

THE LAW IN GENERAL

The Act and Its Purpose

Section 8(a) (5) of the NLRA (or Act) makes it "an unfair labor practice for an employer to refuse to bargain collectively with the representatives of his employees."[1] Section 8(b)(3) places a parallel duty upon a union.[2] According to Section 8(d) of the Act, "to bargain collectively is the performance of the mutual obligation . . . to meet at reasonable times and confer in good faith with respect to wages, hours, and other terms and conditions of employment."[3] Taken together, these sections provide the statutory basis that obligates employers and unions to share information.[4]

The flow of information is necessary to enable parties to bargain intelligently, to police their collective-bargaining agreements, and to prepare for future negotiations. Furthermore, disclosure is favored since it facilitates early settlements between unions and employers and thus promotes industrial peace.

Requests for Information

The party requesting information must make a demand for it,[5] which should be specific,[6] though it need not be precise.[7] If the request is ambiguous, the recipient is obligated to ask for clarification before it can be relieved of the obligation to furnish the information sought.[8] A request need not be in writing.[9] Even if the request involves a grievable matter, it need not be preliminarily submitted to an arbitrator for a determination.[10] Defferal to arbitration in such circumstances "would require labor organizations to proceed to arbitration, without the information necessary to full assessment of its claim, and, at that level, for the first time have access to data which might well indicate that the grievance ought never to have been brought in the first place."[11] Once a request is received, an unreasonable delay in producing the requested information violates the duty to disclose.[12] What constitutes an unreasonable delay varies with the facts of each particular case.[13]

Necessary and Relevant Information

In determining whether there is a duty to disclose, courts and the NLRB (or Board) first ascertain whether the information is necessary and relevant. Although the Act does not expressly provide a standard for what is necessary and relevant, the courts and the Board have established a broad "discovery-type standard."[14] Thus, in the absence of some valid countervailing interest, disclosure usually is required as long as the information may possibly have a bearing on the bargaining process.[15] It is not the Board's function, however, to pass on the merits of the underlying claim.[16] A union does not have to demonstrate instances of contract violations or show that the information that triggered the request is accurate, non-hearsay, or ultimately reliable.[17]

Presumptions

A dichotomy exists between information bearing directly on mandatory bargaining subjects and other information. As a general rule, information related to mandatory subjects of bargaining—those items that relate to "wages, hours and other terms and conditions of employment"—is presumptively relevant.[18] An employer can rebut the presumption, for example, by showing that the union was given similar information in the past or that the information will be used to harass employees rather than to bargain or prosecute grievances.[19]

In *Oil, Chemical & Atomic Workers Local Union v. NLRB*,[20] the D.C. Circuit acknowledged that while some courts have applied the presumption solely to wages and related data,[21] other courts have taken a broader approach and have held that any information relating directly to a mandatory subject of bargaining is presumptively relevant.[22] Although the appellate court found it unnecessary to resolve the issue, it suggested that the latter approach should prevail, since the rationale underlying the presumptive relevance rule is the avoidance of bickering over the specific relevance of requested information.[23]

Information unrelated to mandatory subjects is not presumed to be relevant. In such cases, a union is obligated to demonstrate affirmatively the relevance of such information to bargainable or grievable issues.[24] For example, in order for a union to receive information regarding employees whom it does not represent, the union must demonstrate that the information is relevant to a particular bargaining subject or grievance.[25] If, however, there is a claim that non-bargaining unit employees are performing unit work, unions have the right of access to wage data concerning such employees.[26]

A related area recently addressed by the Board and courts concerns "double-breasted" operations. In this situation, an employer operates two corporations: One employs only union members under a contract purporting to recognize the union over a particular geographic area while its counterpart competes in the same area using nonunion workers. In order for a union to gain access to the information regarding the nonunion operation, it must have a reasonable evidentiary basis for suspecting the possibility of "double-breasting," that is, that two firms are in essence the same employer or alter egos.[27]

Burdensomeness As a Defense

A widely used defense for not providing information is that to do so would be unduly costly or burdensome. A categorical refusal, however, to supply relevant information posited on a defense of undue burden is a violation of the Act.[28] The initial onus is on the party from whom the information is requested to substantiate a claim of undue burden.[29] Once the claim is substantiated, the parties must bargain over the allocation of costs involved in producing relevant and necessary information.[30] Ultimately, if the parties cannot agree on what is a proper allocation, the party from whom the information is requested should provide such access that will enable the other party to compile the requested information[31] unless to do so would violate employee privacy rights or would expose confidential business information.

Waiver of Statutory Rights

Since the NLRA was enacted to create a structure for mandatory bargaining irrespective of the bargaining power of the parties, "[n]ational labor policy disfavors waivers of statutory rights by unions."[32] Thus, it is rare that the courts or the Board will infer that a party has waived its right to information.[33] Waiver can occur in three ways: by an express provision in the collective-bargaining agreement, by the conduct of the parties, or by a combination of the two.[34] For an express waiver to be found, the language in the collective-bargaining agreement or other writing must be "clear and unmistakable."[35] A similar standard also applies to waivers established through the conduct of the parties.[36] The mere existence of a grievance procedure is not sufficient to constitute waiver of a union's statutory right to request information from the employer.[37]

DISCLOSURE IN THE BUSINESS SETTING

Concession Bargaining

Employers sometimes are faced with difficult financial situations and seek to cut costs by bargaining for economic concessions. When that occurs, the employer's financial condition may become a major issue, and a union may request that the employer disclose various financial data in order to substantiate its claim of financial straits.

In the leading case, *NLRB v. Truitt Manufacturing Co.*,[38] the Supreme Court ruled that an employer's refusal to substantiate its claim that a raise of more than two and one-half cents per hour would force it out of business was in violation of Section 8(a)(5) of the Act. The Court reasoned that "[i]f such an argument is important enough to present in the give and take of bargaining, it is important enough to require some sort of proof of its accuracy."[39]

However, subsequent decisions of the Board and the courts have narrowly construed *Truitt*. In determining whether an employer is obligated to provide information pertaining to its financial condition, a distinction is drawn between an explicit plea of inability to pay and mere unwillingness to pay. While an employer's expressed inability to pay may give rise to a duty to provide financial information, simple unwillingness to pay does not invoke the obligation to supply information.

In *Atlanta Hilton and Tower*, the Board held that "[a]lthough no magic words are required to express an inability to pay, the words and conduct must be specific enough to convey such a meaning.''[40] There, the Board found that an employer's refusal to furnish records was not unlawful, since vague references to the economy in general and the hotel's occupancy rate were not sufficient to constitute a plea of inability to pay.[41]

Also, an employer's assertion that union concessions are necessary in order for it to remain competitive does not amount to an expression of inability to pay. In *NLRB v. Harvstone Mfg. Corp.*, the Court of Appeals for the Seventh Circuit refused to enforce a Board order requiring three employers to disclose financial data when the employers made such a claim.[42] In determining that the union could not gain access to the employers' books and records, the court stated that the test is whether there is ''substantial evidence in the record as a whole'' to support a finding that the employer pleaded inability to pay.[43] The court noted that the negotiator's statement to the effect that if the employers did not make a reasonable profit ''they would not stay in business,'' was nothing more than a truism and did not trigger a *Truitt* obligation.[44]

Form of Substantiation

An employer may regard its financial situation as highly sensitive and thus may wish to keep it confidential. Yet failure to substantiate a claim of financial inability may support a finding of a failure to bargain in good faith. In dealing with this tension, the courts and the Board agree that disclosure need not be in the exact form requested.[45] In *Truitt*[46] the Supreme Court held that ''[e]ach case must turn upon its particular facts. The inquiry must always be whether or not under the circumstances of the particular case the statutory obligation to bargain in good faith has been met.''[47] Although the Court's language indicates that a refusal to supply properly requested information is not per se bad faith bargaining, the general consensus today is that a blanket refusal to disclose does constitute a failure to bargain in good faith.[48]

In *Yakima Frozen Foods*, the Board agreed that an employer is not under an obligation to ''bare his books'' to a union.[49] There, the union sought access to company records to verify a claim of financial inability to pay a wage increase. The company feared that if the union had access to its sources of supplies, it would face secondary boycotts. Thus, it offered the union its most recent balance sheets and offered to submit its records to a full audit by an independent certified public accountant. The Board found that by such conditional access the employer did not engage in bad faith bargaining.[50]

Recently, in *NLRB v. St. Joseph's Hospital*, the Second Circuit rejected the contention that a hospital interfered with a union's selection of a bargaining representative by insisting that the certified public accountant selected by the union have familiarity with state reimbursement procedures.[51] In overturning the Board, the court found that the hospital's fear of labor strife, if an unqualified accountant erroneously forecasted its income over the next year, was legitimate and reasonable.

Nonfinancial Data

Employers may also resist disclosure of sensitive or confidential nonfinancial data that could damage their business. When a legitimate and substantial claim of confidentiality is raised,[52] the Board and the courts balance the employer's property and privacy interests against the union's need for relevant information necessary for effective bargaining and grievance adjustment.

Personnel Test Data

In *Detroit Edison Company v. NLRB*, the Supreme Court established that a union's interest in relevant information does not always prevail over an employer's interest in preserving confidentiality.[53] There, the collective-bargaining agreement provided that promotions were to be based on seniority whenever the qualifications and abilities of the employees were not considered to be significantly different. Promotion decisions were subject to the contract's grievance procedure, which culminated in arbitration.

Since the late 1920s, the company had used aptitude tests administered by its industrial psychologists to evaluate employees who wished to be considered for promotion. All tests were administered with the express commitment that they would be kept confidential. When ten employees who took the test failed, the union filed a grievance alleging that the recently revised scoring system, which raised the standard for ''acceptable'' ratings, violated the seniority provision of the agreement. The company rejected the grievance. The union proceeded to arbitration requesting Detroit Edison to disclose the test questions, the employee answer sheets, and the scores linked with the names of the employees who received them. When the company offered the raw scores of all the examinees, but refused to link the scores to the names of the employees without their consent, the Board ordered the company to comply with the union's entire request. To protect the employer, the Board instructed the union to refrain from copying the test questions or allowing employee access to them. The Court of Appeals for the Sixth Circuit upheld the Board's order.

In vacating and remanding the case, the Supreme Court ruled that the Board abused its discretion by ordering the company to deliver the question and answer sheets and to disclose the individual test results. In balancing the parties' competing interests, the Court found that the Board's remedy offered scant protection to the legitimate and substantial interest of the employer in maintaining an effective testing program. The company had offered to turn over the test questions and answers to a union-selected industrial psychologist, and the Court deemed such access sufficient. Concerning the privacy interests of the employees, the Court held that any possible impairment of the union's effectiveness in processing grievances was "more than justified by the interests served by conditioning the disclosure of the test scores upon the consent of the very employees whose grievance was being processed."[54]

Personnel Files

Typically, disputes concerning access to personnel files arise in the context of the grievance process after an employer imposes disciplinary action on an employee. For example, in *New Jersey Telephone Co. v. NLRB*, after three employees were disciplined for reporting late to work, the union sought to examine their absence and tardiness records.[55] The company refused to allow the union to examine the records without the consent of the employees, in accordance with its "Employee Privacy Protection Plan," since the records contained details of intimate personal health problems as reasons for absences.

In overturning the Board's order to disclose, the Third Circuit applied the *Detroit Edison* test to employee records. First, the court determined that the information contained in the records was highly sensitive. Second, it found that obtaining the employees' consent placed a minimal burden on the union. Finally, there was no evidence that the privacy plan was instituted to frustrate the union in its role as employee representatives.[56] Access to such records may be required, however, when the files do not contain intimate or possibly embarrassing information or the circumstances suggest that the employees had formed no legitimate expectations of privacy.[57]

Equal Employment Statistical Data

In *Westinghouse Electric Corp.*, to ascertain whether the company was complying with a nondiscrimination clause in the labor contract, the union requested statistical data on the composition of the work force, copies of all charges and complaints filed against the company for alleged discrimination, and copies of the company's affirmative action programs and work force analyses.[58] Applying the standard it uses to determine the relevance of wage data, the Board found that the demand for the statistical breakdown of the company's unit employees was presumptively relevant. In addition, it held that the union had a presumptive right to copies of all charges and complaints filed by unit employees. To protect the identity of the charging parties, however, the Board allowed the company to delete their names. Finally, the Board held that affirmative action programs were not presumptively relevant, since the information did "not appear to be reasonably necessary to enable the Union to administer its contract intelligently and effectively."[59]

The D.C. Circuit modified the Board's order but essentially sustained the agency's position. The court ruled that delivery of actual copies of the complaints was not required. Instead, a compilation of the numbers, types, dates, and alleged bases of the complaints would be sufficient, since it enabled the union to ascertain the possible existence of discrimination while assuring union members that their complaints would be maintained in confidence.

Contemplation of Litigation

Another area in which the Board may find an employer to have a legitimate and substantial interest in confidentiality concerns information obtained in contemplation of litigation. Witness statements need not be furnished during the grievance process, though the names of witnesses should be disclosed.[60] Studies prepared in contemplation of litigation also may be protected.[61]

Health and Safety Data

Access to employee health and safety data is a source of concern to employers because of the potential for disclosure of trade secrets. While unions have legitimate needs for information relevant to the health and safety of their members, employers have an interest in preserving the confidentiality of the composition of their products. In *Oil, Chemical and Atomic Workers Local Union v. NLRB*, the Court of Appeals for the District of Columbia Circuit reviewed three consolidated Board decisions which addressed this issue.[62]

In *Minnesota Mining and Manufacturing Co. (MMM)*, two local unions sought health and safety related data, including the generic names of all substances used and produced at the plant, in order to determine whether the company was in compliance with the health and safety requirements of the federal Occupational Safety and Health Act.[63] The Board found that the union's request was relevant since, without information regarding the chemicals its members were exposed to, the union could not bargain effectively over health and safety matters. The Board, however, refused to impose a duty on the employer to disclose all of the information, since some of the generic data sought by the union constituted trade secrets. Instead, the Board ordered the company and union to return to the bargaining table in order to work out their own arrangement for disclosure. In *Colgate Palmolive Co.*[64] and *Borden Chemical Co.*,[65] the unions made similar requests for health and safety information. Again, the Board determined that the disclosure of information as to which the employers asserted a trade secret defense was a matter for initial resolution through collective bargaining. In enforcing the Board's orders in all three cases, the Court of Appeals stated that *Detroit Edison* did not afford "support for the position that an employer is absolutely privileged from revealing relevant proprietary or trade secret information." Accordingly, it held appropriate the Board's direction to the parties to return to the bargaining table in an effort to accommodate their respective interests. The court further noted that if no solution could be worked out, the cases could ultimately come before the Board again for a balancing of the parties' interests.[66]

In *Goodyear Atomic Corp. v. NLRB*, the union sought from a uranium manufacturer information concerning employee health and safety programs, monitoring and testing systems, devices and equipment, and statistical data related to working conditions to the extent that such information did not include individual medical records from which identifying characteristics had not been removed.[67] Unlike *MMM*, where the employer raised a trade secret defense, here the employer asserted that to comply with the request would violate employee privacy rights and would be prohibitively expensive. The Sixth Circuit rejected the employer's privacy defense, since the Board's order exempted medical data which identified particular employees. In rejecting the burdensome defense, the court held that if substantial costs were involved, the employer could require the union to bargain in good faith over a method of allocating costs; it could not refuse all access to the requested information. Without agreement on the distribution of costs, the employer was required to grant the union access to the records from which the information could be derived.[68]

Access to Plant

Adequate representation on health and safety matters may also depend on union access to the employer's plant. *Holyoke Water Power Co.* provides a recent example.[69] There, the employer operated a power plant, which contained two large fans used to force air into the plant's burners. The fans were extremely noisy, and employees had to enter the fan room to perform maintenance and repair work. The employer had commenced burning coal instead of oil, causing the temperatures of the burners to increase. To cool the burners, fan operation was increased from 60 to 95 percent of the time. To survey possible health problems created by the increased fan use, the union sent an industrial hygienist into the plant. When the company barred access by the hygienist to the fan room, the union filed an unfair labor practice charge.

Prior to *Holyoke*, the Board had treated union requests for plant access in order to obtain health and safety information as simple requests for information.[70] Here, however, the Board rejected that approach. Instead, using the test first adopted by the Supreme Court in *NLRB v. Babcock and Wilcox Co.*,[71] it balanced the union's interest in obtaining access against the company's property interest. In *Babcock and Wilcox*, the Supreme Court held that nonemployee union organizers enjoyed no presumptive right of access to distribute organizational information on company property as long as there were other means of communicating with employees. The Board in *Holyoke* found, however, that the employer's property rights had to yield to the extent necessary to enable the industrial hygienist to conduct the noise-level tests.

While enforcing the Board's order, the First Circuit noted that *Babcock and Wilcox* did not obviously govern, since the cases to which it applied typically arose out of requests for access by nonemployees in organizational settings that posed a more significant threat to the property rights of employers. Moreover, *Babcock and Wilcox* could not possibly have dealt with the information sharing obligations inherent in the statutory duty to bargain with the exclusive bargaining representative of the employees. Despite these reservations, the Court of Appeals declined to reject the Board's balancing test, since the outcome of the case would have been the same if the request for access was treated as a simple request for information. Although the court noted that the scales were necessarily tipped further to the side of the employer under the Board's balancing test, under either approach the company's interest in denying access was insubstantial.[72]

Business Changes

Decisions to close plants, relocate, sell assets, restructure, consolidate, or subcontract can have a profound effect on the availability of union work. As a consequence, unions frequently seek studies and other information used by an employer in making such decisions. Their entitlement to this information usually depends on whether the decision concerns a mandatory subject of bargaining under Section 8(d) of the Act.

The Board directly addressed the duty to supply information in such a context in *Otis Elevator Co.*[73] There, a few years after acquiring Otis, United Technologies commissioned three studies which showed that Otis had outdated technology, resulting in expensive product designs and noncompetitive prices. Based on its review of these problems, United Technologies decided to terminate two research and development operations and to consolidate them at its major research and development center in another state.

Upon hearing the company's plan, the union requested the internal information used in reaching the decision. When the company refused to comply with the request, the Board found a violation of the Act, reasoning that the decision to relocate or consolidate a plant was a mandatory subject of bargaining. The Board thereupon sought enforcement of its order to disclose the information. While the appeal was pending, the Supreme Court decided *First National Maintenance Corp. v. NLRB*, holding that employers must bargain over the effects of a plant shutdown but not over the decision itself.[74] As a result, the Board withdrew its enforcement proceeding in *Otis* in order to reconsider its decision.[75] After such reconsideration, it held that a decision which turns on a fundamental change in the scope, direction, or nature of the enterprise is excluded from mandatory bargaining, whereas a decision which turns primarily on labor costs is subject to such bargaining.[76] The Board found that since the employer's decision to consolidate was made to improve the company's research and development capability and the marketability of its products, rather than to simply reduce labor costs, the consolidation entailed a fundamental change in the nature and direction of the business. Thus, the Board concluded that the employer was not obligated to provide the information requested.[77]

CONCLUSION

This chapter has summarized the current state of the law regarding information sharing obligations. As noted, there has been a general shift in policy in recent years.

Prior to *Detroit Edison*, it was difficult for an employer to refuse to disclose information. In that decision, however, the Supreme Court held that a union's interest in relevant information does not necessarily take precedence over the business interests of the employer, thus providing the legal foundation for the Board and lower courts to become more protective of employer interests.

The shift is apparent in the area of concession bargaining. In the past, an employer's assertion that it could not pay higher wages or fringe benefits and remain competitive would force disclosure of substantiating information.[78] Now, although the Board and courts examine the record as a whole, they are more apt to deny access to financial records by determining that the employer's claim of a need to remain competitive does not amount to a plea of inability to pay under *Truitt*.

In the past, an employer's interest in the confidentiality of requested data was considered secondary to a union's need for relevant information.[79] Today, the confidentiality defense is formidable. This is particularly true when an employer asserts that disclosure threatens exposure of its trade secrets. In such cases, the parties are now required to bargain in good faith over disclosure of sensitive information. If they cannot agree, the Board will balance their interests. Since, as of this writing, no trade secret case has returned to the Board, it is unclear how it will perform the balancing test if the parties cannot work out their differences.

The present propensity of the Board to give more weight to business interests is also illustrated in cases where a union seeks access to an employer's plant. By treating, for example, a request for access to obtain health and safety data as analogous to a request for access by a nonemployee union organizer—to be analyzed under *Babcock and Wilcox*—the Board necessarily tips the scales in favor of management. Since the First Circuit has refused to adopt the Board's logic, however, union access rights in the future remain unclear.

Finally, by ruling that employer decisions which turn on fundamental changes in the scope, nature, or direction of the business are not mandatory subjects of bargaining, the Board has removed the underpinning for claims by unions for information pertaining to business decisions having an enormous impact on unit work. It remains to be seen what effect all these legal developments will have on unions as they seek to cope with the changing business environment.

NOTES

1. 29 U.S.C. § 158(a) (5).

2. 29 U.S.C. § 158(b) (3). Typically, disclosure involves the dissemination of information from the employer to the union. But see Local Union No. 497, Int'l Brotherhood of Elec. Workers, 275 N.L.R.B. 1249 (1985) (union which operated exclusive hiring hall violated Act by denying employer's request for a list of names and addresses of persons subject to referral system). See also Asbestos Workers, Local 80, 248 N.L.R.B. 143 (1980) (union's refusal to furnish information relating to referral system held unlawful, since information was necessary for employer association to evaluate referral practices, test validity of such practices, and formulate contract proposals); Local No. 13, Printing

and Graphic Communications Union, 233 N.L.R.B. 994 (1977), enf'd, 598 F.2d 267 (D.C. Cir. 1979).

3. 29 U.S.C. § 158(d).

4. NLRB v. Acme Industrial Co., 385 U.S. 432 (1967); NLRB v. Truitt Mfg. Co., 351 U.S. 149 (1956).

5. Westinghouse Elec. Co. v. NLRB, 196 F.2d 1012 (3d Cir. 1952) (company did not refuse unlawfully to produce survey since there was no evidence that the union requested disclosure).

6. Western Elec. Co., 223 N.L.R.B. 86 (1976).

7. See Ellsworth Sheet Metal, Inc., 232 N.L.R.B. 109 (1977). See also Cedar Rapids Steel Transport, Inc., 269 N.L.R.B. 400 (1984), enf'd, 758 F.2d 645 (4th Cir. 1985) (employer's inquiries for added specificity did not excuse nonproduction since the union could not provide greater specificity without additional information from employer). Compare Salt River Valley Water Users' Ass'n, 272 N.L.R.B. 296 (1984), enf'd, 769 F.2d 639 (9th Cir. 1985) (employer's obligation to reveal information in personnel file is limited to those items which the union specified in letter to employer since the union had testified that the letter was intended to clarify which information was specifically requested).

8. See United States Postal Svc., 276 N.L.R.B. 1282 (1985).

9. See International Tel. and Tel. Corp. v. NLRB, 382 F.2d 366, 371 (3d Cir. 1967), cert. denied, 389 U.S. 1039 (1968).

10. NLRB v. Acme Indus. Co., 385 U.S. 432, 438 (1967) ("arbitration can function properly only if the grievance procedures leading to it can sift out unmeritorious claims").

11. General Dynamics Corp., Quincy Shipbuilding Div., 270 N.L.R.B. 829, 835 (1984), quoting Worcester Polytechnic Institute, 213 N.L.R.B. 306, 309 (1974).

12. Reed and Prince Mfg. Co., 96 N.L.R.B. 850 (1951), enf'd, 205 F.2d 131 (1st Cir.), cert. denied, 346 U.S. 887 (1953).

13. See Union Carbide Corp., Nuclear Div., 275 N.L.R.B. 197 (1985) (delay of 10-1/2 months not unlawful since the employer expeditiously commenced an expensive task of gathering data, which included 250,000 pages). See also Financial Employees Local No. 1182 v. NLRB, 738 F.2d 1038 (9th Cir. 1984) (employer's delay not unlawful when there was no evidence that the delay was a mere cover-up to frustrate the union).

14. NLRB v. Acme Indus. Co., 385 U.S. 432, 437 & n.6 (1967); NLRB v. Yawman & Erbe Mfg. Co., 187 F.2d 947, 949 (2d Cir. 1951), enf'g 89 N.L.R.B. 881 (1950). However, in practice, a party may not have access to every piece of paper the company has generated explaining a particular bargaining position. Moreover, the Board does not generally require that the information be disclosed in the exact form requested. See Albany Garage, Inc., 126 N.L.R.B. 417 (1960) (union was not entitled to audit the employer's records to investigate a claim of inability to grant a wage increase where the employer furnished financial statements for the preceding years).

15. NLRB v. Acme Indus. Co., 385 U.S. 432 (1967). See also Local 13, Detroit Newspaper Union v. NLRB, 598 F.2d 267, 271–72 (D.C. Cir. 1979) ("[a] broad disclosure rule is crucial to full development of the role of collective bargaining contemplated by the Act"); Conrock Co., 263 N.L.R.B. 1293, 1294 (1982) ("[a]n employer must furnish information that is even of probable or potential relevance to the Union's duties"), enf'd, 735 F.2d 1371 (9th Cir. 1984). But see E.I. Du Pont de Nemours & Co., 276 N.L.R.B. 335 (1985) (employer did not violate the Act when it denied the union's request

for certain income statements and supporting schedules since the requested information was not relevant to bargaining over a restructuring proposal).

16. NLRB v. Rockwell-Standard Corp., 410 F.2d 953, 957 (6th Cir. 1969), enf'g 166 N.L.R.B. 124 (1967).

17. W-L Molding Co., 272 N.L.R.B. 1239 (1984), citing Boyers Constr. Co., 267 N.L.R.B. 227, 229 (1983).

18. NLRB v. F. W. Woolworth Co., 352 U.S. 938 (1956); Curtis-Wright Corp. v. NLRB, 347 F.2d 61, 69 (3d Cir. 1965); Whitman Machine Works, 108 N.L.R.B. 1537, enf'd, 217 F.2d 593 (4th Cir. 1954), cert. denied, 349 U.S. 905 (1955).

19. See Shell Oil Co. v. NLRB, 457 F.2d 615 (9th Cir. 1975) (employer's refusal to supply employee names to the union was not unlawful since there was a well-founded fear that nonstriking employees would have been harassed).

20. Oil, Chemical & Atomic Workers Local Union v. NLRB, 711 F.2d 348 (D.C. Cir. 1983).

21. See Prudential Ins. Co. of America v. NLRB, 412 F.2d 77, 84 (2d Cir.), cert. denied, 396 U.S. 928 (1969).

22. See Equitable Gas Co. v. NLRB, 637 F.2d 980, 993 (3d Cir. 1981).

23. *Oil, Chemical & Atomic Workers*, 711 F.2d at 359, n.26.

24. Press Democrat Publishing Co. v. NLRB, 629 F.2d 1320, 1324 (9th Cir. 1980), citing San Diego Newspaper Guild v. NLRB, 548 F.2d 863, 867–68 (9th Cir. 1977).

25. See, e.g., United Graphics, Inc., 281 N.L.R.B. 70 (1986) (employer violated the Act by denying the union's request for names, addresses, wages, and fringe benefits of temporary workers whom the employer obtained from an employment agency); Safeway Stores, Inc., 268 N.L.R.B. 284 (1983) (no violation occurred when the employer refused to give the union a list of temporary employees hired during a work stoppage). Also, in order for a union to obtain information concerning retirees, it must demonstrate that the data will enable it to bargain more intelligently for active employees. Union Carbide Corp., 197 N.L.R.B. 717 (1972).

26. See Henry F. Budde Publications, Inc., 242 N.L.R.B. 243 (1979) (employer's refusal to supply pay data for employee interns was held unlawful).

27. See Corson & Grumman Co., 278 N.L.R.B. No. 48, (1986) (asphalt company unlawfully refused information concerning the company's ownership and control of two other paving firms since the union reasonably believed that the three firms were alter egos or a single employer). See also NLRB v. Leonard B. Hebert, Jr., & Co., 696 F.2d 1120 (5th Cir.), cert. denied, 464 U.S. 817 (1983) (based on evidence the union had received concerning a possibility of double-breasting, the union had a reasonable basis for seeking information to assist it in confirming suspicions and determining whether to pursue legal action); NLRB v. Lumber and Mill Employers Ass'n, 736 F.2d 507 (9th Cir.), cert. denied, 409 U.S. 934 (1984) (employer association's refusal to provide the union with a copy of the bylaws and membership roster held unlawful since the information could substantiate fear of double-breasted operations). Compare Bohemia Inc., 272 N.L.R.B. 1128 (1984) (Board did not presume data concerning nonunion operation was relevant since the union failed to establish an objective basis for a belief that unit work was being diverted to that operation).

28. International Union of Electrical, Radio and Machine Workers v. NLRB, 648 F.2d 18, 26 (D.C. Cir. 1980).

29. See Queen Anne Record Sales, Inc., 273 N.L.R.B. 671, (1984), enf'd, 772 F.2d

913 (9th Cir. 1985) (employer failed to show that the production of data would be unduly burdensome since there was nothing in the record to substantiate such a claim).

30. *Oil, Chemical & Atomic Workers*, 711 F.2d at 363; Safeway Stores, 252 N.L.R.B. 1323 (1980), enf'd, 691 F.2d 953 (10th Cir. 1982).

31. Globe-Union, Inc., 233 N.L.R.B. 1458 (1977); Food Employer Council, 197 N.L.R.B. 651 (1972).

32. Chesapeake & Potomac Tel. Co. v. NLRB, 687 F.2d 633, 636 (2d Cir. 1982).

33. Metropolitan Edison Co. v. NLRB, 460 U.S. 693, 708, n.12 (1983), citing *Chesapeake & Potomac Tel. Co.*, 687 F.2d 636.

34. *Chesapeake & Potomac Tel. Co.*, 687 F.2d at 636.

35. Timken Roller Bearing Co., 138 N.L.R.B. 15, 16 (1962). See also American Stores Packing Co., Div. of Acme Markets, 277 N.L.R.B. 1656 (1986) (union waived its right to the information necessary to bargain over the employer's decision to close a plant by executing a letter of intent granting the employer the right to remove unilaterally all unit work); United Technologies Corp., 274 N.L.R.B. 504 (1985) (union waived statutory rights by signing a letter of understanding exchanging access to certain records for relinquishment of rights to other information). Compare Clinchfield Coal Co., 275 N.L.R.B. 1384 (1985) (parties' collective-bargaining agreement did not establish a clear and unmistakable waiver by the union); General Dynamics Corp., Quincy Shipbuilding Div., 268 N.L.R.B. 1432 (1984) (Board held that if a waiver clause was intended to include all confidential information, the parties should have used explicit language to that effect).

36. See Emery Indus. Inc., 268 N.L.R.B. 824 (1984) (union waived the right to information concerning the employer's absenteeism policy when the union did not object to the implementation of the policy and failed to object to three modifications of the policy over a four-year period). Compare General Motors Corp., Inc. v. NLRB, 700 F.2d 1083 (6th Cir. 1983) (union did not waive its right of access to original time study data where the bargaining agreement was silent on the subject).

37. Timken Roller Bearing Co., 138 N.L.R.B. 15 (1962).

38. NLRB v. Truitt Manufacturing, 351 U.S. 149 (1956).

39. Id. at 152–53.

40. Atlanta Hilton and Tower, 271 N.L.R.B. 1600 (1984).

41. See Advertisers Mfg. Co., 275 N.L.R.B. 100 (1985) (employer's refusal to pay a year-end bonus, based on the contention that "the level of business in the industry and the Company has been very poor for an extended period of time," did not constitute a plea of inability to pay). Compare Cowin & Co., Inc., 277 N.L.R.B. 802 (1985) (employer expressed a financial inability to pay when it advised the union of "a real question of whether we shall be in business at the termination of this contract unless prior contractual concepts are radically changed"); Conrock Co., 263 N.L.R.B. 1293 (1982), enf'd, 735 F.2d 1371 (9th Cir. 1984) (refusal of information concerning truck maintenance and repair costs was held unlawful since the information was relevant to the reinstatement rights of drivers who had been laid off due to a decrease in the number of trucks, the employer maintained that the trucks were "too costly to maintain", and the collective-bargaining agreement allowed the employer to determine the extent to which it would replace the equipment that had become too costly to operate); NLRB v. Unoco Apparel, Inc., 508 F.2d 1368, 1370 (5th Cir. 1975) (employer's statement that the "employees came to the well . . . the well is dry" constituted a plea of inability to pay).

42. NLRB v. Harvstone Mfg. Corp., 785 F.2d 570 (7th Cir. 1986).

43. Id. at 572.

44. Id. at 576–77. See also Washington Materials, Inc., 276 N.L.R.B. 839, enf'd, 803 F.2d 1333 (4th Cir. 1986) (employers' position that unionized contractors were at a "competitive disadvantage" because nonunion businesses had lower costs did not amount to a claim of inability to pay since the Board will not assume that an employer who no longer wishes to pay wages and benefits it had once agreed to is unable to make such payments).

45. See Emeryville Research Center, Shell Dev. Co. v. NLRB, 441 F.2d 880 (9th Cir. 1971) (refusal to supply salary information in the form demanded was not unlawful since the proposed alternatives were responsive to the union's needs).

46. 351 U.S. at 149.

47. Id. at 153–54.

48. *Harvstone Mfg. Corp.*, 785 F.2d at 579.

49. Yakima Frozen Foods, 130 N.L.R.B. 1269, 1273 n.5 (1961), enf'd in part sub nom., Fruit and Vegetable Packers and Warehousemen Local 760 v. NLRB, 316 F.2d 389 (D.C. Cir. 1963).

50. The union's accountant may perform the audit when the employer makes no claim of confidentiality or misuse of the information by the union. Goodyear Aerospace Corp., 204 N.L.R.B. 831 (1973), enf'd in part, 497 F.2d 747 (6th Cir. 1974). See also United Aircraft Corp., 247 N.L.R.B. 1042, enf'd, 661 F.2d 910 (2d Cir. 1981), cert. denied, 455 U.S. 1001 (1982) (employer may require that the examination be done in the employer's office).

51. NLRB v. St. Joseph's Hospital, 755 F.2d 260 (2d Cir.), cert. denied sub nom., New York State Nurses Ass'n v. St. Joseph's Hospital, 106 S. Ct. 87 (1985).

52. The party asserting the claim of confidentiality bears the burden of proof. See Pfizer, Inc., 268 N.L.R.B. 916 (1984); McDonnell Douglas Corp., 224 N.L.R.B. 881 (1976).

53. Detroit Edison Company v. NLRB, 440 U.S. 301 (1979).

54. Id. at 319.

55. New Jersey Telephone Co. v. NLRB, 720 F.2d 789 (3d Cir. 1983).

56. Id. at 791.

57. See Salt River Valley v. NLRB, 769 F.2d 639 (9th Cir. 1985) (enforcing a Board order requiring the employer to turn over employee personnel records without employee consent because, unlike *Detroit Edison*, where the test results requested by the union theoretically revealed the employees' intellectual capacity and psychological makeup, here the information sought had no bearing on the employee's intelligence or psychological fitness, the employee had no expectation of confidentiality, and management had access and referred to employee records in a grievance procedure); Pfizer Inc., 268 N.L.R.B. 916 (1984), enf'd, 763 F.2d 887 (7th Cir. 1985) (unlike *Detroit Edison*, no commitment was made that the information about employees' promotions would remain confidential, and employees' work records do not involve the same sensitivity as aptitude test scores); Washington Gas Light Co., 273 N.L.R.B. 116 (1984) (employer's refusal to furnish past disciplinary records of four employees who had been disciplined but not discharged for intoxication was held unlawful since there was no past practice of confidentially, employees were not informed that the files would be kept confidential, and the company's own officials had access).

58. Westinghouse Electric Corp., 239 N.L.R.B. 106 (1978), modified on other grounds

sub nom., International Union of Elec., Radio & Machine Workers v. NLRB, 648 F.2d 18 (D.C. Cir. 1980).

59. 239 N.L.R.B. at 109. See also Equitable Life Assurance Society, 266 N.L.R.B. 732 (1983) (failure to supply equal employment opportunity data was held unlawful, but failure to furnish affirmative action plan was permissible). Compare Electrical Workers, Local Union No. 1186, 264 N.L.R.B. 712 (1982), enf'd, 714 F.2d 152 (9th Cir. 1983) (no violation occurred where the union offered employer association access to its hiring hall between 1:30 and 4:30 P.M. and the employer did not present evidence that such limited access was inadequate).

60. Anheuser-Busch, Inc., 237 N.L.R.B. 982 (1978). Compare Square D. Elec. Co., 266 N.L.R.B. 795 (1983) (employer's video tape of two employees in the act of stealing did not constitute a witness statement).

61. See General Dynamics Corp., Quincy Shipbuilding Div., 268 N.L.R.B. 1432 (1984) (since the employer had a legitimate and substantial interest in seeking to preserve the confidentiality of a study prepared in contemplation of litigation by another employer, the Board ordered the parties to bargain in good faith to reach a mutually acceptable accommodation). Compare Asarco, Inc., 276 N.L.R.B. 1367 (1985) (nondisclosure held unlawful since no lawsuits were pending when the union asked for a report).

62. 711 F.2d at 348.

63. Minnesota Mining and Manufacturing Co., 261 N.L.R.B. 27 (1982).

64. Id. at 90.

65. Id. at 64.

66. 711 F.2d at 362–63. See also Kelly-Springfield Tire Co., 266 N.L.R.B. 587 (1983) (employer was required to furnish the union with a listing of all the chemicals used in the plant and copies of handling precaution sheets along with decoding information in order that the union could understand the information; however, with respect to trade secrets, the Board gave the parties an opportunity to bargain in order to reach agreement).

67. Goodyear Atomic Corp. v. NLRB, 738 F.2d 155 (6th Cir. 1984), enf'g 266 N.L.R.B. 890 (1983).

68. Id. at 156–57.

69. Holyoke Water Power Co., 273 N.L.R.B. 1369, enf'd 778 F.2d 49 (1st Cir. 1985), cert. denied, 106 S. Ct. 3274 (1986).

70. See Winona Industries, 257 N.L.R.B. 695 (1981).

71. NLRB v. Babock and Wilcox Co., 351 U.S. 105 (1956).

72. 778 F.2d at 53. See also Asarco, Inc., 276 N.L.R.B. 1367 (1985) (Board found the principles announced in *Holyoke* to be fully applicable in concluding that the need for a union's hygienist to have access to the site of a mine accident outweighed the employer's property interests). Subsequent to the First Circuit's decision, the Board has continued to adhere to its *Holyoke* rationale; however, it did note that the employer has the burden of demonstrating that its property interest outweighs the union's need for access. See Hercules Inc., 281 N.L.R.B. 130 (1986).

73. Otis Elevator Co., 255 N.L.R.B. 235 (1981), modified 269 N.L.R.B. 891 (1984).

74. First National Maintenance Corp. v. NLRB, 452 U.S. 666 (1981).

75. See Baer, "Duty to Provide Information during Collective Bargaining," N.Y.L.J., Mar. 2, 1984, at 3, col. 1.

76. Otis Elevator Co., 269 N.L.R.B. 891 (1984).

77. See also Bostrom Div. UOP Inc., 272 N.L.R.B. 999 (1984) (employer's denial of the union's request for information regarding the economic justification for the decisions

to close two of four plants, consolidate operations at sites of two other plants, and subcontract foam and wood operations was held not unlawful).

78. See Stanley Bldg. Specialties Co., 166 N.L.R.B. 984 (1967), enf'd sub nom., United Steelworkers of America v. NLRB, 401 F.2d 434 (D.C. Cir. 1968), cert. denied sub nom., Stanley-Artex Windows v. NLRB, 395 U.S. 946 (1969); International Tel. & Tel. Corp., 159 N.L.R.B. 1757 (1966), enf'd, 382 F.2d 366 (3d Cir. 1967), cert. denied, 389 U.S. 1039 (1968); Cincinnati Cordage & Paper Co., 141 N.L.R.B. 72 (1963); Taylor Foundry Co., 141 N.L.R.B. 765 (1963), enf'd, 338 F.2d 1003 (5th Cir. 1964).

79. See J. O'Reilly, Unions' Right to Company Information 67–68 (1981).

4

SUCCESSORSHIP OBLIGATIONS

Samuel Estreicher

Editors' Note. Professor Estreicher compares successorship doctrine with the "single employer," "alter ego," and "contract bar" doctrines. He describes successorship in terms of the "*Wiley–Burns–Howard Johnson* triad," and concludes that the basic test for successorship status is "substantial continuity of identity in the business enterprise," with the most significant factor being the extent to which the predecessor's personnel have been retained in the composition of the new work force. The Supreme Court's decisions in this area thus create powerful incentives on the purchaser's part to refuse to hire the seller's union-represented workers, notwithstanding formal labor law principles which bar antiunion discrimination in hiring. The author considers in detail the seller's obligations under various forms of successorship clauses, and explores the availability of arbitral relief and temporary judicial relief in the nature of "reverse *Boys Market* injunctions."

The author gratefully acknowledges the research assistance of Bob Haroche and Chuck Keller.

The Labor Board's successorship doctrine is of enormous importance in today's world of rapid capital transfers, plant shutdowns, and abrogable collective-bargaining contracts. The following remarks offer not so much a full-scale critical perspective on this area of labor law, but an attempt to identify and assess the key practical issues that confront buyers and sellers of businesses, as well as unions and their members.

THE BASIC FRAMEWORK

It may be useful to begin by comparing the successorship doctrine with the "single employer," "alter ago," and "contract bar" doctrines and then follow with a discussion of the leading Supreme Court cases in this area. After the basic framework has been laid out, the substantive successorship issues will be examined.

Dealing with the "Same" Employing Enterprise

The Single Employer Doctrine. The single employer doctrine suggests that there may be situations in which two or more bona fide independent companies can be said to be so closely linked at the operational level that they each share responsibility for the other's labor decisions.

The D.C. Circuit's ruling in *United Telegraph Workers*[1] tells us that the Board must weigh four factors: (1) interrelation of operations, (2) common management, (3) centralized control of labor relations, and (4) common ownership or financial control.[2] In that case, the company had reorganized itself into a parent holding company and five subsidiaries: Western Union Telegraph (called Telegraph in the following discussion) would run the basic common carrier operation, and the various operations not regulated by the Federal Communications Commission (FCC) would be spun off into four other subsidiaries. The NLRB, with the appellate court's approval, held that while Telegraph retained a bargaining obligation with its union, the bargaining duty did not extend to the four other subsidiaries or the parent company. Important to the court was the fact that this was a bona fide reorganization—not animated by a desire simply to be freed of the union—and that the spun-off subsidiary companies in fact enjoyed day-to-day operational autonomy. As then Chief Judge Bazelon's dissent pointedly observed, however, the NLRB and the majority paid little attention to the fact that at least part of the formerly unionized enterprise was now operating under nonunion auspices.

Closely related to *United Telegraph Workers* is the Third Circuit's decision in *American Bell, Inc. v. Telephone Workers.*[3] In that case, AT&T had to reorganize pursuant to a court-approved consent decree with the Justice Department. AT&T proceeded to incorporate American Bell, Inc. (ABI) as a wholly owned subsidiary. AT&T's local carrier subsidiaries, including Bell Telephone of Pennsylvania (Bell), then transferred various assets to ABI. AT&T, again pursuant to the consent decree, proceeded to spin off its local carrier units, including Bell, as fully independent competitor companies. The Telephone Workers Union had a collective agreement with Bell (now an independent company) providing that the agreement would continue in effect for all employees transferred from Bell to its subsidiaries, and that Bell would make sure that any purchaser or transferee of any part of its operations would honor the labor contract. This was, in effect, a successorship clause.

Bell allegedly breached the successorship clause when it transferred its Phone Centers to ABI on January 1, 1983, without obtaining ABI's promise to assume the labor contract with the Telephone Workers Union. The Third Circuit ruled, however, that ABI was not bound by the Bell–Telephone Workers agreement, even though at the time of the assets transfer both ABI and Bell were subsidiaries of the same parent company. Chief Judge Seitz explained that a court "may not disregard at will the formal differences between affiliated corporations" and that "there is no policy of federal labor law, whether legislative or judge-made, that a parent corporation is bound by its subsidiary's labor contracts simply because it controls the subsidiary's stock and participates in the subsidiary's management."[4] The appeals court also noted that ABI enjoyed full, day-to-day control over its labor relations.

A useful contrast may be drawn between these cases and the Eighth Circuit's *Royal Typewriter* decision.[5] The court there found that Litton Industries, Royal's parent, was intimately involved in its subsidiary's labor relations, and thus Litton could be held partially responsible for Royal's illegal plant shutdown. Accordingly, Litton could be ordered to offer preferential hiring for former Royal employees at other Litton operations.

The lesson of these cases is that, despite common ownership and interrelated top management, parents and subsidiaries will ordinarily not be treated as part of the same enterprise, as long as the subsidiaries enjoy substantial day-to-day autonomy in labor relations.[6]

The Alter Ego Doctrine. Although the First Circuit's ruling in *Penntech Papers*[7] suggests that the terms single employer and alter ego may be used interchangeably, this is misleading. While common factors apply to both doctrines, the single employer or joint employer concept "reflects a judgment that two or more nominally separate business entities may properly be considered sufficiently integrated to warrant their unitary treatment, for various statutory purposes."[8] The alter ego doctrine, however, asks a related, but distinct question: Are we really dealing with two bona fide separate companies, or is the new company "a disguised continuance of the old employer"?[9] In short, alter ego status will attach to organizational changes undertaken not for some legitimate business purpose but solely as a device for exorcising the union.[10]

Typically, alter ego cases involve small companies that are not well situated to establish the kind of formally independent organizational structures found persuasive in *Bell* and *United Telegraph Workers*. Moreover, they present circumstances predisposing the court to pierce the corporate veil in order to stymie a principal's attempt to evade its obligations under an unexpired labor contract via transfer of that business to a newly formed company that is owned and controlled by the same individual or group.[11]

The Contract Bar Doctrine. Unlike both the single employer and alter ego theories, the contract bar context clearly deals with the same employer who finds that his labor contract may follow the move to a new plant location.

In *Westwood Import*,[12] the company embarked on a relocation of its business from San Francisco to Hayward, a distance of thirty miles, offering to transfer all San Francisco employees willing to move to Hayward. The Hayward operation began with seven long-term San Francisco employees and six new employees who had been hired in San Francisco with the understanding that they would be going to Hayward. Westwood argued that since less than a majority of its previous San Francisco work force had transferred to the new location, it was free of any obligations under the contract or with the union. The Board, with Ninth Circuit approval, disagreed, finding that the six new hires were still part of the San Francisco unit at the time of the plant transfer. The court left open the NLRB's alternative theory that even if the six could not be counted, the transfer of a "substantial percentage" (seven of seventeen) of long-time San Francisco employees might demonstrate a sufficient work-force continuity to hold the agreement effective at the relocated facility.

Some courts will not uphold application of the contract bar doctrine when the relocation involves a greater distance than was present in *Westwood Import* or a move across state lines or when there is a basis for finding a union waiver, say, in a narrowly framed plant relocation clause.[13]

The contract bar doctrine evidently turns on the employer's hiring its former employees at the new location. Although the employer may not discriminate on account of union membership, American labor law does not require an employer to offer employment to his former employees, unless this is a product of effects bargaining. Here, as in the successorship area generally, strong incentives are set in motion to avoid hiring or transferring former union-represented employees.

Dealing with a "Different" Employing Enterprise

As labor lawyers are generally familiar with the *Wiley-Burns-Howard Johnson* triad, an extensive discussion will be avoided.

Wiley v. Livingston,[14] penned by Justice Harlan, held that the surviving entity of a merger was under a duty to arbitrate under the predecessor's labor contract. The *Wiley* Court was, of course, much influenced by the *Steelworkers Triology*,[15] by the fact that the signatory employer had disappeared in the merger, and, implicitly, by state law rules requiring assumption of the obligations of the merged entity.

But for Justice Harlan, who the following year would author *Darlington*,[16] a more fundamental principle of adjustment of management-employer interests required recognition of successorship obligations. Justice Harlan offered what might be termed a quid pro quo theory: Entrepreneurial freedom mandates exclusion of certain fundamental decisions from the bargaining process, in return for which workers should be assured that they will be protected from a sudden change in the employment relationship. As Justice Harlan put it:

> Employees, and the union which represents them, ordinarily do not take part in negotiations leading to a change in corporate ownership. The negotiations will ordinarily not

concern the well-being of the employees, whose advantage or disadvantage, potentially great, will inevitably be incidental to the main considerations. The objectives of national labor policy, reflected in established principles of federal law, require that the rightful prerogative of owners independently to rearrange their businesses and even eliminate themselves as employers be balanced by some protection to the employees from a sudden change in the employment relationship. The transition from one corporate organization to another will in most cases be eased and industrial strife avoided if employees' claims continue to be resolved by arbitration rather than by "the relative strength . . . of the contending forces."[17]

The Supreme Court did not return to the successorship subject for another eight years, until *NLRB v. Burns International Security Services*[18]—an opinion which many thought sounded the death knell for *Wiley*. It is hard to understand, however, how *Burns* could have come out differently on the issue of whether a prevailing competitive bidder is obligated to assume the losing bidder's labor contract. The Court was unanimous on this point, for good reason.

Burns was a stranger to the preexisting relationship between Wackenhut and the union; it was a third party, pure and simple. This was not a consensual transfer in which the parties can make provision for the costs of unexpired labor contracts. Imposing the contract on *Burns* would clearly violate the liberty of contract principle of Section 8(d) and *H. K. Porter Co. v. NLRB*.[19]

The retreat from *Wiley* really occurred in the 1974 ruling in *Howard Johnson*, which did involve a consensual transfer.[20] There, the Grissoms, the sellers, who had been operating the enterprise under franchises from Howard Johnson, retained the real property and leased it to Howard Johnson which, in turn, would be conducting the identical operation as had the Grissoms.

The Court held that Howard Johnson was free of any obligation to arbitrate under the seller's agreement, or to bargain with the seller's union. *Wiley* was distinguished as a merger case where the signatory employer had disappeared and all of its employees had continued on with the surviving entity. Gone is Justice Harlan's quid pro quo theme. In its place, we are given a test calling for "substantial continuity of identity in the business enterprise"—the most important factor being whether the purchaser hires the predecessor's people rather than an independent work force. The freedom to hire an independent work force—a principle developed in *Burns* in the context of nonconsensual competitive bidding—has now been transposed to this very different setting of negotiated business transfers with the door now wide open to eliminating bargaining relationships as a normal incident of the sale of assets of a business.

The Supreme Court's recent decision in *Fall River Dyeing & Finishing Corp. v. NLRB*[21] essentially reaffirms the *Burns–Howard Johnson* framework. Justice Blackmun's opinion for the five-four majority explains that the existence of a bargaining obligation will turn on the purchaser's hiring decisions:

[T]o a substantial extent the applicability of *Burns* rests in the hands of the successor. If the new employer makes a conscious decision to maintain generally the same business and to hire a majority of its employees from the predecessor, then the bargaining obligation of § 8(a)(5) is activated. This makes sense when one considers that the employer *intends* to take advantage of the trained workforce of its predecessor.[22]

With the general framework set out, I divide the remainder of my remarks between seller obligations and purchaser obligations.

SELLER'S OBLIGATIONS

A seller may face difficulties under the single employer, alter ego, and contract bar doctrines. Here, I defer to the earlier discussion.

A seller may also have obligations under state law that will survive the termination of the labor contract. The Atari lawsuit in California, for example, may be the harbinger of quasi-contract liability for promises of job security dashed by business downturn.[23]

Mention should also be made of state laws requiring advance notice of plant closings. Massachusetts not too long ago passed a measure of this type.[24] Similar proposals are a hot item on the agenda of thirty-eight other states, and they are being taken seriously in Congress.[25] The Supreme Court in 1987 also made it clear that states are free of any ERISA or NLRA preemption barrier in requiring employers who do not have severance pay agreements or plans in place to pay such benefits upon closing their plants.[26]

The principal focus here is on the seller's obligation, if any, to find a purchaser who will assume the unexpired labor contract.

Type of Clauses

Aside from "vested" and "quasi-vested" claims, such as severance pay, which state law or ERISA common law may address,[27] the seller's obligation will stem, if at all, from the successorship clause of its labor contract. Such clauses take a variety of forms:

1. One type involves boilerplate recitals, whether in the preamble to the labor agreement or its penultimate paragraph, that the contract is binding on the parties and their "successors or assigns."
2. A second type of provision might be termed the "evasion" clause, in which the employer promises not to transfer any operation "for the purpose of defeating or evading the agreement."
3. A third is the explicit successorship clause, in which the employer expressly agrees to transfer the operation only to a purchaser who will assume the labor contract.

Arbitration Awards

Although a few arbitrators may find in the boilerplate variant of the successorship clause an obligation to sell only to an assuming purchaser,[28] most arbitrators will either hold that (1) such clauses do not come into play until we have a legally cognizable "successor" under *Howard Johnson* or an assuming purchaser,[29] or (2) such clauses do not provide a sufficiently clear statement of the parties' intent that the employer assume the extraordinary obligation to delay an important business decision until an assuming purchaser can be found.[30]

Some arbitrators will find liability on the basis of an evasion type of clause,[31] although the better interpretation is that such a clause speaks to conduct, such as subcontracting of unit work, occurring while the employer remains fully in operation.

Those employers who have signed explicit clauses disabling them from effecting a sale or transfer of the business except to an assuming purchaser face a serious prospect of liability. Reported arbitration awards suggest that arbitrators may well enjoin sales[32] or, if the sale has already transpired, may assess significant damages for lost wages, benefits, and dues.[33]

Defenses to Liability under Successorship Clauses

Boilerplate Recitals. Employers will argue that the naked "successors and assigns" clause is of no independent substantive import, for it requires a determination of the core legal issue of whether a purchaser is indeed a "successor."

Questioning the Substantive Reach of the Clause. It may be possible narrowly to construe the reach of an explicit successorship provision. The clause may be drafted so as to depend on the occurrence of specific triggering events, such as the sale of a plant or station as a "going business" as opposed to a mere sale of assets. The clause also may be construed so as to merely require the signatory employer to engage his or her best efforts to find a willing purchaser, rather than to serve as a guarantor in the event of the purchaser's refusal to honor the labor contract.[34]

Effect of Expiration of the Contract. The Supreme Court in *Nolde Brothers*[35] held that the presumption of arbitrability extended beyond a contract's termination to a severance pay claim that arguably arose during the life of the agreement. Even though the agreement had expired several days before the plant closing that led to the severance pay demand, the Court explained that the claim could be viewed as one for compensation for past services and thus arguably arose under the expired contract. Although *Nolde* thus might have been read narrowly to encompass only claims that in a sense fully mature during the life of the contract,[36] the Supreme Court's reliance on the *Steelworkers Trilogy* presumption of arbitrability has led many courts to require arbitration of any claim which plausibly can be asserted to have arisen prior to the termination of the agreement.[37]

The Fourth Circuit's ruling in *Mine Workers v. Allied Corp.*[38] suggests a somewhat narrower treatment of *Nolde*. In this case, a seller was held to be free of liability for failing to honor the successorship clause where it had continued to pay health and other nonpension retiree benefits for the contract's duration, and the court refused to presume that even had there been full compliance with the successorship clause, the purchaser would in fact have agreed to carry forward the terms of the expired contract. In short, the court reasoned, there was no legally cognizable injury. A related argument would be that any post-contract loss to employees or the union is entirely speculative and beyond the arbitrator's authority to redress.

Section 8(e) Illegality. Another possible defense might be illegality under Section 8(e) of Taft Hartley, in that a successorship clause compels the employer to "cease doing business" with prospective purchasers who are unwilling to sign agreements with the union. Although some support for this position may be found in *Commerce Tankers Corp.*,[39] the NLRB, with court approval, has made it clear that such successorship clauses do not violate Section 8(e) where sales of plants or parts of operations do not occur in the normal course of the signatory employer's business.[40]

Availability of "Reverse Boys Market" Injunctions. A critical factor in this context is the union's ability promptly to enjoin a proposed sale pending arbitration. It seems clear that Section 10(j) injunctions are not likely to be sought by the NLRB in a post–*Milwaukee Spring II*[41] world, except where there is a plausible claim of discrimination in refusing to hire the predecessor's employees, and even then the Board is likely to face difficulties in the courts.[42]

The key question will be the availability of the "reverse *Boys Market*" injunction to restrain the sale pending the completion of arbitration. Indeed, the courts of appeals are increasingly granting injunctions restraining plant shutdowns and assets sales.[43] The Ninth Circuit, standing perhaps alone, has indicated that such injunctions will not issue in the absence of an express clause obligating the employer to preserve the status quo pending arbitration, although it, too, has left open the possibility of an injunction for situations in which the arbitrator will not be able effectively to restore the status quo.[44] The Second Circuit has indicated its approval in principle of the reverse *Boys Market* injunction, although it may require a stronger showing of probable success on the merits than other courts.[45]

The requirements for a reverse *Boys Market* injunction are (1) arbitrability, (2) probable success on the merits, (3) irreparable injury, and (4) a balance of relative hardships tipping in favor of its issuance. The courts generally do not require very much in the way of arbitrability or probability of success on merits. The Seventh Circuit in the *Panoramic* litigation required only that the union's position on the merits be "sufficiently 'genuine' . . . to support a status quo injunction."[46] With the exception of the Second and Sixth Circuits,[47] most courts are likely to be satisfied with a broad arbitration clause and some type of successorship clause. As for the irreparable injury requirement, the courts are much influenced by the prospect of permanent loss of jobs by union members and the inability of the arbitrator to fashion an effective remedy once confronted with the fait accompli of a consummated assets sale and transfer of operations. Finally, as to the relative balance of hardship requirement, the courts appear to give little weight to the fact that an injunction may bar the seller from a significant business opportunity.[48]

PURCHASER'S OBLIGATIONS

Duty to Arbitrate Grievances Arising under, or to Honor, the Predecessor's Agreement

The federal labor law governing the successorship obligation of a purchaser of the assets of a business provides, with clarity unusual in this area, that a purchaser is ordinarily not legally obligated to assume the seller's collective-bargaining agreement, at least in the absence of "continuity of identity in the business enterprise," which "necessarily includes . . . a substantial continuity in the identity of the work force across the change in ownership."[49] And the Supreme Court's rulings in *Burns* and in *Howard Johnson* also indicate that the purchaser enjoys complete freedom "to operate the enterprise with his own independent labor force,"[50] provided it does not discriminate against the seller's employees because of their union activities. Indeed, some courts have read *Howard Johnson* and earlier Supreme Court decisions to preclude imposition of the substantive terms of the seller's contract—as opposed to any arbitration obligation—on a nonconsenting purchaser, even where the latter has hired virtually all of the predecessor's employees for a business that is identical to the seller's.[51]

A duty to arbitrate grievances under the predecessor's agreement, moreover, may not necessarily entail any substantive obligation on the purchaser's part. This was true of the arbitration award that ultimately was rendered in the *Wiley v. Livingston* case. The arbitrator there held the merged entity's labor agreement unenforceable once its employees "were moved to the Wiley quarters and commingled with the larger Wiley contingent."[52]

There are a few exceptions to the no-assumption rule for purchasers. First, facts giving rise to a finding of alter ego status will lead to liability under the labor contract.[53] Second, stock transfers that do not involve a major alteration of the predecessor's mode of operation do not ordinarily constitute a change in the identity of the employing enterprise.[54] Third, there may be greater latitude in merger situations to require the surviving entity to adhere to the obligations of the disappearing entity's contracts. *Wiley* was not overruled but distinguished in *Howard Johnson* as a situation possibly meriting special treatment because of the disappearance of the signatory employer and the backdrop of state law.[55] Finally, it is possible that a duty to arbitrate might arise where the purchaser hires substantially all of the predecessor's employees without predicating offers on changes in terms and conditions[56] and without making substantial changes in the operation of the enterprise—another way in which *Wiley* was distinguished from *Howard Johnson*.[57]

Duty to Hire Predecessor Employees

As stated, *Burns* and *Howard Johnson* leave no room for doubt that the purchaser is free to hire an independent work force, although it may not discriminate against the predecessor's employees because of its desire to avoid a labor contract.[58]

Furthermore, as Justice White stated in *Burns*, "there will be instances in which it is perfectly clear that the new employer plans to retain all of the employees in the unit and in which it will be appropriate to have him initially consult with employees' bargaining representative before he fixes terms."[59] The Board in *Boeing* and *Spruce-Up*[60] has qualified this suggestion: an employer who offers the predecessor's employees lower terms than those set forth in the predecessor's agreement is under no bargaining obligation until the predecessor's employees constitute a majority of the purchaser's work force. Where offers of employment are extended without making it clear, however, that they are predicated on different terms than those contained in the predecessor's agreement, the purchaser unwittingly may find himself under a duty to bargain precluding unilateral imposition of new terms.[61]

Purchasers are often leery of approaching the union to elicit possible concessions, for fear that such contacts will lead to a bargaining relationship. Sellers can play a useful intermediary role here. In any event, purchasers, who make it clear that their offer of employment is conditioned on agreement to lower or different terms, will not under *Spruce-Up* and its progeny be held to have assumed a bargaining obligation merely because they have approached the union to explore concessions.[62]

Duty to Bargain with Predecessor Union

The factors recited by the Board in fleshing out the "substantial continuity in the business enterprise" standard are as follows: (1) whether there has been substantial continuity of the same business operation; (2) whether the new employer uses the same plants; (3) whether it has the same or substantially the same work force; (4) whether the same jobs exist under the same working conditions; (5) whether the same supervisors are employed; (6) whether the same machinery, equipment, and methods of production are used; and (7) whether the employer manufacturers the same products or offers the same services.

The most important criterion is, of course, work force continuity: a majority of the purchaser's employees must come from the ranks of the predecessor's work force ("successor majority") before a bargaining duty arises. Some decisions suggest that the purchaser must also hire a majority of the predecessor's employees ("predecessor majority"). Both factors were satisfied by the facts in *Wiley* and *Burns*. The Board with judicial approval holds, however, that a successor majority suffices.[63]

The Supreme Court's recent opinion in *Fall River* muddies the waters here somewhat. While reaffirming the successor majority requirement, the Court deferred decision on the predecessor majority element as presenting an issue not properly before it, even though a bargaining obligation was upheld in that case despite the clear absence of a predecessor majority.[64]

A second important requirement for the establishment of a bargaining duty is a basis for continued adherence to the presumption of the predecessor union's majority status. The case law generally provides that the existence of a hiatus period before the purchaser begins operations will not, standing alone, preclude a bargaining obligation where the other preconditions exist. *Fall River* makes it clear that the presence of even a seven-month hiatus is but one factor which is "relevant only when there are other indicia of discontinuity" and may be readily overcome by other factors indicating "substantial continuity."[65]

Although dicta in *Burns* support delay in responding to the union's recognition demand until a "full complement" has been hired,[66] the Board with court approval generally requires bargaining once a "substantial and representative" force has been engaged.[67] *Fall River* plainly opts for the substantial and representative complement approach. The test for determining when the bargaining obligation arises, Justice Blackmun tells us, is "whether the job classifications designed for the operation were filled or substantially filled and whether the operation was in normal or substantially normal operation," including consideration of "the size of the complement on that date and the time expected to elapse before a substantially larger complement would be at work . . . as well as the relative certainty of the employer's expected expansion."[68] The Board in that case required an employer who had purchased the assets of a business that had gone bankrupt to bargain once it had hired 36 of 55 workers from the predecessor's work force, even though full operations ultimately called for the addition of a second shift and a work force three months later of 106 employees among which the predecessor's employees formed a minority.

In the past, the purchaser's polling of hired employees to determine whether the union still enjoys support was legally hazardous. However, the legal atmosphere may have changed. Relatively recent examples include the Sixth Circuit decision in *Landmark International Trucks*,[69] which permits an employer to advise employees of withdrawal rights, and the Board's reliance in *Sofco*[70] on the presale expression of employee preferences following closely on the heels of employer statements of opposition to the union. Also, the Ninth Circuit has generally loosened the standards governing employer interrogation.[71]

Concerning continuity of the bargaining unit, the Board and courts have required bargaining on the basis of a subdivision of what had been a broader inclusive unit. In the D.C. Circuit's 1979 opinion in *Electrical Workers*,[72] bargaining on a multiplant basis was still required, even though the successor had taken over only five plants from the predecessor's larger multiplant unit. In *Saks & Co.*[73] the Second Circuit limited its focus to a subgroup within the predecessor unit, declaring that "the size of the predecessor unit is not an issue of great moment."[74] The employee group in question—garment alteration workers—had been certified as an appropriate unit in other cases.[75]

The decisional law suggests, however, that continuity of identity of operations is not terribly significant. The Board and courts will not reject a successorship finding simply because the buyer effects a change in operations, say, as in *Electrical Workers*, from highly centralized control to a local facility profit center structure, or as in *Fall River* itself, from a converting and commission textile dyeing business to an exclusively commission dyeing firm.[76] The key question is whether the organizational changes are likely to "affect employees' attitudes toward representation"[77]—for, as the Court explains in *Fall River*, "[i]f the employees find themselves in essentially the same jobs after the employer transition and if their legitimate expectations in continued representation by their union are thwarted, their dissatisfaction may lead to labor unrest."[78]

Duty to Redress Predecessor's Unfair Labor Practices

Golden State Bottling[79] holds that a purchaser of a business who buys with knowledge of his seller's unremedied unfair labor practice is subject to the Board's remedial authority. Apparently, notice may be inferred from circumstantial evidence, such as a balance sheet revealing large entries for legal fees and vague references to "union problems."[80]

The courts also have held that *Golden State Bottling* applies to the full range of statutory violations, including apparently an outstanding *Gissel* bargaining order[81]—a ruling which makes little sense unless the purchaser is independently subject to a bargaining obligation.

The issues presented in this chapter are fairly well identified and have been much fought over in the Labor Board and courts. What emerges quite clearly is that management's perceived need to escape from what is viewed as a burdensome labor contract has fueled an enormous amount of litigation, as the parties themselves have been unable to work out solutions in the bargaining process.

In a period of business change, the labor contract is not sacrosanct.

NOTES

1. United Telegraph Workers v. NLRB, 571 F.2d 665 (D.C. Cir.), cert. denied, 439 U.S. 827 (1978).

2. These factors derive from Radio & Television Technicians Local 1264 v. Broadcast Service, 380 U.S. 255 (1965); South Prairie Construction Co. v. Local 627, Operating Engineers, 425 U.S. 800, 802 & n.3 (1976).

3. American Bell, Inc. v. Telephone Workers, 736 F.2d 879, 116 L.R.R.M. 2673 (3d Cir. 1984).

4. Id., 116 L.R.R.M. at 2678–79.

5. Royal Typewriter Co. v. NLRB, 533 F.2d 1030 (8th Cir. 1976). See also the difficulties attending Texas Air Corporation's attempt to spin off the Eastern Air Shuttle

operation from Eastern Airlines into a wholly owned subsidiary which would not be governed by Eastern's labor contracts. See Machinists v. Eastern Airlines, Inc., 849 F. 2d 1481 (D.C. Cir. 1988), vac. judgment, 127 L.R.R.M. 3078 (D.D.C. March 10, 1988); also Machinists v. Eastern Airlines, Inc., 125 L.R.R.M. 3491 (D.D.C. July 2, 1987).

6. Where the requisite autonomy is present, however, the question becomes one of successorship—the set of principles applicable to transfers to third parties.

7. Penntech Papers, Inc. v. NLRB, 706 F.2d 18 (1st Cir. 1983), cert. denied, 464 U.S. 892 (1984).

8. Parklane Hosiery Co., Inc., 203 N.L.R.B. 597, 612, amended on other grounds, 207 N.L.R.B. 991 (1973); see, e.g., Pulitzer Pub. Co. v. NLRB, 618 F.2d 1275 (8th Cir. 1980).

9. Southport Petroleum Co. v. NLRB, 315 U.S. 100, 106 (1942).

10. See, e.g., NLRB v. Tricor Products, Inc., 636 F.2d 266 (10th Cir. 1980); NLRB v. Scott Printing Corp., 612 F.2d 783 (3d Cir. 1979).

11. Common ownership and control may not suffice in alter ego cases. In Alkire v. NLRB, 716 F.2d 1014 (4th Cir. 1983), the Fourth Circuit heightened the Board's burden by requiring a showing that the transferor would, in fact, clearly benefit from the transfer of the business. The *Alkire* court found that the transferor/alleged alter ego would owe more in loan obligations than rents received from the transfer.

12. Westwood Import Co., Inc. v. NLRB, 681 F.2d 664 (9th Cir. 1982).

13. See NLRB v. Massachusetts Marine and Stamping, Inc., 578 F.2d 15 (1st Cir. 1978); NLRB v. Marine Optical, Inc., 671 F.2d 11 (1st Cir. 1982); Towne Ford Sales, 270 N.L.R.B. 311 (1984). For a recent Board ruling, see Central Soya Co., 281 N.L.R.B. No. 173, 124 L.R.R.M. 1026 (1986).

14. John Wiley & Sons, Inc. v. Livingston, 376 U.S. 543 (1964).

15. United Steelworkers of America v. American Mfg., Co., 363 U.S. 564 (1960); United Steelworkers of America v. Warrior & Gulf Navigation Co., 363 U.S. 574 (1960); United Steelworkers of America v. Enterprise Wheel & Car Corp., 363 U.S. 593 (1960).

16. Textile Workers Union v. Darlington Mfg. Co., 380 U.S. 263 (1965).

17. 376 U.S. at 549, quoting in part *Warrior & Gulf*, supra note 15, 363 U.S. at 580.

18. NLRB v. Burns International Security Services, 406 U.S. 272 (1972).

19. H.K. Porter Co. v. NLRB, 397 U.S. 99 (1970).

20. Howard Johnson Co., Inc. v. Detroit Joint Executive Board, 417 U.S. 249 (1974).

21. Fall River Dyeing & Finishing Corp. v. NLRB, 107 S. Ct. 2225 (1987).

22. Id. at 2234–35.

23. See Lewin, "Workers' Rights in a Closing Tested," N.Y. Times, July 19, 1984, at D1. NLRA preemption may be found, however, where the gist of the employees' claim is failure to disclose relevant information to the union or other arguable unfair labor practices. See Serrano v. Jones & Laughlin Steel Co., 790 F.2d. 1279 (6th Cir. 1986).

24. Mass. Gen. Laws Annotated ch. 149, Labor & Indus. L. § 182 (1984). For examples of other state legislation, see Me. Rev. Stat. Ann. Tit. 26 § 625-B; S.C. Code ch. 41, Labor and Employment, § 41–1–40; Wisc. Stat. ch. 109, Wage Payment Claims and Collections, § 109.07.

25. On May 24, 1988, President Reagan vetoed H.R. 3, the Omnibus Trade and Competitiveness Act of 1988, largely because of opposition to a provision requiring sixty days' advance notice of plant closings or layoffs affecting one-third or more of the work

force for at least six months. In July 1988, Congress passed the Worker Adjustment and Retraining Notification Act (S. 2527), requiring sixty days' advance notice of plant closings and "mass layoffs." See generally Report of Secretary of Labor's Task Force on Economic Adjustment and Worker Dislocation (Dec. 31, 1986), reprinted in (BNA) Daily Lab. Rep., Jan. 13, 1987, at D1ff.; Plant Closing Legislation (A. Aboud ed. 1984).

26. Fort Halifax Packing Co., Inc. v. Coyne, 107 S. Ct. 2211 (1987).

27. See generally Note, "Severance Pay Claims after a Sale of Assets: ERISA Sweeps the Field," 60 St. John's L. Rev. 300 (1986).

28. See, e.g., Schneier's Finer Foods, Inc., 72 L.A. 881, 885 (Belkin, 1979); Air Express Int'l Corp. v. Teamsters, Local 851, 83 Civ. 2550 (E.D.N.Y. July 15, 1983). On somewhat special facts, see also Marley-Wylain Co., 88 L.A. 978 (Jacobowski, 1987).

29. See, e.g., Storer Broadcasting Co., 78–1 (CCH) Lab. Arb. ¶ 8087, at 3415 (Ellmann, 1978); Walker Bros., 41 L.A. 844 (Crawford, 1963).

30. Gallivan's Inc., 79 L.A. 253 (Gallagher, 1982); contra, *Schneier's Fine Foods, Inc.*, 72 L.A. at 881.

31. Herbert J. Caplan, Inc., 81 L.A. 22 (Levine, 1983).

32. Sexton's Steak House, Inc., 76 L.A. 576 (Ross, 1981); Hosanna Trading Co., 74 L.A. 128 (Simons, 1980); Martin Podany Assoc., Inc., 80 L.A. 658 (Gallagher, 1983); High Point Sprinkler Co. of Boston, 67 L.A. 239 (Connolly, 1976); *Herbert J. Caplan, Inc.*, 81 L.A. 22.

33. *High Point Sprinkler Co. of Boston*, 67 L.A. 239; *Herbert J. Caplan, Inc.*, 81 L.A. 22.

34. Compare Dawn Farms Corp. v. Teamsters Local 584, 45 L.A. 1075 (Wolff, 1965) (purchaser refused to honor provision assuming predecessor contract); Amalgamated Food Employees Union, Local No. 590 v. National Tea Co., 346 F. Supp. 875 (W.D.Pa.), rem. without op., 474 F.2d 1338 (3d Cir. 1972), with *Walker Bros.*, 4. L.A. 844.

35. Nolde Brothers, Inc. v. Local No. 358, Bakers & Confectionery Workers Union, 430 U.S. 243 (1977).

36. For example, in United Food and Commercial Workers Local 174 v. Hebrew National Kosher Foods, Inc., 818 F.2d 283 (2d Cir. 1987), the court held arbitrable the question of whether the employer's decision to relocate work outside of the union's jurisdiction was made during the term of the agreement, even though the new plant did not open until after the contract's expiration date. This case involved an explicit provision requiring advance notice and effects bargaining if the employer "decides to move its operations to another location outside the jurisdiction of Local 174. . . . " Thus, if the relocation decision was made during the life of the contract, the claim of violation plainly matured while the agreement was in effect.

37. See Rochdale Village, Inc. v. Public Service Employees Union, 605 F.2d 1290 (2d Cir. 1979); Steelworkers v. Fort Pitt Steel Casting, 598 F.2d 1273 (3d Cir. 1979). Under the Board's ruling in Indiana and Michigan Electric Co., 284 N.L.R.B. No.7 (1987), the arbitration clause itself does not continue during the hiatus period between contracts and thus would not govern disputes which arise after contract expiration.

38. Mine Workers v. Allied Corp., 735 F.2d 121 (4th Cir. 1984).

39. Commerce Tankers Corp., 196 N.L.R.B. 1100 (1972), enf'd, 486 F.2d 907 (2d Cir. 1973), cert. denied, 416 U.S. 970 (1974).

40. See Lone Star Steel Co., 231 N.L.R.B. 573 (1977), enf'd in rel. part, 639 F.2d 545 (10th Cir. 1980), cert. denied, 450 U.S. 911 (1981).

41. Milwaukee Spring Div. of Illinois Coil Spring Co., 268 N.L.R.B. 601 (1984).

42. See, e.g., Kobell v. Suburban Lines, Inc., 731 F.2d 1076 (3d Cir. 1984).

43. See, e.g., Teamsters Local 71 v. Akers Motor Lines, 582 F.2d 1336 (4th Cir. 1978); Lever Brothers Co. v. International Chemical Workers Union Local 217, 554 F.2d 115 (4th Cir. 1976); Machinists Local Lodge 1266 v. Panoramic Corp., 668 F.2d 276 (7th Cir. 1981); United Mine Workers v. Fort Pitt Steel Casting, 598 F.2d 1273 (3d Cir. 1979).

44. See Amalgamated Transit Union Division 1384 v. Greyhound Lines, Inc., 550 F.2d 1237, 1239 (9th Cir.), cert. denied, 434 U.S. 837 (1977); compare Electrical Workers v. Simpson Mfg. Co., 115 L.R.R.M. 2149 (N.D. Cal. 1983).

45. Compare Hoh v. Pepsico, Inc., 491 F.2d 556 (2d Cir. 1974), with Jacobson & Co. v. Armstrong Cork Co., 548 F.2d 438, 443 (2d Cir. 1977).

46. *Panoramic*, 688 F.2d at 285.

47. See Hoh v. Pepsico, Inc., 491 F.2d at 561; United Food and Commercial Workers v. Kroger, 778 F. 2d 1171 (6th Cir. 1985), cert. denied, 107 S. Ct. 69 (1986) (''successor and assigns'' language in preamble); UAW v. Lester Mfg., 718 F.2d 818 (6th Cir. 1983).

48. But see Machinists District 147 v. Northeast Airlines, Inc., 473 F.2d 549 (1st Cir.), cert. denied, 409 U.S. 845 (1972).

49. *Howard Johnson*, 417 U.S. at 263.

50. *Burns*, 406 U.S. at 288; *Howard Johnson*, 417 U.S. at 261.

51. See, e.g, Bartenders & Culinary Workers Union Local 340 v. Howard Johnson Co., 535 F.2d 1160, 1163 (9th Cir. 1976).

52. Interscience Encyclopedia, Inc., 55 L.A. 211 (Roberts, 1970).

53. See, e.g, General Teamster Local Union v. Bill's Trucking, 493 F.2d 956 (3d Cir. 1974).

54. See, e.g., EPE, Inc. v. NLRB No. 87–3850 (4th Cir. May 5, 1988) (sale of 100% of stock to multinational corporation); Clothing Workers v. Ratner Corp., 602 F.2d 1363 (9th Cir. 1979) (stock transfer coupled with reorganization as holding company); TKB International Corp., 240 N.L.R.B. 1082 (1979); Topinka's Country House, Inc., 235 N.L.R.B. 72 (1978), enf'd, 624 F.2d 770 (6th Cir. 1980). The Board's 1976 decision in MPE, Inc., 226 N.L.R.B. 519 (1976), suggests that assumption will not be required in the context of a distress sale when the stock purchaser was not aware of the unexpired labor agreement.

55. *Howard Johnson*, 417 U.S. at 263–64.

56. See Little Rock Mailers Union No. 89, 219 N.L.R.B. 707, 709–10 (1975).

57. *Howard Johnson*, 417 U.S. at 258. Assets purchasers have been held to be under a duty to arbitrate under the seller's agreement in United Steelworkers of America v. United States Gypsum Co., 492 F.2d 713, 726 (5th Cir.), cert. denied, 419 U.S. 998 (1974); Graphic Arts International Union v. Martin Podnay Associates, Inc., 531 F. Supp. 169 (D. Minn. 1982); Local 115 Joint Bd. Nursing Home v. B&K Investments, Inc., 436 F. Supp. 1203, 1209 (S.D. Fla. 1977).

58. *Burns*, 406 U.S. at 288; *Howard Johnson*, 417 U.S. at 261. See, e.g., Sousa & Sons, Inc., 210 N.L.R.B. 982 (1974); Hudson River Aggregates, Inc., 246 N.L.R.B. 192 (1979), enf'd, 639 F.2d 865 (2d Cir. 1981); Kallman v. NLRB, 640 F.2d 1094 (9th Cir. 1981). Although discrimination charges are hard to sustain even where the employer states that its objective is to hire an entirely new, inexperienced work force, see, e.g., Inland Co-trainer Corp., 267 N.L.R.B. 1187 (1983), they can sometimes be proven, see, e.g., Shortway Suburban Lines, Inc., 286 N.L.R.B. No. 30 (1987).

59. *Burns*, 406 U.S. at 294–95.

60. Boeing Co., 214 N.L.R.B. 541 (1974), enf. denied, 521 F.2d 587 (4th Cir. 1975); Spruce-Up Corp., 209 N.L.R.B. 194 (1974), enf'd, 529 F.2d 516 (4th Cir. 1975).

61. See, e.g., Spitzer Akron, Inc. v. NLRB, 540 F.2d 841 (6th Cir. 1976).

62. If care is not taken in making the approach, however, the purchaser may be held to have adopted the predecessor's contract by its conduct. See, e.g., Stockton Door Co., 218 N.L.R.B. 1053 (1975), enf'd, 547 F.2d 489 (9th Cir. 1976), cert. denied, 434 U.S. 834 (1977); World Evangelism, Inc., 248 N.L.R.B. 909 (1980), enf'd, 656 F.2d 1349 (9th Cir. 1981).

63. See Spruce-Up Corp., 209 N.L.R.B. at 196; United Maintenance & Mfg. Co., 214 N.L.R.B. 529, 532–34 (1974); Saks & Co. v. NLRB, 634 F.2d 681, 684–86 & nn.2–3 (2d Cir. 1980).

64. *Fall River*, 107 S. Ct. at 2237, n.12.

65. Id. at 2237.

66. *Burns*, 406 U.S. at 295. See Pacific Hyde & Fur Depot, Inc. v. NLRB, 553 F.2d 609 (9th Cir. 1977), which is no longer good law after *Fall River*.

67. See, e.g., Indianapolis Mack Sales & Serv. Inc., 272 N.L.R.B. 690, 694–96 (1984), enf. denied on other grounds, 802 F.2d 280 (7th Cir. 1986); NLRB v. Jeffries Lithograph Co., 752 F.2d 459, 467 (9th Cir. 1985); Aircraft Magnesium, 265 N.L.R.B. 1344, 1345 (1982), enf'd, 730 F.2d 767 (9th Cir. 1984); Hudson River Aggregates, Inc., 246 N.L.R.B. 192, 197–98 (1979), enf'd, 639 F.2d 865, 870 (2d Cir. 1981).

68. *Fall River*, 107 S. Ct. at 2239, quoting Premium Foods, Inc. v. NLRB, 709 F.2d 623, 628 (9th Cir. 1983).

69. Landmark International Trucks v. NLRB, 699 F.2d 815 (6th Cir. 1983) (advising employees of withdrawal rights).

70. Sofco, Inc. v. NLRB, 268 N.L.R.B. 159 (1983) (presale statements by employees).

71. See Mingtree Restaurant v. NLRB, 736 F.2d. 1295 (9th Cir. 1984).

72. International Union of Electrical, Radio and Machine Workers v. NLRB, 604 F.2d 689 (D.C. Cir. 1979) (five plants severed from the larger multiplant unit when acquired by successor remained appropriate; bargaining required on multiplant basis).

73. *Saks & Co.*, 634 F.2d 681 (subgroup of prior bargaining unit).

74. Id. at 685.

75. Accord, Zim's Foodliner, Inc. v. NLRB, 495 F.2d 1131 (7th Cir. 1974), cert. denied, 419 U.S. 838 (1974) (two stores that had been part of a multiemployer unit sold to two separate buyers); NLRB v. Band-Age, Inc., 534 F.2d 1 (1st Cir.), cert. denied, 429 U.S. 921 (1976) (disregarding diminished scale of operations and size of work force of successor).

76. Accord, NLRB v. Winco Petrol. Co., 668 F.2d 973 (8th Cir. 1982); *Zim's Foodliner*, 495 F.2d at 1142 (change from national chain to individual supermarket discounted); International Union of Electrical, Radio and Machine Workers v. NLRB, 604 F.2d at 694 (shift from centralized control to local facility profit center).

77. NLRB v. Jeffries Lithograph Co., 752 F.2d 466. (9th Cir. 1985).

78. *Fall River*, 107 S. Ct. at 2236.

79. Golden State Bottling Co. v. NLRB, 414 U.S. 168 (1973).

80. NLRB v. Winco Petrol. Co., 668 F.2d at 973.

81. See id.

5

THE ROLE OF LABOR ARBITRATION

Daniel G. Collins

Editors' Note. The grievance arbitration system that has been a mainstay of post–World War II labor relations is by its nature, Professor Collins argues, ill-suited, if not counterproductive, to the resolution of disputes concerning major business change decisions that threaten the existence or fundamental shape of a collective bargaining relationship. The author examines the typical arbitral process as it may bear on such decisions, and he notes that, in many instances, the arbitration forum may be exclusive. Yet, in examining reported arbitration awards dealing with express and allegedly implied limitations on business change, he finds a surprising disinclination by arbitrators to recognize substantive rights or, when they have, to provide effective remedies. The author also discusses the availability of interim judicial relief in aid of arbitration.

The author wishes to acknowledge with gratitude the research assistance of Jennifer Conovitz, a student at New York University School of Law.

Justice Marshall, speaking for the Supreme Court in the *Howard Johnson*[1] case, in which a nonassuming assets purchaser was found not to have any duty to arbitrate claims based on its predecessor's collective-bargaining agreements, observed that the unsuccessful plaintiff union had failed to pursue a potential remedy: "moving to enjoin the sale to [the purchaser] on the ground that this was a breach by [the sellers] of the successorship clauses in the collective-bargaining agreements."[2] Since the agreements also contained the "usual arbitration provisions"[3] and the sellers were prepared to arbitrate,[4] an obvious question is what might the union's invocation of arbitration have wrought. This chapter will, in addition to exploring that question, attempt to assess the significance of the arbitral process for business change decisions.

THE USUAL ARBITRAL PROCESS

The typical labor arbitration clause constitutes the culminating stage of a grievance procedure in which disputes involving the meaning of a collective-bargaining agreement between management, on one hand, and individual workers or their union, on the other, are initiated and pass through ascending levels of factual exploration and settlement discussion. The arbitration stage differs fundamentally from the preliminary stages of the grievance procedure in that it utilizes a third, jointly chosen "impartial" party to make a binding decision as to the merits of the dispute.

Arbitration proceedings vary greatly in degree of formality. However, formal prehearing discovery procedures, in contrast to hearing subpoenas returnable at the hearing, are rarely available.[5]

Arbitration pursuant to a collective agreement is, typically, a relatively slow process, encompassing months and sometimes years between the filing of the grievance and the issuance of a final award.[6] That time lag reflects essentially four factors. First, a claim initially must be processed through the prearbitration stages of the grievance procedure. Second, an arbitrator must be selected. Third, a hearing must be scheduled before an arbitrator who, because he is acceptable, presumably is very busy. Fourth, the arbitrator can be expected to allow both parties full opportunity to present evidence and to make arguments, orally and in writing. Of course, since arbitration is a contractual device, it is possible, though not typical, for parties to streamline their contractual machinery to provide for an expedited hearing before a designated "umpire."[7]

Arbitration awards are not self-enforcing. An award must be judicially confirmed before a judgment based on it may issue.[8]

THE FEDERAL LABOR LAW AND ARBITRATION

Congress stated in Section 203 (d) of the Labor Management Relations Act of 1974 (LMRA) that arbitration is the "desirable method" for resolving contract grievances.[9] Building from that stated policy, the Supreme Court has found under the preemptive federal substantive law of collective-bargaining agreements created by Section 301 of the LMRA[10] that agreements to arbitrate are prospectively enforceable[11]; that while arbitrability is for the courts to determine, courts must send to the arbitral tribunal any claim that is arguably within the scope of the arbitration clause[12] unless expressly or by clear implication excluded therefrom,[13] including all disputes involving procedural arbitrability[14]; that arbitral determinations are judicially reviewable not on their merits but only as to whether the arbitrator exceeded his contractual authority, and even then there is, in case of doubt, a strong presumption of legitimacy[15]; that contract grievance and arbitration provisions must be exhausted before any resort may be had to courts, unless the provisions are specified as nonexclusive or the union is found to have breached its duty of fair representation[16]; that a no-strike obligation will be implied from the very existence of, and ordinarily will be deemed coextensive with, the scope of an arbitration clause[17]; and that a strike injunction may issue notwithstanding the Norris–La Guardia Act[18] if the strike is over an arbitral dispute and the employer is willing to arbitrate that issue.[19]

The arbitral process and the decisions emanating from it have long been accorded special deference by the NLRB (or Board) in cases involving conduct that is prohibited both by the contract and under Section 8 of the NLRA.[20] There is no question that the Board has the authority to interpret collective agreements, for example, where the legality of an employer's unilateral action turns on the meaning of the agreement.[21] Under the Board's *Spielberg*[22] doctrine, however, the agency will defer in such matters to an arbitration decision that is obtained in "fair and regular" proceedings and is not "clearly repugnant to the purposes and policies" of the Act. Under its *Dubo*[23] and *Collyer*[24] rules, the Board will defer where the arbitral process has been or may be invoked, and it will thereafter measure any challenge to the award resulting from that process by the *Spielberg* standards. The scope of the Board's deferral policy has varied considerably over the years; the current deferential policy was adopted in 1984.[25]

An important exception to the finality of the arbitration process occurs when the union has breached its duty fairly to represent affected employees. In such a case, it is irrelevant that the employer, who may thus be exposed to further litigation as to the merits of the dispute it had "won," did not in any way contribute to the breach of the union's duty.[26]

It must be noted that the law is not settled as to whether a successor that has neither expressly nor impliedly assumed a predecessor's collective agreement may ever have liability thereunder. In an early case, *John Wiley & Sons v. Livingston*, the Supreme Court required a nonunion employer, into which a collective agreement signatory had been merged, to arbitrate under that agreement alleged rights of the signatory's former employees in the merged operation.[27] The potential breadth of *Wiley* was sharply curtailed by the Court's decision in *NLRB v. Burns International Security Services*.[28] While the later *Howard Johnson* decision expressly declined to offer an opinion as to *Wiley*'s continued viability,[29] the successor's duty to arbitrate is in all likelihood limited to the merger context.[30] Of course, if the transferee is in effect the same entity as the transferor under tests of either common ownership and control or alter ego, the former will not be able to avoid the collective agreement.[31]

Given the nature of the arbitral process, the federal labor law regarding arbitration has significant ramifications for business change decision making. First, the merits of most business change disputes will be decided by arbitral rather than judicial tribunals. For example, if there is a general "successors and assigns" clause, a sale to a nonassuming buyer would present an arbitrable issue as to the seller's liability under a typical arbitration clause, and the arbitration forum would be exclusive. Furthermore, judicial review of any determination made in that forum would be severely limited. The same would be true in the context of a plant relocation or subcontracting where the applicable agreement dealt expressly with those subjects, or, under the Supreme Court's broad arbitrability doctrine, even where the contractual nexus was less explicit. Almost any business change can be arguably defended as authorized and protected under the management rights clause typically found in a collective agreement and, from the union's side, it can be argued that most forms of business change contravene typical recognition, seniority, and compensation clauses.

Second, a union seeking temporary status quo relief will probably want to look beyond the arbitral process to the courts because of the significant delays involved in setting an arbitration in motion, obtaining an award, and then securing judicial enforcement of the award. The question of availability of temporary judicial relief then becomes critical.

A third ramification is that arbitral start-up problems may similarly thwart an employer's effort to bar a union's use of economic force in opposition to business change, citing it as a violation of a standard no-strike clause. The availability of temporary judicial relief in such circumstances will turn, as a threshold matter, on whether the underlying business change dispute constitutes a matter which the union might take to arbitration under the parties' agreement, and, if so, whether the employer is willing to arbitrate that matter.

Fourth, there would be concern about predictability in arbitral litigation concerning business change, given the fact that the only essential qualification of an arbitrator is acceptability; many arbitrators are not legally trained, and, as a matter of law, judicial review of the arbitrator's award is severely restricted.

ARBITRAL TREATMENT OF BUSINESS CHANGE DECISIONS

Reported arbitration awards are plentiful,[32] but there are caveats to their significance. Because arbitration depends on private agreement, the arbitral process and the awards that emanate from that process are private, not public.[33] Publication thus turns not only on editorial selection but also on consent of the parties. Even more fundamental, there is no doctrine of precedent in labor arbitration.[34] It would be a mistake, however, to regard arbitration results as wildly unpredictable or rarely consistent. Typically, awards are monitored by the ongoing decisions of managements and unions as to any particular arbitrator's continued acceptability. Furthermore, substantive as well as procedural aspects of labor arbitration have for decades been the subject of discussion and published commentary by the body of generally acceptable labor arbitrators.[35]

The following prognosis as to arbitrators' responses to business change issues is based on this writer's experience, on his survey of arbitration decisions dealing with business change reported over the past quarter century in one leading labor arbitration reporter, The Bureau of National Affairs' *Labor Arbitration Reports*, and on the secondary literature generally.

On the issue suggested by Justice Marshall—whether a union could obtain an arbitrator's order prohibiting an employer's transfer to a nonassuming purchaser if there is a clause in the collective agreement purporting to make it binding on "successors and assigns"[36]—the reported decisions demonstrate a unanimous, though (from this writer's perspective) problematical, viewpoint. No published award can readily be found holding that an employer signatory to such a collective agreement is in breach when it has threatened to transfer or has transferred to a nonassuming buyer. Indeed, numerous decisions reach the contrary conclusion.[37] Only when there has been an express undertaking by the employer to condition any transfer on the buyer's assumption of the collective agreement have arbitrators found that a threatened or completed transfer to a nonassuming buyer constituted a breach.[38]

The fact that arbitrators have not found, in the presence of a general successors clause of this type, an implied promise to condition transfer on the buyer's assumption of the collective agreement seems at variance with recognized principles of contract interpretation. Such a transferring employer has, by its own action, frustrated the event which the contract expressly contemplates—an assuming successorship. This would seem to be a classic example of breach of an implicit obligation of good faith in performance.[39] Furthermore, since it has been held that such a successors clause does not bind a nonassuming buyer, a holding that it does not create any obligation in the seller means that the clause is deprived of all meaning, a conclusion never favored under canons of interpretation.[40]

When arbitrators have found an express obligation to condition transfer on assumption of the collective agreement, and the transfer has not yet been made, they have as a matter of course prohibited the offending employer from transferring absent an assumption of the contract by the buyer.[41] And where the transfer has been effected, these arbitrators have required the employer to pay damages to workers and their union based on the difference between the contract benefits and those benefits, if any, realized in connection with any employment by the transferee.[42]

In contrast to their unwillingness to imply obligations from the presence of a general successors clause, arbitrators have sometimes, but by no means always, found by implication obligations not to subcontract bargaining unit work or otherwise not to relocate work outside the unit from the very existence in the collective agreement of clauses covering recognition, seniority, compensation, and job classifications.[43] The split, though, among arbitrators as to whether and under what circumstances an implied prohibition against subcontracting or relocation will be found is so deep and contains so many gradations of response that there can be no predictability of result, except on an arbitrator-by-arbitrator basis.[44]

If a contract violation is found in advance of a threatened subcontracting or relocation of work, the obvious and appropriate relief will be an order prohibiting such conduct. However, whereas in the case of an executed assets sale the signatory employer has lost control of the work, the same is not true with respect to subcontracted and relocated work. Confronted with an executed plant shutdown or relocation, arbitrators undoubtedly have the power to order return of the work to the bargaining unit, and in certain instances arbitrators have ordered plants to be reopened. In one such case, an arbitrator issued an order, which a federal district court refused to set aside, that an employer reopen a New York City plant whose former operations had been consolidated into its Savannah, Georgia, facility.[45] However, such relief is exceptional.

In practice, while most arbitrators will order restoration of the *status quo ante* if there has been a relatively simple contract violation, e.g., the assignment of bargaining unit work to nonunit employees in the same facility,[46] they are extremely reluctant to issue a remedy requiring reconstruction of a complex operation. Illustrative of a certain arbitral tendency toward bravado ending with retreat in the face of practicality is the decision in *Pabst Brewing Company*.[47] There, in violation of an express prohibition against transfer of work out of the bargaining unit, the employer closed one of its two breweries because of overcapacity and consolidated its operations. The arbitrator in the first paragraph of his award unequivocally ordered the closed brewery to be reopened and the affected employees made whole. Then in a second paragraph he provided for an "alternative remedy": the employer could seek to negotiate a settlement with the union, with any dispute in negotiation to be referred to the same arbitrator for "final and binding decision."[48] Other decisions offer less posturing and candidly deny specific relief in favor of damages.[49]

It was noted earlier that there may be practical problems to bringing a business change decision to arbitration prior to its implementation. However, if irreparable harm would otherwise result, arbitrators have indicated a willingness to issue a preliminary order (sometimes in the form of a bench decision) preserving the status quo.[50] Of course, any such relief will turn on whether irreparable harm would otherwise result. While such interim relief frequently finds its source in maintenance-of-status-quo clauses, status quo undertakings may not be necessary.[51] An important caveat to the utility of such interim arbitral relief, however, is the judicial doctrine precluding review, either by way of attempts to confirm or vacate, of awards that are less than a final determination of all the issues in the arbitration.[52]

INTERIM JUDICIAL RELIEF

There is no question that interim judicial relief may be granted to preclude an employer's making changes that are or may be the subject of a pending arbitration.[53] For some years, the only questions in this area have involved the criteria for the awarding of such relief. It is well settled that such relief will not be granted unless the grievants would suffer irreparable injury, that is, the arbitration process would be meaningless and any victory for the grievants "empty."[54] In addition, the balance of hardships must favor the grievants.[55] The only lingering questions have been whether there must have been a contractual status quo undertaking, and whether there must be a demonstration of likelihood of success in the arbitration. The Ninth Circuit requires such an undertaking though it may be implied in fact.[56] The prevailing and, to this writer, better view in the circuits is that there only must be a showing that the arbitration process would otherwise be "frustrated" if preliminary injunctive relief were denied.[57] As to the need for demonstrating likelihood of arbitral success, only the Second Circuit has set forth this criterion,[58] but even that court seems to have receded to a requirement of a showing that there are "serious questions going to the merits"[59]—essentially the prevailing test.[60]

CONCLUSION

The American labor law institution of arbitration is more problematical than useful as a means of dealing with business change. In the *Howard Johnson* context, when the union fears that an impending assets sale threatens the existence of its bargaining unit and the jobs of its members, the arbitration forum will be available to assert against the seller a right to have the transfer conditioned on the buyer's assumption of the collective agreement. However, the union will be foreclosed from initially seeking final contractual relief in court. At the same time, the practical difficulty of obtaining interim relief in the arbitral forum will undoubtedly necessitate a court action for such relief. While there is every reason to believe that such relief will be granted, there can be no similar confidence in the ultimate outcome in the arbitral forum. Not only is the typical labor arbitration proceeding ill-equipped procedurally to deal with issues that go to the core of a party's relationship, but the outcome is at best difficult to predict and is essentially unreviewable. Such a situation serves neither the interests of efficiency nor planning and raises questions of fairness as well.

There is no quarrel here with Congress' and the Supreme Court's conclusion that arbitration is an exceedingly valuable method for dealing with "grievances" that arise in the context of an ongoing collective-bargaining relationship.[61] However, where business change decisions would extinguish or fundamentally alter such a relationship, arbitration appears to be a very unsatisfactory method of addressing the contractual bona fides of those decisions. Unfortunately, this important distinction has not, to this point, been judicially appreciated.

NOTES

1. Howard Johnson Co. v. Detroit Joint Executive Bd., Hotel and Restaurant Employees, 417 U.S. 249 (1974), rev'g 482 F.2d 489 (6th Cir. 1973).

2. 417 U.S. at 258 n.3. Justice Marshall's opinion states that both of the agreements in question—one covering motel and the other restaurant operations—contained succes-

sorship clauses. The Sixth Circuit's opinion states that only the motel contract had such a clause. 482 F.2d at 489. The clause, hereinafter referred to as a "general successors clause," stated (id. at 491): "This Agreement shall be binding upon the successors, assigns, purchasers, lessees or transferees of the Employer whether such succession, assignment or transfer be affected voluntarily or by operation of law or by merger or consolidation with another company provided the establishment remains in the same line of business."

The union might have had another remedy in addition to that suggested by Justice Marshall: an action against the purchaser for interference with advantageous contractual relations. See United Mine Workers v. Eastover Mining Co., 603 F. Supp. 1038, 1047 (W.D. Va. 1985).

3. 482 F.2d at 491.

4. Id. at n.4.

5. See F. Elkouri & E. Elkouri, How Arbitration Works 304-10 (4th ed. 1985); O. Fairweather, Practice and Procedure in Labor Arbitration 133–50 (2d ed. 1983). As Fairweather notes, id. at 150–55, information relevant to a grievance may also be obtained via the unfair labor practice provisions in Sections 8(a)(5) and 8(b)(3) of the NLRA. How arduous this route to discovery can be is illustrated by Detroit Edison Co. v. NLRB, 440 U.S. 301 (1979).

6. In Bowen v. United States Postal Service, 470 F. Supp. 1127 (W.D. Va. 1979), rev'd in part and aff'd in part, 642 F.2d 79 (4th Cir. 1981), rev'd, 459 U.S. 212 (1983), the District Court found, in the context of the four-step procedure in the parties' collective-bargaining agreement, that the period between the onset of the claim and its resolution in arbitration was in the normal course approximately seventeen months. This is not inconsistent with impressions related to this author by experienced case administrators in the New York office of the American Arbitration Association. Their estimate is that a year typically elapses between the appeal to arbitration and a decision by a readily "acceptable"—that is, busy—arbitrator.

7. O. Fairweather, supra note 5, at 689–92. The American Arbitration Association has promulgated "Streamlined" and "Expedited Labor Arbitration" rules for adoption by parties. The former rules contemplate a final decision, from the time of appeal to arbitration, within about thirty days; the latter, six days.

8. See, e.g., United States Arbitration Act §§ 9, 13, codified as 9 U.S.C. §§ 9, 13; New York Arbitration Law, N.Y. Civ. Prac. L. & R. (Consol.) §§ 7510, 7514.

9. 29 U.S.C. § 173(d).

10. 29 U.S.C. § 185(a); Local 174, Int'l Brotherhood of Teamsters v. Lucas Flour Co., 369 U.S. 95 (1962).

11. Textile Workers v. Lincoln Mills, 353 U.S. 448 (1957).

12. AT&T Technologies, Inc. v. Communications Workers, 106 S. Ct. 1415 (1986); Steelworkers v. American Mfg. Co., 363 U.S. 564 (1960). For criticism of the application of this "presumption of arbitrability" to actions seeking to enjoin business changes allegedly in breach of contract, see Local Lodge No. 1266, Machinists v. Panoramic Corp., 668 F.2d 276, 283–84 (7th Cir. 1981).

13. United Steelworkers v. Warrior & Gulf Navigation Co., 363 U.S. 574 (1960).

14. John Wiley & Sons v. Livingston, 376 U.S. 543 (1964).

15. Steelworkers v. Enterprise Wheel & Car Corp., 363 U.S. 593 (1960). There is a narrow public policy basis for review. United Paperworkers Int'l Union v. Misco, Inc.,

108 S. Ct. 364 (1987). There is also statutory and decisional authority for reviewability based on fraud, corruption, partiality, and arbitral misconduct. See, e.g., United States Arbitration Act, 9 U.S.C. § 10; New York Arbitration Law, N.Y. Civ. Prac. L. & R. (Consol.) § 7511(b); Holodnak v. Avco Corp., 381 F. Supp. 191 (D. Conn. 1974), modified on other grounds, 514 F.2d 285 (2d Cir.), cert. denied, 423 U.S. 892 (1975).

16. Compare Republic Steel Corp v. Maddox, 379 U.S. 650 (1965), with Vaca v. Sipes, 386 U.S. 171 (1967).

17. *Lucas Flour Co.*, 369 U.S. 95.

18. Norris–La Guardia Act, 29 U.S.C. § 101–15.

19. Buffalo Forge Co. v. Steelworkers, 428 U.S. 397 (1976); Boys Markets v. Retail Clerks, Local 770, 398 U.S. 235 (1970).

20. 29 U.S.C. § 158.

21. NLRB v. C&C Plywood Corp., 385 U.S. 421 (1967).

22. Spielberg Mfg. Co., 112 N.L.R.B. 1080 (1955).

23. Dubo Mfg. Corp., 142 N.L.R.B. 431 (1963).

24. Collyer Insulated Wire, 192 N.L.R.B. 837 (1971).

25. Olin Corp., 268 N.L.R.B. 573 (1984); United Technologies, Inc., 268 N.L.R.B. 557 (1984).

26. Hines v. Anchor Motor Freight, Inc., 424 U.S. 554 (1976). The union will be primarily liable, however, for employees' losses that its breach of the duty of fair representation exacerbated. Bowen v. United States Postal Serv., 459 U.S. 212 (1983).

27. *Wiley* 376 U.S. at 543. The fact that an agreement has terminated does not in and of itself preclude arbitration if the rights asserted allegedly arose under that agreement. Nolde Bros., Inc. v. Bakery Workers, 430 U.S. 243 (1977).

28. NLRB v. Burns International Security Services, 406 U.S. 272 (1972).

29. *Howard Johnson*, 417 U.S. at 256.

30. Id. at 256–57.

31. See Service Employees Int'l Union v. Commercial Property Services, Inc., 755 F.2d 499, 504, 507 (6th Cir. 1985); American Bell Inc. v. Federation of Tel. Workers, 736 F.2d 879, 886–89 (3d Cir. 1984). See also Carpenters Local Union No. 1478 v. Stevens, 743 F.2d 1271, 1276–77 (9th Cir. 1984), in which the court vacated an arbitrator's award against a nonsignatory employer that the NLRB had found was not part of a single bargaining unit, an alter ego, or a joint employer.

32. The series *Labor Arbitration Awards* has been published by Commerce Clearinghouse since 1961; *Labor Arbitration Reports* has been published by the Bureau of National Affairs (BNA) since 1946. See "How Representative are Published Decisions," in Proc. of 37th Ann. Meeting of the National Academy of [Labor] Arbitrators 170 (1984).

33. Arbitrators have no independent authority to permit publication of their decisions. See National Academy of Arbitrators, American Arbitration Association & Federal Mediation and Conciliation Service, Code of Professional Responsibility for Arbitrators in Labor-Management Disputes, Pt. 2C.1.c (1974 rev. ed.).

34. Id. at pt. 2G.

35. See, e.g., The Proceedings of the Annual Meeting of the National Academy of [Labor] Arbitrators, published by BNA, which is now in its 38th volume.

36. For an example of such a clause, see supra note 2.

37. Wyatt Mfg. Co., 82 L.A. 153 (Goodman, 1983); Kroger Co., 78 L.A. 569 (Howlett, 1981); National Tea Co., 59 L.A. 1193 (Joseph, 1972); Walker Bros., 41 L.A. 844 (Crawford, 1963).

38. Herbert J. Caplan, Inc., 81 L.A. 22 (Levine, 1983); Martin Podany Associates, 80 L.A. 658 (Gallagher, 1983); Sexton's Steak House, Inc., 76 L.A. 577 (Ross, 1981); Hosanna Trading Co., 74 L.A. 128 (Simons, 1980); High Point Sprinkler Co. of Boston, 67 L.A. 239 (Connolly, 1976). For judicial confirmation of such an award, see TTL Distribution, Inc. v. Local 99, 111 L.R.R.M. 3147 (S.D.N.Y. 1982).

39. See American Law Institute (ALI), Restatement (Second) of Contracts §§ 205, 237, illus. 4 (1979).

40. Id. at § 203(a).

41. *Sexton's Steak House, Inc.*, 76 L.A. 577; Hosanna Trading Co., 74 L.A. 128.

42. *Herbert J. Caplan, Inc.*, 81 L.A.22; *High Point Sprinkler Co.*, 67 L.A. 239; *TTL Distribution*, 111 L.R.R.M. 3147. Cf. *Martin Podany Associates*, 80 L.A. 658.

43. If work is lost, there is no principled reason to distinguish between relocation and subcontracting. However, some published awards have relied on such a distinction in addressing the question of whether relocation violates an express prohibition against subcontracting, and they have held that it does not. Lever Bros., 65 L.A. 1299 (Edes, 1976); Metal Textile Corp. 42 L.A. 107 (Rubin, 1964).

44. For a detailed analysis of the subcontracting cases, with quotes from many arbitrators, see O. Fairweather, supra note 5, at 469–90. The relocation cases not surprisingly reflect a similar split and spectrum of opinion. See, e.g., *finding no contract violation*: Continental Telephone System, Indiana Division, 80 L.A. 1355 (Wren, 1983); Leeds-Dixon Laboratories, 74 L.A. 407 (Kramer, 1980); E-lite Co., 66 L.A. 800 (Kronish, 1976), and *finding a violation*: Douwe Egberts Superior Co., 78 L.A. 1131 (Ellmann, 1982); T & S Coal Co., 73 L.A. 882 (Leahy, 1979); Sealtest Dairy, 65 L.A. 858 (Blum, 1975). The Board in applying section 8(d) of the NLRA, 29 U.S.C.A. § 158(d), currently takes the position that such contract clauses do not support the existence of an implied obligation not to relocate—a marked turnabout from its earlier position. See Milwaukee Spring Division of Illinois Coil Spring Co., 268 N.L.R.B. 601 (1984).

45. Atomic Uniform Corp. v. ILGWU, 86 L.R.R.M. 2331 (S.D.N.Y. 1973).

46. O. Fairweather, supra note 5, at 551 n.245, cites only Ohio Edison Co., 46 L.A. 801 (Alexander, 1966) and West Virginia Pulp & Paper Co., 48 L.A. 657 (Rubin, 1966), for the proposition that arbitrators have ordered employees to reopen plants and return machinery to plants.

47. Pabst Brewing Co., 78 L.A. 772 (Wolff, 1982).

48. Id. at 777. Essentially the same kind of an award was issued in *Douwe Egberts Superior Co.*, 78 L.A. at 1137.

49. *Sealtest Dairy Co.*, 65 L.A. 858.

50. United States Postal Service, 67 L.A. 133 (Garrett, 1976) (preliminary relief granted); McCall Printing Co., 63 L.A. 627 (McDermott, 1974) (granted); Armour & Co., 68 L.A. 1076 (Goetz, 1977) (denied); Oakland Tribune Co., 60 L.A. 665 (Koven, 1973) (denied).

51. See *United States Postal Service*, 67 L.A. 133, in which the national arbitrator for the Postal Service and the National Association of Letter Carriers granted interim relief without the benefit of a status quo clause.

52. Michaels v. Mariforum Shipping, S.A., 624 F.2d 411 (2d Cir. 1980). Most recently, a federal district court in the same circuit refused to find this doctrine applicable to interim arbitral relief, confirming an award in the nature of a temporary injunction. See Southern Seas Navigation v. Petroleos Mexicanos, 606 F. Supp. 692 (S.D.N.Y. 1985).

53. The availability of such relief, both pre- and post-*Buffalo Forge*, is treated in two admirable articles: Cantor, "*Buffalo Forge* and Injunctions against Employer Breaches of Collective Bargaining Agreements," 1980 Wis. L. Rev. 247; Gould, "On Labor Injunctions Pending Arbitration: Recasting *Buffalo Forge*," 30 Stan. L. Rev. 533 (1978).

54. See Local Lodge No. 1266, Machinists v. Panoramic Corp., 668 F.2d at 285–88.

55. Id. at 288–89. There may also be procedural prerequisites such as a hearing pursuant to Norris–La Guardia Act § 7, 29 U.S.C. § 107; see United Telegraph Workers v. Western Union, 771 F.2d 699 (3d Cir. 1985).

56. See Amalgamated Transit Union, Div. 1384 v. Greyhound Lines, Inc., 550 F.2d 1237, 1238–39 (9th Cir.), cert. denied, 434 U.S. 837 (1977).

57. See Local Lodge No. 1266, Machinists v. Panoramic Corp., 668 F.2d at 282; United Steelworkers v. Fort Pitt Steel Casting, 598 F.2d 1273, 1279, 1282 (3rd Cir., 1979); Lever Bros. Co. v. International Chemical Workers, Local 217, 554 F.2d 115, 120–23 (4th Cir. 1976); Columbia Local, American Postal Workers v. Bolger, 621 F.2d 615 (4th Cir. 1980); Aluminum Workers International Union v. Consolidated Aluminum Corp., 696 F.2d 437, 443 (6th Cir. 1982).

58. See Hoh v. Pepsico, Inc., 491 F.2d 556, 561 (2d Cir. 1974).

59. The Second Circuit most recently articulated alternative tests: irreparable harm coupled with likelihood of success on the merits, or irreparable harm coupled with a "serious" question on the merits and an adverse balance of hardship. Compare *Hoh*, 491 F.2d 556, with American Postal Workers Union v. United States Postal Service, 766 F.2d. 715, 721 (2d Cir. 1985), cert. denied, 106 S. Ct. 1262 (1986).

60. See, e.g., Local Lodge No. 1266, Machinists v. Panoramic Corp., 668 F.2d at 284–85.

61. United Steelworkers v. Warrior & Gulf Navigation Co., 363 U.S. at 580–82.

6

ERISA CONSIDERATIONS IN BUSINESS CHANGE TRANSACTIONS

Brookes D. Billman

Editors' Note. Professor Billman describes the relationship of the Employee Retirement Income Security Act of 1974 to the Internal Revenue Code's regulation of "qualified" retirement plans. He points out that ERISA was essentially concerned with ensuring adequate funding of "defined benefit plans," but that loopholes in the law quickly appeared. Congress responded by enacting amendments in 1986 and 1987: to prohibit "standard" termination or withdrawal unless plan benefits, not merely minimum statutory benefits, are adequately funded, and to restrict "distress" terminations. The author then looks at the implications of ERISA and Code liability for business change transactions, and cautions that both internal employer revamping and sales of assets may involve significant ERISA liabilities for all parties. In contrast, he notes, a mere change in corporate identity or a stock sale in and of itself will not have ERISA implications. Professor Billman explores the use of plan termination as a financing device to obtain recovery of plan assets in excess of adequately funded benefits, including the important question of what interest rate may appropriately be projected. He also questions whether the fiduciary obligations of plan trustees necessarily restrict their use of plan assets to prevent takeovers.

The purpose of this chapter is to highlight and analyze selected issues that may arise under ERISA in the course of business change transactions. This chapter examines the basic questions affecting pension plans in business change transactions.

As a preliminary matter, some basic definitions should be established and some terminology clarified. First, ERISA[1] means different things depending upon the context. It is both (1) a statute that significantly amended the Internal Revenue Code of 1954 in the qualified retirement plan context and (2) a separate statute beginning at 29 United States Code section 1000 (the so-called "labor provisions" of ERISA). In this chapter, ERISA will be used when referring to 29 United States Code, and the Code will be used when referring to the Internal Revenue Code provisions.

Second, "pension plan" is a phrase with varying meanings under ERISA and the Code. When used herein, pension plan refers to an "employee pension benefit plan" as defined in section 3(2) of ERISA—any plan, fund, or program that provides for the payment of retirement income to employees or for the deferral of income by employees to a date beyond the termination of employment. "Defined benefit plan" and "defined contribution plan" will be used to describe the two major categories of qualified pension plans under the Code.[2]

One cannot examine the effect of ERISA upon business change transactions without considering various tax issues that may arise in those transactions. The reasons for this are quite straightforward. First, ERISA and the Code are an interrelated, integrated pair of statutes. Legal issues affecting pension plans arise under both statutes. Second, for most pension plans, the tax law plays a critical role in their existence and operation. Code sections 401–418E contain a series of rules establishing a special "qualified" status for pension plans. Significant tax benefits for both employers and employees attach to securing this status.[3] Employers will normally not engage in business change transactions without determining whether those transactions will adversely affect these tax benefits. Thus, the following discussion will attempt to integrate important considerations under both the Code and ERISA for pension plans in business change transactions.

THE BASIC ISSUES

One can isolate several different types of issues that may affect pension plans in business change transactions. First, there is a series of what may be called "direct liability" issues. These direct liability issues may arise in a number of different contexts. Some business changes do not involve a change of ownership of the employer (for example, plant closings, reductions in force). In such a case, for an employer who has been maintaining a pension plan, a basic issue is whether the *fact* of the business change will create or increase that employer's liability under the plan. Where the business change involves a change of ownership of either the employer's assets or stock, both the target and acquiring entities must be concerned about whether this change of ownership will create new liabilities for the target or acquiring companies.

Second, there is a set of "fiduciary responsibility" issues. The basic question here is the extent, if any, to which pension plans may be used by their creators or sponsors as crucial parts of business change transactions. For example, may a pension plan be used to prevent a hostile takeover of an employer or to facilitate the acquisition of that employer through the purchase of employer stock?

EMPLOYER LIABILITY UNDER ERISA

In most common business change transactions, there are several potential sources for an employer's liability, including statutes (ERISA and the Code), the plan documents, and perhaps even side agreements, such as union contracts. These various sources weave a complex web of potential liability issues.

Liability under Plan Document

A pension plan is essentially a contract between an employer and its employees. Thus, it is logical to look first to the plan documents to determine the nature and extent of an employer's liability in establishing and maintaining a pension plan. If one examined most pension plans, however, it would become clear that an employer's liability under those plans is quite limited. Plans frequently reserve in the employer the right to terminate the plan and to cease making contributions to the plan, giving the employees upon such a termination a vested right only to the extent of the benefit accrued to the date of the termination, and then only to the extent that such benefit is funded on the date of the termination. Moreover, the Code itself, even after ERISA, seemed to impose no greater obligation upon any qualified plan.[4]

Thus, if an employer can terminate a plan at will and can thereby terminate the basic obligation to contribute under the plan, unless the plan document specifically goes further and imposes greater employer liability, the plan document is generally not a source of extensive liability for employers who maintain pension plans. Hence, for many transactions, the pension plan documents would impose little or no impediment. The employer, in all likelihood, would have reserved in those documents the right to terminate the plan and to cease making contributions to the plan at any time. A more interesting question is whether plans that do not contain language so limiting the employer's liability may be amended in the midst of a business change to provide such a limitation.[5]

A related source of employer liability may be union contracts. Even though the language of a pension plan clearly permits termination of the plan at any time, a separate obligation to continue to make contributions to such a plan may arise under a collective agreement. In such a case, the termination of the plan could give rise to a liability under the contract. Hence, any type of side agreement must be examined to determine whether there is a contractual obligation to maintain and contribute to a pension plan that will be triggered by its termination.

Statutory Liability

The extent and degree of any statutory liability arising out of the operation of a pension plan depends upon the type of plan involved. One important distinction made is whether the plan is a defined benefit plan or a defined contribution plan.[6] As a general matter, neither ERISA nor the Code imposes any special statutory liability upon defined contribution plans.[7] On the other hand, title IV of ERISA imposes potential liability upon an employer who maintains a defined benefit plan.[8]

A second important distinction for the purpose of assessing the statutory liability of defined benefit plans is whether the plan is a "multiemployer plan"[9] or is subject to the single employer plan termination rules.

Basis for Statutory Liability. Liability under title IV of ERISA is limited to defined benefit plans.[10] Why is the statute so limited? The answer lies in the basic nature of the employer's legal obligation or promise under various types of plans.

In a defined contribution plan, the employer makes a promise regarding its contribution to the plan. That contribution will be either fixed (for example, a money purchase plan or a stock bonus plan) or discretionary (for example, a profit-sharing plan.)[11] In either event, the employer's basic obligation to the plan and to the employees who participate in it ends with the employer's contribution to the plan. Thus, in a defined contribution plan, the employer promises no particular level of benefits to employees.[12] An employee's benefit in a defined contribution plan is the balance in his plan account.[13] If the employer is obligated only to make contributions to the plan and if that obligation may be terminated at any time, the employer's liability under a defined contribution plan essentially ends when such a plan is terminated.[14]

In a defined benefit plan, by contrast, the employer promises to pay a specific or definitely determinable benefit.[15] While the employer's obligation is thus to pay a benefit, the plan may be somewhat vague as to the precise manner in which that promised benefit will be funded.[16] Normally, defined benefit plans employ an actuarial funding method under which employer contributions are calculated each year.[17] There is, however, substantial latitude under these actuarial funding methods as to what portion of the promised benefit is funded each year.[18]

With defined benefit plans, termination of the plan and the cessation of employer contributions may take on considerable significance. The employer has promised to pay a benefit that will accrue and will be funded over a period of years. The employer also has reserved the right to terminate the plan and to cease making contributions to the plan. There is a basic tension between the promise to pay a benefit and the right to terminate the plan. If the employer has not been funding the promised benefit at a sufficiently rapid rate during the existence of the plan, the plan's assets will not be sufficient to cover the benefits accrued as of the date of the termination of the plan. If the employer's right to cease making contributions to the plan is absolute under the plan, and if the employees' rights are limited to the accrued benefits to the extent then funded, employees in an underfunded plan might have no source from which to recover the unfunded portion of their benefits.

Title IV of ERISA, as well as other parts of ERISA and the Code,[19] reflect a basic policy decision by Congress to deal with the problem of underfunding of defined benefit plans. When an employer promises to pay a benefit to employees under such a plan, various statutory protections may be necessary to ensure that this promised benefit (at least to the extent accrued as of any termination date) will ultimately be funded and paid. By adopting and maintaining this type of plan, an employer assumes this statutory liability, regardless of what rights may be reserved to the employer in the plan document.

Over time, Congress has recognized that the problem of underfunded benefits must be attacked from a number of different angles. Most importantly, if the employer must, by statute, make regular and substantial contributions to the plan, it is less likely that underfunding will result. Thus, the minimum funding rules obligate employers adopting defined benefit plans to engage in this type of ongoing funding of such plans.[20]

Moreover, Congress has backed up the minimum funding standards to deal with those plans that become underfunded despite satisfaction of minimum funding requirements—the termination provisions of title IV of ERISA. So long as an employer cannot permanently evade the funding requirements by terminating the plan—it is hoped—the regulatory scheme will work. It is this aspect of title IV that has been the subject of considerable abuse and study since the passage of ERISA resulting in recent amendments to bolster funding obligations.

Thus, Congress has structured statutory liability regarding pension plans on the basis of the employer's promise under the plan. When an employer promises a defined benefit, statutory liability may arise to fund that benefit (to the extent accrued), even though the plan itself imposes no such obligation. Because of the stakes involved in the application of title IV to a pension plan and the imposition of statutory liability over and above the obligations imposed by the plan document, litigation has ensued over the proper classification of a particular plan under this statutory scheme.[21]

Single Employer Liability under Title IV. With certain exceptions,[22] for defined benefit plans that are not "multiemployer plans,"[23] statutory liability under title IV of ERISA will be triggered only when the plan terminates.[24] Thus, in absence of a plan termination, most business change transactions will not, in and of themselves, produce statutory liability. The statute also specifically identifies a number of corporate readjustments that are not events triggering liability under the single-employer rules.[25]

Title IV is an outgrowth of the absence of any pre-ERISA rules protecting employees whose defined benefit plans were terminated and whose accrued benefits were underfunded. Title IV regulates primarily this underfunding situation. As a result of the Single Employer Pension Plan Amendments Act of 1986 (SEPPAA)[26] and title IX of the Omnibus Budget Reconciliation Act of 1987 (the 1987 Act),[27] the structure of title IV has been substantially revised to deal with the significant number of plan terminations that occurred in the first decade after ERISA was enacted. Following a brief review of the operation of title IV prior to SEPPAA and the 1987 Act, this chapter turns to an examination of the current, revised structure of title IV.

Title IV prior to SEPPAA. The basic premise of title IV prior to SEPPAA was relatively straightforward. The statute established a guaranteed benefit to which each participant in a defined benefit plan was entitled upon termination of the plan. Under ERISA section 4022(a), the vested accrued benefit of a participant at the time of termination was guaranteed (other than the portion of the benefit that became vested solely because of the termination). The statute did, however, place several limits upon this guaranteed amount, including an annually adjusted maximum dollar limit.[28] The 1987 maximum dollar limit upon guaranteed benefits was $1,857.95 per month.[29]

When a plan terminated, the Pension Benefit Guaranty Corporation (PBGC)[30] determined whether the plan's assets were sufficient to pay the guaranteed benefits under the statute. Under ERISA section 4044, the plan's assets were allocated to various categories of benefits payable under the plan. If the assets allocated to the guaranteed benefits under ERISA section 4044(a)(4) fell short of the value of such benefits, employer liability arose to the extent of the lesser of (1) the excess of the guaranteed benefits over the allocated assets or (2) 30 percent of the employer's net worth.[31]

Hence, the basic liability of an employer under a defined benefit plan and the single employer termination provisions of title IV prior to SEPPAA and the 1987 Act was to pay the guaranteed benefits under title IV, up to a limit of 30 percent of the net worth of the employer. If, as frequently happened, even this liability of the employer did not produce sufficient assets to fund the guaranteed benefits, the PBGC would pay those guaranteed benefits to the terminated plan's participants. The PBGC obtained the funds to pay the guaranteed benefits through a premium that was assessed against all defined benefit plans covered by title IV.[32] In this sense, after the employer's liability was exhausted, title IV did operate to provide termination insurance for the statutorily guaranteed benefits.

Title IV under SEPPAA and the 1987 Act. After almost ten years of experience under title IV, a number of loopholes and abuses of the statutory scheme came to light.[33] In particular, Congress determined that the 30 percent of net worth cap on employer liability was frequently too low, thereby causing the PBGC to assume obligations for guaranteed benefits, even when the employer (and related entities) might have survived a period of financial distress and returned to profitability.[34] The revised statute thus both increases the general extent of employer liability and reduces the occasions under which liability may be transferred to the PBGC.

In addition, Congress also was concerned about the number of plan terminations by profitable employers. Under prior law, as long as the plan assets were sufficient to cover the benefits *guaranteed* by the statute, the employer was not responsible upon plan termination for any additional benefits that might have accrued under the plan in excess of the statutory guarantee. Even if the plan promised greater benefits than title IV guaranteed, a beneficiary under that plan was guaranteed only the statutory minimum benefit and, upon plan termination, would lose any unfunded benefit accruals in excess of the statutory guarantee.[35] Hence, plan termination became a mechanism by which employers could avoid satisfying fully their plan obligations, while at the same time incurring no obligation to the PBGC (because plan assets covered statutorily guaranteed benefits).[36] Congress responded to these practices by restricting the circumstances under which an employer that was not in financial distress could terminate a defined benefit plan and by conditioning such nonhardship terminations upon the payment of most benefits accrued under the plan as of the date of termination.

Standard Terminations. Under SEPPAA and the 1987 Act, revised section 4041(a) of ERISA establishes the exclusive means by which a defined benefit plan may be terminated—either through a standard termination or a distress termination. Unlike prior law, the statute imposes not only potential liability on the PBGC upon plan termination, but also sets forth the circumstances under which employers may terminate such plans in the first instance. Thus, although the new statute continues to respect the basic right of employers to terminate defined benefit plans, it regulates the manner by which employers may seek to avoid contractual plan liability through the termination device. The revised statute carefully defines the circumstances under which financial hardship of the employer may allow the transfer of pension obligations to the PBGC.

A standard termination is one in which the "benefit liabilities" of the plan can be satisfied from the assets of the plan.[37] Benefit liabilities are the benefits of employees and their beneficiaries under the plan under Code section 401(a)(2).[38] Under Code section 401(a)(2), "liabilities" includes both fixed and contingent obligations to employees.[39] Although the precise meaning of "benefit liabilities" may have to be worked out on a case-by-case basis, one basic premise is clear in the revised statute: An employer may terminate a defined benefit plan without further obligation to the PBGC (and obtain a reversion of assets) only if all the benefits accrued to the date of the termination are satisfied by the assets of the plan.

The new notion of standard termination contemplates a self-executing category of terminations. Once the substantial layer of procedural requirements is met,[40] standard terminations can proceed without the PBGC's taking over the assets of the plan because of the definition of standard termination—a termination in which the assets of the plan are sufficient to satisfy the benefit liabilities under the plan. Except for PBGC verification of the sufficiency of assets, such a termination can proceed without further agency action. In other words, standard terminations do not involve underfunding and are to be executed with a minimal amount of government intervention.

This potentially smooth mechanism for standard terminations should not obscure the major substantive change inherent in this area. Congress substantially increased the level of plan assets required before a termination is deemed to involve "sufficient" assets. Prior to SEPPAA, so long as plan assets covered guaranteed benefits, the PBGC did not get involved. Under current law, by contrast, assets must cover benefit liabilities under the plan, not just the lesser level of statutorily guaranteed benefits. Employers may not abrogate their promised benefits under the plan through a plan termination. In any plan under which the assets are not sufficient to cover benefit liabilities, the standard termination procedures may not be used; in such circumstances, the plan may be terminated only if the criteria of a ''distress termination'' are satisfied.

Distress Terminations. Under SEPPAA and the 1987 Act, a defined benefit plan may be terminated by the employer under only two circumstances: the standard termination and the distress termination.[41] The effect of this structure is to require a PBGC finding of ''distress'' before a plan that cannot meet benefit liabilities may be terminated by the employer.

Distress requires a basic finding that the termination cannot be avoided due to the financial problems of the employer. There are three basic distress criteria: (1) the employer is involved in a liquidation case under the bankruptcy laws; (2) the employer is involved in a reorganization case under the bankruptcy laws and the bankruptcy court determines that, without the termination, the employer will be unable to pay its debts under the reorganization plan and will be unable to continue in a business outside the reorganization plan, and thus approves the termination; or (3) the PBGC determines that, without the termination, the employer will not be able to pay debts and continue in business, or the employer's costs of pension coverage are unreasonably burdensome solely as a result of a decline in the employer's work force.[42]

In a distress termination where there is by definition some degree of underfunding,[43] statutory liability to the PBGC arises to the extent of the unfunded benefit liabilities of the plan.[44] This is a significant change from prior law, in that there is no cap on an employer's statutory obligation for benefit liabilities to employees. To enforce this liability, the PBGC has a statutory lien against the assets of the employer, up to 30 percent of the net worth of the employer.[45] Thus, the role of the 30 percent of net worth cap has been altered from one of the alternative limits on an employer's overall liability to merely the limit on the PBGC's lien against employer assets. Even in a distress termination, an employer with sufficient assets in excess of 30 percent of net worth would still have statutory obligations up to the plan's benefit liabilities on the date of termination under the revised statute. The enforcement of these unsecured liabilities in excess of 30 percent of the employer's net worth would also be in the hands of the PBGC.

Moreover, unlike pre-SEPPAA law, the statute takes a very broad view of the ''employer'' for purposes of satisfying the PBGC lien. Under ERISA section 4062(a), the contributing sponsor of the plan and all members of the contributing sponsor's controlled group[46] are jointly and severally liable for the plan's obligation to the PBGC. This represents a major change in prior law, under which only the employer itself was responsible to the PBGC. Under the prior regime, it was possible for a plan to be quite underfunded and for the PBGC to have recourse against only one member of a controlled group of corporations—the sponsoring employer. If that employer had no assets, the PBGC had little recourse. The revised statute allows the PBGC to satisfy its lien against any member of the controlled group of corporations of which the employer is a part. In effect, the present form of the statute makes the form of business structure irrelevant to the satisfaction of PBGC liability. It also prevents a circumstance that Congress found quite troubling—the PBGC's taking over the obligations of an underfunded plan with no assistance from the assets of the employer, while other members of the employer's controlled group enjoyed continued profitability. The form of doing business and allocation of assets among members of a controlled group no longer affect obligations to the PBGC for benefit liabilities.

Thus, in business change transactions, if plan termination is being considered as a component of the transaction, the enhanced level of statutory liability for plan benefit liabilities clearly should be carefully considered. The statute no longer allows avoidance of plan liabilities through the termination device, absent a showing of distress. Where distress is present, a plan may be terminated, but the statutory obligation to pay benefit liabilities remains intact; only the PBGC's lien is limited to 30 percent of the net worth of the employer and its controlled group. If the PBGC's lien does not fully discharge benefit liabilities, those liabilities remain an outstanding obligation of the employer. Only when the employer and its controlled group do not have assets sufficient to satisfy the PBGC's lien will the excess benefit liabilities go unpaid.[47]

Multiemployer Liability under Title IV. As defined in ERISA section 3(37)(A), a multiemployer plan is a plan to which more than one employer is required to contribute, and which is maintained pursuant to one or more collective bargaining agreements between one or more employee organizations and one or more employers. Title IV, as a result of the Multiemployer Pension Plan Amendments Act of 1980,[48] contains a different set of rules regarding employer liability under this type of plan.

At the outset, it is important to focus upon the types of plans that are not multiemployer plans under title IV. There may be many plans in which more than one employer contributes that are not multiemployer plans. For example, in a controlled group of corporations, all members of the group may contribute to a plan. Since all members of a controlled group are treated as a single employer under title IV for this purpose,[49] this is considered a "multiple employer plan," rather than a multiemployer plan, and it will be governed generally by the rules set out above for single employers. Even if the employers contributing to a plan are not related, if the contributions are not made pursuant to a collective bargaining agreement, the plan will not be treated as a multiemployer plan for the purpose of title IV, but will be governed by the single employer termination rules. The single employer termination portion of title IV contains a special set of withdrawal rules for these multiple employer plans under ERISA section 4063, and the termination of a multiple employer plan is governed by ERISA section 4064.

Events Triggering Multiemployer Plan Liability. In the multiemployer plan situation, termination of the plan is a somewhat unlikely event. In most cases, several employers contribute to the plan, and the withdrawal of one or more employers from the plan would not necessarily mean that the whole plan would terminate. Hence, the single employer termination rules, which treat the termination of a plan as the crucial employer liability event, are not well-suited to the multiemployer plan context. Title IV provides separate rules governing employer liability under multiemployer plans, which are designed to ensure that when employers withdraw from such plans, they do not shift their liability for promised benefits to the remaining employers.

Generally, employer liability under a multiemployer plan arises when there has been a ''withdrawal'' of an employer from the plan.[50] A withdrawal may be either complete[51] or partial.[52] Numerous business change transactions may fall under the scope of either of these types of withdrawals, thereby raising the possibility of employer liability under title IV.

(1) Complete Withdrawal. The statute lists two circumstances that qualify as a complete withdrawal from a multiemployer plan: (1) permanently ceasing to have an obligation to contribute under the plan or (2) permanently ceasing all covered operations under the plan.[53] Thus, the statute does not focus as much upon the type of transaction that produces the complete withdrawal as on the fact of the withdrawal. Several transactions could produce a complete withdrawal as defined, including a plant closing, a union decertification, or a withdrawal from the plan pursuant to negotiation.

(2) Partial Withdrawal. A partial withdrawal occurs when there has been either (1) a 70-percent contribution decline or (2) a partial cessation of the employer's obligation to contribute under the plan.[54] The 70-percent contribution decline test focuses upon the number of ''contribution base units''—units with respect to which an employer has an obligation to contribute under a multiemployer plan, as defined in ERISA section 4001(11). There are two critical time periods for this test. First, there is the three-year testing period, the plan year in question and the two immediately preceding plan years. Second, there is the five plan years immediately preceding the three-year testing period. Within the five-year period, the average of the contribution base units in the two years in that period in which such units were the highest is measured. This average becomes the ''high base year.'' The 70-percent test is satisfied if the contribution base units during the three-year testing period do not exceed 30 percent of the contribution base units during the high base year.[55]

A ''partial cessation'' of the obligation to contribute under the plan occurs in two situations: (1) when an employer ceases to have an obligation to contribute under one or more, but less than all, of the collective bargaining units under which it was previously obligated to contribute, but the employer continues to perform work of the type previously covered by the agreement or transfers such work to another location (the ''agreements rule''); and (2) when the employer ceases to have an obligation to contribute to the plan for work performed at one or more, but less than all, of the facilities previously covered by the plan, but the employer continues to perform work at the facility of the type previously covered by the agreement (the "facilities rule").[56]

A complex series of events must occur in order for there to be a partial withdrawal. Under the agreements rule, the employer must have an obligation to contribute to a single plan under more than one collective bargaining unit. The obligation to contribute must permanently cease under one or more, but less than all, of these agreements. In addition, for this event to be a partial withdrawal, the employer must continue to perform work of the type for which the contributions were previously required or must transfer that work to another location. An example of a partial withdrawal under this rule would be the decertification of the union at one or more, but not all, of the facilities under a single plan, where there were separate collective bargaining agreements for each of the facilities with each requiring contributions to the plan.

Under the facilities test, a partial withdrawal arises only when there are a single plan and one or more collective bargaining agreements covering multiple facilities under the plan. A partial withdrawal would occur only if the obligation to contribute at one or more, but not all, facilities ceased, but work continued at the other facilities for which contributions would continue. Hence, the closing of the facility would not give rise to a partial withdrawal under the facilities rule.

The permanent closing of a facility may give rise to partial withdrawal liability under two possible circumstances. In one situation, each facility is covered by a separate bargaining agreement and a single plan, and the obligation to contribute at one facility ceases when it is closed. This will give rise to partial withdrawal liability under the agreements rule if the employer continues to perform the work under the jurisdiction of the agreement at another location. A second situation occurs when the 70-percent contribution decline rule is met as a result of the closing. If all facilities are covered by a single agreement and if one facility is closed, there can be no partial cessation. In such circumstances, the only possibility for partial withdrawal liability is the 70-percent test.

Sales of Assets. Given the definitions of complete and partial withdrawals under title IV, it is easy to see that many common corporate transactions involving the sale and purchase of assets could trigger withdrawal liability for the employer. For example, if an employer sells the assets of a particular division, that sale could be a complete withdrawal from the plan, if the division was the only covered operation under the plan or was the only source of an obligation to contribute under the plan. This potential liability could certainly have an impact upon such transactions, perhaps even eliminating an asset sale as a viable transactional alternative. In anticipation of the possible negative effect of withdrawal liability on these corporate transactions, the statute contains a mechanism by which the seller and purchaser can avoid such liability.

(1) Requirements for Avoiding Withdrawal Liability. ERISA section 4204 provides that withdrawal liability may be avoided in a sale of assets, even though the sale causes the seller to cease covered operations or to cease to have an

obligation to contribute under the plan. The statute sets forth three preconditions, all of which must be met to secure this favorable treatment. First, the purchaser must have an obligation to contribute to the plan (with respect to the purchased operations) involving substantially the same number of contribution base units as the seller had prior to the sale.[57] Second, the purchaser must provide to the plan, for a period of five plan years after the plan year in which the sale occurs, a bond or escrow in the amount of the greater of the seller's average required annual contribution to the plan over the three plan years preceding the year of sale, or the annual contribution of the seller for the last plan year prior to the year of sale. The bond stands as protection to the plan for the five-plan-year period following the year of the sale, if the purchaser withdraws from the plan or fails to make a required contribution to the plan during that period.[58] Third, the sales contract must provide that if the purchaser withdraws from the plan during the five-plan-year period following the sale, the seller is secondarily liable for any withdrawal liability it would have had to the plan with respect to the operations sold to the purchaser.[59] If these conditions are satisfied, no withdrawal liability arises as a result of the transfer to the purchaser. A subsequent withdrawal of the purchaser from the plan, however, may result in withdrawal liability for the purchaser or, if not paid, for the seller.[60]

(2) Criteria for Avoiding Bond/Escrow and Sale Contract Requirements. The bond/escrow and sale contract requirements of ERISA section 4204 may be waived by applying to the PBGC[61] or by demonstrating compliance with certain requirements set forth in PBGC regulations.[62] Under these regulations, if the seller and purchaser inform the plan in writing that the asset sale is covered by section 4204 and if one of three criteria is met, both the bond/escrow and sale contract requirements will be waived. Generally, the three exemptions are for (1) pre-January 1, 1981, sales, (2) "de minimis" transactions, or (3) transactions in which either a net income or a net asset test is satisfied.[63]

A transaction is de minimis if the bond or escrow otherwise required of the purchaser does not exceed the lesser of $250,000 or 2 percent of the average annual contributions made by all employers to the plan for the three plan years ending before the plan year in which the seller's withdrawal would otherwise have occurred as a result of the asset sale (herein referred to as the "seller's deemed withdrawal").[64] If the purchaser's net income after taxes (as defined in the regulations) for the three most recent fiscal years ending before the date of the seller's deemed withdrawal from the plan, reduced by any interest expense arising from the asset purchase for the fiscal year following the date of the seller's deemed withdrawal, exceeds 150 percent of the bond or escrow required, that requirement (and the sale contract requirement) will be waived.[65]

If the purchaser's net tangible assets (as defined in the regulations[66]) at the end of the fiscal year preceding the seller's deemed withdrawal from the plan equal or exceed one of two amounts, a waiver of these section 4204 requirements will be granted. If the purchaser was not obligated to contribute to the plan before the asset purchase, the purchaser's net tangible assets must exceed the amount of the unfunded vested benefits allocable to the seller under the plan (from the purchased operations) as of the date of the seller's deemed withdrawal. If the purchaser already had an obligation to contribute under the plan prior to the purchase, then the purchaser's net tangible assets must exceed the amount of the unfunded vested benefits allocable to both the purchaser and the seller (from the purchased operations) as of the date of the seller's deemed withdrawal.[67]

Other Nonliability Events. Tracking the single employer termination provisions,[68] ERISA section 4218 provides that a withdrawal will not be found to exist merely because an employer ceases to exist as a result of certain corporate transactions[69] or a liquidation to do business in unincorporated form, so long as the transaction causes no interruption in employer contributions or the employer's obligation to contribute under the plan. In each such case, the successor employer or other entity resulting from the change will be considered the original employer for purposes of the withdrawal liability sections.

The legislative history also attempts to make clear that no withdrawal liability should be found to arise merely because of a stock sale transaction. In that case, the original employer, in fact, still exists, and there should be no withdrawal liability in such a transaction. Of course, the seller or the buyer, or both, could be liable for withdrawal liability if an obligation to contribute ceases as part of the stock sale transaction.

Other Liability Issues. The 1987 Act has expanded the potential liability issues that should be considered in the context of certain business change transactions. Most relate to an acquiring employer considering a target company for possible takeover, although similar questions can arise outside of the acquisition context.

In a defined benefit plan, there are rules that operate to ensure that the plan is properly funded in accordance with reasonable actuarial principles. If the plan is qualified under the Code, Code section 412 imposes minimum funding standards upon the plan.[70] Failure to satisfy these minimum funding standards may result in an excise tax being imposed upon the employer under Code section 4971. Defined benefit plans are also required to pay premiums to the PBGC to fund the PBGC's mandate to insure minimum statutory guaranteed benefits in underfunded plans.[71] This premium obligation is a current liability of every defined benefit plan.

The 1987 Act attempts to strengthen the Code and ERISA in dealing with underfunded plans by requiring more rapid funding of underfunded liabilities,[72] by requiring quarterly payment of minimum funding obligations,[73] and by expanding the potential liability for minimum funding violations to the controlled group of the employer sponsoring the underfunded plan.[74] With the PBGC's suffering ever-widening losses, it seemed appropriate for Congress to attack the problem of underfunding before it reaches the PBGC. If more plans are properly funded before plan termination becomes an issue, the PBGC will have to assume fewer plan obligations, and fewer plans will be underfunded with respect to benefit liabilities.

The 1987 Act substantially increased the premiums payable to the PBGC by defined benefit plans. For plan years beginning after December 31, 1987, the basic premium is $16.00 per plan participant, up from $8.50 per participant under prior law.[75] In addition, for plans that have unfunded vested benefits, the premium may increase to as much as $50.00 per participant.[76] This latter provision is intended to impose, at least in part, a risk-related premium structure in the PBGC funding scheme. Plans that may pose in the future the greatest risk to the PBGC (that is, those currently with unfunded vested benefits) must pay substantially greater premiums to the PBGC.

Acquiring companies certainly should examine the funded status of plans of target companies and should carefully weigh the potential cost of compliance with the requirements of title IV of ERISA as part of the overall cost of any acquisition. The increased PBGC premiums, coupled with the accelerated funding requirements for underfunded plans and the inability to get out from under plan obligations through the termination vehicle, should make acquiring companies quite reluctant to take over underfunded plans without substantial concessions from the current plan sponsors reflecting the increased costs of operating defined benefit plans.

In addition, sponsoring employers in general will be reevaluating their commitments to defined benefit plans in light of the multifaceted attack on underfunded plans evidenced in the 1987 Act. The current environment, if not outrightly hostile to defined benefit plans, has certainly reduced the attractiveness of this basic form of retirement income security vehicle.

As an additional matter, any successor or purchaser who will be assuming the qualified plans of the predecessor or seller should review those plans for any possible qualification deficiencies. If, for any reason, an acquired plan ceased to be qualified as a result of a failure of the successor or purchaser, not only would the tax consequences of operating the plans change adversely for the successor or purchaser, but also the successor or purchaser could subject itself to suit by employees whose tax consequences are also adversely affected by the disqualification of the plan.

REVERSION OF PLAN ASSETS

Over the past few years, the Internal Revenue Service (IRS) and the PBGC have been faced with a different type of problem concerning the termination of qualified defined benefit plans: What happens if the assets of the trust are more than sufficient to pay all of the vested benefit liabilities on the date of the termination of a plan? May the excess assets revert to the employer? Due to the strong performance of the stock market between 1982 and 1987 and the generally conservative actuarial assumptions employed by defined benefit plans in determining employer contributions, a significant number of plans have found themselves in this enviable position. Several issues have arisen in these cases.

A Review of Relevant Authority

Although defined benefits plans are frequently drafted to reserve the right in the employer to terminate the plan and to cease to fund the plan, the issue of whether excess plan assets could revert to the employer has been more complicated than this plan language would suggest.[77] Under Code section 401(a)(2), a qualified plan cannot permit any plan assets to be diverted to any purpose other than the exclusive benefit of employees until all of the liabilities of the plan with respect to those employees have been satisfied. The regulations under section 401(a)(2) have always permitted assets to be recovered by the employer after all liabilities have been satisfied if the surplus was due to ''erroneous actuarial computation''—defined to mean

> the surplus arising because actual requirements differ from the expected requirements even though the latter were based upon previous actuarial valuations of liabilities or determinations of costs of providing pension benefits under the plan and were made by a person competent to make such determinations in accordance with reasonable assumptions as to mortality, interest, etc., and correct procedures relating to the method of funding.[78]

The 1987 Act affirms the basic right of the employer to receive a reversion of excess plan assets, so long as the plan provisions authorizing such a reversion have been in the plan for a minimum statutory period of time.[79]

In 1983, the IRS clarified its asset reversion policy by issuing a ruling that updated the regulations for ERISA and took into account PBGC regulations as well. In particular, the IRS ruling stated that in determining whether the plan's assets were sufficient to cover the accrued liabilities of the plan, the PBGC's regulations regarding the valuation of benefits could be used.[80] This ruling revoked a prior IRS policy that required that the valuation rates used in valuing benefits be no less conservative than the interest assumptions used in determining costs under the plan during its existence.[81]

This new IRS position had a logical basis. If the PBGC is in the business of valuing benefits at termination of defined benefit plans, why should the IRS require the use of different assumptions for its termination and asset reversion policy? Thus, Revenue Ruling 83–52 brought IRS benefit valuation rules into line with those of the PBGC.

Upon further examination, however, there is less to be said for the ruling. Its effect is to allow plans to use interest rates in valuing accrued benefits at the termination of a plan that are a good deal higher than the interest rates that had been used to fund the plan over its existence. The higher the interest rate used for valuation of benefits, the lower the present value of those benefits. The lower the present value of the benefits, the greater the surplus of assets available to revert to the employer as a result of actuarial error. Hence, the new IRS position sanctioned a lower valuation of benefits and, thereby, also produced a greater amount of actuarial surplus in the plan to revert to the employer.

Although the strong performance of the stock market led a number of plans to consider termination to obtain a reversion of the actuarial surplus, the IRS position seemed to ''grease the skids'' for these terminations because it enhanced the potential actuarial surplus. Several highly publicized reversion transactions led to an overall review of the asset reversion policy at IRS, PBGC, and the Department of Labor (DOL) and to a congressional inquiry into what several members of Congress termed an alarming rate of terminations for defined benefit plans.

Types of Asset Reversion Transactions

Asset reversion transactions have taken several forms in the past. In each case, the employer starts out with a defined benefit plan that has a significant actuarial surplus. In some cases, the defined benefit plan is terminated and nothing is substituted in its place. Of course, before the reversion can take place, the benefit liabilities of all plan participants (including those benefits that must be vested because of the termination[82]) as of the date of termination must be funded. Usually, the plan will purchase commercial annuity contracts to discharge these liabilities of the plan. Once these annuity contracts have been purchased, the remaining assets (the actuarial surplus) will be available for return to the employer.

In other cases, the employer terminates the defined benefit plan, paying off the vested benefit liabilities with an annuity contract and then establishes a defined contribution plan, such as a money purchase plan, stock bonus plan, or employee stock ownership plan (ESOP). Again, the reversion is allowed to take place once the liabilities of the defined benefit plan have been satisfied.

In yet other cases, a spin-off takes place within the existing defined benefit plan. The plan is split into two parts. One part covers only those individuals in retired status. Assets sufficient to purchase commercial annuity contracts for the retired employee benefits are allocated to this portion of the plan. A second part of the plan covers existing employees. Again, assets sufficient to fund the existing accrued benefits of the current employees are allocated to this part of the plan. This usually leaves a surplus that will revert to the employer. Thus, the defined benefit plan is continued, but the excess assets are stripped out for the employer's use.

In this last type of transaction, two criticisms have been raised. First, by splitting off the retired employees and funding their benefits with annuities, the employer may have dramatically limited the assets available to fund cost-of-living increases for those employees. If the employer remains healthy, those increases could be funded in the future, but if the employer's fortunes turn sour, assets that were once in the plan and that could have been used for this purpose are no longer available. Second, with respect to the current employees' plan, a similar concern is raised. Although the employer's financial well-being and ability to fund the plan in the future may not be in doubt at present, if the employer's financial status deteriorates, assets that could have provided a funding cushion for the current employees' future accrued benefits have been stripped from the plan. From the policy perspective of ensuring that promised benefits are funded, this reversion transaction may raise serious problems.

Asset Reversions and Business Change Transactions

The pool of surplus assets in a pension plan is an attractive source of funds for any number of reasons. One negative aspect of the recent explosion in asset reversion cases is that the management of certain employers may have had motives for engaging in the plan termination and asset reversion transactions that were in conflict with the best interests of plan participants.

One obvious reason to recover an asset surplus is to improve the employer's overall financial position. The surplus could also be used to make needed capital improvements. One such case involved the Great Atlantic & Pacific Tea Company (A&P), which sought to terminate its defined benefit plan, replace it with a defined contribution plan, and recover approximately $250 million in surplus assets for use by the company. Individuals critical of the reversion charged that the plan was intended to "repair the sagging fortunes" of the company. Although litigation arose regarding the termination and reversion, A&P ultimately received approval of a settlement under which approximately $200 million would revert to the company; the remaining $50 million was to be used for the benefit of current and retired employees covered by the terminated plan.[83]

Another use of the surplus assets is to avoid potential or threatened takeovers. In one litigated case, Harper & Row decided to terminate its defined benefit plan and to replace it with an employee stock ownership plan. The surplus assets were used to purchase a large block of the company's stock that would otherwise have been sold on the open market. Moreover, the establishment of the employee stock ownership plan was criticized as a means by which the company could resist hostile takeover offers because of the large block of employer stock that the plan would hold (and presumably vote in favor of current management).

Another interesting facet of this case is that Harper & Row decided to use a 15-percent interest rate in valuing the benefits under the terminated defined benefit plan for the purposes of determining the actuarial surplus. The district court dismissed most of the claims against Harper & Row, including the alleged breach of fiduciary duty against the trustees, who also served as Harper & Row management, in using the defined benefit plan assets to purchase employer stock.[84] The court did not dismiss, however, the issue concerning the reasonableness of the 15-percent interest rate used in valuing plan assets at termination.[85] Both the Code and ERISA mandate that pension plans be operated for the "exclusive benefit" of covered employees and their beneficiaries.[86] Although critics of asset reversions charge that the exclusive benefit rule may be violated in such cases, the court in the *Harper & Row* case saw things differently. In general, the court found that the decision to terminate a defined benefit plan and to recover true actuarial surplus was not subject to the fiduciary responsibility rules under

ERISA.[87] Rather, since the right to terminate the plan and receive a reversion was specifically reserved under the plan, the company had the right to do so, so long as the rule regarding the funding of all plan liabilities was satisfied.[88] Of course, a significant issue was left to be decided in the Harper & Row litigation—whether the interest rate used to value the assets was reasonable.

The Current Regulatory Position

With all of the publicity attending certain asset reversion cases, Congress began to exert considerable pressure upon the IRS, the PBGC, and the DOL to review its asset reversion/plan termination policy. In late May 1984, the three agencies released a new set of guidelines that were intended to deal with the problem areas in these transactions.[89] Two aspects deserve mention here. First, the guidelines criticize the technique of using very high interest rates to value accrued benefits under the plan. Hence, although not backing away from Revenue Ruling 83–52 completely, the IRS seems to have recognized that the rates used by the PBGC to value benefits in terminated plan situations (when the plan assets are insufficient) can possibly be different from the rates used in adequately funded plans which are terminated in order to secure reversion of actuarial surplus.

Second, the spin-off termination transaction came under particular scrutiny. The release reminds employers that a major requirement of plan qualification under the Code is that the plan be permanent.[90] Hence, the guidelines warn against engaging in a series of these spin-off transactions with respect to the same plan. In general, the guidelines suggest that an employer should engage in such a transaction only once every fifteen years. Also, stricter funding requirements will be imposed upon a resulting plan in the portion of the spin-off transaction that covers current employees. The purpose of these rules is to ensure that the benefits of these employees will be funded on a sufficiently rapid basis so that their future accrued benefits will not be jeopardized.

The debates in Congress regarding the Tax Reform Act of 1986 and the 1987 Act continued to question the basic policy of allowing employers to obtain reversions of excess assets from overfunded, terminated plans. In particular, a number of proposals to alter the basic regulatory scheme were floated in the course of the 1987 Act debate. Once all of the dust had settled, however, only limited changes were made to the basic operational guidelines for plan terminations, although at the administrative level the requirements for successful plan terminations seem to be constantly under review.

Of substantial significance was the clarification of the level of benefits that had to be satisfied before a surplus of assets could be deemed to exist. By requiring plans to satisfy all benefit liabilities, Congress clearly reduced both the potential for reversion and the amount of reverting assets.[91]

In addition, in the Tax Reform Act of 1986, Congress sought to reduce the tax incentives toward the creation of reversion situations, by imposing a 10-percent excise tax on reversion distributions.[92] Beyond whatever income tax results to the employer upon the receipt of a reversion,[93] Code section 4980 imposes an additional 10-percent tax upon the amounts returned to the employer. The avowed purpose of this extra tax is to restore to the federal fisc the benefit of the use of the tax-exempt status of the qualified plan trust to the extent that the funds originally contributed for retirement income of employees are not so used. A reversion to the employer signals an inconsistency with the basic premise of the tax exemption for the trust, and, to the extent that funds return to the employer, they have been enjoying tax-exempt status inappropriately. The 10-percent extra tax attempts to recoup for the treasury the approximate value of the benefit of tax-exempt status over time.[94]

FIDUCIARY RESPONSIBILITY IN BUSINESS CHANGE TRANSACTIONS

One important achievement of ERISA was the enactment of fiduciary responsibility rules to establish a standard of conduct required of all fiduciaries of pension plans. "Fiduciary" is a broadly defined term under ERISA section 3(21) (A). Any person who exercises discretionary authority or control over the management of the plan or the plan's assets or any person with discretion in the administration of the plan is a fiduciary. Under part IV of title I of ERISA, these fiduciaries are required to carry out their fiduciary duties in accordance with statutory standards. Under part V of title I of ERISA, plan participants or beneficiaries, as well as the Secretary of Labor, may bring suit in federal court to remedy a breach of these fiduciary duties.

Section 404(a) (1) of ERISA contains the basic duties applicable to fiduciaries of pension plans. A fiduciary must discharge its duties under the plan solely in the interest of the participants and beneficiaries and for the exclusive purpose of providing benefits to participants and beneficiaries and defraying the reasonable expenses of the plan.[95] Fiduciaries must use the care, skill, prudence, and diligence that a prudent man in a like capacity, familiar with the conduct of a similar enterprise and with like aims, would use.[96] A fiduciary must also diversify the investments of the plan unless it is clearly prudent not to do so, and it must administer the plan according to its terms.[97]

It is easy to see that these rules may raise questions regarding the participation of a pension plan in business change transactions. For example, in a hostile takeover situation, would it violate the fiduciary duties of plan trustees to purchase sufficient employer stock with plan funds to prevent the takeover attempt? Would such action be for the exclusive benefit of participants and beneficiaries? It is important to understand that, in this situation, one or more plan trustees may also be members of the top management of the company whose position would be most jeopardized by the takeover. Would the answer to the above questions depend upon whether the purchase price for the employer's stock was a bargain price, the current market value, or a premium price?[98]

Is there a fiduciary violation if there is no actual takeover plan pending, but management desires to use a pension plan to make the chances of a takeover in the future less likely? In *Donovan v. Bierwirth*, the court pointed out that a benefit arising to the employer from a pension plan's action does not automatically signal a violation of the fiduciary responsibility rules.[99] Rather, there must be evidence that one or more fiduciaries did not carry out their statutory duties to participants and beneficiaries. The precise line between an incidental benefit to the employer and a violation of fiduciary duty remains to be fully drawn.

Thus, there is some degree of risk of fiduciary liability when a pension plan is an active participant in the business change transaction. The purchase of employer stock by a pension plan is particularly subject to that risk. Although section 407 of ERISA permits plans to hold employer stock to varying degrees, the issue in this purchase transaction is the fair market value of the stock purchased. Especially if the stock is purchased at a premium to ensure that the plan acquires a sufficient amount of the stock, a fiduciary responsibility violation may be found because plan assets are being used to fund the purchase price premium.[100] That premium may be for the benefit of current management, but it is not necessarily for the exclusive benefit of plan participants and beneficiaries.

NOTES

1. Employee Retirement Income Security Act of 1974, Pub. L. No. 93–406, 88 Stat. 829 (1974).

2. See 26 U.S.C. §§ 414(i), 414(j).

3. For employees, the primary benefit from qualified plans is the deferral of any income tax consequences arising from owning an interest in such a plan until the plan interest is distributed (frequently at retirement). See 26 U.S.C. § 402(a). Despite this deferral for employees, employers enjoy an immediate deduction (within statutory limits) for contributions to these plans. See id. § 404(a). Finally, the vehicle holding the funds of a qualified plan (usually a trust or trust-like entity) will generally be exempt from income taxation for transactions that arise in carrying out the exempt purpose of the trust, namely, the accumulation of retirement income for employees and their beneficiaries. See id. § 501(a).

4. See 26 U.S.C. § 411(d)(3). See also id. § 401(a)(2) and Income Tax Regs. § 1.401–2. The latter Code and regulation sections seem to focus upon both fixed and contingent liabilities of the employer under the plan, but neither imposes statutory liability or requires a plan to obligate an employer to pay those benefits. Rather, those sections merely prevent a reversion of plan assets to the employer until those liabilities are satisfied. Hence, an underfunded plan would remain qualified under these sections as long as no assets reverted to the employer on termination, even though the Code could not force the employer to remedy the underfunding upon termination.

5. Cf. Wilson v. Bluefield Supply Co., 819 F.2d 457 (4th Cir. 1987); Bryant v. International Fruit Products Co., 793 F.2d 118, 123 (6th Cir. 1986); 29 U.S.C. § 1344(d)(2), as amended by the Omnibus Budget Reconciliation Act of 1987.

6. A defined contribution plan is a pension plan that provides for an individual account for each participant and for benefits based solely upon the amount contributed to that account, plus any income, gain, expense, or loss allocated to the account under

the plan. See 26 U.S.C. § 414(j), 29 U.S.C. § 1002(34). A defined benefit plan is any pension plan other than a defined contribution plan. See 26 U.S.C. § 414(i), 29 U.S.C. § 1002(35).

7. See 29 U.S.C. § 1321(b)(1).

8. See id. § 1321.

9. See id. § 1002(37) (A).

10. See id. §§ 1321(a), 1321(b).

11. For plan years beginning after December 31, 1985, under 26 U.S.C. § 401(a)(27), a plan may qualify as a profit-sharing plan, even though employer contributions may be made in years in which the employer does not have profits. Hence, after that date, the primary distinguishing feature of a profit-sharing plan is that it will involve discretionary rather than fixed contributions. Under this scheme, which was put in place by the Tax Reform Act of 1986, defined contribution plans are truly of only two varieties—fixed and discretionary contribution plans.

12. See 26 U.S.C. § 414(i), 29 U.S.C. § 1002(34).

13. See 26 U.S.C. § 414(i).

14. For a discussion of the different statutory treatment of defined contribution and defined benefit plans, see Hickerson v. Velsicol Chemical Corp., 778 F.2d 365 (7th Cir. 1985).

15. See Income Tax Regs. § 1.401–1(b) (1) (i).

16. Although 29 U.S.C. § 1102(b) requires every pension plan to establish and maintain a funding policy, the exact nature of that policy need not be spelled out in the plan.

17. See 26 U.S.C. § 412, 29 U.S.C. §§ 1081–1085, regarding actuarial methods and minimum funding standards for defined benefit plans.

18. For example, when using a normal cost/past service liability actuarial method, the past service liability must be amortized over no more than thirty years to satisfy the minimum funding standards, but it may be amortized over as little as ten years for tax deduction purposes. Employers are afforded a good deal of discretion within these minimum and maximum levels to make annual contributions.

19. See, e.g., 26 U.S.C. § 412, 29 U.S.C. §§ 1081–1085.

20. Id.

21. See, e.g., Connolly v. Pension Benefit Guaranty Corp., 419 F. Supp. 737 (C.D. Cal. 1976), rev'd, 581 F.2d 729 (9th Cir. 1978), cert. denied, 440 U.S. 935 (1979).

22. The primary exception is a withdrawal of a substantial employer from a plan that has more than one substantial employer but that is not a multiemployer plan under ERISA. Under 29 U.S.C. § 1363(b), the general measure of liability for such a withdrawal is the substantial employer's pro rata share of the statutory termination liability that would arise if the plan were terminated on the date of withdrawal. In addition, id. § 1368(f) provides that the cessation of operations at a facility resulting in a more than 20-percent reduction in the employees who participate in a single-employer plan (due to termination of employment) shall be treated as a withdrawal of a substantial employer under id. § 1363(b).

23. See id. § 1002(37) (A).

24. See id. § 1362(a).

25. See id. § 1369(b). Even though the sponsoring employer ceases to exist in many of the transactions covered by id. § 1369(b), a successor employer always steps into the shoes of the sponsoring employer. Unless the successor actually terminates the plan, the provisions of title IV do not produce liability as a result of the business change.

26. Single Employer Pension Plan Amendments Act of 1986, Pub. L. No. 99–272, §§ 11001–11019, 100 Stat. 82, 237 (1986).

27. Omnibus Budget Reconciliation Act of 1987, Pub. L. No. 100–203 101 Stat. 1330–374 (1987).

28. See 29 U.S.C. § 1322(b)(3).

29. See 29 C.F.R. § 2621.3 (1986).

30. The PBGC is established under 29 U.S.C. § 1302. It is an independent government corporation whose purposes are to encourage and maintain the voluntary private pension plan system and to provide timely and uninterrupted payment of benefits to plan participants. See id. § 1302(a).

31. See id. § 1362(b) prior to its amendment by SEPPAA and the 1987 Act.

32. See id. §§ 1306, 1307, establishing the basic obligation of each defined benefit plan to pay a premium to the PBGC.

33. See, e.g., H.R. Rep. No. 99–300, 99th Cong., 1st Sess. 282 (1985).

34. Id.

35. This occurred because, as noted above, the plan would reserve in the employer the right to terminate the plan and to pay only the benefits accured *to the extent then funded*. The statute modified this employer obligation only to the extent of the guaranteed benefit. Benefit accruals in excess of the statutory guarantee that were not funded at the time of termination were lost.

36. See H.R. Rep. No. 99–300, 99th Cong., 1st Sess. 282 (1985).

37. 29 U.S.C. § 1341(b)(1)(D).

38. See id. § 1301(a)(16).

39. See Income Tax Regs. § 1.401–2(b)(2).

40. See 29 U.S.C. §§ 1341(b)(2), 1341(b)(3).

41. Under id. § 1342, the PBGC on its own motion may also terminate a plan. The discussion in the text focuses upon cases in which the employer seeks the termination.

42. See id. § 1341(c)(2)(B).

43. There are two possible levels of underfunding in a distress termination: (1) assets are not sufficient to satisfy even guaranteed benefits or (2) assets are sufficient to satisfy guaranteed benefits but not benefit liabilities.

44. 29 U.S.C. § 1362(b)(1)(A).

45. Id. § 1368(a).

46. A controlled group is all persons under common control, with common control being defined in a consistent manner with the entity aggregation rules under 26 U.S.C. §§ 414(b) and 414(c). See 29 U.S.C. § 1301(a)(14).

47. The PBGC remains obligated to pay the guaranteed benefits under 29 U.S.C. § 1322(a). If plan assets are sufficient to satisfy guaranteed benefits, but do not meet benefit liabilities, the PBGC is not obligated to pay the unfunded benefit liabilities. The PBGC will, however, take over the administration of benefit payments under the terminated plan and will use available employer assets to pay benefit liabilities above guaranteed benefits. See 29 U.S.C. § 1322(c), as amended by the 1987 Act.

48. Multiemployer Pension Plan Amendments Act of 1980, Pub. L. No. 96-364, 94 Stat. 1208 (1980).

49. See 29 U.S.C. §§ 1301(a)(2), 1301(b)(1).

50. See id. § 1381(a).

51. See id. § 1381(a).

52. See id. § 1385(a).

53. See id. § 1383(a).
54. See id. § 1385(a).
55. See id. § 1385(b)(1).
56. See id. § 1385(b)(2)(A).
57. See id. § 1384(a)(1)(A).
58. See id. § 1384(a)(1)(B).
59. See id. § 1384(a)(1)(C).
60. See id. § 1384(a)(4).
61. See id. § 1384(c).
62. See 29 C.F.R. §§ 2643.10–2643.15.
63. See id. § 2643.11(a).
64. See id. § 2643.13.
65. See id. § 2643.14(a)(1).
66. See id. § 2643.14(d).
67. See id. § 2643.14 (a)(2).
68. See 29 U.S.C. § 1369(b).
69. The cross-reference in 29 U.S.C. § 1398(a)(1)(A) should probably be to "a change in corporate structure described in section" 1369(b), reflecting a rearrangement of sections under SEPPAA.
70. A nonqualified pension plan is generally subject to similar funding requirements under 29 U.S.C. §§ 1081–1085, unless a statutory exemption is available.
71. See 29 U.S.C. § 1306.
72. See 26 U.S.C. § 412(l), as added by the 1987 Act.
73. See id. § 412(m), as added by the 1987 Act.
74. See id. § 412(c) (11), as added by the 1987 Act.
75. See 29 U.S.C. § 1306(a)(3)(A), as amended by the 1987 Act.
76. See id. § 1306(3)(E), as amended by the 1987 Act.
77. Several cases have considered whether a defined benefit plan that did not provide for return of excess assets to the employer could be amended to so provide. See, e.g., Wilson v. Bluefield Supply Co., 819 F.2d 457 (4th Cir. 1987); Bryant v. International Fruit Products Co., 793 F. 2d 118, 123 (6th Cir. 1986). 29 U.S.C. § 1344(d)(2), as amended by the Omnibus Budget Reconciliation Act of 1987, specifically regulates the ability to add such a provision to a plan.
78. See Income Tax Regs. § 1.401–2(b)(1).
79. See 29 U.S.C. § 1344(d)(2), as amended by the 1987 Act.
80. See generally 29 C.F.R. pt. 2619.
81. Compare Rev. Rul. 83–52, 1983–1 C.B. 87, with Rev. Rul. 71–152, 1971–1 C.B. 126.
82. See 26 U.S.C. § 411(d)(3).
83. See Walsh v. Great Atlantic and Pacific Tea Co., 96 F.R.D. 632, 635 (D.N.J.), aff'd, 726 F. 2d 956 (3d Cir. 1983).
84. See District 65, UAW v. Harper & Row, Publishers, 576 F. Supp. 1468 (S.D.N.Y. 1983).
85. Id. at 1480.
86. See 26 U.S.C. § 401(a)(2); 29 U.S.C. § 1104(a)(1).
87. 576 F. Supp. at 1477–78.
88. Id. at 1478.
89. PBGC News Release No. 84–23 (May 23, 1984).

90. See Income Tax Regs. § 1.401–1(b)(2).

91. See 29 U.S.C. §§ 1362(b), 1344, as amended by the 1987 Act.

92. 26 U.S.C. § 4980.

93. Under the nonstatutory tax benefit rule, since all monies contributed by the employer to the plan gave rise to deductions when contributed under 26 U.S.C. § 404(a), a return of those funds will be a ''recovery'' of previously deducted items and will be gross income to the employer.

94. See Joint Committee on Taxation, ''General Explanation of the Tax Reform Act of 1986,'' 99th Cong. 2d Sess. 751 (1987).

95. 29 U.S.C. § 404(a)(1)(A).

96. Id. § 404(a)(1)(B).

97. Id. § 404(a)(1)(C)-(D).

98. See, e.g., Donovan v. Bierwirth, 680 F.2d 263 (2d Cir. 1982), cert. denied, 459 U.S. 1069 (1983) (breach of fiduciary duty found in an action brought by the Secretary of Labor against trustees arising from purchase of shares of Grumman Corporation common stock by a pension plan in a successful attempt to thwart a tender offer by LTV Corporation). On remand, the district court found that no loss had been sustained by the pension plan as a result of the breach of fiduciary duty as the stock investment performed better than other investments of the pension plan and trust over the period. 636 F. Supp. 540, 542 (E.D.N.Y. 1986).

99. 680 F.2d 263, 271 (2d Cir. 1982), cert. denied, 459 U.S. 1069 (1983).

100. See DOL Opinion No. 76–52 (May 19, 1976) (employee stock ownership plan is prohibited from purchasing employer stock at a premium above market value).

7

UNION DIRECTORS AND FIDUCIARY DUTIES UNDER STATE CORPORATE LAW

Helen S. Scott

Editors' Note. Recent heightened takeover activity has brought into sharp focus, for courts and corporations, the question of what fiduciary obligations are owed by corporate directors. At the same time unions, for a variety of reasons, have become involved with placing representatives on corporate boards. Professor Scott observes that the judicial decisions tend to emphasize the duty of the directors to the shareholders, and that this view poses substantial conflict-of-interest problems for directors who appear to be serving "other" interests, such as those of labor. The very fact of union representation on a board may trigger a special duty of care on the part of the other directors. The author concludes that, on a case-by-case basis, pitfalls can probably be minimized, if not avoided entirely, by precautions such as disclosure and abstention, but she is less certain that legal risks can be completely eliminated without legislative change.

The author wishes to thank Richard Revesz for his helpful comments and Cindy Goldberg and Jeffrey Resler for their assistance and to acknowledge the generous support of the Filomen D'Agostino and Max E. Greenberg Research Fund of New York University School of Law.

Placing a representative of labor on the board of a public corporation is not a new idea, but it nonetheless is an idea that continues to raise difficult legal questions concerning the potential for conflicts of interest.[1] At first glance, the phenomenon may seem to be no more than an appropriate advance in the trend toward increased employee participation in the corporation through the formation of labor-management committees and the creation of employee stock ownership plans.[2] As the legal obligations of corporate directors are spelled out, however, the concept of direct labor representation on the board of a public corporation presents deeper and more troublesome problems, for the shareholder directors as well as the union directors.[3] For the union director, the conflict arises because in pursuing the union's objectives, he is representing a constituency that may be seeking something other than the maximization of the value of the firm's shares. Even where stock is owned by employees, directly or indirectly, the same potential conflict of interest exists.[4] The fact that the employees are also shareholders does not alter the labor director's dilemma, for his behavior will still be measured against the traditional corporate law standard of the welfare of the shareholders as a whole.

Recent developments are bringing these issues into sharper focus. First, we now have experience, albeit limited, with union directors in major public corporations. The most celebrated example in this country[5] came about in 1980 with the election of then United Auto Workers President Douglas Fraser to the board of directors of Chrysler Corporation. More recently, several labor representatives were elected to the board of directors of Eastern Air Lines.[6] Second, over the last year or two, influential courts have made major statements on the content of the fiduciary duties of directors under state corporate law. Much of the action in corporate law over the last few years has been the result of increased takeover activity. Takeovers provide dramatic factual settings in which to assess the performance of directors. The prevalence and sophistication of the defensive tactics used by corporations that are targets of takeover attempts have forced courts to face, head on, questions about the scope of fiduciary duties. In the process, the courts have developed new or refined tests for the duty of loyalty, and they have invoked the duty of care to closely scrutinize the actions of corporate management.

As a result, even when viewed solely from the perspective of corporate fiduciary analysis, the role of the union director presents a dilemma. Under corporate law, a director owes a duty of loyalty to the corporation, which may make it necessary for him to abstain from certain decisions, to absent himself from certain meetings, or to refrain from receiving certain information in order to avoid tainting a board decision with a disabling conflict of interest.[7] On the other hand, he cannot constantly decline to perform his directorial duties by reason of conflicting interests because he is also under a duty of care which requires him to keep informed, to participate in board deliberations, and to engage in active decision making on behalf of the corporation.[8]

DIRECTORS AS FIDUCIARIES

To whom the corporate director's duty as a fiduciary flows is both an old and a new question. The 1919 decision in *Dodge v. Ford Motor Co.*,[9] involving a challenge brought by two Ford stockholders to the decisions of Ford's board to cut automobile prices and use earnings for expansion rather than dividends, articulated what has become the classic formulation of a director's obligation:

A business corporation is organized and carried on primarily for the profit of the stockholders. The powers of the directors are to be employed for that end. The discretion of directors is to be exercised in the choice of means to attain that end, and does not extend to a change in the end itself, to the reduction of profits, or to the nondistribution of profits among stockholders in order to devote them to other purposes.[10]

The court agreed with the shareholders that the board's action exceeded its authority and ordered the payment of a special dividend, but it did not restrict the company's expansion plans, because of yet another general principle of corporate law—the business judgment rule.[11] Under that principle of deference to board decision making, the court declined to substitute its judgment for that of the board in making business decisions that accommodate the myriad influences operating upon the corporation.[12]

These two principles—primary responsibility to the shareholders and broad discretion in the directors to make business decisions—have won wide acceptance. Yet, at least since 1932, the tension between the two principles has also generated debate[13] over the extent to which the concept of reasonable business discretion may act to temper the primacy of the board's obligation to shareholders by allowing it to consider and act upon a broader range of factors than the criterion of maximizing shareholder wealth.[14] The debate has been couched in terms of corporate governance and corporate social responsibility. The high water mark of the corporate social responsibility movement occurred in the late 1970s with the proliferation of proposals for federal corporate chartering and the creation of directorships to represent special constituencies or the general interest of the public.[15]

Recent cases addressing the fiduciary responsibility of boards of directors when defending against a takeover attempt have shed light on the limits of board discretion to consider factors other than shareholder wealth. During the last year, both the Supreme Court of the State of Delaware, and the federal Court of Appeals for the Second Circuit have injected new life into the notion that directors are to serve the shareholders first, foremost, and, whenever their interests conflict with any others', exclusively.[16] In order to understand the fiduciary problems confronting union directors, it is first necessary to understand why the courts deem shareholder welfare to be central to the director's fiduciary duties.

WHY DO FIDUCIARY DUTIES RUN TO THE SHAREHOLDERS?

Shareholders are not the only persons associated with the modern public corporation whose capital is at risk. Among others contributing capital to the corporation, labor ranks high: "Labor capital" is necessary to the operation of the business, and, in many cases, is far less fungible than investment capital.[17] To the extent that worker "investments" in training and other skill acquisition have value only to the corporation, labor becomes captive to the corporation;

workers cannot by securing employment elsewhere receive a comparable return for their human capital investments. Where this holds true, labor is vulnerable to abusive behavior on the part of management because the cost of tolerating some abuse is lower than the cost of moving elsewhere. A shareholder of a large public corporation, by contrast, can always sell its shares and cash out its investment. Why, then, if labor's contribution to the value of the firm is often more at risk than the shareholders' equity stake, is the traditional legal construct of the corporation aimed solely at the protection of shareholders, and why do the courts adhere to that construct so vigorously?

The usual response is that the shareholders are the "owners" of the corporation.[18] Viewing the large public corporation as an entity, which evolved organically from the sole proprietorship, management is seen as a surrogate for the shareholders. The board of directors stands in for the shareholder, exercising powers which belong to the shareholders at large but which can no longer be conveniently exercised by them, due to the wide dispersion of equity holdings.[19] The board can exercise only such powers as are delegated to it (directly by the shareholders or by statute) and only in a way that benefits the delegator shareholders.[20]

Due to the complexity of operations in the modern corporation and the difficulty of convening a meeting of the shareholders, the board must be given broad discretion to meet situations as they arise. Although this broad delegation of power is necessary to run the corporation effectively, it creates the possibility that, though nominally the agent, the board may exercise its powers to advantage itself, or some other group, and not the principal shareholders. As a result, the law enters to ensure the fidelity of the agent to its principal by labelling the relationship as "fiduciary," subjecting directors' actions to a high level of judicial scrutiny.[21] This model of the modern public corporation as just a larger version of a sole proprietorship is the one reflected in most corporate statutes.

There are also functional reasons for designating the shareholders as the "owners" of the corporation because they serve as the ultimate monitors of managerial performance. In any enterprise, when gains can be generated through the coordination of activities (teamwork), the problem of slacking off by some of the parties may arise.[22] That is, the parties to a transaction may be inclined toward some level of nonperformance, as long as their gains from teamwork still exceed their losses from nonperformance. If A and B can each separately produce 10x, and A and B working together can produce 25x, then B may be tempted not to perform to his capacity, as long as A and B together still produce more than 20x. Since losses (or lower production rates) are shared, as gains are shared, the nonperformer does not have to bear the full cost of his nonperformance. As a result, a principal role of managers is to supervise, or monitor, the performance of their subordinates. Of course, managers are subject to the same disincentives to perform, and shareholders may then be viewed as the ultimate supervisors, or monitors, of corporate performance through their ability to replace the managers.[23]

In other settings, the negotiation of detailed contract terms might provide a means of policing managers' discretion. But, in the context of the modern public corporation, there are serious impediments to shareholder contract negotiation. It would be difficult and costly for shareholders to identify and communicate with each other for the purpose of coordinating their activities.[24] Contract negotiation is further complicated by the fact that shareholders' investments are not associated with particular assets, that is, shareholders have invested in the corporation generally—unlike a creditor, for example, which can protect itself by securing its debt by a claim against specific assets of an ascertainable market value.[25] As long as there are public securities markets and as long as private investment is encouraged, it will remain infeasible and costly in the extreme for shareholders to negotiate the terms of their "contracts" for each investment.[26]

Thus the law's enforcement of fiduciary duties running from the directors to the shareholders may be viewed as lowering the transaction costs that would obtain were shareholders compelled to protect their interests through contract. The legal rules creating fiduciary duties lower the cost to shareholders of investing in corporations and thereby encourage such investments.[27]

From a somewhat different vantage point, shareholders may be seen as simply more successful at claiming fiduciary duties than workers precisely because they have a choice that workers do not. Before commencing employment with a firm, labor's range of possible employers is less than shareholders' range of possible investments. After employment, as labor becomes specific to the enterprise, its mobility is further decreased. By contrast, investment capital remains mobile, and therefore managers must induce continued investment. However, once money is conveyed by the shareholder to the corporation, the monitoring problems addressed above arise: the enormous costs to shareholders of coordinating their activities, their relative lack of expertise in recognizing and evaluating management inefficiency, and the disincentive to any shareholder of engaging in such costly activity relative to the expected return.

If investors can be assured that the likelihood of managers acting on the basis of their own self-interest is low, investments are more likely to be forthcoming. Because investors' money can move easily, it is in the self-interest of managers to convince shareholders to trust them. One way to do this is to promote the requirement that managers act as fiduciaries for the shareholders. This fiduciary relationship, which may at some point subject managers to personal liability if they engage in behavior to the disadvantage of the shareholders, is a price paid to secure investment capital. By contrast, managers do not have the same incentive with respect to workers, whose mobility and, thus, negotiating leverage is less in this respect than that of shareholders. Again, the law imposing fiduciary obligations encourages private investment in public corporations by providing rules that facilitate the formation of the investment relationship in a context where other mechanisms would prove to be so costly as to deter investment.

Thus, from both an economic and a functional perspective, shareholders are well-suited to enforce the goal of productive behavior within the corporation.

And the imposition of a fiduciary duty running from the board to the shareholders is an efficient mechanism for the protection of the shareholders' interests. But stating that the existence of such a fiduciary duty is logical is not enough to determine its effect on the union director. The content of the duty must be explored as well.

THE CONTENT OF THE FIDUCIARY DUTY TO SHAREHOLDERS

General Principles

The relationship between shareholders and directors, although characterized as fiduciary, involves neither absolute dependence on the part of shareholders, nor absolute selflessness on the part of directors.[28] Directors have obligations to shareholders, but they are not required to act toward them as trustees would act toward beneficiaries. For example, most modern corporate statutes contain provisions regulating but not prohibiting contracts between the corporation and one of its directors despite a possible conflict of interest.[29] Compliance with the statutes will not avoid judicial review of the transaction, but it may work to shift the burden of the challenge back to the plaintiff laboring under deferential business judgment standards.[30] If directors were trustees of the shareholders, such transactions would always have to meet a far higher standard of complete fairness, or they would be prohibited.[31]

Therefore, the courts seek to accommodate the legitimate range of discretion that accompanies corporate management[32] with the obligations that management owes shareholders. The principles used by the courts in this task are the business judgment rule, protecting management discretion, and the duties of care and loyalty, protecting the interests of the shareholders.

When a board decision is challenged, ordinarily application of the business judgment rule will insulate the directors from liability for the decision or its consequences, even if the decision caused a loss to the corporation. Procedurally, the business judgement rule acts as "a presumption that in making a business decision, the directors of a corporation acted on an informed basis, in good faith and in the honest belief that the action taken was in the best interests of the company."[33] Thus, directors must satisfy both the duty of care—that they acted on an informed basis—and the duty of loyalty—that they acted in good faith and in the honest belief that the action was in the best interests of the company. If the board fails to fulfill either duty, it loses business judgement rule protection and must shoulder the burden of proving that the transaction was inherently fair to the corporation. This shifting of the burden of proof onto the board generally signals that there will be more intense judicial scrutiny of the transaction. If the board does not prevail, the transactions can be undone,[34] and the directors can be held personally liable for any damages suffered by the shareholders.[35]

To fulfill his duty of care, a director must inform himself "prior to making a business decision, of all material information reasonably available" to him.[36] The duty of care is a negligence-based concept,[37] and, like other negligence principles, it creates varying obligations depending upon the circumstances in which a decision is being made. It has long been recognized that possession of facts which should put a director "on notice" that there might be a problem is sufficient to raise the level of diligence required to meet the duty of care.[38]

An increased level of diligence will be triggered by the existence of a conflict of interest, either in the person supplying information to the board, or in the board itself. Such a conflict frequently arises in the takeover context. Where the corporation is a target, a takeover threat immediately raises the possibility of real divergence of interest between the directors, particularly the manager-directors (who, presumably, seek to avoid the takeover in order to retain their positions) and the shareholders (who, presumably, are interested in at least ascertaining, if not obtaining, the highest price their shares will command). Courts are extremely sensitive to this inherent danger of conflict of interest "when a threat to control is involved."[39]

In *Smith v. Van Gorkom*, the board of directors approved the sale of the Trans Union Corporation, based on a brief oral presentation by Van Gorkom, the chairman and chief executive officer.[40] Although the sale price was at a premium over the market price at which the company's stock had been trading, the Delaware Supreme Court found a breach of the duty of care on the part of the board, based principally on the directors' failure to "adequately inform themselves as to Van Gorkom's role in forcing the 'sale' of the Company and in establishing the price . . . [and] . . . as to the intrinsic value of the Company."[41]Relying on those findings, despite the board's vast knowledge of and experience in managing the company, the court found the directors to have been "grossly negligent" in approving the sale.[42]

Just a few months later, the Second Circuit in *Hanson Trust v. ML SCM Acquisition, Inc.*[43] found that the directors of SCM Corporation had violated their duties of care by agreeing to grant options on two major assets of the corporation to a group, including certain members of management, proposing a leveraged buy-out. A competing independent offer to purchase the company was pending at the same time. The board had received advice from outside counsel and an outside financial advisor on the option prices. Nevertheless, the court found the directors to have "failed to take many of the affirmative directorial steps" that would have been necessary to satisfy their duty of care.[44]

Implications for Union Directors

Of particular relevance to the issue of union directors on a corporate board is the insistence of both courts that the presence of a conflict of interest in some members of the board triggered a heightened duty of care in the remaining directors. In *Van Gorkom*, the board did not even discover the conflict of interest, which was readily discernible had they simply questioned the chief executive officer; after such discovery, the reliability of Van Gorkom's report would have been called into question, and the directors "could not reasonably have relied thereupon in good faith."[45] Similarly, *Hanson Trust* emphasizes the expanded obligations of disinterested directors in the face of a conflict of interest on the part of other directors:

> And this duty of care is, if anything, heightened—it certainly is not weakened—when the favored buyer obtaining the lock-up [option] is a consortium including within it the management/non-independent directors who will have a substantial participation in the future equity of the potential buyer. . . . This directorial duty of care is heightened because management interests are then in direct conflict with those of the shareholders of the target corporation to obtain the highest price either for their shares or for the company's assets.[46]

Thus, in light of these recent rulings, to the extent shareholder interests in any particular decision conflict with interests represented by a union director, the burden on the rest of the board will be heightened, and the diligence with which the conflict is explored and information relevant to the decision is sought will be subject to intensified judicial scrutiny. This would be true even where the tainted director recuses himself, as the interested directors did in *Hanson Trust*.[47]

The duty of care has another aspect with implications for the union director. The vision of the board of directors reflected in the corporate statutes is that of a deliberative body.[48] Directors must act; they cannot simply refuse to learn the necessary facts or refuse to participate in board deliberations. While they need not have any expertise whatsoever in business affairs, what they must do is "faithfully give such ability as they have to their charge."[49]

This requirement of active participation by board members is important to consider in connection with the other major fiduciary obligation imposed on corporate directors—the duty of loyalty.[50] As discussed below, one mechanism developed to cure a duty of loyalty problem is the abstention from decision making of a director with a conflict of interest. If the conflict pervades a broad range of decisions, however, the abstaining director risks a duty of care problem for nonparticipation in corporate decision making.

The traditional context in which duty of loyalty questions arise occurs when a corporation enters into a transaction with one of its directors. If, for example, a director owned a piece of property that the corporation wanted to buy, the transaction could take place, even though the director's interest in a high price and the corporation's interest in a low price would obviously be in opposition. As one would expect, the relevant corporate rules preclude the seller director, who is "interested" in the transaction, from making the decision or conducting the negotiations on behalf of the corporation.[51] In addition, the interested director is required to disclose his interest in the transaction and all material information he possesses about the property to the other "disinterested" directors who can then evaluate the transaction and vote on it.[52] If the directors are all interested, or if they so choose, the appropriate disclosures may be made to the shareholders, who can then sanitize the transaction by a vote. Even in the absence of board or shareholder ratification, the transaction will nonetheless be upheld if it is "fair."[53]

This combination of disclosure and abstention by the director with a conflict, coupled with active investigation by the other directors, has been applied to other conflict situations not covered by statute.[54] As devices to remove the bias from a judgment, they are most effective in case-by-case applications. Indeed, the "interested director" provisions in the corporate statutes are addressed to discrete transactional circumstances.

In the takeover context, where the duty of loyalty of the entire board is frequently called into question (a circumstance unlikely to be created solely by the presence of a union director), the Delaware Supreme Court has evolved a two-part test[55] to determine whether a board of directors was acting primarily to perpetuate its employment, in which case the decisions it made to ward off an acquirer would be tainted, or was acting in the best interests of the corporation, in which case the business judgment principle would attach to those decisions. First, the directors must show that they had "reasonable grounds for believing that a danger" to the corporation existed by virtue of the takeover threat. This burden is met by showing "good faith and reasonable investigation" by the board.[56] Second, the board must show that the action taken was "reasonable in relation to the threat posed."[57]

Again, the courts turn, when faced with conflict problems that may be embedded in the transaction or in the composition of the board of directors, to the decision-making record: Did the board use all the time it had available? Did it omit to ask any of the right questions? Did it consult outside advisors? For how long? Did it acquire all possible relevant information? Imposing these requirements on fluid situations where complex decisions must be made at best greatly slows the decision-making process and, at worst, could paralyze a board or force its members to take the course most likely to minimize their own risk of personal liability.

In the continuing conflict situation, abstention is of little use. The abstaining director would violate either his duty of loyalty by his inability to act with unbiased judgment on behalf of the corporation or his duty of care by his inability to engage in active decision making for the corporation; the remaining directors would have to be constantly on their guard against making decisions based on investigations which could later be deemed insufficient when measured against a heightened standard. A board of directors, and its individual members, face potential liability whenever they make decisions in a context where a conflict of interest is present. Bringing union directors into the boardroom raises precisely this problem of continuing conflict and exposure to potential liability.

CONFLICTING INTERESTS OF SHAREHOLDERS AND EMPLOYEES: MAY A DIRECTOR ACT IN THE INTERESTS OF A NONSHAREHOLDER CONSTITUENCY?

The shareholder and the employee have interests in common,[58] but there are many circumstances in which their interests tend to diverge. As a supplier of investment capital, the shareholder is most concerned about his investment in a particular corporation as compared with other investments he could make. The shareholder is much less concerned with the day-to-day operational setting and working conditions in the corporation in which he has invested than the employee, whose quality of life is directly affected by these factors. The employee is concerned about maintaining his job, which may require preserving both the existing nature of the corporate operations and its location. The economic stability of his community is more likely to be tied to that of his employer than the shareholder's fate is linked to the stability of any single company in which he has invested. Similarly, few stockholders commit as large a percentage of their capital to a single company as do employees.

In addition, the employee's financial interest lies in maximizing his compensation package; the shareholder's in maximizing the return on his investment. Both are seeking to draw from the same fund. Consequently, while both are interested in the current financial health and in the increasing future prosperity of the corporation, they are financially in competition with each other.

Recent developments in takeovers underscore this divergence of interests. Use of employee stock ownership has increased dramatically, and it is uniformly perceived as a repellent to a takeover attempt.[59] Employees, it is felt, will be less quick to tender their shares to a hostile acquirer than will other shareholders, due to their special concerns about maintaining the status quo and their jobs.[60]

While there has been no litigation alleging a breach of directors' fiduciary duty to shareholders by reason of actions taken on behalf of employees, conflicts between shareholders and other constituencies have been considered in the courts. In *Revlon, Inc. v. MacAndrews & Forbes Holding, Inc.*,[61] the Supreme Court of Delaware was called to rule upon the hostile attempt by Pantry Pride, Inc. to gain control of Revlon. As one of a set of defensive maneuvers, the Revlon board had issued $10 million of notes in exchange for Revlon shares. The notes contained covenants dramatically limiting the company's ability to incur additional debt, sell assets, or pay dividends unless otherwise approved by the non-management members of the board. When it later appeared that the board would waive these covenants to enable a friendly bidder to finance its acquisition of the company, the market value of the notes dropped precipitously, and the noteholders became irate. It was in this context that the Revlon board granted an option to purchase certain key assets to the friendly bidder, who was willing to support the par value of the notes.

The court found the granting of the option to be a breach of the directors' fiduciary duty because the board had acted to favor the noteholders at the expense of the shareholders, depriving the shareholders of the opportunity for a higher price for their shares by effectively halting the bidding for the company. Recognizing that a board may properly consider the interests of corporate constituencies other than shareholders, the court declared that: "Although such considerations may be permissible, there are fundamental limitations upon that prerogative. A board may have regard for various constituencies in discharging its responsibilities, provided there are rationally related benefits accruing to the stockholders."[62]

The *Revlon* court found the board's preference for the noteholders over the stockholders particularly inappropriate because the noteholders' "rights . . . already were fixed by contract" and therefore they "required no further protection."[63] Thus, not only are directors precluded from favoring the interests of nonshareholder groups when those interests conflict with the interests of the shareholders, but their discretion with respect to nonshareholder groups is even more circumscribed when the rights of such groups are "fixed by contract."[64] Aside from creditors, the major ongoing constituency of the corporation whose rights are generally "fixed by contract" is, of course, the unionized employees. The presence of a union director on a board of directors, then, may open up the board's actions to challenge whenever the interests of shareholders and employees do not completely coincide.

MODELS FOR LABOR PARTICIPATION ON THE BOARD UNDER EXISTING CORPORATE LAW

While the recent developments in director liability under state corporate law may appear to bode ill for labor representation on boards of directors, there are several models to examine that can both satisfy the goals of labor representation and minimize the liability exposure of all the directors.

The Fraser Model

When Douglas Fraser joined the board of Chrysler, questions of conflicts of interest were, of course, considered by both the corporation and the union. Two key operating principles were adopted by the parties. First, where shareholder and employee interests diverged, it was assumed that any threat of liability to the board would be removed by virtue of the fact that Fraser would be outvoted by the other directors.[65] This assumption seems to have little support. Shareholder directors might disagree over where the best interests of shareholders lie. If they are closely divided, the union director could tip the balance, by argument if not by vote. Second, where there was a conflict, Fraser would simply act as though he were an "interested director" and decline to participate, abstain from the vote, or both.[66] The problem with this second safeguard is that it requires that very difficult judgments be made at virtually every board meeting. For example, Mr. Fraser observed: "I do, however, intend to participate fully in deliberations on all other matters, and vote on them, including but not limited to collective bargaining policies and other worker concerns such as health and safety, plant closing and transfers, new technology, product planning, major investments, and equal employment opportunity policies and practices.''[67] Whether, in a retrospective judicial review, Fraser's determination of those particular issues as to which he had (or did not have) a disabling conflict of interest would be upheld is questionable.

Furthermore, if a broad view is taken of the number of occasions on which shareholder and employee interests diverge, then the interested director mechanism would effectively nullify the union director's voting power. That is, employee representation on the board would be permissible, but only as long as the union director's vote is rarely counted.[68]

Finally, it is interesting to note that, during the entire period of his directorship, Fraser was never able to agree with Chrysler management about the nature of his role.[69] While Chrysler management insisted that Fraser was nominated to the board because of his outstanding abilities as an individual and not as a representative of labor, Fraser believed he represented the workers and was reported to have said that he had ``no intention of representing Chrysler's shareholders.''[70] However, in spite of the publicity attending his remarks, Fraser's statement of his role in Chrysler's proxy materials to the shareholders, sent after UAW lawyers had analyzed court decisions on fiduciary responsibility,[71] was quite conciliatory, and expressed the hope that his directorship would advance the interests of the ``broad Chrysler community—shareholders, workers, suppliers, dealers, consumers and the public.''[72]

Changing the Nature of Employee Representation

Part of the confusion surrounding Fraser's role on the Chrysler board can be attributed to differences between what he hoped to accomplish on the board and what directors of corporations are supposed to do in general. In light of Fraser's public statements, the voting function of his directorship may have, in fact, been less important than his mere presence in the boardroom.[73]

Commentators have identified various goals to be attained through union directorships, none of which appear to require that the union representative actually be a voting director of the corporation. The common thread in the discussions is the ``window'' or information exchange function:[74] The union directorship provides both a window for the union on board deliberations and financial information about the company,[75] and a window for the board on employee concerns and views on the management of the business.[76]

This cross-informational function[77] could be fulfilled by some position other than director, which carried with it the right to attend board meetings.[78] Indeed, freed of the conflicting fiduciary duties of a director, such a representative could be more passionate in his advocacy.[79] While his influence might be reduced if a difference in stature were perceived by the other directors, this might be no more of a risk than if he were a voting, but contentious and hence uninfluential, director.

Changing the Nature of the Board

Another way to minimize the number of occasions when the presence of a union director is problematic for a board is to change the kind of decisions the board makes. To remain within the confines of current corporate law, the overall role of the board of directors cannot be drastically changed. However, the specific activities of the board can be tailored in a way that makes it more closely resemble the two-tier system of boards of directors in Europe. In Germany, for example, labor sits on the supervisory board, which meets infrequently, supervises management in a general way, and reports to the shareholders. The actual, day-to-day management functions are run by a managing board. Important transactions, like mergers, are subjects for the supervisory board, as are the appointment and removal of the managers. Otherwise, the conduct of the business is left largely to the managing board.[80]

Separation of the board of directors of a United States corporation into two distinct entities would clearly require amendment of the statutes. Even if such a separation could be made,[81] many of the decisions reserved for the supervisory board would still give rise to conflict problems. However, some effective separation, and, consequently, some reduction of the problems, can be accomplished by the use of an executive committee, which is typically authorized by statute.[82] Under the Delaware provision, for example, the executive committee may be delegated almost all powers of the board.[83]

Changing the Directors' Fiduciary Duties

If shareholders could decide that employee representation were so desirable that they would rather have a union director than have the benefit of the full panoply of fiduciary duties owed to them by the board, an informed vote of the shareholders might be sufficient to cure many of the care and loyalty problems outlined above. Whether or not shareholders can acquiesce in the creation of directorships which entail less than full-fledged fiduciary duties is a question to which there is no satisfactory answer under current law.

Certainly, Fraser thought he was obtaining the informed consent of Chrysler's shareholders at the time of his election:

> The statement to the stockholders [in the proxy materials] said basically this: that I viewed my position on the Board as different than other Board members, that I viewed myself going in there as a representative of the workers. I think I also said that I see nothing inconsistent with this. So that people who voted for me voted with their eyes wide open, which probably explains why I got fewer votes than anybody else.[84]

There are, however, serious questions about whether a general statement in the proxy materials circulated in connection with an election of directors would be sufficient to generate the informed consent of the shareholders to a change in the nature of Fraser's fiduciary duties. Even if he were correct, and at least a majority of the shareholders did knowingly consent to his representation of interests other than their own, the question remains as to whether the courts would accept such a view of the vote.[85]

The answer must be sought in the nature of the relationship between the shareholders and the directors. To the extent that such a relationship is deemed fiduciary, rather than simply contractual, the shareholders may not have the power to "consent out" of the protections to which they are entitled. "When a fiduciary relation is deemed to exist, the parties cannot waive the courts' supervision over the fiduciary; they cannot 'shake off' judicial intervention. Courts insist on a continuing role in the fiduciary relation, perhaps because they are skeptical that an entrustor's general waiver to unspecified violations of fiduciary duties can be informed and independent."[86] Indeed, even the interested director statutes, which contemplate the waiver of conflicts of interest in particular transactions by means of an informed shareholder vote, do not eliminate all judicial review.[87] And so, to the extent that the courts characterize the relationship between shareholders and directors as fiduciary, consenting out may not foreclose all judicial scrutiny.[88]

If, however, the public corporation is viewed as simply a larger version of the small corporation (or sole proprietorship), it should be possible for the corporate documents to be more flexibly drafted to allow for such choices. Indeed, some flexibility has been made statutorily available to the small corporation.[89]

Whether the courts will look favorably upon attempts to extend this flexibility to the large public corporation remains to be seen. To the extent that public corporations faced with takeover threats have revised their certificates of incorporation for defensive purposes to include new "contract terms" like a classified board of directors or authorization of additional stock, judicial determinations of validity have turned not on the legality of the devices themselves, which are permissible under the relevant statutes, but on whether the board of directors breached its fiduciary duty in its use of such devices.[90]

CONCLUSION

The standards of care and loyalty to which corporate directors are held as a matter of fiduciary obligation have recently been the subject of intense judicial scrutiny. The traditional notion that the fiduciary relationship runs from directors to shareholders, as opposed to any other corporate constituency, has been reaffirmed. Indeed, to the extent that fidelity on the part of one or more directors to the shareholders may be questioned, the remaining directors take on a heavier burden of justification to avoid liability for breach of duty.

Employee representation on the board of directors presents problems under this fiduciary analysis, both for the union director and for the other directors. However, several corporations facing severe economic pressure have nominated union directors to their boards in connection with obtaining the financial benefits of employee wage and benefit concessions. This path may be pursued by more corporations in the future. There are various corporate techniques that may be tried in order to minimize the fiduciary problems created by these directorships, but their legal effectiveness remains a disturbingly open question.

NOTES

1. Although this chapter deals exclusively with corporate law problems, it should be noted that employee representation on the corporate board also raises serious problems in labor law and antitrust law. For a discussion of some of these problems, see Hamer, "Serving Two Masters: Union Representation on Corporate Boards of Directors," 81 Colum. L. Rev. 639, 640–52 (1981); Abramowitz, "Broadening the Board: Labor Participation in Corporate Governance," 34 Sw. L.J. 963, 969–75 (1980); Note, "Labor Unions in the Boardroom: An Antitrust Dilemma," 92 Yale L.J. 106 (1982).

2. See Fraser, "Worker Participation in Corporate Government: The U.A.W.–Chrysler Experience," 58 Chi.-Kent L. Rev. 949, 967–973 (1981); "ESOPs: Revolution or Ripoff?," Bus. Week, Apr. 15, 1985, at 94; "The Risk of Putting a Union Chief on the Board," Bus. Week, May 19, 1980, at 149; but see Reisman & Campa, "The Case for Adversarial Unions," Harv. Bus. Rev., May-June 1985, at 22.

3. I will refer to a representative of labor on the board of directors as a "union director," for the sake of brevity, because, to the extent the phenomenon has occurred in the United States, the labor representative has been an official or designee of the union. Questions regarding the mechanism for selection of the representative, either by the union or directly by employees, are beyond the scope of this chapter.

Similarly, when necessary for clarity, the nonlabor representatives on the board of directors are referred to as "shareholder directors." This is not to imply that such directors may not also represent interests which, at times, may come into conflict with the interests of the shareholders, for example, when a director is an official of a large creditor of the corporation, but to leave those conflicts for exploration elsewhere.

Throughout this chapter, the term "shareholder" describes a shareholder with a minority interest in a large, widely held corporation.

4. The degree of discomfort to which union directors are subject is, in fact, even greater. Union officials take on a fiduciary role under the various provisions of U.S. labor laws—most clearly under section 501 of the Labor-Management Reporting and Disclosure Act of 1959, 29 U.S.C. § 501(a) (1976)—which bear on their performance as corporate directors. Union directors are thus immediately subject to two sets of fiduciary duties—labor-law-generated and corporate-law-generated—and run a risk from the outset of being caught in an irreconcilable conflict. See Hamer, supra note 1.

5. Labor representation in corporate management is far more common in Europe, particularly in Germany. See, e.g., Hopt, "New Ways in Corporate Governance: European Experiments with Labor Representation on Corporate Boards," 82 Mich. L. Rev. 1338 (1984); Vagts, "Reforming the 'Modern' Corporation: Perspectives from the German," 80 Harv. L. Rev. 23 (1966).

6. On the subject of Chrysler, see Chrysler Corporation Proxy Statement (March 21,

1980); ''UAW's Fraser to Speak Out for Labor, Public in Role as Director at Chrysler,'' Wall St. J., Oct. 29, 1979, at 6, col. 2; ''GM Chief Hits Chrysler's Plan to Seat Fraser,'' Wall St. J., Nov. 8, 1979, at 4, col. 1; ''Chrysler Is Likely to Name UAW's Bieber to Board; Union Seen Controlling Seat,'' Wall St. J., Oct. 4, 1984, at 5, col. 1; F. Baldwin, Conflicting Interests 83–84 (1984). On the subject of Eastern, see Eastern Air Lines Proxy Statement (March 1984); ''Eastern Air Union Head Is Nominated a Director,'' Wall St. J., Mar. 2, 1984, at 35, col. 5 (eastern ed.); ''New Era for Eastern's Unions,'' N.Y. Times, Apr. 20, 1984, at D1, col. 3; ''Labor's New Role inside Eastern Airlines Seems to Be Succeeding,'' Wall St. J., Oct. 31, 1984, at 1, col. 6; ''Will the Labor-Management Revolution Survive at Eastern?,'' Bus. Week, Jan. 20, 1986, at 64.

7. This conflict of interest would arise for the union director whenever the interests of employees with respect to a particular decision differed from those of the shareholders. As discussed later (see text accompanying notes 59–65, infra), this might occur quite often. The conflict of interest would arise regardless of the fiduciary obligations created by labor law.

8. Furthermore, one director's conflict of interest may heighten the obligations of the other directors.

9. Dodge v. Ford Motor Company, 170 N.W. 668 (Mich. 1919).

10. Id. at 684.

11. See text accompanying notes 33–36, infra.

12. See, e.g., Zapata Corp. v. Maldonado, 430 A.2d 779 (Del. Sup. Ct. 1981), in which, in the context of a corporate decision to terminate a shareholder derivative suit, the Delaware Supreme Court recognized that a business judgment requires ''a balance of many factors—ethical, commercial, promotional, public relations, employee relations, fiscal as well as legal.'' Id. at 788, quoting Maldonado v. Flynn, 485 F. Supp. 274, 285 (S.D.N.Y. 1980).

13. Dodd, ''For Whom Are Corporate Managers Trustees?,'' 45 Harv. L. Rev. 1145 (1932); Berle, ''For Whom Corporate Managers *Are* Trustees: A Note,'' 45 Harv. L. Rev. 1365 (1932).

14. The usual example of judicial acceptance of such broader criteria is the permissibility of corporate charitable giving. This is, however, the only example of consistent judicial acceptance which can be cited. F. Baldwin, supra note 6, at 29–31.

15. R. Nader, M. Green & J. Seligman, Taming the Giant Corporation (1976); Schwartz, ''A Case for Federal Chartering of Corporations,'' 31 Bus. Law. 1125 (1976).

16. Revlon, Inc. v. MacAndrews & Forbes Holdings, Inc., 506 A.2d 173 (Del. Sup. Ct. 1986); Hanson Trust PLC v. ML SCM Acquisition, Inc., 781 F.2d 264 (2d Cir. 1986).

17. See, e.g., Williamson, ''Corporate Governance,'' 93 Yale L.J. 1197, 1199–1200 nn.8–11 (1984); Note, ''An Economic and Legal Analysis of Union Representation on Corporate Boards of Directors,'' 130 U. Pa. L. Rev. 919, 927 (1982). Of course, labor and investment capital are both parts of the single overall financial picture of the corporation. It is interesting to note that, in the cases of both Chrysler and Eastern, the union directorships were part of ''concessionary bargaining'' packages negotiated in connection with severe economic pressures on the corporations involved. The combination of wage and benefit relief for the corporation, on the one hand, and employee ownership participation and representation in management, on the other hand, illustrate that labor capital may sometimes be exchanged for investment capital.

18. Berle, supra note 13, at 1368–70.

19. The residual power of the corporation remains with the shareholders. See Auer v. Dressel, 306 N.Y. 427 (1954). Small, privately held corporations, of course, do not have the same shareholder coordination problem, and modern corporate statutes recognize this by providing for greater flexibility in those corporations to distribute powers between the shareholders and the directors, e.g., New York Business Corporation Law § 620(b) (McKinney's 1985)[hereafter cited as NYBCL]. Under Delaware law, the board may even be dispensed with entirely, and management may be vested directly in the shareholders. See Delaware General Corporation Law, Del. Code Ann. tit. 8, § 351 [hereafter cited as Del. GCL].

20. See e.g., Brudney, "Corporate Governance, Agency Costs, and the Rhetoric of Contract," 85 Colum. L. Rev. 1403, 1436 (1985).

21. See generally, Frankel, "Fiduciary Law," 71 Calif. L. Rev. 795 (1983).

22. Alchian & Demsetz, "Production, Information Costs and Economic Organization," 62 Amer. Econ. Rev. 777, 779–81 (1972); Jensen and Meckling, "Agency Costs and the Theory of the Firm," 3 J. Fin. Econ. 305, 308–309 (1976).

23. See Levmore, "Monitors and Freeriders in Commercial and Corporate Settings," 92 Yale L.J. 49, 60 (1982); Jensen & Ruback, "The Market for Corporate Control," 11 J. Fin. Econ. 5 (1983); Easterbrook & Fischel, "The Proper Role of a Target's Management in Responding to a Tender Offer," 94 Harv. L. Rev. 1161 (1981).

Higher levels of supervisors could be imagined, of course, but each would suffer the same mixed incentives (to keep his job or increase his personal power as well as maximize returns) until the ultimate "owners"—those whose well-being varies more directly with the productivity of the enterprise and not with their other relationships to the enterprise—were reached.

24. It might be argued that, if the ability to function as a monitor of management is the key to the creation of a fiduciary obligation running to the monitor from the person monitored, then workers, not shareholders, should be the beneficiaries of those duties. Workers are ideally situated to monitor certain types of managerial performance. Workers may even have better access to information about managerial inefficiency and greater expertise in evaluating that information than do shareholders. However, the aspects of managerial behavior which workers are likely to monitor are those which bear on the terms and conditions of their employment—aspects of managerial performance different from those the shareholders would most want monitored. Worker monitoring, then, would not substitute for shareholder monitoring in any event.

It is also far easier for workers than shareholders to protect themselves by contract against the particular abusive behavior they want to avoid; workers can relatively easily identify each other, communicate with each other, and coordinate their activities. While compliance with contract provisions also has to be monitored, the costs of negotiating, drafting, and policing a contract that covers the vulnerability of workers are far less than those costs would be for widely dispersed shareholders. Union representation acts to facilitate the making and administration of such contracts.

25. Williamson, supra note 17, at 1210.

26. Frankel, supra note 21, at 813. The "contracts" of shareholders are the certificate of incorporation and bylaws of the corporation (as well as certain statutory rules which provide a background for those documents). Those documents have been long in place by the time most existing shareholders in most major public corporations buy their shares. Moreover, no individual shareholder would have the incentive to instigate a revision of the corporation documents (or the statute) because the costs of such an undertaking to

that shareholder would be enormous, whereas any benefits would accrue to all of the shareholders, not in proportion to their efforts. See Levmore, supra note 23 at 53–54; Easterbrook and Fischel, supra note 23, at 1170–71.

The question whether corporate documents should be viewed as a species of contract will again be important in discussing the possibility that shareholders can waive—or consent out of—the fiduciary duties otherwise owed to them. See text accompanying notes 85–90, infra.

27. It has been argued, however, that an active capital market may, in fact, act to discourage monitoring by making it more profitable for a shareholder who discovers a problem to sell before that information has affected the stock price than to act to correct it. Levmore, supra note 23, at 63–64. Cf. Easterbrook and Fischel, supra note 23, at 1169, who take the position that the risk of takeover, made possible by an active capital market, is the factor that most effectively exerts discipline on managements.

28. Frankel, supra note 21, at 800–01.

29. See, e.g., Del. GCL § 144; NYBCL § 713. See text accompanying notes 51–54, infra.

30. See Aronoff v. Albanese, 85 A.D.2d 3, 446 N.Y.S.2d 368 (App. Div. 1982). But see Fleigler v. Lawrence 361 A.2d 218 (Del. Sup. Ct. 1976).

31. Brudney, supra note 20, at 1433–34; J. Slain, C. Thompson & F. Bein, Agency, Partnership and Employment: A Transactional Approach 3–25 to 3–26 (1980).

32. Such discretion may include the situation in which it is to the corporation's advantage to transact business with one of its directors, for example, when the director wishes to sell to the corporation an asset which would be valuable in its business.

33. Aronson v. Lewis, 473 A.2d 805, 812 (Del. Sup. Ct. 1984).

34. See, e.g., Norlin Corporation v. Rooney, Pace, Inc., 744 F.2d 255 (2d Cir. 1984).

35. See, e.g., Smith v. Van Gorkom, 488 A.2d 858 (Del. 1985). After the directors were found to have breached their duties of care in approving a sale of the company, the case was remanded to the trial court for a determination of the amount of damages to be awarded. The parties settled out of court; the directors agreed to pay the shareholders $23.5 million, only $10 million of which was covered by insurance. "Focus on Corporate Boards, Directors Feel the Legal Heat," N.Y. Times, Dec. 15, 1985, § 3, at 12, col. 3. It is now within the power of the shareholders of Delaware corporations to eliminate the board's liability to them for mere negligence (see note 89, infra). Such disclaimers do not extend, however, to the board's liability for recklessness or for breach of the duty of loyalty, or the directors' personal responsibility for damages in those cases.

36. Aronson v. Lewis, 473 A.2d at 812.

37. The duty of care has been codified in some states. A typical statutory formulation is New York's, which requires a director to use "that degree of care which an ordinarily prudent person in a like position would use under similar circumstances." NYBCL § 717.

38. See, e.g., Bates v. Dresser, 251 U.S. 524 (1920).

39. Cheff v. Mathes, 199 A.2d 548, 554 (Del. Sup. Ct. 1964) quoting Bennett v. Propp, 187 A.2d 405, 409 (Del. Sup. Ct. 1962).

40. Smith v. Van Gorkom, 488 A.2d 858 (Del. Sup. Ct. 1985).

41. Id. at 874.

42. Id.

43. Hanson Trust v. ML SCM Acquisition, Inc., 781 F.2d 264 (2d. Cir. 1986).

44. Id. at 275.

45. *Van Gorkom*, 488 A.2d at 877.

46. *Hanson Trust*, 781 F.2d at 284 (Oakes, J., concurring).

47. The interested directors in *Hanson Trust* had obvious direct pecuniary interests in conflict with those of the shareholders. In the case of the union director, personal pecuniary interests are unlikely to be present. However, direct conflicts between employee interests and shareholder interests are quite likely. Since the duty of care varies, the result may turn on a judicial determination of how direct the conflict is in any particular case.

48. For example, unlike shareholders, directors may not meet by proxy—even meetings by telephone are permissible only as specifically provided in the statutes—and may act without a meeting only by unanimous written consent. Cf. Del. GCL § 212 with Del. GCL §§ 141(f) and 141(i).

49. Barnes v. Andrews, 298 F. 614 (S.D.N.Y. 1924). "A director is not an ornament, but an essential component of corporate governance." Francis v. United Jersey Bank, 432 A.2d 814, 823 (N.J. 1981).

In the *Van Gorkom* case, one defense asserted by the directors was that their failure to act with due care was cured by the fact that they had sent the decision on the merger to the shareholders for a vote. However, Del. GCL § 251 requires action by the board—the "adoption of a resolution approving an agreement of merger"—before the matter may be submitted to a shareholder vote. As the court explained: "[c]ertainly in the merger context, a director may not abdicate that duty by leaving to the shareholders alone the decision to approve or disapprove the agreement." 488 A.2d at 873.

50. A serious and related problem not addressed by this chapter is access by the union director to confidential corporate information. Both the duty of care and the duty of loyalty are implicated here as well. Fulfillment of the duty of care requires the director to keep himself fully informed about corporate affairs. However, it may be difficult for the union director to preserve the confidentiality of the information—a duty of loyalty concern—when it relates to employee interests. See Note, supra note 17, at 952; Abramowitz, supra note 1, at 968–69. Nonetheless, at both Chrysler and Eastern, union directors have been given access to company books. See "Will the Labor-Management Revolution Survive at Eastern?," supra note 6; "Strains of Fraser's Dual Role," N.Y. Times, May 1, 1983, § 3, at 1, col. 1.

51. See Del. GCL § 144, on which this description is based.

52. Even though the interested director may be present at the meeting, his vote may not be counted in determining whether the "majority of the disinterested directors" approved of the transaction. Id.

53. Once the duty of loyalty of one director comes into question, the remaining directors will be on notice of facts which heighten their obligation of care.

54. See, e.g., Zapata Corp. v. Maldonado, 430 A.2d 779 (decision to dismiss a shareholder derivative suit naming some, but not all, of the then directors as defendants).

55. Unocal Corp. v. Mesa Petroleum Co., 493 A.2d 946 (Del. Sup. Ct. 1985).

56. Id. at 955.

57. Id.

58. Hamer, supra note 1, at 654–55, n.107. See also Small, "The Evolving Role of the Director in Corporate Governance," 30 Hastings L.J. 1353, 1368 (1979).

59. Block & Miller, "The Responsibilities and Obligations of Corporate Directors in Takeover Contests," 11 Sec. Reg. L.J. 44, 60 (1983); "ESOPs: Revolution or Ripoff?," supra note 2.

60. If labor has become specific to the firm, presumably the "value" of its employment

in the firm should be larger than that of other employees that could be brought in. This suggests that employees should be indifferent to takeovers wherever the acquirer plans to continue running the business. This has not, however, been observed.

The phenomenon that employees as a group tend to side with management much more frequently than nonemployee shareholders in a takeover situation was noted by the Chief Executive Office of Grumman Corporation in a letter to Grumman shareholders sent in response to a tender offer for Grumman by LTV Corporation. The letter, quoted in Donovan v. Bierwirth, 680 F.2d 263, 266–67 (2d Cir. 1982), stated: "We're very optimistic about our chances of defeating the takeover bid. About a third of all shares are held by Grumman's employee investment and pension plans. These plans are managed by Grummanites who will look long and hard at how well their fellow members would be served by selling off Grumman stock. Much of the rest is owned by Grumman people who, I believe, understand their future is worth more than a quick return on a block of shares."

See also "How Citizens and Businesses Rally Round When a Takeover Threat Strides into Town," Christian Sci. Monitor, Apr. 22, 1985, at 13, col. 2; "Hometown Fights for Phillips," N.Y. Times, Feb. 11, 1985, at D1, col. 3. But compare the actions of Charles Bryan, head of the International Association of Machinists and a member of the Board of Directors of Eastern Airlines, who refused to make wage concessions already accepted by other unions in order to prevent a sale of the company to Texas Air Corporation. Mr. Bryan's actions have been attributed at least in part to his long-standing enmity toward Frank Borman, at that time Eastern's chief executive officer. "Eastern Air's Borman Badly Underestimated Obduracy of Old Foe," Wall St. J., Feb. 25, 1986, at 1, col. 1.

61. Revlon, Inc. v. MacAndrews & Forbes Holding, Inc., 506 A.2d 173.

62. Id. at 182.

63. Id.

64. It can be argued that *Revlon* applies only when the decision has been made to sell the entire company to one of the competing bidders, and shareholders will have no choice but to relinquish their stock for some price. The opinion of the District Court in GAF Corporation v. Union Carbide Corporation, 624 F. Supp. 1016 (S.D.N.Y. 1985), might be cited for the proposition that directors may consider nonshareholder interests in a takeover contest where the fate of the target company has not yet been determined. However, that opinion does not deal with the question of what is permissible when there is a conflict between the interests of the shareholders and the interests of some other group. In one passage of the opinion, the *GAF* court observed: "[T]he exercise of independent, honest business judgment of an enlightened and disinterested Board is the traditional and appropriate way to deal fairly and even-handedly with both the protection of investors, on the one hand, and the legitimate concerns and interests of employees and management of a corporation who service the interests of investors, on the other." Id. at 1020. In another passage, the court clearly stated that "[The board's] duty is solely to the welfare of Carbide's investors and to deal with the interests of Carbide's employees and management fairly, in furtherance of those interests of investors." Id. at 1019.

65. When Fraser was nominated to the Chrysler board, he was to be one of twenty directors. See Proxy Statement of Chrysler Corporation, March 21, 1980. The NLRB stressed this fact in advising the union that Fraser's presence on Chrysler's board would not violate sections 8(b)(1)(A) and 8(b)(3) of the NLRA, 29 U.S.C. §§ 158(b)(1)(A) and 158(b)(3) (1976). International Union, UAW (Chrysler Corp.), Advice Mem. Case No.

7-CB-4815, 1980–81 NLRB (CCH), para. 20,269 [hereafter cited as UAW–Chrysler Memorandum] at 33,476 (Oct. 22, 1980).

Commenting on the conflicts inherent in Fraser's dual role, Professor Alfred F. Conard noted that Fraser would most likely be outvoted by the other directors on those issues in which the worker's interests were opposed to those of other shareholders. Conard was reported to have said that "there is no significant chance that a court will find that a board, made up as this one is, voted for something that the directors did not reasonably believe would be in the best, long-term interests of the corporation." "The Risk of Putting a Union Chief on the Board," supra note 2.

Another commentator has suggested that it would be appropriate for a court to intervene in the decision of a board with a union director "only when there is a significant probability that the board has compromised the interests of the corporation. This danger is more likely to be present when the employee representative votes on a matter directly affecting employees, and his vote is decisive." Hamer, supra note 1, at 658. The determination of when a "significant probability" of "compromise" exists would presumably have to be developed by case law, as would the determination of the equally elusive notion of when a union director's vote on a deliberative body like a board of directors is "decisive."

66. Fraser openly acknowledged his intention to leave the room and to not vote whenever the Chrysler board discussed collective-bargaining strategy. See Proxy Statement of Chrysler Corporation, March 21, 1980, at 10. See also "UAW's Fraser to Speak Out for Labor," supra note 6.

67. Proxy Statement of Chrysler Corporation, March 21, 1980, at 10.

68. This may also raise duty of care problems for the union director. See text accompanying notes 49–51, supra.

In the case of Continental Steel Corporation, a director representing the United Steelworkers recently resigned when the company's law firm concluded that he could not discuss or vote on labor issues without generating a potential conflict of interest. See "Power-Sharing between Management and Labor: It's Slow Going," Bus. Week, Feb. 17, 1986, at 37. See also Ferguson & Gaal, "Codetermination: A Fad or a Future in America?," 2 Employee Rel. L.J. 176, 191 (1984).

69. See, e.g., "Strains of Fraser's Dual Role," supra note 50; "Chrysler Is Likely to Name UAW's Bieber to Board," supra note 6.

70. "UAW's Fraser to Speak Out for Labor," supra note 6.

71. "The Risk of Putting a Union Chief on the Board," supra note 2.

72. Proxy Statement of Chrysler Corporation, March 21, 1980, at 10.

Indeed, the NLRB contemplated Fraser's continued allegiance to the employees and, in part for that reason, took the position that his directorship would not violate the NLRA: "Further, Fraser has stressed publicly and in his proxy statement that his prime interest in being on the Board of Directors is to represent the interest of the employees he represents, particularly with respect to matters which affect terms and conditions of employment, e.g., plant closings. There is nothing in Fraser's conduct which suggests that he has behaved inconsistently with this prime interest in representing employees." UAW–Chrysler Memorandum, supra note 65, at 33, 476–77.

73. The demand of the UAW for a seat on the Chrysler board "came about because [the employees] reached the conclusion that they don't have a voice in their own destiny and their own future unless they have representation at the point the decisions are made or before the decisions are made." Fraser, supra note 2, at 953.

74. Schwartz, "Governmentally Appointed Directors in a Private Corporation—The Communications Satellite Act of 1962," 79 Harv. L. Rev. 350, 353 (1965).

75. See, e.g., Note, supra note 1, at 109–10; Abramowitz, supra note 1, at 977–78.

76. See, e.g., Note, supra note 17, at 939–40.

77. This disclosure and exchange of information raises serious problems of confidentiality and permissible use of data. See supra note 50.

78. See, Williamson, supra note 17, at 1205–06. As Professor Williamson has observed: "Labor membership on boards of directors can be especially important during periods of actual or alleged adversity, especially when firms are asking workers for give-backs. Labor's board membership might mitigate worker skepticism by promoting the exchange of credible information." Id. at 1209.

79. One function of employee representation which would make a nondirectorial position more comfortable is the "gadfly" role:

> Mr. Fraser made it clear that his nomination and election to the Chrysler Board will not require his silence in the interest of corporate unity, in the event he disagrees with corporate policy. "If you don't go public to apply pressure, what have you got?" he is reported to have stated.

"Special Interest Directors," Report of Committee on Corporation Law, 35 Record of the Assn. of the Bar of the City of N.Y. 26, 33 (Jan.-Feb. 1980) quoting Wall St., Oct. 29, 1979, at 6, col. 6.

80. See Vagts, supra note 5, at 50–52.

81. Although this section addresses solutions that require no change in the existing corporate statutes, it is assumed that the board could be bifurcated by amending the statute. No states have as yet taken this route.

Legislative activity could take other forms, if a specific response to the union director problem were sought. For example, the statutes could provide for either mandatory or permissive employee representation on the board, with an accompanying change in the fiduciary duties of the employee representative. Such a change raises questions about the nature and source of fiduciary duties. See text accompanying notes 85–90, infra.

82. See, e.g., Del. GCL § 141(c).

83. For example, the Delaware statute reserves certain powers which may not be delegated: The executive committee may not amend the certificate of incorporation or authorize organic changes to the corporation. The executive committee may, however, be specifically authorized to declare dividends and to issue stock. Id.

84. Fraser, supra note 2, at 956.

85.

> Even if adequate disclosure could be forced, there would still remain the question of the adequacy of the volition with which investors respond. Consent by dispersed investors in the context of a particular transaction to which alternatives are rarely offered is hardly the kind of consent a single principal can give to resolve uncertainty about his agent's discretion . . . A single owner might well reject a fully disclosed 'take-it-or-leave-it' proposition that dispersed stockholders solicited by the proxy system are constrained to accept. At the very least, he might make a counteroffer that would produce a more favorable result than is possible for dispersed stockholders

Brudney, supra note 20, at 1437.

86. Frankel, supra note 21, at 821.

87. See Fleigler v. Lawrence, 361 A.2d 218 (1976).

88. "Special Interest Directors," supra note 79, at 135.

89. See, e.g., Del. GCL §§ 341–356 (special provisions applicable to close corpo-

rations). Courts have been willing to uphold arrangements in small, or close, corporations that would otherwise have violated statutory norms. See, e.g., Galler v. Galler, 32 N.E.2d 577 (Ill. 1964)

On June 18, 1986, the Governor of the State of Delaware signed into law a new provision of the state's corporate statute which would, in effect, give the shareholders of all corporations incorporated in the state the option of consenting to give up the right to seek monetary damages for certain breaches of the duty of care. Waiver of liability would not be permitted however, (i) for any breach of the director's duty of loyalty to the corporation or its stockholders, (ii) for acts or omissions not in good faith or which involve intentional misconduct or a knowing violation of law, (iii) under section 174 of [the Del. GCL], or (iv) for any transaction from which the director derived an improper personal benefit'' Delaware State Senate, 133rd General Assembly, Senate Bill No. 533, effective July 1, 1986. The availability of equitable remedies, such as injunctive relief or recision, would not be affected.

90. See, e.g., Moran v. Household International, Inc., 500 A.2d 1346 (Del Sup. Ct. 1985); Norlin Corporation v. Rooney, Pace, Inc., 744 F.2d 255; Revlon Inc. v. MacAndrews & Forbes Holdings, Inc., 506 A.2d 173.

8
COMPARATIVE PERSPECTIVES

Clyde W. Summers

Editors' Note. Professor Summers describes basic American labor and employment law concepts and compares them with those of selected Western European nations and Japan. In the author's view, Western European and Japanese labor systems are founded on principles of individual employee rights to job security and collective rights to participation in management decision making, which differ radically from the basic premises of the American system. This theme is developed through a description of the approaches these other countries have taken to business change decisions, including notification requirements, consultation as to decisions and codetermination as to impact, and successor obligations.

Comparisons in labor law require sailing between the Scylla of generalization, which distorts with oversimplification, and the Charybdis of specifics, which obscures with details. There is no safe passage; at best, one suffers partial losses on both sides. The dangers are increased by the lack of any sure compass and the risk of misperceiving crucial landmarks. Comparisons are inevitably based on perceptions of one's own labor law and labor relations system; only through such an imperfect lens can we attempt to observe the dominant features and details of an unfamiliar terrain.

The purpose of this chapter is to provide a basis for comparing the way in which different labor law systems, particularly those of Germany, Sweden, Great Britain, and Japan, deal with employment relations problems arising out of major changes in the enterprise. This requires, first, describing in broad strokes certain fundamental differences between labor law in the United States and that in

Western European countries and Japan. It requires, second, describing in some detail the legal rules of other countries in particular areas, such as worker participation in decision bargaining, information sharing, termination of employment, and successorship obligations, and how they apply in various situations of major business change. The hope is that these generalizations, though oversimplified, will provide a context and framework for understanding and organizing the details.

The description presented here is not truly comparative in two respects. First, it deals almost entirely with the legal rules and not with the institutional structures or industrial practices which in labor law are crucially important to understanding how the legal rules actually function in the labor relations system. Second, only limited reference is made to specific legal rules in the United States, and a limited effort is made to draw explicit comparisons. The relevant legal rules have been elaborated in the preceding chapters, and the comparisons are to be drawn primarily by the readers.

FUNDAMENTAL DIFFERENCES

The Employment Relation

The most fundamental difference in labor law between the United States, on the one side, and most Western European countries, on the other, is the character of the employment relation. In the United States, the employment relation is characterized by employment at will. In the absence of an agreement to the contrary or an explicit statutory prescription, the employment relation may be terminated by either party at any time for any reason or no reason, and for the great majority of employees there is no agreement or statutory rule to the contrary. The courts in the past have been markedly unwilling to imply from employer representations, employee reliance, or general practices any limitations on the employer's freedom to dismiss without notice or reason.[1]

Most collective agreements provide employees with seniority rights and prohibit discharge without "just cause," but collective agreements cover less than 25 percent of the work force.[2] Various statutes prohibit discrimination because of race, creed, nationality, sex, age, and union membership, but these leave the employer free to dismiss for any other reason, no matter how arbitrary or whimsical. During the last ten years, a number of courts have found implied contractual limits on dismissals and tort liability for abusive discharge.[3] However, employment at will remains the dominant characteristic of the employment relation in the United States.

Employment at will leaves the employment contract a hollow shell, for the ability to terminate at any time deprives it of any core of continuing or future obligations. The contract of employment contains little more than the obligation to pay for work already performed; the terms of future performance can be changed at any time and in any way. This inevitably stunts the development of any law of the employment contract.

Employment at will is not only the dominant legal rule, but it also expresses a common social attitude that the employment relation creates no continuing tie between the employer and the employee. Employment is the purchase of a worker's labor, when and if wanted; past services create no future obligations.[4] Collective agreements, with seniority provisions and prohibitions against unjust discharge, are built on a different premise. The individual has a continuing right in the job, subject to the employer's continuation of the job. Collective agreements commonly permit the employer nearly unlimited freedom to eliminate jobs, deciding when and how many employees to lay off, subject to seniority principles. Notice of lay off or termination is limited to a few days, and only a minority of agreements provide for any severance pay. Even accumulated pension benefits may be wiped out if vesting periods are not met.[5]

In contrast, Western European countries and Japan have rejected the doctrine of employment at will; all have statutes prohibiting unfair dismissals.[6] The law even prior to these statutes viewed the employment relation as creating a substantial and continuing legal obligation. In Great Britain the common law required reasonable notice of termination, and other countries by law or practice had similar rules. The individual contract of employment has traditionally been the core of British labor law, and it is a central concept in the labor law of other countries, of at least equal importance to the collective contract.

Less tangible, though perhaps more important, is an underlying attitude of a tied relationship between the employer and the employee which views the employee not as a supplier of labor but as a member of the enterprise. To some extent this seems to have quasifeudal roots, with remnants of nineteenth-century master-servant law which imposed on the master certain obligations for the social welfare of his servant. To some extent it finds expression in the establishment of works councils and employee representation on corporate boards, which are integral parts of the industrial relations system in most Western European countries. This attitude varies in strength from Great Britain, where it seems nearly nonexistent, to Japan, where lifetime employees in an enterprise are described as members of the "family" and a range of institutions and practices create a close relationship which competes with the family for time, attention, and loyalty.[7]

The centrality of the employment contract expresses a view of the employment relation as creating a web of continuing rights and obligations. In addition, the employment contract provides a framework for adding to those rights and obligations by legally mandating certain terms such as severance pay or protection against unfair dismissal. Although a concept of a tied relationship or membership in the enterprise does not negate the dominant-subordinate nature of the employment relation, it does encourage the creation of additional employer obligations and supports the employees' claim to have a voice in decisions of the enterprise.

Collective Representation of Employees

The second fundamental difference that significantly affects the way in which different labor law and labor relations systems deal with problems arising out of major changes in the enterprise is the role of collective representation of employees. Congress, in 1935, declared in the National Labor Relations Act (Wagner Act) the national policy of encouraging the practices and procedures of collective bargaining, and it described collective bargaining as "fundamental to the friendly adjustment of industrial disputes." One of the purposes of the Act was to provide a measure of industrial democracy by giving employees a voice in the decisions that govern their working life. With the passage of the 1947 Taft-Hartley amendments, however, the policy of encouraging collective bargaining shifted to one of legal neutrality or indifference; collective bargaining is now viewed by the Board and the courts not as a process for friendly adjustment of disputes, but as an essentially adversarial process between combatants relying on economic power. The larger purpose of enhancing industrial democracy or worker participation is all but forgotten.

From the beginning, American employers have almost uniformly resisted the establishment of collective bargaining, commonly conducting massive campaigns to persuade their employees that they have no need for collective representation, and that unions will be detrimental to both the employees and the enterprise. Employer resistance is often not limited to lawful persuasion, but extends to coercive and retaliatory conduct. National Labor Relations Board statistics show that for every seven votes in favor of a union in a representation election, one employee is discharged for union activity.[8] Even employers who have established bargaining relationships often seek to unseat the union and return to individual bargaining. The dominant attitude of American employers is resistance to collective representation of their employees. This, at least, contributes to the result that only one employee out of four enjoys such representation.

In contrast, the policies and purposes originally expressed in the Wagner Act have, in fact, been largely followed in Western Europe and Japan, and collective representation is the dominant pattern of the labor relations systems in those countries. Collective agreements in Western Europe are typically negotiated on an industry-wide basis between unions and employer associations which include most employers in the industry.[9] Although the collective agreement may be legally binding only as to union members, or in Britain not legally binding at all, employer association members, in fact, generally apply it to all employees whether they are union members or not.[10] As a result, in Germany, for example, only 40 percent of workers belong to unions, but more than 90 percent are, in fact, covered by collective agreements.[11] In many of the countries, the applicability of the collective agreement may be legally extended by administrative or executive order to all employers in the industry.[12]

Industry-wide agreements are limited mainly to economic terms such as wages, hours, vacations, and severance pay, and for those the agreement establishes only minimum terms. The full and actual terms of employment relation are determined at the plant or enterprise level. In every Western European country, there is established by law or practice a comprehensive system of plant representation.[13] In West Germany the Works Constitution Act[14] provides for the creation of works councils elected by the employees in every establishment having more than five employees, as well as a system of combined works councils in multiplant enterprises. The works council negotiates economic benefits above the agreement minimum, and it is vested by statute with extensive representation rights concerning other matters such as manpower planning, guidelines for recruitments and dismissals, introduction of new production processes, transfer of employees, and partial or total closure of operations.[15]

Similar worker representation committees are created by statute or national inter-confederation agreements in other continental countries such as Austria, Belgium, France and Italy.[16] The high level of unionization in Sweden enables unions to provide representation at nearly every workplace without the aid of legislation.[17] Plant level representation is less comprehensive in Great Britain, for shop stewards function only where there is a substantial union membership.[18] Even so, representation is more extensive there than in the United States, because unions need not demonstrate majority support before collective bargaining can begin.[19]

Japan presents a different picture. Unions are limited to single enterprises, and although they may join on an industry or national level in an annual wage offensive, collective agreements are negotiated at the enterprise level. Most larger enterprises (those with more than 500 employees) have collective agreements.[20] However, union membership and collective agreements are limited to lifetime employees; so-called temporary and part-time workers are excluded from the system.[21] In larger enterprises, lifetime employees constitute about 70 percent of the employees, but lifetime employees overall constitute no more than 30 percent of the national work force.[22] Collective representation, therefore, is quite comprehensive for the 30 percent of workers who enjoy lifetime employment but is nearly nonexistent for all others.

More important than the pervasiveness of collective representation in other countries is the acceptance of collective representation by employers. In none of these countries do employers actively resist unionization and collective bargaining. No other country has, or needs to have, such elaborate legal protection of the right to organize, nor such extensive enforcement machinery to curb illegal employer conduct as the United States. Even the lawful antiunion practices used by many American employers would make them social pariahs in Germany, Sweden, and Japan.

Employers in most of Western Europe not only accept, but seem to prefer, collective representation. Many join employers associations, thereby voluntarily becoming a part of the collective-bargaining system even though few of their employees are union members. Although French and German employers seek to limit unions to representation at the industry agreement level, French employers accept and German employers actively support works councils at the plant level.[23] The dominant attitude of British employers is less one of acceptance of collective representation than unwelcome toleration, but rarely do they actively campaign to persuade their employees not to unionize.[24]

Along with acceptance of collective representation is a tempering of the adversarial attitude, a recognition on both sides—expressed in use of the term "social partners"—that they have common as well as adverse interests. This is, as might be expected, least true in Great Britain, where the tie between employer and employee is the weakest, and most true in Japan where enterprise unionism and the view of lifetime employees as members of the enterprise family combine to place primary emphasis on the welfare of the enterprise. It is exemplified by Section 2 of the German Works Constitution Act, which states: "The employer and works council shall work together in a spirit of mutual trust . . . for the good of the employees and of the establishment."[25] These words, unlike the phrase "friendly adjustment of disputes" in the Wagner Act, express the dominant reality of the German employment relationship.

Finally, acceptance of collective representation as a fundamental element in labor relations has been reinforced in Western Europe by the movement for increased worker participation in decisions of the enterprise.[26] In Germany, the role of the works council was significantly strengthened in 1972, and employee representation on corporate boards was increased in 1976.[27] In Sweden, union representation on corporate boards, first enacted in 1972, was expanded in 1976.[28] A Codetermination Act giving unions greatly increased influence at the plant level was adopted in 1976;[29] and Workers Funds legislation providing for acquisition of ownership shares and ultimate control of the enterprise was passed in 1983.[30] In the last fifteen years, every Western European country except Great Britain has taken steps in one or more of these directions toward increased worker participation.[31] In Britain, proposals for employee representation on corporate boards were developed by the Bullock Commission in 1976, but these were pushed aside with the onset of the Thatcher Administration.[32]

European employers originally opposed worker participation in decisions of the enterprise, for they saw it as encroaching on areas where management had previously exercised unquestioned control. They have now accepted it as a part of the system of collective representation, but only within a limited area of shared control. The crucial fact, however, is that the area of shared control has been significantly expanded, and worker representatives now have a voice in many decisions which most American employers insist are exclusively management prerogatives.

These two fundamental differences in the basic employment relation and in worker participation in decisions have been described with broad and bold strokes. As emphasized at the outset, such generalizations are oversimplified, and the differences are overstated. The employment relation in the United States is, in practice, not as transitory as the legal rules describe, or as employers insist the law should continue to allow. In Western Europe, the contract of employment loses substance, and the tied relationship becomes looser with increased unemployment and the proliferation of temporary, part-time, and other forms of irregular employment. Collective bargaining in the United States can be cooperative, emphasizing common concerns, while union-employer relations in Japan can at times display all the antagonism of a family fight. In Germany, many small employers have no works council or the ones in place are moribund, and, even in Sweden, active union "clubs" do not exist in many small plants. However, when the dominant patterns of legal rules, employment practices, and social attitudes are examined, the fundamental differences between American and European labor systems cannot be gainsaid. They will appear even more clearly as we examine the particular legal principles and institutional practices used by different countries in responding to business changes which significantly affect employees.

COMPARATIVE LEGAL OBLIGATIONS

Comparing labor law in the United States applicable to situations of business change with that in other countries requires distinguishing those situations in which employees are represented by a union and those in which they are not. In the latter context, governed by employment at will, the employees in the United States have no substantial rights, individual or collective, other than to be paid wages earned. The employer can dispose of the plant, the jobs, and the employees as he sees fit. There are no restrictions on employer discretion and hence no basis for making comparisons. As a result, the focus is on the law of collective bargaining. It must be kept in mind, however, that collective bargaining is applicable to less than one-fourth of the workers in this country and also that the law applicable in other countries includes both individual employment rights and collective representation rights.

Participation in Decisions: Negotiation, Consultation, Codetermination

In the United States, the legal right of employees to participate in the decisions of the enterprise is defined by the duty to bargain, which encompasses rules prescribing when the parties are obligated to bargain, how they are to conduct themselves in negotiations, and what subjects must be bargained about. The effectiveness of participation depends on the union's bargaining power as evidenced by its ability to inflict economic costs on the employer. Other countries have legal rules which, although they perform similar functions, have a significantly different content.

Sweden. In Sweden, Section 10 of the Codetermination Act of 1976 imposes on the employer a duty to negotiate with the local union organization on "any matter relating to the relationship between the employer and any member of the organization who is or has been employed by the employer." These words are not intended to limit the scope of negotiations but to be "so wide that no questions are excluded over which it is important for workers to obtain influence," including questions which "relate to the enterprise's production, business management, work management or other matters." The subjects on which the union can call for negotiations are, for legal and practical purposes, unlimited.[33]

In addition, Section 11 requires an employer to initiate negotiations before making a decision on a somewhat narrower, but still broad range of matters. This includes any "important alteration of his activities" or any "important alteration of working or employment conditions for employees." These words were clearly intended to reach all decisions that "one would typically expect a union to wish to have an opportunity to negotiate about"[34]—including decisions to reduce operations, close existing plants, open new plants, or change the location of the enterprise. The Swedish Labor Court, a court of last resort, has held that the employer must initiate negotiations before deciding to introduce a new type of machinery, move control of a plant from one subsidiary to another, sell the company, or merge with another company.[35] In these areas, which are, in American terms, at the "core of entrepreneurial control," the employer is required to engage in "decision bargaining" and cannot make the decision until negotiations have reached an agreement or an impasse.

The union can exert its influence on these decisions not only by persuasion but also by economic force. Indeed, although a statutory no-strike obligation is imposed during the term of a collective agreement, the Codetermination Act specifically provides in Section 44 that the union can reserve the right to strike on these codetermination issues during the contract term.[36] Unions, however, have not asserted or used this surviving right to strike during the contract, but have relied on the process of persuasion. Employer acceptance of unions and commitment to resolving problems by negotiation reduces the need for a strike club to induce employers to listen and give substantial weight to their employees' views in making decisions.[37]

The declared purpose of the Codetermination Act was to establish "democracy at the workplace" by giving employees a voice in the decisions of the enterprise that directly or indirectly affect them. This premise was first laid down in 1972 in the statute giving employees the right to elect two members on corporate boards,[38] thereby explicitly recognizing that employees were members of the enterprise entitled to participate in all of its decisions. As stated by those proposing the legislation: "Representation on the board would serve to indicate that workers are part of the firm and that they have a right to give their views on its activities before any final decision is taken."[39] Board membership would not create dual loyalties, for it was "quite incorrect to regard workers' interests as being opposed to the firm's. In fact, the workers are a part of the firm, so they cannot be at variance with it."[40] Swedish law thus articulates the principle that there is no area of management prerogative shielded from participation by the employees through the union representative. Although management may determine the final decision, it is only after the employees have been heard, their interests have been considered, and efforts have been made to reach an agreement.[41] They are entitled to influence the decisions of the enterprise that lie at the ''core of entrepreneurial control.''

Germany. A substantial number of collective agreements in Germany include provisions protecting employees subject to loss of earnings or dismissal due to changes in technology and organization. However, the primary method of protecting employees from changes in the enterprise is not through collective bargaining with unions at the industry level but through participation in works councils at the plant and enterprise level. Works councils are elected by all employees, other than members of the executive staff, at the workplace and are institutionally separate from the union. However, unions play a major role in these elections; 75 percent of works councils members are elected from union-sponsored slates.[42] The employer and works council are, according to the Works Constitution Act, to meet at least once a month and ''discuss the matters at issue with an earnest desire to reach agreement.''[43]

Works councils have the right to participate in a wide range of decisions, and that participation takes two different forms. For some decisions, participation is limited to ''consultation,'' which requires the employer to discuss the matter before taking action but allows the employer to make the decision. Participation in these discussions is limited to persuasion, because the works council is barred by law from striking or engaging in other forms of economic action. For other decisions, the works council has the right to ''codetermination,'' which requires the parties, if they are unable to agree, to submit the dispute to a ''conciliation commission'' made up of members representing each side and a neutral chosen by the parties for binding determination.[44]

Consultation with the works council is required on any plans concerning changes in work processes or operations, changes in jobs, any new construction (including alterations or extensions of the plant), and any matters relating to manpower planning, including present and future staffing needs, staff movements, and vocational training.[45]

Codetermination extends to a much broader range of decisions, including setting of work schedules, introduction and application of incentive pay systems, institution of health and safety measures, implementation of vocational training programs, and the promulgation of guidelines for the hiring, transfer, promotion, and dismissal of employees. In all of these matters, if no agreement is reached, the decision is made by what is, in effect, compulsory interest arbitration by a tripartite panel.[46]

Special procedures for codetermination are prescribed when the firm proposes changes which ''entail substantial prejudice to the staff or a large sector thereof.'' This includes changes caused by reduction of operations or partial or total plant closures, transfer of production to other plants, plant mergers, reorganization of operations, modification of products, and introduction of new work methods and production processes. The ''prejudice to the staff'' may consist of dismissal, loss of earnings, increased work load, more undesirable hours, or any other material disadvantage, and it will be considered "substantial" if it affects at least 20 percent of the work force.[47]

If such a change is contemplated, the employer is required to inform the works council "in full and in good time" and to consult with the works council in developing a "social plan" for dealing with the impact of the changes on the employees. The social plan may provide for transfer of employees to other work or to other locations, moving costs, retraining, supplements for reduced earnings, early retirement, and severance pay for those dismissed. The plan may also include provisions for the timing of the changes and for the number of employees to be transferred or dismissed at various stages. If the parties are unable to reach an agreement on the compensation to be paid employees prejudiced by the change, the matter is submitted to the conciliation commission which draws up a binding social compensation plan.[48]

The compensation provided by social plans can be very substantial. Severance pay for employees dismissed is based on length of service, age, and pay. In a financially healthy enterprise, the amount may be equivalent to a year's pay or more for an older employee of fifteen years of service and one month's pay for a young employee of five years of service. In a financially weak enterprise, the amount may be only half that amount because one of the considerations in determining the amount of compensation is what the employer can pay and still continue to operate.[49]

Poverty does not obviate the obligation to develop a social plan, for there is a strong social feeling, reflected in conciliation commission decisions, that employees should receive some compensation, however meager, for this dislocation, and it is an accepted view that an enterprise which is unable to pay such compensation will not long survive in any case. Even insolvent employers undergoing reorganization are obligated to develop a social plan if they have any unsecured assets. Obligations under a social plan have first rank among unsecured creditors, but severance pay is statutorily limited in insolvency cases to two and one-half months' pay, and such obligations may not claim more than one-third of the unsecured assets.[50]

It should be noted that the provisions concerning social plans give the works council only consultation rights in the decision to make changes in the enterprise and codetermination rights only in decisions concerning how to handle the impact of those changes on the employees. In American terms, this is not "decision bargaining" but "effects bargaining." However, the prospect of a works council insisting on a costly social plan often causes employers to work out an agreement in advance with the works council in order to minimize the impact on the work force or avoid a social plan entirely.

Participation in decisions concerning changes in the enterprise may also take place through employee representation on corporate boards. Representation is limited, however, to the supervisory board; it does not extend to the management board. In the German two-tier board structure, the functions of the supervisory board can be, and normally are, limited to appointing the managing directors and examining accounts, so that the kinds of decisions with which this chapter are concerned are often made by the managing directors without any consultation of the supervisory board.[51] Only in the coal and steel industry, where there is full labor-management parity on the supervisory board and employee members select the labor director does board representation provide much opportunity for employees to influence such business decisions.[52]

Great Britain. Great Britain, at present, imposes no general legal obligation on employers to recognize or bargain with unions. The Industrial Relations Act of 1971, in a sharp break with the voluntarist tradition, created procedures for requiring an employer to recognize and bargain with the union. This was modified by the Employment Protection Act of 1975. The Employment Act of 1980 abolished these procedures and returned to the voluntarist tradition.[53]

The procedures created by the 1971 and 1975 legislation are, however, of special interest. First, determination of whether a particular union should be recognized was not based on majority rule. Often no election was held, but instead the Advisory, Conciliation and Arbitration Service (ACAS) would investigate the employees' attitudes toward collective bargaining. The issue was not the simple one of majority choice to be determined by balloting, but the more complex, practical one of whether there was adequate support within the group to sustain effective bargaining. ACAS might determine that effective bargaining was possible even though the union currently lacked majority support or that effective bargaining would not be possible even though the union had a majority in the plant because the employer, as a member of an employer's association, was already bound by a controlling national agreement with another union. Second, recognition was limited to those subjects on which the parties agreed to bargain. The employer, by refusing to bargain about certain matters, could circumscribe its recognition obligation. Third, the ultimate sanction for refusing recognition was not to compel directly recognition or bargaining, but to order the employer to raise wages or improve terms and conditions of employment as determined by the Central Arbitration Committee (CAC) of the ACAS—a form of interest arbitration.[54]

The lack of a legal obligation in Great Britain to recognize and bargain with the union does not necessarily ensure employers unilateral control. The union is free to use economic force against an employer to compel him to bargain, and this may include bargaining on subjects which do not relate directly to terms and conditions of employment. Strikes or other forms of direct economic action are legally permissible if they are "in contemplation of furtherance of a trade dispute."[55] This includes economic action against managerial acts that may lead to reduced employment, such as the use of outside contractors or purchasing from outside sources. The economic action may be directed against the management decision itself, not merely to protect employees from the effects of the decision.[56]

Although there is no general legal obligation under current British law for employers to deal with unions, there are bits and pieces of such an obligation.

First, publicly owned industries routinely have been compelled under their statutes to recognize unions. Although these provisions give the employer broad discretion because it was assumed that nationalized companies did not require the spur of legal obligation to deal with unions, this assumption has proved to be less than entirely correct.[57]

Second, the Health and Safety at Work Act of 1974 gives recognized unions the right to appoint safety representatives and imposes on the employers a duty to consult with such representatives concerning measures to ensure health and safety at work. Regulations under the statute spell out the functions of such representatives in some detail. Disputes between employers and unions concerning failure to consult or observe the regulations are to be resolved by bargaining, and only if that fails by legal procedures.[58]

Third, and directly relevant to the problems of business change, the Employment Protection Act of 1975 requires the employer to consult with a recognized union before reducing his work force because of lack of work. Consultation must begin "at the earliest opportunity" and at least ninety days before the first dismissal if one hundred or more employees are to be dismissed and at least thirty days before the first dismissal if ten or more employees are to be dismissed. The employer must inform the union about the reasons for the proposed dismissals, the number and types of workers involved, and the proposed procedures for selecting the employees to be dismissed. The time limits are modified where special circumstances render it not reasonably practicable to comply. Because there is no duty to consult until the employer has been able to develop a proposal to reduce the work, consultation in many cases of insolvency may be very truncated.[59]

Fourth, regulations issued to comply with the Directive of the European Economic Community (EEC) on Transfers of Undertakings require an employer to consult over a proposed transfer of the business. These regulations apply only to a transfer of the business itself as a going concern and do not apply to transfer of control by takeover bids or sale of shares, or to a sale only of the assets previously used in the business. The employer is required to inform the union of the time of the transfer, the reason for the transfer, the effect on the employees, and the measures, if any, proposed by the transferor or transferee with reference to employees. This information must be provided "long enough before a relevant transfer to enable consultations to take place."[60]

It should be noted that, in cases of redundancies and business transfers, the employer's duty is not to bargain, only to consult. In the British context, consultation gives the union little practical influence. Moreover, the obligation to consult extends, not to the decision to transfer the business, but only to the impact on the employees who will be affected. However, the union can legally use economic force to compel bargaining on the underlying business decision. In practice, consultation is but the prelude to negotiations, which move through stages of trying to reduce the number to be terminated, establishing the criteria for selecting those to be terminated, and determining the payments to those terminated.[61]

Japan. The Japanese Labor Relations Act[62] was modelled after the National Labor Relations Act and adopted during the post-war occupation. It contains a general duty to bargain, but, because there is no principle of exclusive representation, the duty runs to every union that has any members in the work force. In practice, significant bargaining on general terms and conditions of employment takes place with the union recognized by the employer as the dominant union in that enterprise, usually the majority union.[63]

The law has little relevance to the bargaining process, for employers accept the principle of joint decision making with the enterprise union.[64] The obligations regarding notice, consultation, and negotiation are those provided by collective agreements.

In practice, unions insist on the right to participate in any decisions concerning business changes that might lead to work-force reductions, and this right is accepted by management. Management normally notifies the union of proposed changes early enough to allow time to persuade the union and the employees involved of the necessity to reduce the work-force. The information usually includes detailed information on the economic and technological reasons for the change and the number of employees affected. Discussion begins with consultation, which is considered a process of finding an accommodation. If no accommodation is reached, negotiation turns into confrontation bargaining with failure to agree potentially ending in economic action.[65] In plant closures, the workers may respond by occupying the plant, a nominally illegal but tolerated practice.[66] Negotiations seldom, however, reach the stage of confrontation, even less often economic conflict, because the enterprise-based union recognizes its interest in the economic welfare of the enterprise, and management accepts collective representation and responsibility for providing continued employment to its lifetime employees.[67]

Summary. This examination of the legal rules concerning the right of workers to participate in decisions of the enterprise, which in the United States are generally encompassed by the duty to bargain, leads to three general observations.

First, in all except perhaps Great Britain, the workers' representatives have more voice in the decisions of the enterprise than they do in the United States. This is particularly true of plant closures and other major changes which affect the employment relation. The right extends to the managerial decision itself, by law in Sweden, and by practice in Japan. Although the right extends legally only to the effects on employees in Germany, the availability of compulsory settlement gives the works council a practical voice in the decision-making process. Although there is no legal duty to bargain in Great Britain, the union can use economic action to compel the employer to give the union an effective voice in managerial decisions. In contrast, the limited duty to bargain in the United States shields as "management prerogatives" a broad area of decision making from employee influence through collective action because the union's use of economic action to compel agreement on a nonmandatory subject constitutes a refusal to bargain under section 8(b)3 of the NLRA.

Second, giving employees a greater voice in decisions of the enterprise is accompanied by a less adversarial and more collaborative relation. Sweden, Germany, and Japan have affirmative policies of increasing employee participation in managerial decisions when those decisions affect the employees—Sweden and Germany by law, and Japan by practice. In these three countries, there is a marked spirit of collaboration in collective labor relations. In Great Britain, the law might be considered neutral because the scope of participation is determined by relative economic strength. The law in the United States, in contrast, encourages and protects management in asserting its prerogatives because the employer is given legal protection against the union insisting, through economic pressure, on consideration of its views. In both Great Britain and the United States, union-employer relations are characterized by confrontation.

Separating cause and effect is difficult, but a study of the various systems suggests that it is participation in managerial decisions that creates in the employees' representative a sense of responsibility for the welfare of the enterprise and makes collaboration possible. When the employer refuses to recognize the employee's representative as a partner, the sense of common purpose is discouraged, and the prospect of confrontation is increased.

Third, other systems recognize the usefulness of forms of participation short of bargaining with potential resort to economic force. Swedish unions, in dealing with problems such as plant closures, relocation, technological change, and reorganization, rely on the employer's obligation to inform and negotiate prior to the decision when the union is bound by a no-strike obligation. German works councils have only the right to be informed and consulted on decisions such as changes in working processes, operations, or job content, with the right to make the decision remaining in the employer. In Japan, consultation with no contemplation of economic action is the normal method of deciding issues other than annual wage increases.

In the United States, by contrast, mandatory negotiation or consultation without the strike weapon has been largely shunted aside in the private sector. The limited duty to bargain during the contract term on matters not previously discussed can be and often is barred by so-called zipper clauses. In public sector bargaining, the use of the strike is, in most states, not legally allowed but is frequently used. Negotiation without the availability of the strike is commonly denigrated as meaningless.

The effectiveness of consultation is, of course, not guaranteed by making it mandatory, but it is likely to help foster a collaborative attitude on the part of the parties. Requiring an employer to inform and consult on a subject declares to both the employer and the employees that the employees are entitled to a voice in that decision, and the mandated process provides an opportunity for rational discussion to persuade on both sides. These are prerequisites for promoting collaboration.

Sharing of Information

The right to information is closely related to the right to participate because meaningful and constructive participation in decision making requires knowledge of all relevant information. This is true whether participation is through consultation or bargaining. The duty to disclose rests almost entirely on the employer, for the union has little information not available to the employer. This is particularly true concerning changes in the enterprise.

In the United States, the employer has a duty to disclose information only upon the union's request, and only information which the NLRB and the courts consider relevant to mandatory subjects of bargaining. This approach normally excludes information concerning production costs, profitability, capital investments in new equipment, product changes, new plants, or the financial condition or plans of the company.

In Germany and Sweden, the employer's duty to disclose is more significant in two respects. First, the employer has the affirmative obligation to provide relevant information regularly, whether or not requested by the employee representative. Second, the scope of the information that must be provided is much more extensive, not only because the area of participation is broader, but also because of a much more inclusive view of what is deemed relevant.

The German Works Constitution Act provides for the appointment by the works council of a finance committee in all companies of more than one hundred employees. The employer is required to inform the finance committee "in full and good time of the financial affairs of the establishment." Among the financial matters covered are the "economic and financial situation of the company," "the production and marketing situation," "the production and investment programs," "rationalization plans," new work methods, reduction of operations, partial or total plant closures, relocation or mergers, changes in plant organization or the products, and "any other circumstances or plans that may materially affect the interests of the employees."[68]

The Swedish statute is less detailed, but no less broad. It requires the employer to keep the union "continuously informed about how his activity is developing in respect to production and economically." This is interpreted to include salaries of executives and others not covered by the collective agreement, unit costs of production, number of units produced, sale prices and profit margins, and plans for expansion or contraction, introduction of new products, new technologies or new production process, changes in the capital structure, or any other changes in the activities of the enterprise. The union is by statute entitled to examine the books, accounts, and other documents to the extent needed "to take care of its members' interests in relation to the employer."[69]

The British employer, under the Employment Protection Act of 1975, has a much narrower duty to disclose: the limitations all but swallow the obligation.[70] First, the union's right to information is an incident of recognition, and the employer may recognize the union for purposes of bargaining over only certain subjects. If the employer recognizes the union for bargaining only over salaries, he is required only to provide information relevant to salaries. As stated earlier, there is no legal requirement of recognition, so the employer is required to provide information only on those subjects for which he has agreed to bargain, either voluntarily or because of the union's economic strength.[71] Second, the employer is not required to disclose all information, but only that "without which the union would be to a material extent impeded in bargaining" and "information it would be in accordance with good industrial relations practice for the employer to disclose."[72] The administrative and judicial decisions have held that the first limitation "narrows considerably the test from one of relevance to one of importance"[73] and that the second requirement does not impose the best available practice but only the standard of "a good practitioner" in the industry.[74] Third, the employer is not required to disclose any information that "would cause substantial injury to the firm." This qualification apparently privileges nondisclosure of unit costs of products, marketing or pricing policies, and analysis of investment policies. Fourth, the employer has no affirmative obligation to provide the union with information on a regular basis, but only to provide it at the union's request.[75]

The duty to disclose raises a special problem when the information is confidential or secrecy needs to be maintained for other reasons. In the United States and Great Britain, the solution is to allow the employer to withhold the information. In Germany and Sweden, by contrast, where the duty to disclose is much broader and hence the problem is more acute, the solution is not to deprive the works council or union of the information, but to impose an obligation on those receiving the information to preserve its confidentiality.[76]

The Commission of the European Economic Community has proposed a Draft Directive—the "Vredeling" proposal—which would give employees extensive information and consultation rights in large complex enterprises employing more than one thousand employees. This proposal has been extensively debated, but it has not yet been adopted.[77]

The marked differences in the duty of the employer to disclose information follow the lines distinguishing between adversarial and collaborative labor relations systems. When employees are viewed as members of the enterprise and unions or works councils as social partners in the enterprise, their right to full information concerning the activities, plans, and financial affairs of the enterprise on a continuing basis follows naturally—indeed, it is deemed essential for the spirit and substance of collaboration. Even in an adversarial relation, full disclosure might be thought to lead to more rational and objective bargaining; production costs and profit figures in particular could make the union's demands more realistic instead of endangering jobs and could even make the union more receptive to the changes required to enable the enterprise to survive. However, the emphasis present in American law on viewing the parties as adversaries with opposing interests—each seeking gains at the other's expense—makes it seem inappropriate to require one party to provide information which the other may use to its advantage.

Termination of Employment

The most significant impact on employees of business changes such as plant closures, relocations, robotization, and reorganizations is the termination of those whose jobs disappear. On this, the law in the United States has little to say. The employment-at-will doctrine leaves the employer free to terminate any number at any time without notice or severance pay. Other countries do not give the employer such a free hand, but rather impose a series of procedural and substantive obligations.[78]

First, the employer may be required to give notice of any such changes to public officials and, in some cases, to obtain their approval. For example, in Great Britain, the employer must give advance notice to the Department of Employment of a proposed dismissal of ten or more employees within a thirty-day period.[79] In West Germany, the employer is required to notify the employment office without delay when foreseeable changes in the establishment within the next twelve months are likely to lead to collective dismissals or other staff reduction. The employer is barred from carrying out any such actions until one month after notice unless the employment office approves an earlier date, and the office may postpone the dismissals for an additional month.[80] In France and the Netherlands, all dismissals for economic reasons require authorization by the labor office, and it may refuse or delay permission if the workers have poor prospects of finding jobs and if the employer's need is not especially urgent.[81]

Second, the employer may be required to inform and consult with the employees' representative prior to effecting collective dismissals. Notice and commencement of consultation in Great Britain must be "at the earliest opportunity" but, in the absence of "special circumstances," at least thirty days in advance if ten or more are to be dismissed and ninety days if the number is one hundred or more.[82] Dismissals are void in Germany unless the works council is first consulted, and this must be done before the employment office is notified and before employees are given the required notice of dismissal, which may be as much as three months prior to dismissal.[83] In France, the works committee must be notified at least fifteen days before a request for authorization to dismiss may be filed.[84]

Third, the individual employees to be dismissed must be given advance notice. This is required in almost every country for all dismissals, whether individual or collective. The length of notice varies between countries, and within each country the length of notice typically increases with length of service. In Japan, the notice period is a flat thirty days.[85] In Great Britain, it is one week after four weeks of employment up to two years, and one week per year of service thereafter, up to a maximum of twelve weeks.[86] In Germany, it is scaled from two weeks during the first five years of service to three months after twenty years.[87] In Belgium, the notice period varies not only with the length of service, but also with the category of work and salary so that a high salaried white collar worker may be entitled to as much as two years' notice.[88] In Sweden, the length of notice is not based on length of service but on age, with an employee at age twenty-five entitled to two months' notice and an employee over forty-five to six months' notice.[89]

Fourth, the employee given notice of dismissal may be entitled in some countries such as Sweden, Germany, and Great Britain to time off from work with pay to seek new employment. This is generally limited to two or three days' pay.[90]

Fifth, the employer may be restricted in selecting the employees to be dismissed. The Swedish statute establishes a simple seniority standard, but this can be modified by collective agreement to allow dismissal of older employees eligible for early retirement.[91] The German statute, similar to measures in other countries, requires a more complex selection. Dismissal is ''socially unjustified'' if personal and social factors are not considered. Not only length of service, but age, family responsibilities, and ability to find other work must be considered. There is no formula for the weights to be given to the various factors, but guidelines can be established by codetermination with the works council.[92] The only limit on the British employer's selection is one of bare reasonableness—that it not be one which no reasonable management could make, and that it not discriminate on the basis or race or sex. This leaves the employer with essentially a free hand.[93]

Sixth, the employer may be required to pay those employees who are dismissed some form of severance pay. The most notable example is the British Redundancy Payments Act. Although not applicable to all dismissals due to economic conditions and technological changes, it is generally applicable to plant closures, relocations, and other business changes discussed here. The amount of the redundancy or severance pay is based on the employee's age, length of service, and rate of pay—for each year of service between age twenty-two and forty, one week's pay; and for each year between age forty and sixty-five, one and one-half week's pay, with a maximum of twenty years used in the calculation. Benefits for employees over sixty-four (sixty for women) are reduced by one-twelfth each month so that employees of retirement age receive no severance pay. The payment is made by the employer who is then given a rebate from the Redundancy Fund, which is financed by employer contributions.[94]

Germany has no general severance pay requirement, but, as discussed earlier, when business changes have substantial impact on employees, the employer is required to work out a social compensation plan with the works council. The major element of that plan is severance pay for the employees who are dismissed, and the amount may be a year or more pay for an older employee of long service.

Severance pay becomes in substance a legal requirement because, if the employer and works council cannot agree, a tripartite commission makes a legally binding determination.[95]

Although employers are generally given wide discretion in determining how many employees within each category are needed, staff reductions are nevertheless subject to limitation. In France, the labor office may refuse to authorize dismissals because the severance pay or employer's efforts to find other places in the enterprise for affected employees are considered inadequate. It will authorize dismissals where the employer is in economic difficulties, but refuse to authorize any dismissal that would simply increase profits when the displaced employees would have little chance of finding jobs.[96] The German dismissal law treats as socially unjustified the dismissal of an employee if there is available in the same plant or another plant in the enterprise work which the employee can perform with reasonable retraining and experience. Provisions for transfers and retraining are customary in social plans for partial closures and relocations.[97]

The European Economic Community in 1978 adopted a Council Directive on collective redundancies, which is binding on the ten member states.[98] It sets forth the minimum protection to be given employees by the laws of the member states. Briefly, the directive requires that the employer shall first consult with the workers' representative "with a view to reaching agreement," and these negotiations shall cover at least the ways of avoiding the collective redundancies or reducing the number of workers affected. The employer is then required to notify the competent public authority and report to it the results of consultation with the workers' representative. The redundancies are not to take effect until at least thirty days after notice. This period is to be used by the public officials "to seek solutions in the problems raised by the proposed redundancies." The directive is obviously directed only to consultation and efforts to mitigate the effects of redundancies; it apparently does not reach the question of notice to the employee, time off to seek other work, the selection of employees, or severance pay.

In Japan, the process of work force reduction takes a significantly different form because of the institution of lifetime employment, which is not considered a legal status but a social practice. The need to reduce the work force can often be accomplished by dismissal of part-time or temporary workers (those who do not have lifetime employment and who, in larger establishments, may constitute from 20 to 30 percent of the work force), by terminating subcontracting and giving the work to employees, and by eliminating overtime. If this does not suffice, some lifetime employees may be assigned to other companies which are affiliated, or even other industries where they are needed, with the employer making up any differential in pay; or the plant may be temporarily closed with the employees receiving substantially full pay. If such measures prove inadequate, selected lifetime employees are asked to resign "voluntarily." These are commonly selected among the youngest, the oldest, and those judged to be the least productive. Those who resign are given "retirement pay," which is based on the rate of pay and the length of service. This varies among employers but often is approximately one month's pay for each year of service. With the aid of these devices, employers can avoid any formal dismissal of lifetime employees even though the overall work force may, in fact, be halved. None of this is required by law; it is a matter of practice, with the retirement or severance pay sometimes fixed by collective agreement.[99]

It must be emphasized that, in every country, the legal rules prescribe only minimum requirements, and collective agreements commonly place additional limitations on employers. The length of notice to be given dismissed employees is often lengthened; rationalization agreements in Germany make it nearly impossible to dismiss employees over fifty years of age with ten or fifteen years of service; and British unions regularly negotiate for more than the statutory redundancy pay.[100]

The contrast between the protection against termination provided in other countries and that provided in the United States is glaringly obvious. Few collective agreements in the United States provide as much protection as the legal minimum in these other countries. This difference runs deeper than legal rules; it is rooted in basic conceptions of the employment relation. The employment-at-will doctrine is not followed in other countries because it is contrary to underlying conceptions and values. Protection against termination is rooted, in part, in acceptance that an employee has a property right in his job; beyond that, it is recognition that an employee is a member of the enterprise. This may be expressed in different ways. The British redundancy law has as its express purpose making employees more willing to accept needed economic and technological changes. But this was an acknowledgment that the workers had an undeniable claim against the enterprise for their past contributions and that they would use economic force to assert that claim. Severance pay under German social plans is viewed not as payment for economic loss but as payment for loss of membership in the work group and the enterprise. The use of plant occupations to block mass terminations, in countries as diverse as France and Japan, has roots in the same sense of membership in and claim against the enterprise. The unwillingness of law enforcement officials to take action against this plainly illegal conduct reveals social acceptance of the underlying view.

These underlying conceptions of a property right in the job and membership in the enterprise impose on the employer a responsibility for the employees beyond payment for labor performed. The employment relation is viewed as a continuing relation, which is not to be severed when that can be avoided and then only with compensation for the severance. Not every country, of course, recognizes in full measure these conceptions of the employment relation and the obligations which follow. But it is the formal recognition of these conceptions and the values they express which makes the law in other countries so very different from that in the United States.

Successorship Obligations

When a business is transferred in the United States, the relevant labor law is concerned almost exclusively with collective bargaining—the obligations to recognize the union and to observe the collective agreements. The rights of individual employees are limited to unpaid wages, accrued vacations, and, possibly, severance pay and pension benefits. In the absence of collective bargaining, there are no significant labor law problems because employment at will gives both the transferor and the transferee a nearly completely free hand.

In other countries, the questions center around the continuing obligations under the individual contract of employment and the statutory protection of individual employees against termination. The impact of the transfer on the status of the employees' representative and on the collective agreement is a secondary concern.

Great Britain. Under traditional contract principles, transfer of the enterprise dissolves the employment contract. The employment contract is legally viewed as creating a personal relationship between the employer and the employee. The rights are nonassignable and the duties, nondelegable. This was the English common law rule. Other countries, however, have evolved modifications of this principle, particularly in commercial and industrial employment,[101] and it no longer governs British labor law, which is now subject to the EEC Council Directive of 1971.[102]

Sweden. Swedish law starts from the individual contract model so that transfer of the business terminates the employment contract. Under the Employment Protection Act of 1974, dismissals can be only for "objective cause," but that includes, of course, lack of work. When the employer transfers the business, he no longer has work to be performed, so dismissal is for "objective cause." However, the transferee employer is viewed as a successor with respect to the employee's seniority rights, so that Section 25 of the Act entitles the dismissed employee to preferential hiring if any vacancies occur in the business within one year. If the successor employer hires any new employees, he must first hire those of the transferor, and they are entitled to seniority rights from the date they were hired by the transferor.[103] The collective agreement, under Section 28 of the Codetermination Act of 1976, continues to be applicable as against the new employer, unless he is already bound by another collective agreement. The union, however, may terminate the collective agreement by giving notice of termination.[104]

European Community Member States. The general principles applicable to the ten members of the EEC are stated in the Council Directive, adopted in 1977 on safeguarding the employees' rights in transfers of undertakings.[105] The directive is applicable to transfers of all or part of a business, whether by sale of assets or merger. The obligations imposed on the employers may be outlined as follows.

1. *Duty to Inform and Consult with Representatives of Employees*. Both the

transferor and the transferee are required to inform the representatives of their respective employees affected by the transfer of the legal, social, and economic implications of the transfer for the employees and the measures contemplated for them. The information must be given "in good time before the transfer and the employees are affected." If either the transferor or the transferee envisions measures such as dismissal or reassignment of employees, he must consult with the representatives of his employees "in good time with a view to seeking agreement."

2. *Continuation of Employee Representatives*. If the business preserves its autonomy, the status and function of the employee representatives is preserved. The union or works council continues unchanged.

3. *Right to Continued Employment*. The transfer shall not itself constitute grounds for dismissal by either the transferor or transferee. Dismissals, however, may take place if there are economic, technical, or organizational reasons which would require changes in the work force.

4. *Continuation of Employment Contract Rights and Obligations*. The transferor's rights and obligations under the contract of employment shall be transferred to the transferee. Member states may, in addition, provide that the transferor shall continue to be liable for all obligations.

5. *Continuation of Obligations under the Collective Agreement*. The transferee is obligated to continue to observe the terms and conditions of the collective agreement applicable to the transferor. Employee rights under supplementary disability, retirement, or survivors' benefits under employer pension plans are not covered by these provisions, but the member states are urged to adopt measures to protect those rights.

6. *Summary*. The core of the EEC Directive is rejection of the traditional contract principle that rights and obligations in the employment relation are not transferable. Transfer of the business does not sever the relationship; the employer's obligations under the individual contract of employment and the collective agreement are transferred with the business to the successor. The relation continues substantially as if there had been no change in employers. Refusal of the successor to continue an employee is an unfair dismissal for which the successor employer is liable unless there are economic, technical, or organizational reasons for termination. If there are such reasons, then, under the German social plans and the British redundancy pay provisions, for example, the transferor employer is liable for severance pay. Employees who are continued on by the successor are not entitled to severance pay, but their length of service continues unbroken from the original date of hiring by the transferor. The employment relationship is, in a sense, with the establishment rather than with the employer.

CONCLUSIONS

The comparison between labor law in the United States and the law in Western Europe and Japan applicable in situations of business change which cause dislocation of large number of workers can be summarized rather simply.

In the United States, the law leaves the employer largely unrestrained and unburdened in plant closures, plant relocations, and transfers of business. In the absence of a collective agreement, which is the case for three-fourths of the workers, the employer can close, move, or sell the plant and dismiss the employees without any notice, any severance pay, or any obligation to offer them openings in the relocated or transferred plant. Even with a collective agreement, the employer need not notify the union in advance and need not explain or justify its reasons for its action. The employer is required to bargain about the effects of a decision, but only after the decision and at a time when the union may have little or no bargaining power. Most collective agreements will require only short notice to the employees, with little or no severance pay or relocation rights. Indeed, the employer can, by relocating or selling the plant, reduce the collective agreement to a scrap of paper and strip the union of bargaining rights in the middle of a contract term.

In Western Europe, other than Britain, the employees' representative (union or works council) has continuous knowledge of the employer's financial condition so as to be warned of plant closure, relocation, or transfer. The employer is required to notify and to negotiate with the representative in advance, either concerning the decision itself or its effects. In every country, the employer is required to negotiate with the union prior to notifying employees of the intent to dismiss, and employees must be given notice substantially in advance of dismissal. Other than in Britain, the employer must try to find other jobs within the enterprise for dismissed workers, and, if the plant is relocated, employees have prior rights to jobs in the relocated plants. In most countries, those dismissed will be entitled to substantial severance or redundancy pay. When the business is transferred, the collective agreement and seniority and other employment rights continue in the transferred business.

This comparison bespeaks a fundamental difference in the nature of the employment relation: the rights of an employee in his job, the responsibility of the employer for his employees, the interest of the employee in the enterprise, and the legitimate role of the employees' representative. In perhaps oversimplified terms, the worker in the United States is legally viewed essentially as a supplier of labor bought and sold as a commodity on the market. In most other countries, the employee is legally viewed as a member of the enterprise with a continuing relationship, which entitles the employees to a voice in the enterprise through his or her representative and which imposes on the enterprise continuing responsibilities for the employee. Employment is not viewed as a purchase and sale of labor but as an established relationship of the employee within and as a part of the enterprise.

NOTES

1. Blades, "Employment at Will v. Individual Freedom: On Limiting the Abusive Exercise of Employer Power," 67 Colum. L. Rev. 1404 (1967); Summers, "Individual

Protection against Unjust Dismissal: Time for a Statute,'' 62 Va. L. Rev. 481 (1976); Note, ''Implied Contract Rights to Job Security,'' 26 Stan. L. Rev. 335 (1974).

2. Existing data make possible only an estimate of the proportion of employed workers covered by collective agreements. The Census Population Survey of 1984 shows that 19.1 percent of wage and salary workers are union members. Adams, ''Changing Employment Patterns of Organized Workers,'' 108 Monthly Lab. Rev., Feb. 1985, at 25, 26. It is generally assumed that the number covered by collective agreements is somewhat larger.

3. Linzer, ''The Decline of Assent: At-Will Employment as a Case Study of the Breakdown of Private Law Theory,'' 20 Ga. L. Rev. 323 (1986); Comment, ''Wrongful Termination of Employees at Will: The California Trend,'' 78 Nw. U.L. Rev. 259 (1983).

4. P. Selznik, Law, Society and Industrial Justice 134–36 (1969).

5. Sector 203(a) of ERISA, 29 U.S.C. § 1056(a) establishes maximum periods for vesting, but an employee who is terminated before completing ten years of service could forfeit all pension rights. The Tax Reform Act of 1986 has now reduced the maximum vesting period to five years.

6. Estreicher & Wolff, Report of Committee on Labor and Employment Law, ''At-Will Employment and the Problem of Unjust Dismissal,'' 36 Record of the Assn. of the Bar of the City of N.Y. 170, 175–80 (April 1981); Estreicher, ''Unjust Dismissal Laws: Some Cautionary Notes,'' 33 Am. J. Comp. L. 310 (1985); Hepple, ''Security of Employment,'' in Comparative Labour Law and Industrial Relations, ch. 20 (R. Blanpain & F. Millard eds. 1982).

7. A. Whitehill & S. Takezawa, The Other Worker, ch. 12 (1968).

8. NLRB statistics show that, during fiscal year 1981, 184,933 votes were cast for union representation. In that same year, back pay was awarded to 26,091 workers who had been discriminated against for union activity. See 46th NLRB Ann. Rep. 13, 18 (1981).

9. Cordova, ''Collective Bargaining,'' in Comparative Labour Law and Industrial Relations 307, 312–19 (R. Blanpain ed. 1986).

10. Schmidt & Neal, ''Collective Agreements and Collective Bargaining,'' in 15 International Encyclopedia of Comparative Law, Labour Law, ch. 12, at 17–18, 36–37, 44–45, 63–70 (R. Hepple ed. 1984); Cordova, supra note 9, at 327–28.

11. Summers, ''Worker Participation in the U.S. and West Germany: A Comparative Study from an American Perspective,'' 28 Amer. J. Comp. L. 367, 377 (1980).

12. Schmidt & Neal, supra note 10, at 15, 44–45, 68–69.

13. W. Kolvenbach, Employee Councils in European Companies (1978); Merrifield, ''Worker Participation in Decisions within Undertakings,'' 5 Comp. Lab. L.J. 1 (1982).

14. Works Constitution Act, 1972, translated in Federal Minister of Labour and Social Affairs, Codetermination in the Federal Republic of Germany 103–92 (1980).

15. Ricardi, ''Worker Participation in Decisions within Undertakings in the Federal Republic of Germany,'' 5 Comp. Lab. L.J. 23 (1982); Summers, supra note 11.

16. W. Kolvenbach, supra note 13.

17. Summers, ''Worker Participation in Sweden and the United States: Some Comparisons from an American Perspective,'' 133 U. of Pa. L. Rev. 175, 181 (1984).

18. W. Daniels & N. Millward, Workplace Industrial Relations in Britain (1983); E. Batstone, I. Boraston & S. Frenkel, Shop Stewards in Action (1977).

19. P. Davies & M. Freedland, Labour Law: Text and Materials 124–27 (2d ed. 1984).

20. Suna, "Recent Trends in Collective Bargaining Agreements in Japan," 18 Japan Lab. Bull. No. 7 (1979).

21. T. Hanami, Labour Law and Industrial Relations in Japan 103 (1979); Shirai, "A Theory of Enterprise Unionism," in Contemporary Industrial Relations in Japan 119 (T. Shirai ed. 1983).

22. R. Cole, Work Mobility and Participation 120 (1979).

23. Glendon, "French Labor Law Reform 1982–3: The Struggle for Collective Bargaining," 32 Am. J. Comp. L. 449, 459–65 (1984); Hetzler & Schienstock, "Federal Republic of Germany," in Toward Industrial Democracy 40–42 (B. Roberts ed. 1979).

24. Lewis, "The Role of the Law in Employment Relations," in Labour Law in Britain 20 (R. Lewis ed. 1986).

25. Works Constitution Act, § 74 (1).

26. Roberts, "Introduction," in Toward Industrial Democracy 19–22 (B. Roberts ed. 1979).

27. The Codetermination Act of 1976, translated in Federal Minister of Labour and Social Affairs, Codetermination in the Federal Republic of Germany 7–72 (1980), increased the number of employee representatives on corporate boards of corporations having more than 2,000 employees from one-third to one-half, with the shareholders representatives electing the chairman and the chairman empowered to cast a second vote to break a tie.

28. F. Schmidt, Law and Industrial Relations in Sweden, ch. 6 (1977).

29. Translated in F. Schmidt, id. at 234–45; Victorin, "Co-Determination in Sweden: The Union Way," 2 J. Comp. Corp. L. & Sec. Reg. 111 (1979); Berquist, "Worker Participation in Decisions within Undertakings in Sweden," 5 Comp. Lab. L.J. 65 (1982).

30. "Sweden: Employee Funds Law Enacted," Eur. Ind. Rel. Rev. 120 (Jan. 1984); R. Meidner, Employee Investment Funds (1978).

31. W. Kolvenbach, supra note 13; Merrifield, supra note 13; Hanami "Workers' Participation in the Workshop and the Enterprise," in Comparative Labour Law and Industrial Relations, ch. 14 (R. Blanpain & F. Millard eds. 1982).

32. Report, Committee on Inquiry on Industrial Democracy, cmnd 6706 (London HMSO, 1977); Hepple, "Great Britain," in International Encyclopedia of Labor Law and Industrial Relations 176–77 (R. Blanpain ed. 1980).

33. Summers, supra note 17, at 197–98.

34. Id. at 199.

35. Schmidt, "Conflict and Community in Decision-Making within the Undertaking," 5 Comp. Lab. L.J. 197, 201–5 (1982); Gospel, "Trade Unions and the Obligation to Bargain: An American, Swedish and British Comparison," 21 Brit. J. of Indus. Rel. 343, 347–48 (1983).

36. F. Schmidt, supra note 28, at 147–48.

37. Summers, supra note 17, at 212–13.

38. Act on Board Representation for Employees 1972; F. Schmidt, supra note 28, at 85–86.

39. Summers, supra note 17, at 203–4.

40. Id. at 204.

41. Schmidt, supra note 35, at 199.

42. Summers, "The Usefulness of Unions in a Modern Industrial Society—A Comparative Sketch," 58 Tul. L. Rev. 1409, 1416 (1984).

43. Works Constitution Act, § 74 (1).

44. Ramm, ''Federal Republic of Germany,'' in International Encyclopedia of Labor Law and Industrial Relations 177–81 (R. Blanpain, ed. 1979).

45. Works Constitution Act, §§ 90, 92.

46. Works Constitution Act, §§ 87, 95, 98; Ramm, supra note 44, at 181–86.

47. Works Constitution Act, §§ 111, 112; Dose-Digenopoulos & Holand, ''Dismissal of Employees in the Federal Republic of Germany,'' 48 Mod. L. Rev. 539, 546 (1985).

48. Bosch, ''West Germany,'' in Managing Workforce Reduction: An International Survey 164, 179–84 (M. Cross ed. 1985).

49. Id. at 183.

50. Arbeit und Recht, Feb. 1985, at 55; Plett & Gessner, ''Insolvency and the Worker: The Case of the Federal Republic of Germany,'' 12 Int'l. J. Sociol. L. 307 (1984).

51. Davies, ''Employee Representation on Company Boards and Participation in Corporate Planning,'' 38 Mod. L. Rev. 254, 267 (1975).

52. Daheim, ''The Practice of Codetermination on the Management Level of German Enterprises,'' in Participation in Management (W. Albeda ed. 1977); Report of the Biedenkopf Commission, ''Codetermination in the Enterprise'' (1970).

53. Dickens & Bain, ''A Duty to Bargain? Union Recognition and Information Disclosures,'' in Labor Law in Britain, ch. 3 (R. Lewis ed. 1986); L. Wedderburn, The Worker and the Law 278–89 (1986).

54. P. Davies & M. Freedland, supra note 19, at 127–37; Gospel, supra note 35, at 349.

55. P. Davies & M. Freedland, supra note 19, at 792–817; L. Wedderburn, supra note 53, at 553–71.

56. P. Davis & M. Freedland, supra note 19, at 804–05, 816–17.

57. Id. at 198.

58. Safety Representatives and Safety Committees Regulations 1977, SI 1977, no. 500; P. Davies & M. Freedland, supra note 19, at 230–37.

59. Anderman, ''Unfair Dismissals and Redundancies,'' in Labour Law in Britain 439–42 (R. Lewis ed. 1986); P. Davies & M. Freedland, supra note 19, at 237–43; L. Wedderburn, supra note 53, at 294–98.

60. Hepple, ''Transfer of Undertakings (Protection of Employment) Regulations,'' 11 Indus. L. J. 29, 38–40 (1982); P. Davies & M. Freedland, supra note 19, at 250–52.

61. Gennard, ''Great Britain,'' in Workforce Reductions in Undertakings 107, 128–29 (E. Yemin ed. 1982).

62. Trade Union Law, 1949, translated in Ministry of Labour, Labour Laws of Japan (1980).

63. Sugeno, ''The Coexistence of Rival Unions at Undertakings and Unfair Labor Practices,'' 23 Japan Lab. Bull. No. 10 (1984); Sugeno, ''Collective Bargaining with Rival Unions—The Supreme Court's More Significant Second Ruling,'' 24 Japan Lab. Bull No. 10 (1985).

64. Klee, ''Worker Participation in Japan: The Temporary Employee and Enterprise Unionism,'' 7 Comp. Lab. L. J. 365 (1986); Hagizawa, ''Procedures and Structures for Collective Bargaining at the Enterprise and Plant Levels in Japan'' 7 Comp. Lab. L. J. 277 (1986).

65. Hanami, ''Japan,'' in Workforce Reductions in Undertakings 173–76 (E. Yemin ed. 1982); Okamoto, ''Japan,'' in Toward Industrial Democracy 197–210 (B. Roberts ed. 1979).

66. T. Hanami, supra note 21, at 126.

67. Shirai, ''A Theory of Enterprise Unionism,'' in Contemporary Industrial Rela-

tions in Japan 135–40 (T. Shirai ed. 1983); Shirai, ''Characteristics of Japanese Management,'' id. at 369, 374–77.

68. Works Constitution Act, §§ 106–10.

69. Codetermination Act of 1976, § 19; Fahlbeck, ''The Swedish Act on Joint Regulation of Working Life,'' in Law and the Weaker Party 145, 156–59 (A. Neal ed. 1981).

70. Dickens & Bain, supra note 53, at 96–99.

71. Bellace, ''Disclosure of Information to Unions in the United States and Britain,'' in Proceedings of the Fiftieth Anglo-American Conference on Law, in London, England (1982); Bellace & Gospel, ''Disclosure of Information to Trade Unions: A Comparative Perspective,'' 122 Int'l. Lab. Rev. 57, 63–67 (1983).

72. Employment Protection Act, 1975, § 17(1).

73. CAC Award no. 78/353, Daily Telegraph Ltd. and Institute of Journalists. (June 19, 1976).

74. CAC Award no. 79/484, Standard Telephones & Cables, Ltd. and Ass'n of Scientific, Technical and Managerial Staffs (Sept. 3, 1979).

75. Bellace, supra note 71, at 13.

76. The German Works Constitution Act, § 120, makes it a crime to divulge trade or business secrets which the employer has expressly stated are to be kept confidential. The Swedish Codetermination Act, § 56, provides that any employee who breaches the duty of confidentiality shall be liable in damages.

77. Docksey, ''Employee Information and Consultation Rights in Member States of the European Communities,'' 7 Comp. Lab. L. 32 (1985); Aaron, ''Plant Closings: American and Comparative Perspectives,'' 59 Chi.-Kent L. Rev. 941, 958–60 (1984); R. Blanpain, F. Blanquet, F. Herman & A. Mouty, The Vredeling Proposal: Information and Consultation of Employees in Multinational Enterprises (1983).

78. See Estreicher, supra note 6; ''Termination of Employment on Initiative of the Employer,'' 5 Comp. Lab. L.J. 221 (1982) (Reports of 10th International Congress of International Society of Labour Law and Social Security, General Report, Britain, Israel, Romania, Singapore, United States, ILO).

79. Gennard, supra note 61, at 107, 109–10.

80. Bosch, supra note 48, at 164, 177–78.

81. Pelissier, ''France,'' in Workforce Reductions in Undertakings 64–66 (E. Yemin ed. 1982); Blanpain, ''Structural Adjustment and Industrial Relations: Labour Law Aspects,'' 10 Lab. & Soc'y 175, 184–85 (1985).

82. L. Wedderburn, supra note 53, at 294–98; Gennard, supra note 79, at 108–09.

83. Works Constitution Act, §§ 92, 111; Dose-Digenopoulos & Holand, supra note 47, at 544–46; Sengenberger, ''Federal Republic of Germany,'' in Workforce Reductions in Undertakings 88–89 (E. Yemin ed. 1982).

84. Pelissier, supra note 81, at 60.

85. Labour Standards Act (Japan), § 20; T. Hanami, supra note 21, at 81.

86. Employment Protection Act of 1975 (Great Britain) § 49 (1); Gennard, supra note 61, at 110–11.

87. Sengenberger, supra note 83, at 86–87.

88. Blanpain, ''Belgium,'' in International Encyclopedia of Labor Law and Industrial Relations 116–17 (R. Blanpain ed. 1985).

89. Employment Security Act of 1974, Sweden, § 11.

90. Yemin, ''Comparative Survey,'' in Workforce Reductions in Undertakings 26 (E. Yemin ed. 1982).

91. Employment Security Act of 1974, Sweden, § 14.

92. Sengenberger, supra note 83, at 98–99.

93. S. Anderman, Unfair Dismissal 199–210 (3d ed. 1985).

94. Daniel, ''The United Kingdom,'' in Managing Workforce Reductions: An International Survey 67, 69 (M. Cross ed. 1985).

95. Bosch, supra note 48, at 164, 179–84.

96. Pelissier, supra note 81, at 64–65.

97. Weiss, ''Germany,'' in Encyclopedia for Labor Law and Industrial Relations (R. Blanpain ed. 1987).

98. Council Directive, 75/129/EEC, 17 Feb. 1975, on Collective Redundancies.

99. Anthony, ''Japan,'' in Managing Workforce Reduction: An International Survey 92 (M. Cross ed. 1981); Inagami, ''Employment Adjustments in Japan,'' 25 Japan Lab. Bull. No. 7 (1984); Koike, ''Internal Labor Markets: Workers in Large Firms,'' in Contemporary Industrial Relations in Japan 46–50 (T. Shirai ed. 1983); Hanami, supra note 65, at 167–72, 178–80.

100. Bosch, supra note 48, at 164, 169–70, 185–86; Daniel, supra note 94, at 67, 72–74, 80–82.

101. Eklund, ''A Look at Labour Law in the Context of Transfers of Undertakings,'' 7 Comp. Lab. L. J. 71 (1985); Hepple, supra note 60, at 29.

102. S. Anderman, supra note 93, ch. 14; P. Davies & M. Freedland, supra note 19, at 583–87.

103. Eklund, supra note 101, at 82–86.

104. F. Schmidt, supra note 28, at 144.

105. Council Directive, 77/187/EEC, 14 Feb. 1977, on the Safeguarding of Employees' Rights in the Event of Transfers of Undertakings, Businesses or Parts of Businesses.

PART II
TRANSACTIONAL PERSPECTIVES

9
SALE OF ASSETS, MERGERS, AND ACQUISITIONS: A MANAGEMENT VIEW

Marvin Dicker

Editors' Note. The form of the corporate transaction may well determine, Mr. Dicker maintains, whether bargaining representatives must continue to be recognized and collective agreements must still be observed. The author finds that a merger or stock purchase, in contrast to an assets acquisition, will not offer either management or union an opportunity to avoid a preexisting collective bargaining agreement. He describes and analyzes, in the case of assets transfers, the rules by which a successor's contractual and bargaining liabilities are determined. He also considers the extent to which business transformation decisions may affect the NLRB's presumptions as to the incumbent union's majority status. Finally, he discusses ERISA implications.

Marvin Dicker is a member of Proskauer, Rose, Goetz & Mendelsohn, New York, N.Y.

The author wishes to thank Thomas S. Rosenthal for the extraordinarily hard work he put into helping prepare this chapter.

A determination of the rights and obligations of a company involved in a corporate transaction—from the perspectives of both the selling and purchasing entities—requires a careful analysis of the overall impact on labor-management relations. Unfortunately, although the corporate and tax consequences of a transaction are examined extensively, all too often the labor consequences are accorded little or no consideration. By focusing on the labor-management relations dimension at an early stage, and by continuing to analyze those considerations during and after the corporate transformation, management will best be able to structure the transaction in a manner beneficial to its interests. Thus, careful planning is necessary if management desires control in determining its labor relations in the new or restructured corporate entity.

The sale, merger, or acquisition of a corporation offers an opportunity to reassess the state of labor relations and to implement changes, if desired. Because the form a corporate transaction takes will critically influence management's ability to structure its subsequent labor relations, management must carefully assess its goals and needs: whether it wishes to maintain or avoid a collective-bargaining agreement, to recognize and bargain with an existing union or to avoid union obligations so as to bring about a cost-effective and efficient labor situation. In formulating these goals, it should learn as much as it can about the history of labor-management relations in the business enterprise, the current state of relations with employees, and the qualities and experience of the employee complement. This will inform the decision whether to structure the transaction so as to maintain the labor force, to utilize only those employees management deems effective or efficient, or to avoid the existing complement altogether.

Management should carefully evaluate the corporation as it exists prior to the transformation. The seller may command a higher acquisition price if labor relations are peaceful or existing collective-bargaining agreements are advantageous. The purchaser should carefully evaluate whether or not the corporation is successful, as the success of the ongoing concern may be attributable, at least in part, to stable labor relations. On the other hand, if the business is struggling, the purchaser may want to alter existing relations. The purchaser should also assess its financial position and that of its predecessor; it is possible that, if the seller obtained labor concessions because of troubled business, the purchaser will want to assume the concessions by adopting its predecessor's agreements instead of initiating new terms or conditions of employment.

These issues represent just a sampling of the labor considerations to be evaluated when embarking upon a transaction. The practical application of these and other issues during the transactional process enables management to shape an approach which takes advantage of favorable labor considerations and to avoid any entanglements, legal and otherwise, that could significantly alter the expected labor consequences of the deal.

THE CHOICE BETWEEN STOCK PURCHASE AND ASSETS PURCHASE

Stock Acquisition

An essential consideration in the acquisition of a company is whether to assume the seller's collective agreement with its union. As a general rule, the acquisition of a majority of the stock of an enterprise is not sufficient to alter the bargaining obligations of that business. Thus, since the corporation remains unchanged after a stock purchase, that corporation is obligated to bargain with the preexisting union and to adhere to the existing labor agreement.[1] As explained by the NLRB, "the stock transfer involves no break or hiatus between two legal entities, but is, rather, the continuing existence of a legal entity, albeit under new ownership.[2] Although there may be special exceptions to the general rule (where, for example, the enterprise undergoes a significant organizational or structural transformation),[3] a purchaser of stock is presumptively bound by its predecessor's collective agreement.

This presumption offers the purchasing entity an opportunity to structure the transaction so as to optimize its labor relations impact. Where the preexisting agreement is advantageous or is a desirable asset of the enterprise to be acquired, the purchaser is well advised to make a stock acquisition.[4] It is conceivable that a union might attempt to repudiate the existing agreement when the purchaser takes over, especially in those situations in which the purchaser has a "deeper pocket" than the seller or the seller had obtained labor concessions because of its financial plight. The purchaser therefore is advised to inform the union before the transaction is completed that the existing collective-bargaining agreement will be maintained after the transfer. If the union does not object at the time it is informed, it may be estopped at a later date from attempting to repudiate the agreement. If the union does raise a timely objection, it does not necessarily gain any substantive rights, and the purchaser at least is on notice that the transaction's labor consequences may not be as beneficial as otherwise indicated. Although the matter is not free from doubt, the present state of law suggests that the purchase of stock will allow the purchaser to maintain the existing collective-bargaining agreement,[5] with or without union acknowledgment. Thus, in a stock purchase, additional language in the purchase agreement or a separate agreement with the union would ordinarily not be necessary.

If, however, the existing collective-bargaining agreement is a liability or if it contains onerous terms and conditions of employment, a stock acquisition may not be advisable, and the purchaser should consider structuring the transaction in a manner that allows it to set initial terms and conditions of employment before hiring any employees. If a stock acquistion is the only reasonable transactional alternative and if the seller's preexisting labor relations are not beneficial, the purchaser may attempt to condition the sale on the seller's negotiation of a new collective-bargaining agreement. Alternatively, if the purchaser has an option to structure the transaction as either a stock acquisition or an asset acquisition, the employees' bargaining representative could be informed of the impending transaction and asked to negotiate a new bargaining agreement in exchange for a promise to adhere to the agreement after the corporate transformation. If the union refuses and the purchaser acquires the assets only of the seller, it probably will be able to avoid the seller's collective agreement.

Obviously, the approach to be taken and the business decisions to be made must be determined on a case-by-case basis. Important considerations include whether the purchaser wants to retain the collective-bargaining agreement and whether the purchaser wants to keep the existing work force. Dealing with the union before the transaction is consummated will depend upon a host of factors, such as the need for secrecy in the transaction, the relationship between the seller and the union, and the relationship that the purchaser may have with the seller's union or other unions with which the purchaser may have to deal.

Assets Acquisition

The purchaser of the assets, as opposed to the stock, of a business is normally not required to assume or adopt the seller's existing labor agreement. Whether the purchaser is obligated to recognize and bargain with a union representing the seller's employees is determined by an analysis of the "successorship" doctrine as articulated in court and Board decisions.[6] Generally, when the assets of a unionized enterprise are purchased without an alteration of the basic nature of the business and the personnel formerly employed constitute a majority of the employee complement hired by the buyer, the purchaser may unilaterally set the initial terms and conditions of employment (provided it clearly announces its intentions before hiring the seller's employees).[7] The assets purchaser may be required, however, to recognize and bargain with the union representing the seller's employees.

The existence of a bargaining obligation will turn on whether there is a "substantial continuity of identity in the business enterprise."[8] This inquiry requires an examination of the "totality of the circumstances" to ascertain whether there has been a substantial and material alteration in the employing enterprise.[9]

A key question will be whether the new employer has hired "a majority of its employees from the predecessor." Other factors include:

> [W]hether the business of both employers is essentially the same; whether the employees of the new company are doing the same jobs in the same working conditions under the same supervisors; and whether the new entity has the same production process, produces the same products, and basically has the same body of customers. . . .
>
> In conducting this analysis, the Board keeps in mind the question whether "those employees who have been retained will understandably view their job situations as essentially unaltered." . . . If the employees find themselves in essentially the same jobs after the employer transition and if their legitimate expectations in continued representation by their union are thwarted, their dissatisfaction may lead to labor unrest.[10]

It is thus necessary to conduct a careful assessment of these factors and employee expectations in deciding whether the duty to bargain attaches, when it attaches, and what management can do to influence the scope and nature of its obligations.

FACTORS GOVERNING THE PURCHASER'S DUTY TO BARGAIN

Is There a Successor Majority?

For purposes of successorship status and the concomitant duty to bargain with the seller's union, the most significant factor is "whether a majority of the new employer's bargaining unit employees were members of the predecessor's unit work force at or near the time it ceased operations.''[11] Without a finding of ''majority,'' the purchaser is under no obligation to bargain with the bargaining representative of the seller's employees regardless of the presence of other indicia of enterprise continuity.[12] Indeed, where the predecessor's employees do not constitute a majority of the purchaser's unit work force, the Board may not even bother to analyze the other successorship factors.[13] On the other hand, successorship may be found where continuity of the work force is the only significant factor present.[14]

The existence of a hiatus between the cessation of the former employer's business and the new employer's commencement of operations has been found to be a relevant, if not controlling, factor in the successorship determination. Although a substantial hiatus may suggest that the new employer should not be deemed a successor and is thereby free of a bargaining duty, the decisions so holding generally have also involved a lack of continuity in the work force or a change in production methods, the kind of products manufactured, or the type of market supplied.[15] Where the hiatus has not been accompanied by substantial changes in the work force or its business operations, the new employer has been found to be a successor.[16] Thus, where a two-month hiatus has been accompained either by a change in production methods, products, and customers, or by a bankruptcy, successorship obligations have been rejected.[17] However, even a seven-month hiatus accompanied by evidence that a majority of the purchaser's employees were employed by the predecessor and that little or no change occurred in the enterprise will not defeat successorship obligations.[18]

The time at which a determination is made regarding the continuity of the work force may have a substantial impact on the successorship determination. While the successor majority inquiry often can be made at the time of transfer or when the purchaser assumes operations of the enterprise, there are situations in which the determination is delayed, perhaps because the purchaser is operating at a reduced capacity or is rebuilding a business. The Supreme Court has approved the Board's '' 'substantial and representative complement' rule for fixing the moment when the determination as to the composition of the successor's workforce is to be made.''[19] As the Court stated, in determining whether a substantial and representative complement exists, the Board will consider

> ''whether the job classifications designated for the operation were filled or substantially filled and whether the operation was in normal or substantially normal production'' . . . In addition, it takes into consideration ''the size of the complement on that date and the time expected to elapse before a substantially larger complement would be at work . . . as well as the relative certainty of the employer's expected expansions.''[20]

The purchaser should also be aware that a mere delay in hiring employees in the seller's work force to avoid a bargaining obligation may not necessarily avoid a successorship finding at some later date. The Supreme Court has approved the "continuing demand" rule, namely, "when the union has made a premature demand that has been rejected by the employer, this demand remains in force until the moment when the employer attains the 'substantial and representative complement.' "[21]

Selecting the New Work Force

The purchaser should be careful not to allow union animus to influence its selection of employees. It is not obligated to hire any of the seller's employees, so long as it does not refuse to hire anyone for antiunion reasons.[22] In selecting its employees, the purchaser may not discriminatorily refuse to hire the predecessor's employees either because of union membership or activities or because of the purchaser's desire to avoid unionization. If the union would have enjoyed majority status in the purchaser's employee complement but for the discriminatory refusal to hire, the purchaser probably will be ordered to bargain with the union.[23]

A purchaser may have difficulty in refusing to hire the predecessor's employees who appear to possess the requisite skills and abilities. It may be advisable for the purchaser to establish minimum or standard requirements for the employee complement it seeks to hire. It should also be helpful for the purchaser to obtain from the seller a profile of the seller's employees to aid the purchaser in determining which of the seller's employees it may wish to hire. Moreover, such evidence of a reasoned and objective assessment of the seller's employees may aid in avoiding the appearance of a discriminatory refusal to hire. Of course, the profile will be helpful in any event to the purchaser who presumably seeks to employ a qualified complement of employees and to avoid undesirable employees. The purchaser is therefore advised to obtain such a profile whether or not it seeks to avoid a bargaining obligation.

In setting the terms and conditions of employment offered to employees by the purchaser, consideration should be given to whether such new terms and conditions will encourage or discourage the former employees from applying to the purchaser for employment. For example, a wage and fringe benefits package which is substantially less favorable than that formerly enjoyed by the employees may discourage many employees from taking a position with the new employer.

Overcoming the Presumption of Majority Status

The purchaser should be aware that, even though it may be deemed a successor upon its assumption of the seller's operations, its obligation to recognize and bargain with a union may be extinguished in certain circumstances. Although a union is entitled to an irrebuttable presumption of majority status for the year following its certification as the employees' exclusive-bargaining representative (with that presumption surviving the transfer to a successor employer who has hired a majority from the predecessor's employees),[24] the presumption of continued majority status is rebuttable following the certification year.[25] Thus, the purchaser successor may withdraw recognition if it establishes a good faith doubt of the union's continued majority support based on objective considerations in a context free of unfair labor practices.[26] Of course, if, after the first year of certification, the successor can prove that the union, in fact, does not represent a majority of the unit employees, it may lawfully withdraw recognition.[27]

The bargaining obligation may be substantially influenced by the scope and nature of the purchaser's preexisting business entity. In any merger or consolidation, management of the surviving entity must assess the impact of the transaction upon existing employee bargaining units. If one or more parties to a merger or consolidation is unionized, the transaction may alter the status and size of the bargaining unit. Under certain circumstances, employees of one entity may be "accreted" into an existing bargaining unit. An accretion has been defined as "the incorporation of employees into an already existing larger unit when such a community of interest exists among the entire group that the additional employees have no separate unit identity [and thus are] properly governed by the larger group's choice of bargaining representative."[28]

Several factors inform the accretion inquiry, including (1) actual interchange of employees between the bargaining units, (2) common control or supervision, (3) common control over labor relations, (4) integration of operations, (5) integration of machine and product lines, (6) similarity of working conditions, (7) geographical proximity, (8) collective bargaining history, and (9) the number of employees in the group to be accreted as compared with the existing unit.[29]

The significance of the accretion doctrine to acquisition planning is its impact on the employer's ability to control or influence the representation of its employees. If the enumerated factors weigh against accretion, it is possible that the new enterprise will have two or more bargaining representatives. In such circumstances, management has a concomitant duty to recognize and bargain with each of those representatives. It is possible that, prior to a merger or consolidation, the separate enterprises could negotiate with their employees' representatives a peaceful and beneficial transition. If management of the new enterprise ignores accretion issues, however, it may well find that recognition of a bargaining representative for a group of employees without their consent or insistence that employees of the merged enterprise accrete to the surviving entity's existing bargaining unit constitutes an unfair labor practice.

The merger or consolidation of two or more entities may result in a significant corporate alteration or very little change in the nature of the operation. If there is little change in the nature of the operations or the work force, a previously existing bargaining obligation remains in effect after the transformation, even if the status of the operation is changed and the employees are moved from one facility to another.[30] On the other hand, a previously existing bargaining obligation may cease if the merger or consolidation involves a substantial change in the nature of the new enterprise's operations, such as a consolidation of the administration of previously separate units of employees, centralized control of labor relations, and employee interchange in a physically consolidated operation where all employees are performing similar functions under common terms and conditions of employment. Moreover, if two or more unions represented the employees prior to the transformation, it is possible that an election will be ordered to determine the exclusive representative in a single unit of employees.[31]

A purchaser often will acquire only a small portion of the seller's business. The courts and Board decisions will nevertheless tend to enforce a bargaining obligation as long as a majority of the purchaser's employee complement is made up of the seller's employees, even though that majority was but a small portion of the seller's unit work force.[32] Thus, management must be careful not to assume, merely because its new business is smaller than that of the selling entity, that successorship obligations can be successfully skirted.

Setting the Initial Terms and Conditions of Employment

Although, in most instances, the purchaser unilaterally may set the initial terms and conditions of employment for its employee complement, there are situations in which the purchaser will be obligated to consult with the bargaining representative before establishing those terms and conditions. To avoid this obligation, management is advised to set the terms and conditions of employment and to announce them to the seller's employees prior to the takeover. The purchaser should offer employment only on the terms announced. The more formal and open the announcement and hiring process is, the better the purchaser will be able to withstand a challenge to the new terms and conditions of employment. If the purchaser indicates that employment will continue without change in underlying terms and conditions, it may bind itself to a bargaining obligation under the terms of the predecessor's agreement. Thus, the Supreme Court has said that ''there will be instances in which it is perfectly clear that the new employer plans to retain all of the employees in the unit and in which it will be appropriate to have him initially consult with the employees' bargaining representative before he fixes terms.''[33] The purchaser should not make any empty promises or otherwise allow employees to draw the inference that pay scales will not be altered or that other employment conditions will be maintained. If the purchaser is careless, it may be estopped from invoking its right to establish initial terms and conditions of employment unilaterally.[34]

If the sale of assets is a disguised continuance of the former business enterprise, undertaken so that the seller can avoid its collective agreement with its employees' union, it is likely that the Board will find that the sale of assets is merely a sham transaction and that the ''purchaser'' is an ''alter ego'' of the seller, thereby binding the purchaser to the terms of the seller's collective-bargaining agreement.[35]

The purchaser of assets may, for valid business reasons, choose to recognize the union and assume the seller's collective-bargaining agreement.[36] The purchaser of a successful going concern should consider the advantages of stable labor relations in the same manner as a purchaser of a failing business considers the need to change labor policies. While there seems to be no reported decision as to the right of the purchaser of assets to assume a collective-bargaining agreement over the union's objections, most unions in practice would welcome the assumption of such a contract. Nevertheless, it would seem prudent for the purchaser of assets to announce in advance its intention to assume the contract. A union might well be barred from subsequently objecting if it did not object at the time that the purchaser made its announcement. Of course, the safest course would be to get the union to agree to the assumption of the existing contract at or prior to the purchase.

If the purchaser seeks to set initial terms and conditions of employment unilaterally, it should be careful not to adopt or assume its predecessor's agreement. Generally, clear evidence of consent and intention is needed to bind the purchaser. Adoption has been found where the purchaser of assets has applied the substantive terms of the seller's agreement and has consulted and negotiated with the seller's employees' union.[37] Moreover, if a successor is deemed to have adopted an agreement, it will be required, to the same extent as the predecessor, to bargain about changes in employment practices, such as bonuses, even though the written contract is silent on such matters.[38] Therefore, management should be careful, if it seeks to avoid labor obligations (both those explicitly set forth in the predecessor's agreement and those implicit in the seller's past practice), to announce clearly and unambiguously its intention to set initial terms and conditions of employment different from those in the seller's collective agreement.

REVIEW OF EXISTING LABOR RELATIONS AND LABOR AGREEMENTS

A careful assessment of the predecessor's relations with its employee complement and the predecessor's collective-bargaining agreement not only aids in determining the structure of the corporate transaction, but further gives the parties an opportunity to avoid undue surprise and potential liabilities.

Pending Unfair Labor Practices

If the purchaser acquires a business entity with notice of pending unfair labor practice charges against the predecessor and there is no substantial change in operations, employee complement, or supervisory personnel, the purchaser as a successor will be subject to joint and several liability for its predecessor's actions. Thus, the purchaser will be liable for back pay and may be required to offer unlawfully discharged employees immediate reinstatement to their former or substantially equivalent positions.[39] Successor employers also have been required to provide redress to individual victims of a predecessor's employment discrimination[40] and to comply with the terms of a consent decree entered into by the predecessor.[41] Thus, the purchaser is advised to request from the seller an accounting of potential or unresolved liabilities. The purchaser is then in a position to negotiate for the seller's resolution of pending charges or liabilities or for a purchase price which reflects the possibility that the purchaser will be held accountable for its predecessor's actions.

Successorship Obligations Flowing from the Predecessor's Agreement

Each party to a corporate transaction should analyze the seller's collective-bargaining agreement exhaustively. Collective-bargaining agreements often contain a ''successors and assigns'' clause. Both the seller and the buyer should be aware that, if the buyer does not adopt the collective agreement, the union may be able to forestall the corporate transaction. Courts have enjoined the sale of a business in which the successors and assigns clause of the seller's agreement was not followed. The injunction generally is not issued to enforce the clause, but rather to preserve the status quo by prohibiting the sale (or completion of the sale) of the company pending arbitration over whether the seller breached the successors and assigns clause by selling to a purchaser which does not adopt the collective-bargaining agreement.[42]

It is also possible that the union will seek arbitration against the purchaser on the basis of the Supreme Court's decision in *John Wiley & Sons, Inc. v. Livingston*.[43] The Court there held that an employer was required to arbitrate under a collective-bargaining agreement between the union and another corporation that had merged with the employer.[44]

Wiley was narrowed in *NLRB v. Burns Int'l Security Services, Inc.*, and *Howard Johnson Co. v. Hotel Employees*,[45] where the Supreme Court held that a new employer who simply purchased the predecessor's assets should be permitted to make changes in operations without being bound by the substantive provisions of a preexisting agreement that it had not assumed. There is some lower court authority, however, compelling a successor employer to arbitrate under the terms of a preexisting collective-bargaining agreement it had not assumed.[46] In fact, notwithstanding *Howard Johnson*, there is a risk that arbitration may be ordered where successorship occurs not only by merger but by a purchase of assets, even when the successor expressly refuses to assume the collective-bargaining agreement.[47]

Thus, purchasers and sellers should not be surprised if unions attempt to circumvent or challenge their ability to structure the transaction without union consent. It is possible for the seller to negotiate with the union regarding the effects of the proposed deal.[48] Indeed, the purchaser could condition the sale on the seller's successful negotiation of a close-out agreement with the union. Thus, the seller could offer the employees additional severance pay, extension of fringe benefits, and similar economic sweeteners to induce such a agreement.

A careful examination of the successors and assigns clause itself should provide management with enough information to determine whether the clause will be construed to require the seller to obtain a purchaser to assume the seller's collective-bargaining agreement. A bare successors and assigns clause normally will not bind the seller because the seller should not be made to account for the decisions of the buyer unless the collective agreement identifies that responsibility in no uncertain terms. Most arbitrators would subscribe to the following:

> there is a significant difference between a seller who agrees that the contract shall be binding upon its successors and assigns and the seller who (a) agrees to continued liability if the buyer does not assume the agreement or, (b) obligates itself to find a buyer who will assume the agreement as a condition of sale, or (c) covenants to refrain from performing any act which evades or avoids the terms of the agreement.[49]

Although the seller normally will be required to stand behind the contract with respect to accrued earnings and other benefits due employees through the date of sale, the seller probably will not be found in breach of contract where the purchaser does not assume the contract unless the successors and assigns clause imposes an "active duty" requirement upon the seller. As one arbitrator has noted: "The obligation to require assumption is imposed if it is set out in express terms; it is not imposed if the clause is nothing more than a recitation that successors are to be bound."[50] Of course, the interpretation of contract language by an arbitrator is subject to greater variation and unpredictability than might be expected from courts.

SOME ERISA CONSIDERATIONS

Contingent pension liabilities under both single employer and multiemployer pension plans arise pursuant to ERISA, 1974, as amended by the Multiemployer Pension Plan Amendments Act of 1980.[51] Title IV of ERISA (the "plan termination insurance" provisions) establishes an insurance program that is designed to protect employees from forfeiting all or part of their vested, accrued pension benefits. Such forfeitures most often result from the termination of a defined benefit pension plan (due to the sale of a business or another reason) prior to the full funding of benefits.

Typically, defined benefit pension plans (both single employer and multiemployer) are not fully funded and, upon plan termination, assets accumulated thereunder may be insufficient to provide the total amount of pension benefits promised. This insufficiency is commonly characterized as "unfunded, vested pension liability." Consequently, the aggregate amount of unfunded, vested pension liabilities of all plans to which the seller contributes could be a major factor in the purchaser's ultimate decision to purchase the seller's business and a key determinant of the price it will insist upon in negotiations.

Under Title IV of ERISA, an employer maintaining a single-employer defined-benefit pension plan is liable upon plan termination to the PBGC for the amount of the unfunded, vested pension benefits guaranteed by the agency. The PBGC is the government corporation established pursuant to ERISA to insure benefits under most defined-benefit pension plans.

With respect to multiemployer pension plans, liability under Title IV is triggered by a ''complete'' or ''partial'' withdrawal from the plan, rather than plan termination itself. Upon such withdrawal, a contributing employer will be liable to the multiemployer plan (instead of the PBGC) for a proportionate share of the plan's entire unfunded, vested pension liabilities. The precise amount of the liability will vary among each multiemployer plan and generally will depend on the withdrawal liability assessment rules selected by the particular plan (or imposed by statute) and the ratio of the employer's contributions to the total contributions made to the plan by all contributing employees measured over a period of time (usually five years).

Contingent pension liabilities frequently are a significant aspect of negotiations concerning the purchase of a business. Crucial to the determination of the purchaser's assumption of such liabilities, through its purchase of the seller's business, is whether the acquisition will be effected pursuant to a purchase of stock or assets.

When the stock of a corporation maintaining a single-employer pension plan (or contributing to a multiemployer pension plan) is purchased, either for cash or for stock, the corporation itself will remain in existence and, therefore, will continue to be the plan sponsor (or contributor). Consequently, the purchaser will assume the contingent pension liabilities relating to both single-employer and multiemployer plans maintained by the seller because there has been no plan termination or withdrawal, as the case may be. Thus, if the proposed acquisition is effected by the purchaser's purchase of the seller's stock and if the seller's plans are subsequently terminated, the purchaser will be contingently liable for the unfunded, vested pension benefits of all such plans.

Although the stock purchase agreement can be drafted to alter the impact of such liability as between purchaser and the seller's shareholders, the agreement cannot relieve the seller from its contingent liability for unfunded, vested pension benefits. The purchaser could, of course, seek to eliminate contingent pension liabilities by negotiating a termination of the seller's single-employer plans and satisfaction of liabilities thereunder by the seller prior to the sale of stock. Presumably, however, there would be a corresponding reduction in the value of the stock being purchased. It might also be difficult to obtain union agreement where this is necessary.

If the acquisition of the seller's business involves a sale of assets and if the purchaser elects to continue the seller's single-employer pension plans on behalf of the employees transferred in connection with the sale, such plans may be continued either by assuming the contingent pension obligations thereunder or by establishing comparable plans (which may grant credit for service performed by the transferred employees of the seller). In either event, the purchaser would become contingently liable for ERISA liability upon any subsequent plan termination. Obviously, an adjustment in the purchase price of the assets, reflecting the purchaser's assumption of such contingent obligations, should be negotiated.

On the other hand, if the purchaser purchases the seller's assets, but does not continue the seller's single-employer plans, the seller will be primarily responsible for the ERISA liabilities associated with such plans. Similarly, any asset acquisition involving the multiemployer pension plans to which the seller currently contributes would place primary liability upon the seller for unfunded, vested pension benefits accrued to the date of the acquisition. Of course, since contributions to such multiemployer plans presumably will continue on behalf of former seller employees transferred in connection with the acquisition, the purchaser should expect to become contingently liable for a share of the withdrawal liability under each multiemployer plan.

It is crucial to note that, for purposes of determining PBGC liability (with respect to a single-employer plan) and for purposes of assessing withdrawal liability under a multiemployer plan), ERISA provides that all employees of trades or businesses which are "under common control" shall be treated as if employed by a single employer, and all such trades and businesses shall be treated as a single employer. Under this concept, liability for unfunded, vested pension benefits may be satisfied from the assets of any member of the "controlled group." Thus, by assuming the contingent pension liabilities of the seller (pursuant to either a stock purchase or asset purchase involving plan continuation), the purchaser may expose its entire controlled group of companies to contingent pension liabilities.

The foregoing is merely an overview of the major pension considerations that must be evaluated in connection with the purchaser's proposed acquisition of the seller. Obviously, it is essential that the purchaser know what pension obligations and liabilities, if any, it will be undertaking when purchasing the seller's business.

Initially, an inventory should be made of each employee pension benefit plan maintained by the seller or to which it contributes, as well as a determination as to whether such plans are subject to Title IV of ERISA. A computation of the extent of the unfunded, vested liabilities attributable to each plan should be conducted by an actuary reviewing both the terms of the plan itself and any pertinent financial and actuarial reports.

The terms of each plan should also be reviewed to confirm that each comports with the requirements of ERISA and the Internal Revenue Code. Copies of each plan's annual report and other disclosure documents should be examined to ascertain compliance with ERISA's reporting and disclosure rules. Summary plan descriptions should be reviewed to confirm that each is consistent with the plan provisions it purports to describe. Inclusion of appropriate representations and warranties in the contract of sale may alleviate the need for this type of intensive review.

NOTES

1. See, e.g., Western Boot & Shoe, Inc., 205 N.L.R.B. 999 (1973); Topinka's Country House, Inc., 235 N.L.R.B. 72 (1978). Although not obligated, the purchaser of the assets of a company may also adopt an existing collective-bargaining agreement.

2. TKB Int'l Corp., 240 N.L.R.B. 1082, 1083 n.4 (1979).

3. See, e.g., MPE, Inc., 226 N.L.R.B. 519 (1976); Spencer Foods, Inc., 268 N.L.R.B. 1483 (1984), enf'd in part and rev'd in part, 768 F.2d 1463 (D.C. Cir. 1985).

4. In a stock acquisition, the stock price may reflect the prevailing state of labor relations. If a collective-bargaining agreement is favorable to management, the stock price could be higher than if the agreement is considered a liability. Consequently, the purchaser may "pay the price" for a beneficial labor agreement if the transaction is structured as a stock acquisition. The purchaser should weigh the increased cost of acquisition against the benefits of acquiring a subsisting agreement before deciding on the transactional form.

5. See supra note 1.

6. See, e.g., Fall River Dyeing and Finishing Corp. v. NLRB, 107 S. Ct. 2225 (1987); Howard Johnson Co. v. Hotel Employees, 417 U.S. 249 (1974); NLRB v. Burns Int'l Security Services, Inc., 406 U.S. 272 (1972); Airport Bus Service, Inc., 273 N.L.R.B. No. 84 (1984); Miami Industrial Trucks, 221 N.L.R.B. 1223 (1975).

7. Caution is advised in setting the terms of employment. If nothing is done to such terms and conditions, it may be held that the existing terms in the union contract continue in effect.

8. *Howard Johnson Co.*, 417 U.S. at 263 (citation omitted). See also Miami Industrial Trucks, 221 N.L.R.B. at 1224.

9. *Fall River Dyeing*, 107 S. Ct. at 2236–37. See also NLRB v. Band-Age, Inc., 534 F.2d 1, 3 (1st Cir.), cert. denied, 429 U.S. 921 (1976).

10. *Fall River Dyeing*, 107 S.Ct. at 2236 (citations omitted). Accord, NLRB v. Jeffries Lithograph Co., 752 F.2d 459, 465–66 (9th Cir. 1985); NLRB v. Hudson River Aggregates, Inc., 639 F.2d 865, 869 (2d Cir. 1981); Premium Foods, Inc., 260 N.L.R.B. 708, 714 (1982), enf'd, 709 F.2d 623 (9th Cir. 1983); Border Steel Rolling Mills, Inc., 204 N.L.R.B. 814, 815 (1973).

11. Airport Bus Service, Inc., 273 N.L.R.B. 561 (1984).

12. See, e.g., G.W. Hunt, 258 N.L.R.B. 1198 (1981).

13. Airport Bus Service, Inc., 273 N.L.R.B. 561.

14. Premium Foods Inc., 260 N.L.R.B. 708 (1982), enf'd, 709 F.2d 623 (9th Cir. 1983).

15. See, e.g., Radiant Fashions, Inc., 202 N.L.R.B. 938 (1973); Norton Precision, Inc., 199 N.L.R.B. 1003 (1972).

16. Daneker Clock Co. Inc., 211 N.L.R.B. 719 (1974), enf'd, 516 F.2d 315 (4th Cir. 1975); C. G. Conn, Ltd., 197 N.L.R.B. 442 (1972), enf'd, 82 L.R.R.M. 3092 (5th Cir. 1973).

17. Norton Precision, Inc., 199 N.L.R.B. 1003; Gladding Corp., 192 N.L.R.B. 200 (1971).

18. *Fall River Dyeing*, 107 S. Ct. 2236; *Daneker Clock*, 211 N.L.R.B. 721, See also C.G. Conn, Ltd., 197 N.L.R.B. 447 (4–1/2-month hiatus).

19. *Fall River Dyeing*, 107 S. Ct. at 2238 (footnote omitted).

20. Id. at 2239 (citations omitted).

21. Id. at 2241 (citation omitted).

22. *Howard Johnson Co.*, 417 U.S. at 262; *Burns*, 406 U.S. at 280–81 n.5.

23. See, e.g., J.R.R. Realty Co., 273 N.L.R.B. 1523 (1985), enf'd, 785 F.2d 46 (2d Cir. 1986); Blu-Fountain Manor, 270 N.L.R.B. 199 (1984), enf'd, 785 F.2d 195 (7th Cir. 1986).

24. *Blu-Fountain Manor*, 270 N.L.R.B. 208 Ranch-Way, Inc., 203 N.L.R.B. 911 (1973).

25. Sun Coast Foods, Inc., 273 N.L.R.B. 1642 (1985); Virginia Sportswear, 226 N.L.R.B. 1296 (1976).

26. Landmark Int'l Trucks, Inc. v. NLRB, 669 F.2d 815 (6th Cir. 1983); Harley-Davidson Transportation Co., 273 N.L.R.B. No. 192 (1985); B&B Gallo Pest Control Services, Inc., 265 N.L.R.B. 535 (1982). See also Silver Spur Casino, 270 N.L.R.B. 1067 (1984).

27. Golden Poultry Co., 271 N.L.R.B. 925 (1984).

28. Matlack, Inc., 278 N.L.R.B. No. 36 (1986), quoting NLRB v. Security Columbian Banknote Co., 541 F.2d 135 (3d Cir. 1976).

29. Safeway Stores, Inc., 276 N.L.R.B. No. 99 (1985).

30. Westwood Import Co., Inc., 251 N.L.R.B. 1213 (1980), enf'd, 681 F.2d 664 (9th Cir. 1982).

31. Martin Marietta Chemicals, 270 N.L.R.B. 821, 822 (1984).

32. See e.g., Zim's Foodliner, Inc. v. NLRB, 495 F.2d 1131 (7th Cir.), cert. denied, 419 U.S. 838 (1974); Louis Pappas' Homosassa Springs Restaurant, Inc., 275 N.L.R.B. No. 213 (1985). But see also W&W Steel Co. v. NLRB, 599 F.2d 934 (10th Cir. 1979).

33. *Burns*, 406 U.S. at 294–95. Cf. International Association of Machinists v. NLRB, 595 F.2d 664 (D.C. Cir. 1978), cert. denied, 439 U.S. 1070 (1979).

34. See, e.g., Stewart Granite Enterprises, 255 N.L.R.B. 569 (1981); Sorrento Hotel, 266 N.L.R.B. 350 (1983); Joe Costa Trucking Company, 238 N.L.R.B. 1516 (1978), enf'd, 631 F.2d 604 (9th Cir. 1980).

35. See, e.g., Watt Electric Company, 273 N.L.R.B. 655 (1984); Fugazy Continental Corp., 265 N.L.R.B. 1301 (1982), enf'd, 725 F.2d 1416 (D.C. Cir. 1984). A determination of alter ego status involves consideration of the following factors: (1) common management and ownership; (2) common business purpose, nature of operations, and supervision; (3) common premises and equipment; (4) common customers; (5) nature and extent of the negotiations and formalities surrounding the transaction; and (6) whether the purpose behind the creation of the alleged alter ego is legitimate or, instead, whether its purpose is to evade responsibilities under the contract or labor laws.

36. White-Westinghouse Corp., 229 N.L.R.B. 667 (1977), enf'd, 604 F.2d 689 (D.C. Cir. 1979).

37. Stockton Door Co., 218 N.L.R.B. 1053 (1975), enf'd, 547 F.2d 489 (9th Cir. 1976), cert. denied, 434 U.S. 834 (1977).

38. Pepsi-Cola Distributing Co., 241 N.L.R.B. 869 (1979), enf'd, 646 F.2d 1173 (6th Cir. 1981), cert. denied, 456 U.S. 936 (1982).

39. See, e.g., Golden State Bottling v. NLRB, 414 U.S. 168 (1973); Trucking Water Air Corp., 276 N.L.R.B. 158 (1985); *Blu-Fountain Manor*, 270 N.L.R.B. 200.

40. Slack v. Havens, 522 F.2d 1091 (9th Cir. 1975); Musikiwamba v. ESSI Inc., 760 F.2d 740 (7th Cir. 1985).

41. Bates v. Pacific Maritime Ass'n, 744 F.2d 705 (9th Cir. 1984).

42. See, e.g., Nursing Home and Hospital Union, Local No. 434 v. Sky Vue Terrace, Inc., 759 F.2d 1094 (3d Cir. 1985); Local Lodge No. 1266, Int'l Ass'n of Machinists and Aerospace Workers v. Panoramic Corp., 668 F.2d 276 (7th Cir. 1981); United Steelworkers of America v. Fort Pitt Steel Casting, 598 F.2d 1273 (3d Cir. 1979); Local 115 Joint Bd. Nursing Home v. B&K Investments, Inc., 436 F. Supp. 1203 (S.D. Fla. 1977). But see United Food & Commercial Workers Union Local No. 626 v. Kroger Company, 778 F.2d 1171 (6th Cir. 1985), cert. denied, 107 S. Ct 69 (1986).

43. John Wiley and Sons, Inc., 376 U.S. 543 (1964).

44. Id. at 548.

45. See supra note 4.

46. See, e.g., United Steelworkers of America v. United States Gypsum Company, 492 F.2d 713 (5th Cir.), cert. denied, 419 U.S. 998 (1974); Graphic Arts International Union v. Martin Podnay Associates, Inc., 531 F. Supp. 169 (D. Minn. 1982); *B&K Investments*, 436 F. Supp. at 1209.

47. *United States Gypsum Co.*, 492 F.2d at 726 (pre–*Howard Johnson* ruling; purchaser hired all but three of the predecessor's employees and retained substantially the same conditions of employment as obtained prior to the sale).

48. See Anderson v. Ideal Basic Industries, 120 L.R.R.M. 2039 (E.D. Tenn. 1985).

49. Wyatt Manufacturing Co., 82 L.A. 153, 163 (Goodman, 1983).

50. Gallivan's Inc., 79 L.A. 253, 253 (Gallagher, 1982).

51. 29 U.S.C. § 1001 et seq.

10

SALE OF ASSETS, MERGERS, AND ACQUISITIONS: A UNION VIEW

Wilbur Daniels and Seth Kupferberg

Editors' Note. Messrs. Daniels and Kupferberg argue that there is no general rule excluding asset sales, mergers, and acquisitions from the obligation of decision bargaining; the question is not one of form but of whether the possible gains from bargaining are outweighed by the possible costs to the employer. In any event, the authors conclude, the employer has a duty to engage in effects bargaining and to give sufficient notice to permit a union to exercise this right meaningfully. The authors explore the possibility that an employer's concealment of an impending business change may constitute bargaining in bad faith. The authors also consider other statutory, administrative, and contractual restraints on business change decisions that affect workers rights, and they examine the obligations of successor employers.

In the last decade, American business has undergone a wave of consolidation, corporate and financial restructuring, and comparative indifference to actual production unprecedented since the appearance of a stable, legally accepted labor movement.[1] The instability which has always marked such "secondary sector" industries as clothing, leaving workers peculiarly vulnerable, has spread to industries in which the disappearance or transfer to new hands of a plant may have catastrophic consequences for an entire community. Financial action increasingly separate from productive investment has fueled an economic "recovery," but workers remain unemployed, existing capacity is still unused, and popular needs continue to be unmet and ignored.

Traditional labor law developed in a different context. Capital was less mobile: companies rarely changed their business; and corporate decisions were based on labor and other production and sales costs, with relatively little attention paid to the possibilities of shifting investment elsewhere. In such circumstances, collective bargaining about conditions of employment usually sufficed to protect workers' immediate interests. Unions rarely focused on investment decisions, and neither did the law. The consequences of this limited focus are being felt today.

Current law protects workers and unions against corporate actions specifically intended to undermine union rights, and it guarantees unions some input into decisions with sufficiently direct impact on labor concerns. Thus, corporate actions taken out of dislike for unions are illegal, and organized workers are entitled to bargain over the effects of actions that directly affect their jobs, and sometimes over the decisions themselves. But this legal focus is inadequate for workers and communities vulnerable to mobile capital. Real legal protection for those affected by mergers, sales of assets, and acquisitions, and the plant closings and other drastic changes to which they often lead, requires legal reform unlikely without political change.

The law concerning the impact on workers of sales of assets, mergers, and acquisitions is heavily dependent on a half-dozen Supreme Court decisions. Laudably, the Court has refused "to adopt a mode of analysis requiring the Board to distinguish among mergers, consolidations, and purchases of assets,"[2] and it has encouraged examination of underlying realities rather than formal or legalistic distinctions. The Court has called for an inquiry into whether there is "substantial continuity" between two firms in such matters as the nature of the business, the production process, and the customers. Above all, it has looked to "whether those employees who have been retained will understandably view their job situations as essentially unaltered"—an "emphasis on the employees' perspective."[3] As the Supreme Court recently observed: "The focus of the analysis, in other words, is not on the continuity of the business structure in general, but rather on the particular operations of the business as they affect the members of the relevant bargaining unit."[4]

Even while recognizing continuities between firms, however, the Supreme Court has limited the responsibilities of a predecessor when a corporate shift is not motivated by labor considerations, and the responsibilities of a successor when a majority of its work force is not hired from the predecessor's ranks. The Court has declined to make continuing responsibility a general rule; successorship as a concept, we are told, is "simply not meaningful in the abstract."[5]

John Wiley & Sons, Inc. v. Livingston,[6] the Supreme Court's first major ruling on the implications of corporate reorganization for employees, included the following general statement:

"Employees, and the union which represents them, ordinarily do not take part in negotiations leading to a change in corporate ownership. The negotiations will ordinarily not concern the well-being of the employees, whose advantage or disadvantage, potentially great, will inevitably be incidental to the main considerations. The objectives of national labor policy . . . require that the rightful prerogative of owners independently to rearrange their businesses and even eliminate themselves as employers be balanced by some protection to the employees."[7]

The law's development has been shaped by the continuing struggle between "the rightful prerogative of owners" and the workers' acknowledged need for "some protection."

The discussion below is divided into two broad topics: rights against the original employing entity (for convenience, despite the Court's caveat about the meaningfulness of labels, called the "predecessor") and rights against the employing entity that emerges from the merger or other transaction (the "successor"). Workers' rights under current law and strategies to protect those rights are emphasized.

RIGHTS AGAINST THE PREDECESSOR

Decision Bargaining

The case law relevant to decision bargaining over changes in employing entities' legal identity stems from the Supreme Court's ruling in *Fibreboard Paper Products Corp v. NLRB*,[8] which involved not a sale of assets but a company's decision to contract out maintenance work previously done by its own unionized employees. In an opinion by Chief Justice Warren, the Court found this plan must first be discussed with the union because no fundamental alteration in the company's basic operation was contemplated, as the company simply aimed to economize by cutting labor costs, something "peculiarly suitable for resolution" by collective bargaining.[9]

In an influential concurrence,[10] Justice Stewart emphasized that Fibreboard officials continued to supervise the maintenance work and pay for it on a cost-plus basis so that "all that is involved is the substitution of one group of workers for another to perform the same task in the same plant under the ultimate control of the same employer." The concurring opinion cautioned against

imposing a duty to bargain collectively regarding . . . managerial decisions, which lie at the core of entrepreneurial control. Decisions concerning the commitment of investment capital and the basic scope of the enterprise are not in themselves primarily about conditions of employment . . . It is possible that in meeting these problems Congress may eventually decide to give organized labor or government a far heavier hand in controlling what until now have been considered the prerogatives of private business management. That path would mark a sharp departure from the traditional principles of a free enterprise economy. Whether we should follow it is, within constitutional limitations, for Congress to choose. But it is a path which Congress certainly did not choose when it enacted the Taft-Hartley Act.[11]

Thus, while *Fibreboard*'s holding was a victory for workers, Justice Stewart's concurrence implied that they could be completely excluded from "entrepreneurial" decisions, even though the Court had acknowledged the need for "some protection" for affected workers in *Wiley* a short time before.[12]

In 1981, the Court made this exclusion explicit in *First National Maintenance Corp. v. NLRB*,[13] holding that a company need not bargain before closing one of several locations. Justice Blackmun's opinion, while recognizing the union's "legitimate concern over job security," held that this concern must yield to management's "need for speed, flexibility, and secrecy. . . . [S]ignificant tax or securities consequences [may] . . . hinge on confidentiality. . . . The publicity incident to the normal process of bargaining may injure the possibility of a successful transition. . . .

> Management must be free from the constraints of the bargaining process to the extent essential to the running of a profitable business. . . . [I]n view of an employer's need for unencumbered decisionmaking, bargaining over management decisions that have a substantial impact on the continued availability of employment should be required only if the benefit, for labor-management relations and the collective-bargaining process, outweighs the burden placed on the conduct of the business.[14]

Relying on *Fibreboard*, the First Circuit had earlier found no duty to bargain over a corporate merger.[15] *First National Maintenance* provided the impetus for the Board to rule in *Otis Elevator Co.*[16] that a company need not bargain over a partial shutdown that does not turn on labor costs (or, according to two of the NLRB's four members, some other factor likely to be resolved through bargaining). Three Board members even implied that assets sales are never mandatory bargaining subjects because such decisions are inherently managerial.[17]

While it is true that, under *First National Maintenance*, unions have no right to bargain over decisions not "amenable to resolution through the bargaining process,"[18] this should not be misread to mean that simply structuring a transaction as a sale, merger, or acquisition eliminates a need for bargaining if bargaining might, in fact, affect the outcome. On the contrary, the *First National Maintenance* Court stressed that decisions "such as . . . sales . . . are to be considered on their particular facts" and cited with seeming approval a case implying that a sale to another company, which continued to run the transferred operation, was indeed a mandatory bargaining subject.[19] Bargaining was not required in *First National Maintenance*, as it had been in *Fibreboard* because labor considerations could have had no impact on First National Maintenance's decision to sever all connection with a particular user of its services, which, according to the Court, depended solely on the customer's unwillingness to pay a higher fee.[20] Neither case involved a sale of assets; the legal form a transaction may take cannot explain the different results.

Another post-*Fibreboard* case, in which bargaining was not required, illuminates why certain decisions, but not others, need not be negotiated with unions, and the inadequacy of looking only at a transaction's formal structure. General Motors (GM) sold a truck center to a franchisee; the NLRB and D.C. Circuit held that this decision need not be bargained with the union.[21] However, two Board members and then Chief Judge Bazelon of the D.C. Circuit saw the sale, in which GM continued to have ultimate control through a franchise agreement, as similar to *Fibreboard*'s decision to contract out work, not as a change in the truck center's basic operation.

These dissenters would have required GM to bargain over the decision, even though the GM transaction was structured as a sale of assets. The appellate court's majority opinion, authored by retired Justice Clark (who had been part of the *Fibreboard* majority), cautioned that "GM's tagging of the contract as a sale is, of course, not decisive." Critical to the court's reasoning was its recognition of "a national GM policy to switch its remaining manufacturer-owned and operated retail outlets to independent franchises or dealerships."[22] Presumably, bargaining at a particular dealership could not have affected this national decision to utilize independent dealerships.

When, by contrast, negotiation does have the potential to influence an ostensibly entrepreneurial decision, unions should insist on the right to bargain even if the decision takes the form of a sale of assets, mergers, or acquisition. If, for example, a company sells a plant because it considers labor costs too high or because it has personnel concerns such as absenteeism or lack of discipline, which might be addressed through collective bargaining, nothing in *First National Maintenance* precludes union insistence on the right to bargain over the decision. *First National Maintenance* calls for balancing possible gains from bargaining against possible costs to an employer if management's freedom to act unilaterally is limited; the case does not permit an employer to evade its duties simply by structuring a transaction as a transfer to a legally distinct entity.

Resistance to an expansive reading of *First National Maintenance* is essential because employers can easily manipulate the form of a transaction if that is all that is needed to escape a bargaining obligation. In applying *First National Maintenance*, the courts and the Board should look to the underlying reality, and ask whether bargaining could conceivably affect a decision. This is consistent with the normal practice of disregarding a transaction's form and continuing to hold employers legally responsible for obligations for which they are, in fact, responsible.[23]

Effects Bargaining

Even if there is no duty to bargain over the *decision* to merge or transfer assets with another company, *First National Maintenance* reiterated that a union "must be given a significant opportunity . . . [for] the 'effects' bargaining mandated by Section 8(a) (5). . . . [B]argaining over the effects of a decision must be conducted in a meaningful manner and at a meaningful time, and the Board may impose sanctions to insure its adequacy."[24] Cases dealing with effects bargaining make it clear that an employer must give the union timely notice of its decision "so that good faith bargaining does not become futile or impossible." What "timeliness" means in this context depends on the particular facts. An emergency might justify precipitous action by a company, but, in the more usual situation in which a decision is planned in advance, a company must discuss it with the union while its implementation is still under consideration and the union still has influence and economic strength.[25] Gossip or rumors of a possible closing "cannot take the place of formal notice."[26]

If an employer does not give timely notice, the Board, recognizing that "[m]eaningful bargaining cannot be assured unless some measure of economic strength is restored" to workers no longer employed by the wrongdoer, has ordered, in addition to bargaining, payment of wages to workers until either an agreement or impasse is reached, with a minimum of two weeks pay to the workers who lost their jobs.[27]

In simple plant closing cases, the most important subject for effects bargaining is usually severance pay,[28] since there is little prospect the employees can continue working. In the case of a sale of assets or merger, by contrast, union demands relating to a decision's effects as well as "legitimate concern over job security"[29] should often include much more—even though, in the haste and furor that accompanies a sale, it is particularly difficult for unions to plan properly or assert all legal rights effectively.

For example, a demand that the predecessor company's agreement with its successor provide for the latter's adherence to the union contract "implicates the effect of the decision [to sell], rather than the decision itself," and it is properly deemed a mandatory bargaining subject.[30] The same is presumably true of less restrictive demands related to the merger or sale agreement—for instance, that the successor agree to employ current workers, give them preference in hiring, or recognize or transfer seniority or pension rights. Since such demands are "vital to the protection of . . . employees' previously negotiated wages and working conditions," they involve a mandatory bargaining subject, and a union can legally strike the predecessor to obtain them.[31] In a particular situation, there may be other, less typical, but equally proper and important effects demands[32] or a need for timely union concessions.[33]

Relatively few reported cases deal with this kind of broader effects bargaining; there appears to be some reluctance to find that employers have evaded their effects bargaining responsibilities.[34] Yet, there is no basis in NLRB or court precedent to preclude a requirement of broader effects bargaining, which is well within the logic of *First National Maintenance*. In fact, one reason the Court there did not find a duty to bargain over the decision to close was that it thought effects bargaining could satisfy unions' legitimate interests without thwarting the decision itself.[35] There is a need for imagination and stubbornness on the unions' part in pressing for expansive effects protection of their members' jobs and contractual expectations. If such efforts do not produce agreements to preserve jobs, they may at least establish a basis for legal action against any employers that fail to bargain in good faith.

It is unclear from the case law whether, in circumstances where timely negotiations might have produced continuing job security rather than merely severance pay, there is occasion for additional remedies for refusals to bargain beyond the normal bargaining order and minimum two weeks' pay.

Employer Dishonesty

While *Fibreboard* and *First National Maintenance* recognize employer needs for "freedom to manage the business" and for "speed, flexibility, and secrecy," they do not authorize employers to deceive workers or unions. If an employer goes beyond simply keeping future plans confidential and actively misleads organized workers, it may violate the NLRA's requirement of good-faith bargaining. For example, an employer fraudulently seeking union concessions to keep a plant open while concealing its predetermined resolve to shut down anyway may lay itself open to charges under Section 8(a)(5).[36] There is no reason to limit this principle to concession bargaining. Besides violating Section 8(a)(5), deceit by an employer may violate the collective bargaining agreement.[37]

If workers are deceived in ways not governed by federal labor law, employers may be liable for misrepresentation or breach of contract under state law.[38] Thus, workers without union representation, or who were individually deceived outside of the collective-bargaining process, may be able to bring a state law claim (or possibly, if company promises were sufficiently unambiguous, a federal promissory estoppel claim) if a company deceives them.[39] Where the claim against a company is predicated on federal law, state law may furnish a basis to hold liable corporate affiliates or other coconspirators who share responsibility for an employer's breach of contract.[40]

A claim of contract violation is governed by federal law but may be brought in either federal or state court.[41] While unions might prefer to bring misrepresentation claims in state tort actions rather than under Section 8(a)(5) before the NLRB, the Sixth Circuit (rejecting an argument that fraud claims are deeply rooted in local law and should not be preempted) has required that they be brought before the NLRB.[42] Since the Supreme Court has also found preemption in analogous cases in which employees sought to raise tort claims arising in a collective-bargaining context,[43] Section 8(a)(5) may be the only available avenue.

Transactions for Antiunion Reasons

In addition to indicating that bargaining about the effects of mergers, sales, or acquisitions is required by Section 8(a)(5) of the NLRA, *First National Maintenance* reiterated that Section 8(a)(3) "prohibits partial closings motivated by antiunion animus."[44] When a company involved in a merger or transfer of assets does not go out of business completely, Section 8(a)(3) prohibits any transaction undertaken for antiunion reasons.[45] As a practical matter, however, even when timing and other circumstances make a transaction suspect,[46] it is often extraordinarily difficult to prove that the employer's motive in shutting one of its facilities was to avoid dealing with a union or to inhibit the use of rights by employees at remaining plants. In one International Ladies' Garment Workers' Union (ILGWU) case, a lawyer worked virtually full-time for months exhuming circumstantial evidence of a firm's antiunion motivation in closing a union plant while acquiring a new facility nearby.[47] Although she obtained a satisfactory settlement, such an effort is not ordinarily feasible even in those cases in which it could theoretically achieve results.

Contractual Constraints

As set forth above, unions may legally obtain, if necessary by striking, contractual commitments that employers will not merge or sell assets unless the successor employer first assumes the collective bargaining agreement or otherwise agrees to respect workers' rights.[48] While *First National Maintenance* held that employers are not required to bargain over decisions to close parts of their business, it also said that unions "may secure in contract negotiations provisions implementing rights to notice, information, and fair bargaining"[49]—a comment that should also apply to mergers or sales that affect job security.

Such commitments are probably most feasibly obtained as part of boilerplate in contracts covering multiemployer or multiplant bargaining units, in situations in which a union has economic strength and, for the employers who agree to such language, in circumstances in which freedom to escape the union agreement is not a concern or option. For example, many ILGWU affiliate contracts with employer associations provide that, if a firm merges or transfers assets to another, the successor must respect the employees' rights in specified ways.[50] Unions may also legally obtain, through strikes if necessary, protections that impose practical limits on the terms under which an employer can acquire a new plant by prohibiting the relocation of union employees' work or the undercutting of their standards.[51] Contractual clauses facilitating union organizing at any newly acquired sites,[52] or providing for an existing contract to be extended to newly acquired sites if workers select union representation,[53] are desirable and have been held proper.

Even without a specific contractual commitment, it may be arguable that especially egregious corporate actions, particularly those eliminating jobs wholesale, violate the labor agreement's implicit obligation of good faith and fair dealing or its prohibition of unjust discharge. While it would be difficult to stop a closing based solely on such general language, a contract's general commitments may help resolve ambiguities in specific clauses relied on by a union and may strengthen its hand if there are settlement negotiations.

Contracts restraining employers' unilateral action or requiring them to obtain successor guarantees of workers' rights can be enforced through litigation, arbitration, or any other means that would be used to enforce any other contracts.[54] In addition to damages after the fact—and far more effective in protecting workers' rights—injunctive relief should be available to stop a transaction pending resolution of the contractual claim.[55]

Other Legal Restraints

This article does not address general legal restraints on mergers and analogous corporate transactions (such as antitrust law); similarly, it does not address responses such as offers to buy companies outright (which unions sometimes make). Both general legal restraints and ordinary corporate law rules, however, can be quite important to workers and unions. The Sixth Circuit has held, for example, that a company's flat refusal to deal with a union which wants to buy a plant to avert its closing may violate antitrust law.[56]

There are also special legal restrictions on mergers in some regulated industries, which are directly relevant to workers and their unions. For example, before airline deregulation, the Civil Aeronautics Board (CAB) "developed a set of rules called Labor Protective Provisions . . . which it normally requires carriers to adopt as a condition to its approval of their mergers." The provisions required compensation to workers who lost jobs and arbitration of disputes.[57] The Department of Transportation still has power to impose such requirements, although its current normal policy is to defer to collective bargaining.[58] Similarly, Congress has imposed protections for merged railroads' workers;[59] the Interstate Commerce Commission requires that merging railroads protect workers' interests even if collective bargaining fails to yield protective arrangements.[60] Under federal law, a government service contractor, whether or not it buys a predecessor's assets, must match the standards prescribed in a predecessor's labor agreement unless the Secretary of Labor finds them substantially at variance with the local going rate.[61] Such special rules (which no doubt exist in other industries as well) recall Justice Stewart's general observation that Congress "may eventually decide to give organized labor or government a far heavier hand in controlling" private prerogatives that affect workers and the public.[62]

RIGHTS AGAINST THE SUCCESSOR

As a preliminary matter, it is important to note that a corporate transaction may take the form of a merger, assets sale, or other transfer to a legally distinct entity, and yet the "successor" may be deemed an alter ego of the "predecessor."[63] In that case, workers have the same rights after as before the transaction. Although some courts have required proof of intent to evade union rights for a finding of alter ego status, the better view, expressly adopted in the Second and Sixth Circuits, is that a specific intention to evade the union is not a necessary element of proof, or that where there is a sufficiently strong showing of identity between two nominally distinct firms, any necessary employer intent can be inferred.[64]

Even so, proof of alter ego status is difficult to mount; in one case I am aware of, an ILGWU lawyer succeeded only after spending an inordinate amount of time examining two nominally distinct companies' insurance and utility bills and payments, records of transactions between the companies, and other business records obtained through an NLRB subpoena.[65] At least one reported arbitration case finds such an inquiry so important, and employer efforts to conceal continuity so egregious, that pilferage of confidential documents by employees in an effort to prove continuity may be excused.[66] The following remarks assume that there has been a genuine change in the employing entity.

Carryover of Collective Bargaining Agreements

Three Supreme Court rulings deal with the carryover of collective-bargaining agreements following a merger, sale of assets, or acquisition. Together, they make clear that the successor employer's actions, rather than the language in the union's contract with the predecessor, determine whether the contract can be enforced against the successor.[67]

John Wiley & Sons, Inc. v. Livingston[68] was the first of these Supreme Court rulings. Interscience, a publisher with 40 unionized workers, merged with Wiley, a much larger publisher with about 300 employees. The union sought arbitration under its Interscience contract of claims that Wiley had to recognize the Interscience workers' seniority, vacation, medical, pension, and job-security rights.

The Court held that federal labor law controlled the case, that arbitration would give workers some peaceful protection, and that ''similarity and continuity of operation across the change in ownership . . . evidenced by the wholesale transfer of Interscience employees to the Wiley plant'' made imposing arbitration reasonable even though ''the principles of law governing ordinary contracts would not bind to a contract an unconsenting successor to a contracting party.''[69] As later cases acknowledged,[70] this unsupported distinction between a collective-bargaining agreement and ''ordinary'' contracts, under which a successor presumably could not have been compelled to arbitrate, was misleading. The *Wiley* opinion itself referred both to ''the general rule . . . in the case of a merger [that] the corporation which survives is liable for . . . contracts of the one which disappears'' and to a state law relied on by the union providing ''that no 'claim or demand for any cause' against a constituent corporation shall be extinguished by a consolidation.''[71]

When the union's claim was arbitrated as required by the Supreme Court, Interscience's labor contract was found effective after the merger only ''until there is a change of conditions that altered the separate identity [of former Interscience employees] within the new business enterprise.'' Union members' rights continued for three months, until ''the former Interscience employees were moved to the Wiley quarters and co-mingled with the larger Wiley contingent.''[72]

The Supreme Court's second ruling about the survival of collective-bargaining agreements came in *NLRB v. Burns International Security Service.*[73] This case did not involve any kind of business reorganization; Burns had replaced a competitor company at a customer's premises. Most of the guards Burns hired had worked for its competitor, however, and the NLRB had found that both the union's bargaining rights and labor agreement carried over to the new employer.

The Court, although agreeing that bargaining rights continued, unanimously held that the contract did not carry over. Justice White's opinion distinguished *Wiley* because *Burns*, instead of being a merger or sale of assets case, involved "an [unconnected] employer . . . doing the same work in the same place with the same employees as his predecessor." But the opinion also said, seemingly more generally:

> [H]olding either the union or the new employer bound to the substantive terms of an old collective-bargaining contract may result in serious inequities. A potential employer may be willing to take over a moribund business only if he can make changes in corporate structure, composition of the labor force, work location, task assignment, and nature of supervision. Saddling such an employer with the terms and conditions of employment contained in the old collective-bargaining contract may make these changes impossible and may discourage and inhibit the transfer of capital.[74]

In *Howard Johnson Co. Inc. v. Hotel and Restaurant Employees Detroit Local*[75] the Court found that a union's contract with the owner of a franchised Howard Johnson's outlet did not bind Howard Johnson when it bought the contractor's assets and hired new employees. Although Justice Marshall's opinion noted that *Wiley*'s and *Burns*' logic were "to some extent inconsistent," the Court in *Howard Johnson* did not overrule *Wiley*.

The majority distinguished *Wiley* on three grounds: (1) its "background of . . . the general rule that in merger situations the surviving corporation is liable . . . which suggests that holding Wiley bound . . . may have been fairly within the reasonable expectations of the parties"; (2) Howard Johnson's former franchisee remained in existence and retained assets to pay any damages to the union (whereas Interscience had disappeared into the merged company); and (3) "[e]ven more important," Howard Johnson had not hired most of the old workers after buying the franchisee's assets, whereas Wiley "hired *all*" of Interscience's workers, who continued to operate (for the period during which the arbitrator found the contract remained in effect) in the same way as before the merger.[76] In these circumstances, the Court found *Burns*' deference to the new employer's freedom of action, rather than *Wiley*'s concern for protection of workers' rights, controlling.

Subsequent to *Howard Johnson*, courts have generally found that a successor does not have to arbitrate disputes with a union under a predecessor's agreement; it "is ordinarily free to set initial terms on which it will hire the employees of a predecessor, . . . and . . . is not bound by the substantive provisions of the predecessor's collective-bargaining agreement.''[77] However, since the Court in *Howard Johnson* distinguished rather than overruled *Wiley*, there may still be circumstances in which a successor is bound by the arbitration promise provided for in the predecessor's labor agreement.

Soon after *Howard Johnson*, the Fifth Circuit discussed what would constitute such circumstances: ''substantial continuity in the identity of the work force'' and ''continuity in identity of the *enterprise*.''[78] While neither concept is well defined, work-force continuity requires that a majority or at least a significant minority of the predecessor's work force be employed by the successor. A merger or purchase of the predecessor's assets would help show enterprise continuity. Moreover, if two companies' work forces are almost identical, this may show enterprise as well as work-force continuity, even without additional evidence.[79] Unless and until *Wiley* is overruled, unions can still seek to compel arbitration by successor employers if there is strong evidence of continuity along the lines suggested above.[80]

Both here and in the more common context (discussed in the next section), in which a union merely seeks the right to bargain with a successor employer, it is significant that an employer cannot legally minimize continuity by discriminating against the predecessor's employees ''because they were union members or to avoid having to recognize the union.''[81] Employer claims that there was some other reason for refusing to hire the predecessor's employees need not be accepted at face value.[82] In one case, an antinepotism rule was found to be a pretext for discrimination, where the new owners knew of a predecessor company's history of poor labor relations and that the old work force included many sets of relatives.[83]

The preceding discussion has assumed that a successor intends not to assume the predecessor's labor agreement. In some mergers, however, the union which represented employees of the predecessor already also has a collective-bargaining agreement with the surviving company. In such a case, the union is free to negotiate a reasonable modification to accommodate displaced workers, for example by dovetailing previously separate seniority lists. Although it may not be welcomed by all union members, such a modification should not contravene the duty of fair representation.[84] Moreover, even in the more usual case in which the successor company is not already bound by a labor agreement, it may choose to adopt the predecessor's agreement, whether expressly or implicitly.

Burns recognized that successors not required to accept union contracts may nevertheless ''find it advantageous . . . to observe the pre-existing contract rather than to face uncertainty'' and that ''in a variety of circumstances involving a merger, stock acquisition, reorganization, or assets purchase, the Board might properly find as a matter of fact that the successor had assumed the obligations under the old contract.''[85] Since *Burns* suggests that it would be as unfair to hold a union as to hold a successor employer to a contract negotiated with the predecessor,[86] the union as well as the employer must agree to this kind of assumption. Where the parties' actions show agreement, even if only implicit, a successor employer cannot later change its mind and repudiate the contract.[87]

Carryover of Bargaining Rights

As discussed above, the Supreme Court held in *NLRB v. Burns International Security Services, Inc.*[88] that a company the majority of whose employees had worked for a competitor at the same location, though not bound by the competitor's labor agreement, did have to bargain with the employees' union. The Court noted, however, that determining when such a duty arises would sometimes be difficult:

> [T]here will be instances in which it is perfectly clear that the new employer plans to retain all of the employees in the unit and in which it will be appropriate to have him initially consult with the employees' bargaining representative before he fixes terms. In other situations, however, it may not be clear until the successor employer has hired his full complement of employees that he has a duty to bargain with a union, since it will not be evident until then that the bargaining representative represents a majority of the employees in the unit.[89]

Here, as with the carryover of contract obligations, the fact that employees are retained is a necessary but not a sufficient condition for finding sufficient continuity so that the successor takes on its predecessor's legal obligations.[90] The NLRB identified several other factors, in addition to work-force continuity: "the Board examines a number of factors: whether the business of both employers is essentially the same; whether the employees of the new company are doing the same jobs in the same working conditions under the same supervisors; and whether the new entity has the same production process, produces the same products, and basically has the same body of customers."[91] But a recent Supreme Court decision makes it clear that these other factors are important only to the extent "*they impinge on union members*," not as they may appear to corporate officials or others who are concerned with business strategy.[92] In this recent ruling, *Fall River Dyeing & Finishing Corp. v. NLRB*,[93] the Court further noted that the existence of a hiatus, even of seven months, when employees are not working does not preclude a finding of successorship. Indeed, *Fall River Dyeing* suggests that an obligation to bargain is activated whenever a business chooses to take most of its employees from a predecessor's work force.[94]

There is, therefore, a major difference in how employee continuity is determined when it is a question of carrying over bargaining obligations rather than requiring the purchaser's adherence to a predecessor's labor agreement. *Howard Johnson*, dealing with rights under the predecessor's collective-bargaining agreement, looks to whether a substantial number of the *predecessor*'s workers have been retained by the successor; *Burns*, dealing with bargaining rights, looks to whether a majority of the *successor*'s employees worked for the predecessor.[95] (Without specifically holding that this is the correct interpretation of *Burns, Fall River Dyeing* acknowledged the prevalence of this dichotomy in the opinions of the NLRB and lower courts and implicitly adopted it.[96]) If, however, two unionized companies of roughly equal size merge, the Board is likely to find "a total integration of . . . two operations" with neither union's prior representation barring an election in the new, consolidated unit.[97]

Since bargaining rights depend on how much of a successor's work force comes from a union-represented predecessor, it is of great importance that an employer not be able to discriminate against its predecessor's employees in order to escape a bargaining obligation.[98] As Justice Blackmun's majority opinion in *Fall River Dyeing* observes: "[T]o a substantial extent the applicability of *Burns* rests in the hands of the successor" which selects its initial employees.[99] It is therefore crucial that unions take legal steps to enforce *Burns*' warning that "an employer who declines to hire employees solely because they are members of a union commits a Section 8(a)(3) unfair labor practice."[100] While outright antiunion hostility is proscribed, it is similarly improper for a successor to discriminate in order to escape a history of bad labor relations or because workers are on strike. If a successor does discriminate, "the conventional remedy [is] reinstatement (or in this case, recall) and back pay for the prior workforce. . . . "[101] Where, but for illegal discrimination, most of the successor's work force would have been carried over, the remedy includes a bargaining order as well.[102]

Fall River Dyeing settled a number of other questions about successor companies' bargaining obligations. First, the Board presumes that the predecessor union continues to enjoy majority support among the predecessor's workers; the corporate transaction, standing alone, does not create a basis for challenging the union's status.[103] Second, once a union makes a demand for bargaining, the demand continues in force, and an obligation to bargain arises if, once a "substantial and representative complement"[104] of employees has been hired, a majority of this work force was previously employed by the predecessor. The significance of this ruling is that the employer cannot wait to respond to a bargaining demand until it has hired all employees, in the hope that predecessor employees might no longer be a majority.[105] Obviously, the union should demand bargaining promptly, but it does not have to make the demand at some preordained moment.

Under *Burns*, as noted earlier, a successor can usually set initial terms of employment unilaterally, even though it may at some point be obliged to bargain with the predecessor's union. However, *Burns* recognized an exception: when "it is perfectly clear that the new employer plans to retain all of the employees in the unit," the employer must "consult with the employees' bargaining representative before he fixes terms."[106] The courts have emphasized that, if an employer does not intend to maintain the terms of employment granted by a predecessor, it must make this clear to the predecessor's employees at the time that they are hired. A successor who tells workers they will be retained while misleading them into a belief that prior conditions of employment will be preserved as well can be required to bargain with the union before instituting changes.[107]

Successor Liability for Unfair Labor Practices

The Supreme Court held unanimously in *Golden State Bottling Co. Inc. v. NLRB*[108] that a company that acquires an employer's assets knowing of an unfair labor practice finding may be ordered to remedy the unfair labor practice. Similar rules of successor liability have been applied in employment discrimination cases.[109] Where the successor does not know about a charge—an affirmative defense that it must prove[110]—it may still sometimes be liable if substantial relief is not available from the predecessor,[111] but this is much more problematic.

CONCLUSION

As profit-seeking capital gravitates less and less to useful production and more and more to financial maneuvering, corporate infighting, and paper transactions employing only lawyers and executives, the limitations of American labor law as it has been interpreted have taken on special poignancy. The impact of corporate actions on working people and their communities can be no less devastating for being unintended; working people and other citizens need to control how and where economic resources are directed, not just discuss less crucial matters after key decisions have been made.

While current law gives unions some room to maneuver, it does not focus on achieving democratic control over decisions that affect their members. It is easy to imagine specific legal reforms which should be adopted: restrictions on plant closings, guaranteed portability of pension rights, more frequent use of the power of eminent domain to facilitate production controlled by local government or by a plant's workers, and an end to tax advantages for corporate transactions that do not result in new, productive investment. More broadly, unions, working people, and other citizens must expand popular influence over entrepreneurial prerogatives. The narrowly circumscribed bargaining which current law promotes leads too readily to troubles like those summarized by a steel worker in *The Wall Street Journal*:

> "USX took the money we gave them and ran and bought Marathon Oil Co.," complains Wayne Mortal, a 52-year-old worker at the company's Irvin works outside Pittsburgh. Steel today accounts for only 30% of USX's revenues. "Basically, they laughed at us, and most people don't like to be laughed at," Mr. Mortal says. "Their attitude seems to be that we're dumb. Their promises [to reinvest in steel operations] aren't promises."[112]

NOTES

1. The last such wave, roughly from the Civil War to the emergence of the giant trusts and centered in such leading sectors of the economy as steel, oil, and the railroads, was chronicled a half-century ago in M. Josephson, The Robber Barons (1962).

2. Golden State Bottling Co. v. NLRB, 414 U.S. 168, 183 n.5 (1973).

3. Fall River Dyeing & Finishing Corp. v. NLRB, 107 S. Ct. 2225, 125 L.R.R.M. 2441, 2447 (1987), quoting Golden State Bottling Co. v. NLRB, 414 U.S. 168, 184 (1973).

4. United Food and Commercial Workers Local 152 v. NLRB, 768 F.2d 1463, 1470 (D.C. Cir. 1985).

5. Howard Johnson Co., Inc. v. Hotel and Restaurant Employees Detroit Local, 417 U.S. 249, 262 n.9 (1974).

6. John Wiley & Sons, Inc. v. Livingston, 376 U.S. 543 (1964).

7. Id. at 549.

8. Fibreboard Paper Products Corp. v. NLRB, 379 U.S. 203 (1964).

9. Id. at 213–14.

10. Id. at 217 (Stewart, J., concurring).

11. Id. at 223, 225–26.

12. *Wiley*, 376 U.S. at 549.

13. First National Maintenance Corp. v. NLRB, 452 U.S. 666 (1981).

14. Id. at 681–83, 678–79.

15. International Association of Machinists and Aerospace Workers v. Northeast Airlines, Inc., 473 F.2d 549, 556–57 (1st Cir.), cert. denied, 409 U.S. 845 (1972) (Railway Labor Act case).

16. Otis Elevator Co., 269 N.L.R.B. 891 (1984).

17. Id. at 893 n.5 (1984) (Chairman Dotson and Member Hunter); id. at 897 n.8 (Member Dennis, concurring).

18. *First National Maintenance*, 452 U.S. at 678.

19. Id. at 686 n.22, citing Young Motor Truck Service, Inc., 156 N.L.R.B. 661, 662–63 (1966).

20. *First National Maintenance*, 452 U.S. at 669, 687–88.

21. General Motors Corp., GMC Truck & Coach Division, 191 N.L.R.B. 951 (1971), enf'd, 470 F.2d 422 (D.C. Cir. 1972).

22. 470 F.2d at 425.

23. See, e.g., Parklane Hosiery Co., 203 N.L.R.B. 597 (1973) (ordering a company to reassume direct control over stores it had transferred to an alter ego franchisee); ACTWU v. Ratner Corp., 602 F.2d 1363, 1370 (9th Cir. 1979) (holding a corporate parent liable under a labor contract although it had transferred manufacturing operations to a subsidiary). Cf. Howard Johnson Co. v. Hotel Employees Detroit Local, 417 U.S. at 249, 266–67 (Douglas, J., dissenting) (arguing "that there was a substantial continuity—indeed identity—of the business operation" before and after franchiser bought the assets of a franchisee).

24. *First National Maintenance*, 452 U.S. at 677 n.15, 681–82.

25. Penntech Papers, Inc. v. NLRB, 706 F.2d 18, 26, 27 (1st Cir.), cert. denied, 464 U.S. 892 (1983).

26. NLRB v. National Car Rental System, Inc., 672 F.2d 1182, 1188 (3d Cir. 1982).

See American Distributing Co., Inc. v. NLRB, 715 F.2d 446, 450 (9th Cir. 1983); NLRB v. Transmarine Navigation Corp., 380 F.2d 933, 939–40 (9th Cir. 1967).

27. Penntech Papers, Inc., 263 N.L.R.B. 264, 265 (1982), enf'd, 706 F.2d 18 (1st Cir.), cert. denied, 464 U.S. 892 (1983); NLRB v. National Car Rental System, Inc., 672 F. 2d at 1191; Transmarine Navigation Co., 170 N.L.R.B. 389 (1968). Cf. Royal Plating and Polishing Co., 160 N.L.R.B. 990 (1966); NLRB v. Winn-Dixie Stores, Inc., 361 F.2d 512 (5th Cir. 1966).

28. See, e.g., *Fibreboard*, 379 U.S. at 208 n.2.

29. *First National Maintenance* 452 U.S. at 681.

30. Lone Star Steel Co. v. NLRB, 639 F.2d 545, 556 (10th Cir. 1980), cert. denied, 450 U.S. 911 (1981).

31. Id. at 553–56. This assumes that there is no contractual prohibition of a strike.

32. For example, in *First National Maintenance*, the maintenance company's customer was unwilling to hire the displaced employees directly because its contract with the maintenance company prohibited direct hiring of the maintenance employees for thirty days after termination of the contract. First National Maintenance Corp. v. NLRB, 452 U.S. 666, 670 (1981). A maintenance company's waiver of that contract provision would have been a reasonable effects demand.

33. For example, in Blu-Fountain Manor, 270 N.L.R.B. 199, 207 (1984), enf'd, 785 F.2d 195 (7th Cir. 1986), the administrative law judge pointed out that failure to notify the union of an impending sale prevented the union from ending a strike before the sale took place.

34. Compare, e.g., International Association of Machinists and Aerospace Workers v. Northeast Airlines, Inc., 473 F.2d at 554, 557–59 (no "unlimited" duty under the Railway Labor Act to bargain over a merger's effects; no duty at all where bargaining "would be ineffectual unless the company could be required to renegotiate the merger," the need for negotiation is not "compelling," there is "no allegation that the notice given the Union of the merger was insufficient," and the union waited six months after the merger agreement before demanding negotiation), with Martin Marietta Corp., 159 N.L.R.B. 905, 907 (1966) ("[i]t may be that where a seller . . . has clear knowledge of the dissolution of the employing entity [planned by the successor] . . . an obligation to *timely* discuss matters flowing from such action exists").

35. *First National Maintenance*, 452 U.S. at 683–84.

36. See Serrano v. Jones & Laughlin Steel Co., 790 F.2d 1279, 1286–87 (6th Cir. 1986). One judge felt that workers might also be entitled to have the value of any concessions which they had granted awarded them by a court. Id. at 1289 (Porter, J., dissenting in part).

37. See, e.g., UAW v. Cardwell Manufacturing Co., Inc., 416 F. Supp. 1267, 1288–89 (D. Kan. 1976); UAW v. Avis Industrial Corp., 56 L.R.R.M. 2632 (E.D. Mich. 1964); Ex-Cell-O Corp., 60 L.A. 1094, 1099–1100 (Sembower, 1973).

38. See generally Belknap, Inc. v. Hale, 463 U.S. 491 (1983); Caterpillar, Inc. v. Williams, 107 S.Ct 2425 (1987).

39. See generally Caterpillar, Inc. v. Williams, 107 S. Ct. at 2425. Atari, Inc. v. Carson, 166 Cal. App. 3d 867, 212 Cal. Rptr. 773 (6th Dist. 1985), is an example of a state suit alleging that a company transferred operations overseas after improperly leading workers to believe it would not. In Steelworkers Local 1330 v. U.S. Steel Corp., 631 F.2d 1264, 1279 (6th Cir. 1980), the court found it unnecessary to reach the question whether oral statements by corporate officials could give rise to promissory estoppel

claims by union and worker plaintiffs. Abbington v. Dayton Malleable, Inc., 561 F. Supp. 1290, 1296–98 (S.D. Ohio 1983), aff'd, 738 F.2d 438 (6th Cir. 1984), is a similar later case. These decisions suggest that, if a company unambiguously commits itself to remaining open in exchange for worker concessions, the company may be liable under promissory estoppel principles if it reneges.

40. See UAW v. Cardwell Manufacturing Co., Inc., 416 F. Supp. 1267, 1289–90 (D. Kan. 1976).

41. Teamsters Local 174 v. Lucas Flour Co., 369 U.S. 95, 101–4 (1962); Charles Dowd Box Co. v. Courtney, 368 U.S. 502 (1962).

42. Serrano v. Jones & Laughlin Steel Co., 790 F.2d 1279 (6th Cir. 1986).

43. Allis-Chalmers Corp. v. Lueck, 471 U.S. 202 (1985); IBEW v. Hechler, 107 S.Ct. 2161 (1987).

44. *First National Maintenance Corp.*, 452 U.S. at 682.

45. See generally Textile Workers Union of America v. Darlington Manufacturing Co., 380 U.S. 263 (1965).

46. For example, in *First National Maintenance*, the union won an election in March, and the company first expressed dissatisfaction with its customer in June. The union requested bargaining on July 12, and termination of the operation was announced on July 25. See 452 U.S. at 668–69. Whatever the actual motivation for such a termination—a matter difficult for unions to investigate, much less litigate—workers would likely sense a connection between the facility shutdown and their exercise of the statutory right to organize. Cf. U.S. Contractors, Inc., 257 N.L.R.B. 1180 (1981), enf. denied on other grounds, 697 F.2d 692 (5th Cir. 1983); Kingwood Mining Co., 210 N.L.R.B. 844 (1974), enf'd, 515 F.2d 1018 (D.C. Cir. 1975) (sale of assets case). Not surprisingly, proof of illegal discrimination to the satisfaction of the Reagan Board has been particularly difficult to muster. See, e.g., Maritz Communications Co., 274 N.L.R.B. 200 (1985) (reversing an administrative law judge's finding of discrimination by a successor employer).

47. The proof, buried in various corporate documents such as Securities and Exchange Commission quarterly reports and production records obtained through subpoena in an NLRB proceeding, included evidence that a new facility had been acquired, that figures used to present an economic justification for the plant closing had been falsified, and that the firm's parent corporation had repeatedly closed union plants in other countries. In addition to seeking to deceive the union and the NLRB, the firm was apparently seeking tax advantages to which it was not entitled.

48. Lone Star Steel Co. v. NLRB, 639 F.2d 545 (10th Cir. 1980), cert. denied, 450 U.S. 911 (1981).

49. *First National Maintenance Corp.*, 452 U.S. at 682.

50. For example, the agreement between the Atlantic Apparel Contractors Association and the ILGWU's Northeast, Western Pennsylvania and Ohio Department and Eastern Pennsylvania Region includes a clause which states:

> An Employer shall not enter into partnership or consolidate or merge with or become the successor or assign of another person, firm or concern in the industry unless the new firm assumes all accrued obligations to the Union, to the benefit funds hereinafter named, and to the workers of the constituent concern. Upon the formation of such a partnership, or upon such consolidation or merger, such new firm shall give preference in employment to the workers of the absorbed concern over all other workers except those then employed by the firm that continues in business.

The agreement between Local 102, ILGWU and five trucking associations in New York's garment center includes similar language and requires "reasonable notice of any such transaction,'' severance pay to any workers ''that merged firm chooses not to employ,'' and carry-over of employee seniority for purposes of vacation eligibility.

51. See generally National Woodwork Manufacturers Assoc. v. NLRB, 386 U.S. 612 (1967) (agreement that union carpenters will not handle prefitted doors); International Brotherhood of Teamsters Local 24 v. Oliver, 358 U.S. 283 (1959) (agreement that trucking companies must pay any owner operators who are employed at least union scale plus costs of operation).

52. See generally, e.g., International Woodworkers Local 3–193 v. Ketchikan Pulp Co., 611 F.2d 1295 (9th. Cir. 1980) (waiving employer's right to require NLRB election rather than card check); Retail Clerks International Local 455 v. NLRB, 510 F.2d 802 (D.C. Cir. 1975) (same); UAW v. Dana Corp., 679 F.2d 634 (6th Cir. 1982) (waiving employer's right to oppose unionization), vacated as moot, 697 F.2d 718 (6th Cir. 1983).

53. See, e.g., Retail Store Employees Local 400 v. Great A&P Co., Inc., 480 F. Supp. 88, 94–95 (D. Md. 1979). The best-known contract including this type of clause is probably the one signed by the Amalgamated Clothing and Textile Workers Union and J.P. Stevens after their historic struggle. A union may not, however, negotiate for workers it does not properly represent.

54. See, e.g., Brotherhood of Locomotive Engineers v. Chicago and North Western Railway Co., 314 F.2d 424, 433 (8th Cir.), cert. denied, 375 U.S. 819 (1963) (agreement to arbitrate merger disputes held enforceable); International Assoc. of Machinists and Aerospace Workers v. Northeast Airlines, Inc., 473 F.2d 549, 555 (1st Cir.), cert. denied, 409 U.S. 845 (1972) (union governed by Railway Labor Act must apply to System Adjustment Board for relief under contract requiring premerger discussion).

55. See, e.g., Machinists and Aerospace Workers, Local Lodge No. 1266 v. Panoramic Corp., 668 F.2d 276, 286 (7th Cir. 1981); ILGWU v. Bali Co., 649 F. Supp. 1083 (D.P.R. 1986), app. dismissed, 815 F.2d 691 (1st Cir. 1987); UAW v. Miles Machinery Co., 34 B.R. 683, 113 L.R.R.M. 3616 (E.D. Mich. 1982); Amalgamated Food Employees Local No. 590 v. National Tea Co., 346 F. Supp. 875 (W.D. Pa. 1972), remanded without opinion, 474 F.2d 1338 (3d Cir. 1972); see generally *Howard Johnson Co.*, 417 U.S. at 258 n.3.

56. United Steelworkers Local 1330 v. U.S. Steel Corp., 631 F.2d 1264, 1282–83 (6th Cir. 1980). For a discussion of some legal problems associated with purchases of companies by employees, see Sutton v. Weirton Steel Div. of National Steel Corp., 724 F.2d 406 (4th Cir. 1983), cert. denied, 467 U.S. 1205 (1984).

57. See Wallace v. Civil Aeronautics Board, 755 F.2d 861, 862 (11th Cir. 1985). In International Assoc. of Machinists and Aerospace Workers v. Northeast Airlines, Inc., 473 F.2d 549, 559–60 (1st Cir.), cert. denied, 409 U.S. 845 (1972), the court held that Congress' grant of authority to the CAB to approve mergers on these terms superseded the Railway Labor Act's or a collective-bargaining agreement's imposition of a duty to bargain over a merger, even if there would otherwise be such a duty.

58. Northwest Airlines–Republic Airlines Acquisition Case, Department of Transportation Order 86–7–81 (July 31, 1986).

59. See generally Brotherhood of Maintenance of Way Employees v. United States, 366 U.S. 169, 172–73 (1961); Matter of Milwaukee Railroad, 713 F.2d 274, 281–82 (7th Cir. 1983), cert. denied, 465 U.S. 1100 (1984); Brotherhood of Locomotive Engineers v. Boston & Maine Corp., 788 F.2d 794 (1st Cir.), cert. denied, 107 S. Ct. 111 (1986).

60. 49 U.S.C. § 11347.

61. 41 U.S.C. § 353 (c). The background of the law is discussed in Boeing Co. v. Machinists, 504 F.2d 307, 312 n.7 (5th Cir. 1974), cert. denied, 421 U.S. 913 (1975).

62. *Fibreboard* 379 U.S. at 225–26 (Stewart, J., concurring).

63. The cases cited at supra note 23 are examples of rulings disregarding the form of a transaction and recognizing an alter ego relationship.

64. NLRB v. Allcoast Transfer, Inc., 780 F.2d 576, 579–82 (6th Cir. 1986), includes a useful survey and discussion of precedent. Cf. Crest Tankers, Inc. v. NMU, 796 F.2d 234, 238 n.2 (8th Cir. 1986).

65. See All Kind Quilting, Inc., 266 N.L.R.B. 1186 (1983). In this case, a company closed during a union drive and sold its machinery to a new company, but there was evidence that the transaction was a sham. The Supreme Court in Textile Workers v. Darlington Manufacturing Co., 380 U.S. 263 (1965), recognized that opening a new plant for the purpose of escaping a union plant ''would involve discriminatory employer action,'' id. at 273–74, and that antiunion motive could be found even where the new plant took the form of a legally distinct corporation, id. at 265–66, 274–77.

66. Franklin Textiles, Inc., 68 L.A. 223 (Kornblum, 1976).

67. Compare *Wiley*, 376 U.S. 543 (no ''successors and assigns'' clause in predecessor's contract but arbitration with surviving entity in merger was ordered) with *Howard Johnson Co.*, 417 U.S. 249 (''successors and assigns'' clause in predecessor's contract but no successor obligation to arbitrate was found).

68. *Wiley*, 376 U.S. 543.

69. Id. at 543, 550, 551.

70. *Burns*, 406 U.S. at 286; *Howard Johnson Co.*, 417 U.S. at 257.

71. *Wiley*, 376 U.S. at 550 n.3, 547–48.

72. Interscience Encyclopedia, Inc., 55 L.A. 210, 218 (Roberts, 1970).

73. *Burns*, 406 U.S. at 272.

74. Id. at 287–88.

75. *Howard Johnson Co.*, 417 U.S. 249.

76. Id. at 254, 257–58.

77. Fall River Dyeing & Finishing Corp., 107 S.Ct. at 2234, 125 L.R.R.M. 2441, 2446 (1987).

78. Boeing Co. v. International Association of Machinists and Aerospace Workers, 504 F.2d 307, 317, 322 (5th Cir. 1974) cert. denied, 421 U.S. 913 (1975) (emphasis added).

79. 504 F.2d at 317–323.

80. In addition to the two elements of substantial continuity in the work force and continuity in the enterprise, *Howard Johnson*'s list of differences from *Wiley* (outlined in the text) suggests that the nonexistence of a meaningful remedy to redress the predecessor company's illegality could point toward holding the successor liable.

81. *Howard Johnson Co.*, 417 U.S. at 262 n.8. Cf. *Fall River Dyeing* 125 L.R.R.M. at 2441, 2446.

82. See, e.g., Kobell v. Suburban Lines, Inc., 731 F.2d 1076, 1086–88 (3d Cir. 1984); NLRB v. Foodway of El Paso, 496 F.2d 117, 119–20 (5th Cir. 1974); NLRB v. New England Tank Industries, Inc., 302 F.2d 273, 276–77 (1st Cir.), cert. denied, 371 U.S. 875 (1962).

83. United Food and Commercial Workers Local 152 v. NLRB, 768 F.2d 1463, 1474–75 (D.C. Cir. 1985).

84. Ekas v. Carling National Breweries, Inc., 602 F.2d 664 (4th Cir. 1979), cert.

denied, 444 U.S. 1017 (1980); cf. Sutton v. Weirton Steel Div. of National Steel Corp., 724 F.2d 406, 412 (4th Cir. 1983), cert. denied, 467 U.S. 1205 (1984). A union must be careful, however, to take into consideration the existing contractual rights of all employees. See Griesmann v. Chemical Leaman Tank Lines, Inc., 776 F.2d 66, 72, 75 (3rd Cir. 1985) (company promise not to add additional workers to a seniority list may be a binding contract, which union must consider).

85. *Burns*, 406 U.S. at 291. The court cited a case, Oilfield Maintenance Co., 142 N.L.R.B. 1384 (1963), in which assumption of a predecessor's contract was found because the successor and predecessor were alter egos.

86. *Burns*, 406 U.S. at 287–88.

87. Stockton Door Co., 218 N.L.R.B. 1053 (1975), enf'd, 547 F.2d 489 (9th Cir. 1976), cert. denied, 434 U.S. 134 (1977); Drivers and Helpers Local 92 v. Strabley Building Supply, Inc., 98 L.R.R.M. 3025 (N.D. Ohio 1978).

88. *Burns*, 406 U.S. at 272.

89. Id. at 294–95.

90. Id. at 280–81; Western Distributing Co. v. NLRB, 608 F.2d 397, 399 n.4 (10th Cir. 1979).

91. Fall River Dyeing & Finishing Corp. v. NLRB, 107 S. Ct. at 2236.

92. United Food and Commercial Workers Local 152 v. NLRB, 768 F.2d 1463, 1474 (D.C. Cir. 1985); see NLRB v. Cablevision Systems Delivery Co., 671 F.2d 737 (2d Cir.), cert. denied, 459 U.S. 966 (1982); Aircraft Magnesium, 265 N.L.R.B. 1344 (1982), enf'd, 730 F.2d 767 (9th Cir. 1984); Fall River Dyeing & Finishing Corp. v. NLRB, 107 S. Ct. at 2236 (''emphasis on the employees' perspective'').

93. 107 S. Ct. 2225 (1987).

94. Id. at 2234–35 (If the new employer makes a conscious decision to maintain generally the same business and to hire a majority of its employees from the predecessor, then the bargaining obligation of Section 8(a) (5) is activated.'').

95. See, e.g., Boeing Co. v. International Association of Machinists and Aerospace Workers, 504 F.2d 307, 318–20 (5th Cir. 1974), cert. denied, 421 U.S. 913 (1975); NLRB v. Band-Age, Inc., 534 F.2d 1, 4 n.6 (1st Cir.), cert. denied, 429 U.S. 921 (1976); United Maintenance & Manufacturing Co., 214 N.L.R.B. 529 (1974).

96. *Fall River Dyeing* 107 S. Ct. at 2237, & a.12.

97. Panda Terminals, Inc., 161 N.L.R.B. 1215, 1220–22 (1966); see The Kroger Co., 155 NLRB 546 (1965).

98. See supra notes 81–83 and the accompanying text.

99. *Fall River Dyeing*, 107 S. Ct. at 2234.

100. *Burns*, 406 U.S. at 280–81 n.5.

101. United Food and Commercial Workers Local 152 v. NLRB, 768 F.2d 1463, 1476 (D.C. Cir. 1985); Blu-Fountain Manor, 270 N.L.R.B. 199 (1984), enf'd on other grounds, 785 F.2d 195 (7th Cir. 1986).

102. Piasecki Aircraft Corp. v. NLRB, 280 F.2d 575, 591 (3d Cir. 1960), cert. denied, 364 U.S. 933 (1961); Mason City Dressed Beef, 231 N.L.R.B. 735, 748 (1977), enf. denied on other grounds, 590 F.2d 688, 691 n.2 (8th Cir. 1978).

103. *Fall River Dyeing* 107 S. Ct. at 2233–34. See also NLRB v. Jarm Enterprises, Inc., 785 F.2d 195, 205–6 (7th Cir. 1986); Indianapolis Mack Sales and Service, Inc., 272 N.L.R.B. 690 (1984), enf. denied on other grounds, 802 F.2d 280 (7th Cir. 1986);

Ranch-Way, Inc., 203 N.L.R.B. 911 (1973); Zim's Foodliner, Inc. v. NLRB, 495 F.2d 1131, 1140 (7th Cir.), cert. denied, 419 U.S. 838 (1974).

104. *Fall River Dyeing* 107 S. Ct at 2237–40. The concept was developed in such earlier cases as NLRB v. Hudson River Aggregates, Inc., 639 F.2d 865, 869–71 (2d Cir. 1981); NLRB v. Premium Foods, Inc., 709 F.2d 623, 630 (9th Cir. 1983); and Jeffries Lithograph Co. v. NLRB, 752 F.2d 459, 467–68 (9th Cir. 1985).

105. *Fall River Dyeing*, 107 S. Ct. at 2241. The union had demanded bargaining at a time when 18 of the successor's 21 employees had worked for the predecessor; 36 of 55 employees hired for an initial shift with a complete range of jobs had worked for the predecessor. However, only 52 or 53 of the 107 employees working several months later had worked for the predecessor. Thus, if the employer had been entitled to delay a response until its full complement had been hired, there would have been no bargaining obligation.

106. *Burns*, 406 U.S. at 294–95.

107. See Spitzer Akron, Inc. v. NLRB, 540 F.2d 841, 845–46 (6th Cir. 1976), cert. denied, 429 U.S. 1040 (1977); Howard Johnson Co., Inc., 198 N.L.R.B. 763 (1972), enf'd, 496 F.2d 532 (9th Cir. 1974); Saks & Co., 247 N.L.R.B. 1047, 1051, enf. denied, 634 F.2d 681, 687 (2d Cir. 1980); Spruce-Up Corp., 209 N.L.R.B. 194, 195 (1974), enf'd, 529 F.2d 516 (4th Cir. 1975); International Association of Machinists and Aerospace Workers v. NLRB, 595 F.2d 664, 671–76 (D.C. Cir. 1978), cert. denied, 439 U.S. 1070 (1979).

108. Golden State Bottling Co. v. NLRB, 414 U.S. 168 (1973).

109. Musikiwamba v. ESSI, Inc., 760 F.2d 740 (7th Cir. 1985).

110. Am-Del-Co., 234 N.L.R.B. 1040, 1041 (1978); cf. NLRB v. Jarm Enterprises, Inc., 785 F.2d 195, 204–5 (7th Cir. 1986).

111. See generally Wheeler v. Snyder Buick, Inc., 794 F.2d 1228 (7th Cir. 1986) (employment discrimination case).

112. Beazeley & Russell, "Steel Union Is Balking at Further Givebacks, Terming Them Futile," Wall St. J., July 29, 1986, at 12.

11

PLANT CLOSINGS, RELOCATIONS, AND TRANSFERS OF UNIT WORK: A MANAGEMENT VIEW

Peter G. Nash and Scott W. Schattenfield

Editors' Note. Messrs. Nash and Schattenfield examine plant closings and work relocations and transfers in the context of the employer's statutory duties to bargain in good faith and not to discriminate because of union affiliation. They analyze in detail the factors that are relevant in determining whether such activities will be deemed motivated by legitimate business considerations rather than antiunion animus, including timing, precipitousness, threats, awareness of union activity, financial condition, production problems, economic efficacy, past practice, removal of plant materials, disparate treatment, documentary corroboration, investment in plant equipment at the old site, availability of work for employees at the new site or operation, misrepresentation or failure to provide information to the union, willingness to engage in decision bargaining, and the degree of unionization at the new facility.

As our nation moves from an industrial to a service economy, as older facilities become obsolete, and as our industries face ever-increasing worldwide competition, managers are faced more and more with the decisions to close, relocate, or transfer existing facilities. In agonizing over these decisions, management must be mindful of its obligations to its employees and the labor law implications such decisions normally import.

The applicable labor law requirements generally fall into two areas of concern: bargaining duties under Section 8(a)(5) and the proscription of antiunion motivation in Section 8(a)(3) of the NLRA.

If an employer must bargain but neglects to do so, he may be liable for back pay to all employees displaced as a result of his decision. However, just because an employer must bargain does not mean he must reach an agreement with the union. Without provisions in a labor agreement restricting the employer's options to close or move, the employer need only bargain in good faith to the point of impasse and may then execute its closing or relocation decision. If an employer's closing or relocation decision is based upon antiunion considerations in contravention of Sections 8(a)(3), that employer may be liable to all displaced employees for back pay and possible job reinstatement.

The application of the foregoing legal principles depends upon the nature of the transaction. For example, a management decision to close a business completely has minimal labor law implications; partial closings, temporary shutdowns, and facility transfers or relocations have far broader legal consequences.

COMPLETE BUSINESS TERMINATIONS

In its 1965 *Darlington* decision, the Supreme Court held that ''an employer has the absolute right to terminate his entire business for any reason he pleases.''[1] The rationale for this holding is that an employer who completely terminates his entire business, even if he is motivated solely by antiunion animus, is not seeking to enhance his future position in relation to his employees.[2]

Even where the employees are union represented, the employer is not required to bargain with the union about the decision to go out of business.[3] However, even though ''decision'' bargaining is not required, an employer may be required to bargain with a union over the decision's effect on unit employees.[4]

PARTIAL, PERMANENT SHUTDOWNS

Duty to Bargain

Prior to 1981, the courts were divided as to whether an employer contemplating a partial closing had to bargain over that decision with the union representing the affected employees,[5] while the NLRB had held that a partial termination was indeed a mandatory subject of bargaining.[6]

In *First National Maintenance Corp. v. NLRB*,[7] however, the Supreme Court made it clear that even an employer whose employees are union represented normally will not be required to bargain over the pure business decision to shut down a plant (but will be required to bargain over the effects of that closing upon employees).[8] The Court recognized that where considerations influencing the decision whether to close are amenable to resolution through the bargaining process (e.g., labor costs), it would be in the employer's best interests to voluntarily bargain with the union.[9] In addition, the effects bargaining obligation provides the union with an avenue through which to make known its views and its willingness to offer concessions which could bring management's closing decision to the bargaining table. The Court ''conclude[d] that the harm likely to be done to an employer's need to operate freely in deciding whether to shut down part of its business purely for economic reasons outweighs the incremental benefit that might be gained through the union's participation in making the decision."[10]

Where the employer's decision is likely to be quite sensitive to labor costs, bargaining over the decision may be required, as illustrated by Court's decision in *Fibreboard Paper Products v. NLRB*,[11] which held that an employer's decision to subcontract maintenance work was a mandatory subject of bargaining. The *Fibreboard* Court focused on the fact that the decision "did not alter the Company's basic operation . . . [that no] capital investment was contemplated . . . [and that therefore] requir[ing] the employer to bargain about the matter would not significantly abridge his freedom to manage his business."[12] *First National Maintenance* is thus a logical outgrowth of the *Fibreboard* decision.[13]

Antiunion Motive

A decision to close or terminate part of a business, such as totally and completely closing a single plant or facility, may violate the antidiscrimination requirement of Section 8(a)(3) or (1) of the NLRA if the decision to close or the timing of the closing[14] is not based on valid business reasons but, rather, is motivated by a desire to chill unionism elsewhere to the benefit of the employer. That latter motive is established by a showing that:

1. The employer has an interest in other plants or businesses that is substantial enough to enable the employer to realize an economic benefit if unionization of the other business is discouraged.
2. The plant was closed for the purpose of obtaining the benefit.
3. And it was realistically foreseeable that the plant closing would generate fears among remaining employees that their plant would also close if they supported unionization.[15]

In summary, an employer who closes part of the business normally need not bargain about the closing decision, must bargain about the effects of that decision on its union-represented employees, and may violate the Act if the decision is not business motivated but, instead, is based upon a desire to chill unionism in other facilities.

TEMPORARY SHUTDOWNS AND LOCKOUTS

Duty to Bargain

An employer whose employees are union represented must bargain about a temporary shutdown decision (but not, of course, about a bargaining lockout)[16] and over the effects of such a shutdown upon the employees.[17] Of course, as discussed earlier, absent labor contract restrictions on an employer's right to close or relocate (and absent antiunion animus), an employer need only bargain to a good faith impasse with its union and is thereafter free to implement its decision unilaterally.[18]

Antiunion Motive

An employer may temporarily shut down the business and lay off the employees without violating NLRB Sections 8(a)(3) and (1) if that decision is based upon valid business reasons, but he may not do so if he is motivated by antiunion bias—a desire to avoid or undercut a union.[19] Furthermore, an employer may temporarily lock out employees in support of a collective-bargaining position as long as the decision is not motivated by union hostility, a desire to discourage union membership, or a desire to avoid bargaining.[20]

PLANT RELOCATIONS

By far the most litigated and most complicated legal requirements concern an employer's decision to relocate or transfer a plant or facility. These decisions may or may not be bargainable, and they are the types of management decisions most susceptible to an inference of antiunion bias. The remainder of this chapter discusses this legally complex management decision.

Bargaining Obligation

In *Otis Elevator II*, the NLRB, following the Supreme Court's lead in *First National Maintenance*, set forth the basic bargaining requirements for employers. If the decision to transfer or relocate a facility turns on labor costs—in the sense that wage, benefit, or working condition concessions may be able to alter the employer's decision to relocate—the relocation decision must be bargained over unless the employer can establish some overriding reason for not bargaining, such as a need for speedy action or a need to keep the decision confidential.[21] If, on the other hand, the relocation decision involves a fundamental change in the nature and direction of the employer's business and, accordingly, does not turn on labor costs, the employer is not required to bargain with the union about that decision. Whether or not the decision to relocate is bargainable, effects bargaining is required.[22]

Antiunion Motive

An employer may close all or part of its business and relocate it elsewhere for valid business reasons, but Sections 8(a)(1) and (3) are violated if that relocation is motivated by antiunion bias.[23] Even if the closing and relocation are lawful, the employer may still violate Sections 8(a)(1) and (3) if the employer denies transfer rights to employees because of their union membership or representation,[24] or if the employer accelerates the decision to transfer for antiunion reasons.[25]

Various factors are used in determining whether business reasons or antiunion feelings prompt a relocation. Generally speaking, a decision to close or relocate a unionized facility (or one subject to union organizing) seldom turns totally on an antiunion bias or totally on pure business considerations. Furthermore, few employers openly state that their decision is based upon a desire to rid themselves of a union. Thus, almost every reported case involves a weighing of economic and business considerations against antiunion considerations in order to determine whether, under all the circumstances, the decision to close or relocate was lawful or unlawful. The NLRB has consistently treated each case individually by considering the particular facts involved without applying any set criteria. The resolution of this issue is primarily a matter of common sense and inevitably turns on whether the business reasons offered by the employer appear, upon analysis, to be credible or pretextual.[26] The NLRB and courts, however, do consider certain factors as particularly relevant in ascertaining motivation.

The Timing of the Decision to Relocate or Close. In *NLRB v. Lloyd Wood Coal Co. Inc.*,[27] no discriminatory relocation was found where the business was operating at a loss, the company accountant recommended selling, and steps were taken to sell the present site and acquire a new site prior to the onset of organizing activities. No violation was found despite evidence of antiunion motivation including shutting down almost immediately after a demand for recognition, an unlawful employee discharge, and several other violations including unlawful interrogation, surveillance, and plant closure threats.

In *Roman Cleanser Co.*,[28] no Section 8(a)(3) violation was found where the business was in a state of decline and losing money, the expansion plans at the old plant did not materialize, and the company president testified (without documentary corroboration) that the decision to relocate was made prior to the union activities. Again, there was some evidence of antiunion motivation: The shutdown occurred two days after the union demanded recognition, and the employer had engaged in illegal, coercive interrogation.

Similarly, in *Mt. Hope Finishing Co. v. NLRB*,[29] the relocation did not contravene Section 8(a)(3) where the business was steadily declining, the relocation was contemplated before union activities began (new sites had been explored before the advent of union activities), and there was a general trend in the textile industry to relocate to the South. Countervailing evidence of antiunion motivation included substantial layoffs two days after the union demanded recognition, closure of the plant six weeks after the union election victory, and a final decision to relocate made soon after the union activities began.

The Employer's Awareness of Union Activity. In *NLRB v. Prineville Stud Co.*,[30] a Section 8(a)(3) discriminatory relocation was found where the plant was closed the day after the union obtained authorization cards from a majority of the employees. The evidence showed that the employer was aware and resentful of the union activity, and there was a two-month supply of raw materials on hand at the time of closure and relocation. In *Lloyd Wood Coal Co.*,[31] the lack of employer awareness of union activity at the time of the relocation was a factor considered by the court in finding no Section 8(a)(3) violation.

The Relocation Is Likely to Alleviate the Asserted Economic Difficulties. In *Local 57, ILGWU v. NLRB* (Garwin),[32] a discriminatory relocation was found where the employer had committed independent unfair labor practices, had operated at a substantial profit over the previous two years, and had failed to show that the relocation would alleviate purported economic problems. The principal economic justification asserted by the employer was the loss of a major customer, but the evidence showed that this had occurred after the relocation decision had been made.

The Sudden Nature of the Closure or Relocation. In *National Family Opinion, Inc.*,[33] the employer was found to have violated Section 8(a)(3) by closing the printing department despite the Board's finding that the employer intended to close the department sometime in the future. The employer had threatened closure prior to the union's election victory and then closed the plant immediately at the outset of negotiations for a collective-bargaining agreement. In *Long Lake Lumber Co.*,[34] a discriminatory closing was found where the shutdown occurred one day after the union organized the employees and the company's foreman made antiunion plant closing threats. The employer asserted that the shutdown was occasioned by bad weather, but the evidence showed that the operation had not been shut down in prior years during more adverse weather conditions.[35]

Employer Threats of Closure. Such threats, themselves Section 8(a)(1) violations, are persuasive evidence of antiunion animus.[36]

The Employer's Past Practice under Similar Circumstances. In *Lloyd Wood Coal Co.*[37] evidence that there was no layoff when the employer relocated on a prior occasion did not establish a discriminatory motive in the present layoff and relocation where the transferee site was not operational at the time of the layoff.[38]

The Removal of Materials from the Plant. In *Sylco Corporation*, the transfer of the plant's knitwear department was not violative of Section 8(a)(3) despite the fact that the plant received a large delivery of raw materials which it then removed to another plant for the manufacturing process.[39] The NLRB noted that, although the removal of material from a plant during a time of union activities can be indicative of an antiunion motivation, it was insufficient in the instant case where the knitwear department was losing money, the decision to close was made before the union activities started, the materials arrived after the decision was made, and the evidence of improved business conditions after the closure decision was based primarily upon vague statements by employees.

The Plant's Financial Condition. In several cases in which the closed plant was losing money, no Section 8(a)(3) violation was found,[40] but economic decline is not an absolute defense.[41] In *Strawsine Manufacturing Company, Inc.*, a Section 8(a)(3) violation was found despite the employer's showing that the closed facility had lost $100,000 in its last year of operation.[42] The fact that another of the employer's plants had lost eight times as much during the same year and was not closed undercut that contention. By contrast, closing a profitable operation does not necessarily lead to a statutory offense. In *International Ladies Garment Workers Union v. NLRB (McLoughlin)*,[43] no Section 8(a)(3) violation was found in the relocation of a unionized plant even though the plant was operating at a profit, was experiencing no financial difficulty, and the employer had failed to bargain with the union over the relocation. Evidence refuting a finding of discrimination included a showing that the present building was antiquated and required heavy upkeep expenditures, that the plant layout caused operational problems, and that there was a large turnover of employees due to a restrictive seniority provision in the collective-bargaining agreement, which resulted in higher payroll expenses. On the other hand, a Section 8(a)(3) violation was found in another case where a profitable plant was closed.[44]

Operational Problems at the Present Site. As mentioned above, no Section 8(a)(3) violation was found in *McLoughlin* where the present site was antiquated and consisted of two buildings which were inefficient.[45] Similarly, in *Robertshaw Controls Company, Acro Division v. NLRB*,[46] the relocation of a unionized plant was held proper, notwithstanding the personnel manager's statements indicating that the move was made to evade the union, where the evidence showed that the move had been carefully planned over a long period of time, where union membership or nonmembership was not a factor in selecting which employees to transfer, and where the new site was necessitated by a change in the employer's production methods.

Disparate Treatment Based on Employees' Union Views. In *Mt. Hope Finishing Co.*,[47] no Section 8(a)(3) violation was found where the employer did not discriminate against union members in layoffs. In *Royal Norton Mfg. Co.*,[48] however, Section 8(a)(3) was violated when the plant relocated notwithstanding the fact that the employer was ordered to vacate the premises by the lessor, and evidence was introduced that showed that land and a modern building were available at a new site for a reasonable price. These apparently valid reasons were undercut by a showing that the employer was hostile toward the union, had threatened employees, had stated that he would use lease problems to get rid of the union, had violated his Section 8(a)(5) bargaining duty, and had selected employees at the new plant on the basis of the applicants' union views.

The Lack of Documentary Corroboration. Although not absolutely required, documentary corroboration of business justifications is helpful. In *Roman Cleanser Co.*,[49] the court questioned the lack of corroboration for the company president's plausible testimony that the relocation was economically motivated.

The Investment of Capital in Plant Equipment. An employer's closing of an entire "slider" department was found to be in violation of Section 8(a)(3) in *Robin American Corporation*,[50] despite the employer's contention that the department was merely "experimental" and temporary. This assertion was contradicted by a showing that the employer had invested substantial capital in moving, reactivating, and supplementing equipment for the department and had achieved successful production prior to closing. In *Lloyd Wood Coal Co.*,[51] on the other hand, the purchase of new trucks and other equipment for use at the present site was deemed consistent with the purpose of relocating where the equipment was movable and usable at the transfer site. Similarly, the fact that equipment was left at the old plant in *Roman Cleanser*[52] was not indicative of a lack of bona fide business reasons where the equipment was not of "high investment" type and could not be economically moved.

The Refusal to Transfer Employees to a Nearby Relocated Facility. The failure to transfer union-represented employees was found, in *Westwood Import Co. Inc.*,[53] to be indicative of the employers' desire to be rid of the union. In *Universal Security Instrument*,[54] however, the employers transfer offer was held not to indicate an antiunion motive despite the requirement that the employees start their seniority anew at the new location.[55]

Misrepresentations Made to Union and Refusals to Provide Information. In *Local 57, ILGWU v. NLRB (Garwin)*,[56] the failure to tell the union that a move to Florida was contemplated and misrepresentations to the effect that a move to another location in New York was being planned were found to be evidence of an antiunion motive. Similarly, in *ILGWU v. NLRB (McLoughlin)*,[57] the company told the union that it was closing and liquidating its business when, in fact, it was contemplating a move from Indiana to Atlanta. However, in *Motoresearch Company*,[58] the Board held that lack of candor, by itself, did not establish a violation of Section 8(a)(3). There, the company told the union that it was subcontracting unit work, but it did not tell the union that it was subcontracting to a subsidiary company; this misrepresentation was found not to be material. In *Production Molded Plastics*,[59] the Board found that although a lack of candor is a factor in the inquiry whether the company's stated reasons for a relocation were pretextual, where the statement was merely an exaggeration rather than a total fabrication, it was entitled to less weight in establishing the company's antiunion motive.[60]

The Refusal to Bargain with the Union. A failure to bargain over the decision to close or relocate is regarded as one factor indicating a lack of antiunion motivation.[61]

Relocation to Another Unionized Facility. When the transferee facility is unionized, an absence of antiunion motivation is indicated.[62]

Attempts to Gain Concessions from the Union. A sincere effort to secure concessions from the union is some evidence of real economic problems and a lack of any antiunion motive.[63]

As mentioned above, none of these factors is dispositive, standing alone, and all are simply tools used to decide whether the economic justifications offered are genuine or pretextual. The Board's task is one of a careful weighing of the evidence.

CONCLUSION

Every management decision to close or relocate all or part of its unionized business raises the question of whether that employer must bargain about the decision itself and about the effects of the decision on the employees. In almost every instance, effects bargaining is required, and with the exception of a total business closure, most decisions to close or move a plant or facility are apt to necessitate bargaining if at least part of the business reason for the decision is the cost of labor. When there is any question, most employers will choose to bargain—for at least three good reasons. First, bargaining about the effects of the decision is required in any event, and it is the unusual case in which the reason for the decision to move or close does not, as a practical matter, become part of that effects bargaining. Thus, if one is going to talk about the decision anyway, why not do it officially? Second, an employer who bargains about its decision to move goes a long way toward refuting any inference that his move is antiunion motivated. Third, a failure to bargain about a decision to move or relocate is apt to be challenged by the union representing a company's employees. That challenge could delay the closing or transfer often resulting in years of litigation—all of which may be avoided by sitting down with the union first and explaining why the company is considering closing or moving.

Similarly, every decision to close or relocate a unionized business, or a business undergoing union organizing efforts, raises serious questions concerning the management's motive—is there a good business reason for the move or closure, or, on balance, is it motivated by antiunion considerations? Here, there is no easy answer. A good rule of thumb for union-sensitive management is to enter the decision-making process without a commitment to move or close and, thereafter, to reach such a decision only if the business reasons are so substantial that no other decision makes sense. It may not be possible to avoid a challenge to the decision, but it ought to be possible ultimately to win any ensuing legal battle.

NOTES

1. Textile Workers Union v. Darlington Manufacturing Co., 380 U.S. 263, 268 (1965). See also First National Maintenance Corp. v. NLRB (*FNM*), 452 U.S. 666 (1981); Otis Elevator Co., 269 N.L.R.B. 891 (1984).
2. *Darlington*, 380 U.S. at 263.
3. *Darlington*, 380 U.S. at 263; *FNM*, 452 U.S. 666; Otis Elevator Co., 269 N.L.R.B. 891 (1984).
4. See *FNM*, 452 U.S. at 684; Brockway Motor Trucks v. NLRB, 582 F.2d 720 (3d Cir. 1978); NLRB v. Transmarine Navigation Corp., 380 F.2d 933 (9th Cir. 1967); Ozark Trailers, Inc., 161 N.L.R.B. 561 (1966) (although the *Ozark* rationale requiring decision bargaining in partial closing cases was rejected by the Supreme Court in *FNM*, the portion of the opinion reiterating the duty to bargain over the effects of the decision enjoys continued vitality). Effects bargaining encompasses such subjects as severance pay, vacation pay, seniority, pensions, and other issues "of particular relevance and importance" to the employees about to be displaced. NLRB v. Royal Plating and Polishing Co., 350 F.2d 191, 196 (3d Cir. 1965).
5. See NLRB v. Winn-Dixie Stores, Inc., 361 F.2d 512 (5th Cir. 1966) (partial

termination is mandatory subject). Compare NLRB v. International Harvester Co., 618 F.2d 85 (9th Cir. 1980); NLRB v. Adams Dairy, Inc., 350 F.2d 108 (8th Cir. 1965), cert. denied, 382 U.S. 1011 (1966); NLRB v. Royal Plating and Polishing Co., 350 F.2d 191 (3d Cir. 1965).

6. Ozark Trailers, Inc., 161 N.L.R.B. 561 (1966).

7. *FNM*, 452 U.S. 666 (1981). See Otis Elevator Co., 269 N.L.R.B. 891 (1984); Columbia City Freight Lines, Inc., 271 N.L.R.B. 12 (1984).

8. *FNM*, 452 U.S. at 684; Otis Elevator, 269 N.L.R.B. at 892; Milwaukee Spring Division of Illinois Coil Spring Co. (*Milwaukee Spring II*), 268 N.L.R.B. 601 (1984), aff'd sub. nom. Intern. Union, United Auto. Aerospace & Ag. v. NLRB, 765 F.2d 176 (D.C. Cir. 1985).

The pre-*FNM* confusion as to whether decision bargaining was mandated in partial closing situations stemmed in part from *Darlington*'s "chill" test, which was intended to focus on unlawful discrimination and, as such, was not intended to distinguish between partial and complete terminations in the bargaining context. The Supreme Court in *FNM* made it clear that normally the partial termination of a business was a nonmandatory subject under Section 8(d) of the Act. In so finding, the *FNM* court applied a balancing test in deciding whether decision bargaining was mandated, stating that "bargaining over management decisions that have a substantial impact on the continued availability of employment should be required only if the benefit, for labor management relations and the collective bargaining process, outweighs the burden placed on the conduct of the business." 452 U.S. at 679. It then applied the test in the abstract, creating an effective per se rule making decision bargaining nonmandatory in partial termination cases. Id. at 681–686.

9. *FNM*, 452 U.S. at 682–683.

10. Id. at 686.

11. Fibreboard Paper Products v. NLRB, 379 U.S. at 203 (1964).

12. Id. at 213.

13. Id. at 222–23 (Stewart, J., concurring). Justice Stewart had proposed three categories of management decisions that were later adopted by the *FNM* Court: (1) decisions directly involving working conditions or the physical dimensions of the working environment which are clearly bargainable under the Act; (2) decisions having only indirect impact on employees, such as those involving financing or advertising, which are clearly not mandatory subjects of bargaining; (3) those decisions which directly impact employees by eliminating jobs but which involve the core of entrepreneurial control and are fundamental to the basic direction of the corporation, which, under Stewart's analysis, would not be mandatory subjects. The facility shutdown in *FNM* fell into this last category.

14. In Electrical Products Div. of Midland-Ross v. NLRB, 617 F.2d 977 (3d Cir.), cert. denied, 449 U.S. 871 (1980), the court held that what otherwise would have been a legitimate economic closing decision became an unfair labor practice when it was announced just prior to an election at another plant for the purpose of influencing that election. Id. at 986–87. See also Purolator Armored, Inc. v. NLRB, 764 F.2d 1423 (11th Cir. 1985).

15. *Darlington*, 380 U.S. at 275–76; *FNM*, 452 U.S. at 666; Frito-Lay, Inc. v. NLRB, 585 F.2d 62 (3d Cir. 1978). See NLRB v. New England Web, Inc., 309 F.2d 696 (1st Cir. 1962); NLRB v. Drennon Food Products Co., 272 F.2d 23 (5th Cir. 1959); NLRB v. Kingsford, 313 F.2d 826 (5th Cir. 1963).

16. Cf. Hawaii Meat Co. v. NLRB, 321 F.2d 397 (9th Cir. 1963) (no duty to bargain

over subcontracting arrangement designed to keep the struck business operating); see supra note 20.

17. See, e.g., *FNM*, 452 U.S. at 666,681; *Milwaukee Spring II*, 268 N.L.R.B. at 603; Columbia City Freight Lines, Inc., 271 N.L.R.B. at 1216; Brockway Motor Trucks, 582 F.2d 720 (3d Cir. 1978); *Midland-Ross*, 617 F.2d at 979.

18. *Milwaukee Spring II*, 268 N.L.R.B. at 603; University of Chicago v. NLRB, 514 F.2d 942 (7th Cir. 1975); Wimberly v. Clark Controller Co., 364 F.2d 225, 228 (6th Cir. 1966); UAW, Local 375 V. Northern Telecom, Inc., 434 F. Supp. 331, 335 (E.D. Mich. 1977).

19. *Darlington*, 380 U.S. at 263, 269; American Ship Building Co. v. NLRB, 380 U.S. 300 (1965); Schmutz Foundry and Machine Co., 251 N.L.R.B. 1494 (1980), enf'd, 678 F.2d 657 (6th Cir. 1982); Armored Transport, Inc., 252 N.L.R.B. 447 (1980), enf'd, 109 L.R.R.M. 2936 (9th Cir. 1982); NLRB v. Lloyd Wood Coal Co., Inc., 585 F.2d 752 (5th Cir. 1978); The Jones' Boys Discount, 218 N.L.R.B. 135 (1975), enf'd, 94 L.R.R.M. 2125 (6th Cir. 1976).

20. American Shipbuilding, 380 U.S. 300 (1965); Challenge-Cook Brothers of Ohio, Inc., 282 N.L.R.B. 2 (1986); Georgia-Pacific Southern Division, Advice Memorandum in Case No. 5-CA-11747, 104 L.R.R.M. 1167 (1980) (lockout lawful even if implemented prior to impasse in absence of evidence of discriminatory motive); Darling & Co., 171 N.L.R.B. 801 (1968), enf'd, 418 F.2d 1208 (D.C. Cir. 1969).

21. *FNM*, 452 U.S. at 682–83; *Otis Elevator*, 269 N.L.R.B. at 893; *Milwaukee Spring II*, 268 N.L.R.B. at 603; Columbia City Freight Lines, Inc. 271 N.L.R.B. at 12, 16–17; Morco Industries, Inc., 279 N.L.R.B. 100 (1986); De Soto, 274 N.L.R.B. 114 (1985); NLRB Gen. Counsel–*Otis Elevator* Guidelines, 116 L.R.R.M. 186 (1984).

22. Id.; Co-Ed Garment Co., 231 N.L.R.B. 848 (1977); American Needle & Novelty Company, 206 N.L.R.B. 534 (1973), motion to transfer petition granted sub. nom. Kronenberger v. NLRB, 496 F.2d 18 (7th Cir. 1974); ILGWU v. NLRB, 463 F.2d 907 (D.C. Cir. 1972).

23. See, e.g., *Otis Elevator*, 269 N.L.R.B. at 891; Strawsine Manufacturing Co., 280 N.L.R.B. No. 63 (1986); *Midland-Ross*, 617 F.2d 977; Smyth Mfg. Co. Inc., 247 N.L.R.B. 1139 (1980); Weather Tamer, Inc., 253 N.L.R.B. 293 (1980), enf'd in relevant part, 676 F.2d 483 (11th Cir. 1982); *Frito-Lay* 585 F.2d at 62, 67; Ethyl Corporation, 231 N.L.R.B. 431 (1977); Joint Industry Board of the Electrical Industry, 238 N.L.R.B. 1398 (1978); Local 57, ILGWU v. NLRB, 374 F.2d 295 (D.C. Cir.), cert. denied, 387 U.S. 942 (1967); NLRB v. Houston Chronicle Pub. Co., 211 F.2d 848 (5th Cir. 1954); Roman Cleanser Company, 188 N.L.R.B. 931 (1971); International Offset Corp., 210 N.L.R.B. 854 (1974); Production Molded Plastics, Inc., 227 N.L.R.B. 776 (1977), enf'd, 604 F.2d 451 (6th Cir. 1979).

24. National Car Rental Systems, Inc., 252 N.L.R.B. 159 (1980), enf'd in relevant part, 672 F.2d 1182 (3d Cir. 1982).

25. NLRB v. Preston Feed Corporation, 309 F.2d 346 (4th Cir. 1962); Bridgford Distributing Co., 229 N.L.R.B. 678 (1977); Carbonex Coal Company, 262 N.L.R.B. 1306 (1982).

26. Great Chinese American Sewing Co., 227 N.L.R.B. 1670, enf'd, 578 F.2d 251 (9th Cir. 1978); NLRB v. Rapid Bindery, Inc., 293 F.2d 170 (2d Cir. 1961); NLRB v. Kingsford, 313 F.2d 826; Wright-Line, 251 N.L.R.B. 1083 (1980), enf'd, 662 F.2d 899 (1st Cir. 1981); *Weather Tamer, Inc.*, 253 N.L.R.B. at 293, 307.

27. 585 F.2d 752.

28. 188 N.L.R.B. 931.

29. 211 F.2d 365.

30. 227 N.L.R.B. 1845. (1977), enf'd, 578 F.2d 1292 (9th Cir. 1978).

31. 585 F.2d 752.

32. 374 F.2d 295.

33. 246 N.L.R.B. 521 (1979).

34. 34 N.L.R.B. 700 (1941), enf'd, 138 F.2d 363 (9th Cir. 1943).

35. See also Prineville Stud Co., 227 N.L.R.B. 1845 (1977); Lloyd Wood Coal Co., 585 F.2d at 752.

36. See *Prineville Stud Co.*, 227 N.L.R.B. at 1845, 1849; *Long Lake Lumber Co.*, 34 N.L.R.B. 700 (1941); *Frito-Lay* 585 F.2d at 62, 66; *Lloyd Wood Coal Co.*, 585 F.2d at 752, 756.

37. *Lloyd Wood Coal Co.*, 585 F.2d 752.

38. See also *Long Lake Lumber Co.*, 34 N.L.R.B. at 700, 709–710.

39. Sylco Corporation, 184 N.L.R.B. 741 (1970).

40. See Mt. Hope Finishing Co., 211 F.2d 365 (4th Cir. 1954); Sylco Corp., 184 N.L.R.B. at 741 (1970); *Lloyd Wood Coal Co.*, 752, 756.

41. *Prineville Stud Co.*, 227 N.L.R.B. at 1845, 1850.

42. 280 N.L.R.B. No. 63 (1986).

43. *ILGWU v. NLRB*, 463 F.2d 907 (D.C. Cir. 1972).

44. *Local 57, ILGWU*, 374 F.2d 295.

45. 463 F.2d at 907.

46. Robertshaw Controls Company, Acro Division v. NLRB, 386 F.2d 377 (4th Cir. 1967).

47. 211 F.2d at 365.

48. Royal Norton Mfg. Co., 189 N.L.R.B. 489 (1971).

49. 188 N.L.R.B. 931 (1971). (Finding no § 8(a)(3) violation).

50. Robin American Corporation, 245 N.L.R.B. 822 (1979), enf'd in relevant part, 654 F.2d 1022 (5th Cir. 1981).

51. 585 F.2d 752.

52. 188 N.L.R.B. 931.

53. Westwood Import Co. Inc., 251 N.L.R.B. 1213 (1980), enf'd, 681 F.2d 664 (9th Cir. 1982).

54. Universal Security Instrument, 250 N.L.R.B. 661 (1980).

55. See also National Car Rental Systems, Inc., 252 N.L.R.B. 159 (1980).

56. 374 F.2d 295.

57. 463 F.2d 907.

58. Motoresearch Company, 138 N.L.R.B. 1490.

59. 227 N.L.R.B. 776 (1977).

60. See also Strawsine Manufacturing Co. Inc., 280 N.L.R.B. No. 63 (1986).

61. Food Fair Stores, Inc., General Counsel's Advice Memorandum in Case No. 4-CA-9925, 103 L.R.R.M. 1503 (1980); see also Co-Ed Garment Co., 231 N.L.R.B. 848 (1977).

62. Production Molded Plastics, 227 N.L.R.B. 776 (1977).

63. Co-Ed Garment, 231 N.L.R.B. 848 (1977); Food Fair Stores, 103 L.R.R.M. 1503 (NLRB, 1980).

12
PLANT CLOSINGS, RELOCATIONS, AND TRANSFERS OF UNIT WORK: A UNION VIEW

Eugene G. Eisner

Editors' Note. Mr. Eisner deplores the structural inadequacy of the NLRA to provide for meaningful collective bargaining over plant closings, relocations, and work transfers—a failing which has been compounded by recent Supreme Court and NLRB decisions. He finds, however, some solace in decisions concerning effects bargaining, but more hope of union success in arbitral enforcement of collective-bargaining agreements, backed by interim judicial relief in the form of "reverse *Boys Market* injunctions." The author provides examples of contract clauses that will enhance union leverage in dealing with corporate transformation. He also considers remedies outside of the NLRA, such as Title VII of the Civil Rights Act of 1964 and ERISA, and he describes proposed federal plant closing legislation.

In 1935 Congress enacted the Wagner Act which declared that "employees shall have the right to self-organization, to form, join, or assist labor organizations, to bargain collectively through representatives of their own choosing, and to engage in other concerted activities for the purpose of collective bargaining or other mutual aid or protection."[1]

From its inception, the key to the success of the modern legal structure governing labor-management relations was the confidence of all parties that protections and proceedings established by the NLRA (or Act) would function effectively and that the law would be even-handed. In recent years, however, this confidence has been shattered by a failure of the Act to provide meaningful protections to vast numbers of American workers who have lost jobs as a result of plant closings. It is no mere coincidence that a recent chairman of the NLRB (or Board) has publicly declared that "collective bargaining frequently means . . . the destruction of individual freedom and the destruction of the marketplace," and that "the price we have paid is the loss of entire industries and the crippling of others."[2]

Professor Clyde Summers, testifying recently before a House Labor Subcommittee on Labor-Management Relations (which conducted hearings to determine whether the labor laws in the United States should be changed), told the panel that the law, as interpreted by the NLRB and the courts, was no longer serving its initial purpose of encouraging collective bargaining.[3]

Professor James Atleson told the same panel that recent decisions by the Board and the Supreme Court involving the scope of bargaining, partial closings, and the stability of working conditions during the life of the collective-bargaining agreement "call into question both the viability of collective bargaining and the concept that the collective bargaining agreement provides both sides with stability and predictability during its term."[4]

Although the courts and the law generally have not been favorable to labor, recent changes in the law in the face of an increasing incidence of plant closings, relocations, and assets sales (and the concomitant loss of millions of jobs) have made matters much worse and have caused unions and their advisers to seek more creative ways of dealing with this enormous problem. This chapter examines some of the methods that unions have recently adopted (1) to prevent threatened employer shutdown or removal of work or, failing that, (2) to cushion the impact of the loss of work.

As part of this developing strategy, it is of course necessary to understand the legal framework in which we currently operate. A brief analysis is in order.

RIGHTS AND REMEDIES UNDER THE NATIONAL LABOR RELATIONS ACT

Nondiscrimination Principle

Section 8(a)(3) of the Act makes it an unfair labor practice to "discriminat[e] in regard to hire or tenure of employment . . . to encourage or discourage membership in any labor organization."[5] Thus, if it can be shown that the proposed shutdown or removal of work is being considered because of antiunion animus, then a valid Section 8(a)(3) charge would lie. The problem of proving antiunion animus in a plant closing situation is obvious: Normally, a corporation can claim some legitimate business purpose for its action. An examination of the corporation's overall conduct is necessary.

An important distinction must be made between an employer who shuts down a plant and goes completely out of business and one who closes only a department in a plant or one plant of several. In *Textile Workers of America v. Darlington Manufacturing Company*,[6] the Supreme Court held that an employer may go completely out of business even for antiunion reasons without violating Section

8(a)(3). However, the Court limited the reach of its holding to a total cessation of operations; a shutdown of only part of an employer's operations may violate the Act if such a closing is designed to "chill unionism in any of the remaining plants."[7] Thus, if it can be established that the closed plant is a "runaway shop" (moving to another location to avoid the union) or was a single plant of a multiplant employer that was closed for the purpose of discouraging union activity at other plants of the same employer, a Section 8(a)(3) violation can be established.[8]

Section 8(a)(3) also applies when an entire plant remains open, and only part of the work is terminated. This may result either from a transfer of bargaining unit work to another plant of the same employer or from contracting out to another business. In *Ethyl Corporation*,[9] the employer transferred a product line from a plant that had recently voted for union representation to a plant in a different city that was not unionized. The transfer resulted in the layoff of some workers at the unionized plant. In finding that the transfer violated Section 8(a)(3), the Board stated that the fear of subsequent strike activity was not an "objective fact" or a "substantial and legitimate business reason" that could be used to justify a transfer. In addition, the Board rejected the notion that the failure to single out union adherents for layoffs established a defense. In a number of other similar situations, the Board has found violations when an employer closes, or contracts out work from, a department in which an organizing effort is under way.[10]

The most effective potential remedy for Section 8(a)(3) violations is an order that the closed operation be reopened and the displaced workers reinstated.[11] An order to reopen is certainly the most effective remedy, and the Board will order resumption of operations in an appropriate case,[12] but the courts typically will decline enforcement because of the hardship to the employer.[13]

Obviously, when the announcement of a proposed plant closing is made, a thorough investigation of the background of the announcement and the company's practices in the recent past should be undertaken. The union should ask the employer to document and verify any statements made at the bargaining table. The union should request, in writing, the detailed reasons for the move, the location where the product will be made after the closing, and data comparing labor costs at each facility that is currently or in the future will be manufacturing the same product. Finally, the union should ask for copies of any written feasibility studies contemplating the closing or removal. If the employer fails to provide the information or discloses damaging information, early processing of a Board charge may enable the NLRB to seek a preliminary injunction against the closing.[14]

Duty to Bargain

Section 8(a)(5) of the Act provides that "it shall be an unfair labor practice for an employer to refuse to bargain collectively with the representatives of his employees."[15] The phrase "bargain collectively" is defined by Section 8(d) of the Act.[16]

In the past, in a plant shutdown context, a refusal to bargain frequently occurred when an employer failed to tell the union of its plans before implementing them, thereby foreclosing the union from bargaining effectively about the decision to close or move.[17] The Supreme Court held in *Fibreboard Paper Products v. NLRB*[18] that an employer was obligated to bargain about a decision[19] to subcontract work previously performed by bargaining unit employees. The Court's rationale was simple: "Experience illustrates that contracting out in one form or another has been brought, widely and successfully, within the collective bargaining framework."[20]

In response to the question of whether there was a need for negotiations under the circumstances in which an employer is undergoing economic hardship and wishes to get out from under, the Supreme Court responded: "The short answer is that, although it is not possible to say whether a satisfactory solution could be reached [with the union], national labor policy is founded upon the congressional determination that the chances are good enough to warrant subjecting such issues to the process of collective negotiation."[21]

In an oft-cited concurrence, Mr. Justice Stewart pointed out that there are many employer decisions which "may clearly imperil job security or indeed terminate employment"[22] but which are not within the scope of mandatory bargaining. Stewart cited several examples, such as management's decision to invest in labor-saving machinery or to liquidate its assets and go out of business. He argued that such decisions lie at the core of entrepreneurial control and may not be subject to mandatory bargaining.

Many circuit courts, which followed Justice Stewart's distinction, found that closing an entire plant was not a mandatory subject of bargaining.[23] A number of courts, however, adopted the position of the Third Circuit in *Brockway Motor Trucks v. NLRB*,[24] which held that a decision to close a plant was presumptively a mandatory subject of bargaining. The court found that this presumption could be overcome only by a showing of certain extenuating circumstances such as dire financial straits or actions by a third party such as condemnation.

The Board and the courts continued to apply the *Fibreboard* and *Brockway* analyses to plant closing situations for several years. However, in 1981, the Supreme Court, in *First National Maintenance v. NLRB*,[25] adopted Justice Stewart's *Fibreboard* concurrence and held that a decision by an employer to shut down part of its business purely for economic reasons is not a mandatory subject of bargaining. The Court went on to say: "In this opinion we of course intimate no view as to other types of management decisions, such as plant relocations, sales, and other kinds of subcontracting, automation, etc., which are to be considered on their particular facts."[26]

Although *First National Maintenance*, by its terms, was a setback for organized labor, union lawyers relying on then General Counsel Lubbers' advice memorandum distinguished the Court's opinion wherever they could.[27] Until

1984 it was still possible to persuade the Board that an employer had an obligation to bargain about work redistribution schemes such as plant relocations, consolidations, and work transfers.

In 1984, however, the ~~Board began to issue a series~~ of so-called lead cases which substantially broadened the reach of *First National Maintenance*. In *Otis Elevator II*,[28] the Board repudiated well-settled legal doctrine and found that a plant relocation, for allegedly economic reasons, was not a mandatory subject of collective bargaining. In the view of the *Otis II* Board, bargaining will be required only in the rare situation in which it can be established that the employer was motivated *solely* by a desire to reduce labor costs. The Board also held that the union was not entitled to information (feasibility studies and reports conducted by Otis) because Otis was not obligated to bargain over the relocation decision.[29]

Otis Elevator II was soon followed by the Board's flip-flop in *Milwaukee Spring II*,[30] wherein it reversed its prior holding in *Milwaukee Spring I*,[31] and decided that an employer was free to remove its entire plant during the term of a collective-bargaining agreement so long as it did so after reaching impasse with the union, and the collective-bargaining agreement did not contain any explicit prohibition on the transfer of the work.[32] Thus, the one-two punch of *Milwaukee Spring* and *Otis* has made it clear that unions can no longer look to the Board for relief in plant relocation cases except when the employer is violating a contract provision barring such a removal.[33]

Finally, even in those rare instances in which the Board finds a Section 8(a)(5) violation in a plant removal situation, the major drawback of a bargaining order is that the remedy lacks any substantive bite. Thus, the duty to bargain in good faith does not require an employer to make any concessions, but only to bargain to a bona-fide impasse. Resumption of operations is rarely ordered by the Board, particularly when the decision to shut down or relocate was made for ostensibly legitimate economic reasons.

Obligation to Engage in Effects Bargaining

Whether or not an employer has a duty to bargain over its decision to close or transfer its work, the law provides that it must always bargain over the *effects* of the closing upon the employees. Effects bargaining would include such topics as severance pay, seniority, pensions, vacation pay, job transfer rights, and early retirement programs.

The scope of this duty is broad: Bargaining over effects must be conducted in a meaningful manner and at a meaningful time (after the decision to close or transfer has been made but before the employer takes unilateral action on any of the bargainable subjects).[34] Timely notice of a closing must be formal and clear.[35] The employer's duty to bargain about the effects of its decision includes a duty to provide the union with sufficient advance notice and information to ensure meaningful negotiations. An employer who refuses to give such notice or information violates Section 8(a)(5) as surely as one who refuses to bargain at all.[36] And, perhaps most important, if the employer is planning to continue operations at other facilities, effects bargaining includes a duty to discuss preferential hiring and transfer rights.[37]

When an employer has refused to consider transfer to other facilities of its union-represented employees, the Board has often inferred a desire to avoid the union in violation of Section 8(a)(3) of the Act. For example, in *NLRB v. National Car Rental*,[38] the employer closed its facility in Newark and relocated twenty miles south in Edison. The company reassigned four of its seven nonunion employees to the new operation but terminated the employment of all thirteen union workers. The entire work force at the new site was nonunion. No bargaining over the decision occurred despite inquiries by several workers; the Board found an 8(a)(5) violation. Also, in *Eastern Market Beef Processing*,[39] the employer notified the union that it was opening a second plant and that it wanted to renegotiate their unexpired collective-bargaining agreement to ensure labor peace in the new facility. However, during negotiations with the union, the company set up the new plant as a separate division of the corporation and recognized another union as the representative of the new workers it was about to hire. Then the company shut down the existing plant, without guarantees of transfers or the preservation of seniority rights for its existing employees. This, too, was found to violate Section 8(a)(5).

To remedy a failure to bargain over effects, the Board will order the employer to bargain to impasse and provide a limited back pay award. Under the formula that the Board established in *Transmarine Navigation Corp.*,[40] an employer is liable for the wages of each affected employee from a date five days after the Board's order until the date of agreement or impasse, or the union fails to bargain in good faith. The award may not be less than two weeks' pay for each employee.[41]

ENFORCING THE COLLECTIVE-BARGAINING AGREEMENT

As a result of the laissez faire approach taken by the NLRB in plant relocation situations, unions have increasingly resorted to negotiating more protective language into their collective-bargaining agreements and attempting to enforce those agreements. If the collective-bargaining agreement contains a provision barring transfer of work or other restrictive language, the union will naturally seek to enforce these restrictions through arbitration. However, even if the employer agrees to arbitrate (but is not willing to maintain the status quo pending arbitration), the remedy that unions will be seeking is a "reverse *Boys Market* injunction."[42] Unions have used this injunction to stop employer actions when there is a disagreement over an arbitrable issue and the union argues that the injunction is necessary to preserve the viability of the arbitrable process. Clearly, the use of such a tactic can be very effective in a plant closing situation.

One of the most often cited cases on this subject is *Lever Bros. Co. v.*

International Chemical Workers Union Local 2,[43] wherein the court concluded that an injunction in aid of arbitration to prohibit an employer from closing its plant pending arbitration was appropriate.[44] Similarly, in *IAM v. Panoramic Corporation*,[45] the employer attempted to sell a division of the company, and the union alleged a violation of a "successors" clause which prevented the sale unless the purchaser and the union agreed to a contract. In granting the injunction, the court explained that the plaintiff must show a likelihood of success on the merits and be threatened with irreparable harm. The court held that the first requirement is satisfied by a showing that the position the union will espouse in arbitration is "sufficiently sound to prevent the arbitration from being a futile endeavor." As to the second requirement, the court stated:

> We follow what we understand to be the practice of most courts and focus into a single concept the twin ideas of irreparable injury and frustration of arbitration. An injunction in aid of arbitration is appropriate, therefore, only when the actual or threatened harm to the aggrieved party amounts to a frustration or vitiation of the arbitration.[46]

Of course, a reverse *Boys Market* injunction is, at best, a holding action. In the absence of language forbidding work removal of any kind, the injunction pending arbitration usually has the effect of only postponing the inevitable. However, given how few options are available to unions faced with an imminent shutdown, it does buy time for the workers (and possibly for the community) to negotiate alternatives.[47]

Of course, workers are in a better position when their union anticipates the danger of a runaway employer and is able to negotiate clear language in the collective-bargaining agreement. In *Jos. Schlitz Brewing Co.*,[48] the union had been concerned since 1964 about the growth of nationwide brewers, and it was able to secure successively stronger language with respect to plant shutdowns. In 1971, the employer decided to shift all production from its Brooklyn plant to a new plant in Winston-Salem, North Carolina. The labor agreement provided that: "The Employer will not import beer from plants not covered by this Contract to service areas it traditionally served by the Employer from plants and depots covered by this Contract which is the cause for layoffs of employees covered by this Contract."[49] It also stated that "there shall be no layoffs except for lack of work."[50] Based on these provisions, the arbitrator found that the employer was barred from shifting production outside of New York during the term of the contract.

In some cases, unions have successfully argued that there is an implied prohibition against plant movement arising from other clauses in the collective-bargaining agreement, such as the recognition clause. For example, in *Vulcan Rivet & Bolt Corp.*,[51] the employer began contracting out bargaining unit work while employees were on layoff. The arbitrator, relying on the recognition clause, found that the employer had guaranteed that work in bargaining unit classifications would be done by regular employees. He noted that there had been no past history of contracting out bargaining unit work. One can argue that, by recognizing the union and by signing the collective-bargaining agreement, the employer has implicitly agreed to have bargaining unit work done under the terms and conditions of the contract.[52]

In other cases, the union has argued that the employer, by transferring operations, has violated an implied covenant of good faith and fair dealing. Often when the threat of a plant shutdown looms, the union will negotiate material concessions with the understanding that this will forestall the cessation of operations. An employer who extracts such concessions with no intention of altering plans to close the plant may have violated an implied covenant of fair dealing with the union. In *Local 461, IUE v. Singer Co.*,[53] the court awarded the union $2 million in damages for the company's failure to live up to its promise to improve the plant in return for concessions from the union. The union had agreed to at least $1.8 million in "give-backs." In return, the company had agreed to invest $2 million to restructure the facility's operations and to use its best efforts to seek defense work in order to keep the plant open. When the company announced it was closing the plant, having failed to honor either promise, the union sought an injunction and damages. Although the court refused to grant the injunction, since it did not find that the agreement absolutely required the company to keep the plant open, it did award the union damages for breach of the two contract provisions. Damages were to be measured by the value of the give-backs (which was disputed) or the $2 million investment commitment, whichever was greater.

Similarly, in *Ex-Cell-O*,[54] before closing two plants and transferring the work to two other facilities, the employer had extracted concessions from the union by promising to keep the plants in operation in return for such concessions. Arbitrator Sembower posed the question: "How far can an employer contemplating closedowns of his plants entice the bargaining representatives of the employees with offers not to close a plant just to see what can be gotten in negotiations?" He answered: "It is little less than cruel to stir hopes in a workforce whose average age is more than fifty years that the plant where they have spent the bulk of their work life will be kept open if only they make enough concessions."[55] As Professor Archibald Cox has observed: "A collective bargaining agreement implies . . . an implied obligation not to seek substitute labor supply at lower wages or inferior standards. The implied promise would prohibit subcontracting for this purpose."[56]

In other cases, courts and arbitrators have relied on a union shop clause, a clause specifying the procedure for filling job vacancies and the frustration doctrine from contract law to find relief for the unions.[57] These arguments are by no means accepted by all courts or arbitrators.[58] They are certainly no substitute for the negotiation of express restrictions or conditions upon closing or moving a facility.

Unions have negotiated a wide variety of restrictions against closing or transfer of work. Some examples of such negotiated clauses that exist in contracts negotiated by District 65 of the United Automobile Workers are as follows:

1. *No Moving*—The employer agrees that so long as it remains in business it shall not move its operations from its present location beyond reasonable commuting distance.

2. *No Layoffs*—There shall be no layoffs except for lack of work.

3. *No Subcontracting*—The employer agrees not to subcontract any work as long as the employees are capable of performing the work.[59]

4. *Transfer of Operations*—

(a) In the event the employer shall move its operations, this agreement shall remain applicable to the plant at its new location.

(b) If the employer permanently transfers its operations to a location beyond reasonable commuting distance, current employees shall be offered employment by seniority; moving and housing allowances shall also be provided in such instance.

(c) In the event that the employer resumes its operations, in whole or in part, within fifty miles from its present location, it agrees to recognize the union as the exclusive bargaining agent for its employees and enter into negotiations for a new agreement. In the event of such resumption, employees will be recalled in the order of seniority.

(d) The employer agrees to give the union six months' notice before closing any of its operations. In such event, the parties agree to meet to discuss ways of avoiding the closing.

(e) When an operation is closed, the employees shall have a right to transfer back to a former company operation in which the employees previously worked with all seniority rights intact.

For many years, it has been well established that, in the absence of restrictive contract language, a purchasing employer who does not hire a majority of his predecessor's employees will not be required to honor the old agreement or to bargain with the union.[60] So long as there is no antiunion motive present, the successor is free to hire new employees. However, where the employer has hired a "substantial and representative" portion of his new employees, he cannot avoid his bargaining obligation by claiming that he has yet to hire his full complement of employees.[61]

In the attempt to secure strong successorship language in collective-bargaining agreements, some unions have successfully negotiated one or more of the following clauses:

(a) In the event that the employer sells or transfers the business, the employer shall nevertheless continue to be liable for the complete performance of this agreement until the purchaser or transferee expressly agrees in writing with the union that it is fully bound by the terms of this agreement.

(b) This agreement shall be binding on any and all successors and assigns of the employer whether by sale, transfer, merger, acquisition, consolidation, or otherwise. The employer shall make it a condition of transfer that the successor or assignee shall be bound by the terms of this agreement.

(c) This agreement, when executed by the parties hereto, shall be binding upon the union and the employer, their transferees, successors, heirs, executors, administrators, assignees, receivers in bankruptcy, receivers in equity, trustees, or any such other equivalent designee, whether voluntary or pursuant to a court decree.[62]

When unions and their counsel have exhausted all their physical and creative energies in an unsuccessful effort to dissuade an employer from shutting down or moving, they will do everything possible to secure the greatest possible compensation for workers. Unfortunately, as recent studies have shown, whatever benefits are obtained cannot remedy the devastating long-term effects of a shutdown on workers and their communities.[63]

LEGAL REMEDIES OUTSIDE THE NLRA OR COLLECTIVE-BARGAINING AGREEMENT

Civil Rights Laws

Depending on the facts of the case, it may be worthwhile to explore the viability of an employment discrimination suit in a plant closing situation. Several cases have alleged that a move of operations from an urban to a suburban location has a disparate impact on minorities in violation of Title VII of the Civil Rights Act of 1964.[64]

ERISA

Also, ERISA[65] makes it unlawful for an employer to discharge or discriminate against a participant ''for the purpose of interfering with the attainment of any right to which such participant may become entitled'' under a pension plan. A plant closing motivated in part by a desire to avoid pension liability to an older work force could be the subject of an ERISA lawsuit.[66]

Eminent Domain

In the desperate search for solutions, unions have begun to persuade some state and local governments to exercise their power of eminent domain to preserve a failing plant. For example, in New Bedford, Massachusetts, after Gulf & Western had announced that it was planning to shut down its local facility, the mayor of the city announced (under pressure from the unions) that, unless the company found a private buyer to continue the operation, he intended to invoke the city's power of eminent domain to condemn the property, take it over, and sell it to a private party to operate it. The company ultimately found a private buyer who continued to operate the plant.[67]

Legislative Solutions

Federal Legislative Initiatives. Each year since 1975 a bill has been introduced in Congress which has sought to address the plant closing problem. A recent version, called the Labor-Management Notification and Consultation Act of 1986 (HR 1616), would have required employers to give adequate notice of plant closings to workers and their communities to enable them to explore alternatives to closing. The bill provided federal financial assistance to employers who are affected by the legislation. It also provided for the payment of shutdown benefits for affected workers and communities, as well as for transfer rights,[68] protection of benefits for a period of time following shutdown or mass layoff, grants and loans to family businesses, economic redevelopment assistance to local governments, and financial assistance to workers in the event of an opportunity to buy a failing business and run it as a worker cooperative.[69]

A much narrower provision requiring 60 days' advance notice of plant shutdowns and major layoffs has recently been enacted into law.[70]

Although the proposed federal legislation falls short of some of the more progressive European legislation—by shielding from review the basic question of whether relocation is necessary—it would provide at least some modicum of protection. Substantive federal restrictions on the corporate power to close or relocate plants probably would require a major mobilization of political forces which has yet to occur.

State and Local Legislation. While the problem of plant closings is plainly a national one—one which would best be addressed through federal legislation—a number of state and local legislatures have already enacted statutes, and others have considered enacting such laws. Most of these laws would require (1) advance notice of a plant shutdown or layoff, (2) severance pay for workers who lose jobs due to a plant closing or relocation away from the community, and (3) payment of adjustment fees to the adversely affected community.[71]

CONCLUSION

Our current laws are not adequately protecting the American workers from the ravages of plant closings. Accompanying this economic disaster is a continuing breakdown of labor-management relations. In this chapter, we have attempted to demonstrate some of the ways in which unions have tried to ameliorate the problem, in part through the use of restrictive contract language. However, this problem is one of national if not global dimensions. National legislation mandating protection for workers faced with a plant closing based on the Western European model would be a positive step. Without massive intervention at the federal or state levels, one could easily predict years of industrial strife, the likes of which we have not seen before.

NOTES

1. 29 U.S.C.§ 157.

2. "House Subcommittee Plans Oversight Hearing on Changes at Enforcement Division of NLRB," (BNA) Daily Lab. Rep., June 7, 1983, at A8.

3. "Statement Examining Question 'Has Labor Law Failed?' before House Labor Subcommittee on Labor-Management Relations," (BNA) Daily Lab. Rep., June 22, 1984, at F6.

4. "Statements before House Labor Subcommittee on Labor-Management Relations Hearing on Labor Law, June 25, 1984," (BNA) Daily Lab. Rep., June 26, 1984, at F9.

5. 29 U.S.C. § 158(a)(3).

6. 380 U.S. 263 (1965).

7. Id. at 275.

8. None of the recent Board cases have changed this fundamental rule. Indeed, in Otis Elevator, 269 N.L.R.B. 891 (1984) (discussed later), the Board reaffirmed the *Darlington* principle by limiting its holding to purely economic decisions of the employer. As a practical matter, however, the Board rarely finds Section 8(a)(3) conduct in the absence of a general pattern of antiunion conduct. Normally, an employer can refute the charge by showing good economic reasons for moving the business. See, e.g., NLRB v. Rapid Bindery, Inc., 293 F.2d 170 (2d Cir. 1961) (economic justification for threat to close plant if the union won election).

9. 231 N.L.R.B. 431 (1977).

10. See, e.g., Smyth Manufacturing Co. and Beacon Industries, 247 N.L.R.B. 1139 (1980). Beacon, an engine manufacturer, acquired control of a separate, unorganized corporation (Smyth) in the bookbinding business. The bookbinder operation was profitable, but it was closed and the work was subcontracted out. About fifteen months after being acquired, the Board found that the Smyth plant had been closed for the purpose of discouraging unionism.

11. Id. at 1142.

12. Hood Industries, Inc., 248 N.L.R.B. 597 (1980).

13. See, e.g., Jays Foods, Inc. v. NLRB, 573 F.2d 438 (7th Cir.), cert, denied, 438 U.S. 859 (1978); NLRB v. Townhouse T.V., Inc., 531 F.2d 826 (7th Cir. 1976).

14. The NLRB is authorized under Section 10(j) of the Act to seek a temporary injunction in the district courts if the underlying unfair labor practice is seriously eroding the injured party's rights. Thus, for example, in Gottfried v. Eichlin, Inc., 113 L.R.R.M. 2349 (E.D. Mich. 1983), the Board obtained a Section 10(j) injunction when the employer sought to transfer its valve machinery and assembly work to another plant without union approval. The court held that the employer must bargain to a good faith impasse over a midcontract work transfer, and it failed to do so by refusing to provide the union with information necessary to the bargaining process. Similarly, in Zipp v. Bohn Heat Transfer Group, 110 L.R.R.M. 3013 (C.D. Ill. 1982), the court found a Section 10(j) injunction "just and proper" when the relocation of work would require laying off 40 percent of the plant's work force in an area of high unemployment. The court reasoned that many workers would leave the area in search of jobs during the resolution of the dispute, thereby irrevocably eroding the union's base of support and making potential restoration impossible. See also Kobell v. Thorsen Tool Co., 112 L.R.R.M. 2397 (M.D. Pa. 1982).

15. 29 U.S.C. § 158(a)(5).

16. Section 8(d) provides: "For the purposes of this section, to bargain collectively is the performance of the mutual obligation of the employer and the representative of the employees to meet at reasonable times and confer in good faith with respect to wages, hours, and other terms and conditions of employment, or the negotiation of an agreement, or any question arising thereunder, and the execution of a written contract incorporating any agreement reached if requested by either party, but such obligation does not compel either party to agree to a proposal or require the making of a concession." 29 U.S.C. § 158(d).

17. Where a company purposely withheld notice for several weeks, that failure was, in itself, a violation of Section 8(a) (5). See NLRB v. Borg Warner Corp., 663 F.2d 666 (6th Cir. 1981), cert. denied, 457 U.S. 1105 (1982). The extent of advance notice which an employer has to give varies with the circumstances. Where an employer has legitimate economic reasons for making a sudden decision and the employer had previously notified the union that he was considering the move, two days' notice has been held sufficient. Chippewa Motor Freight, 261 N.L.R.B. 455 (1982).

18. 379 U.S. 203 (1964).

19. "Decision" bargaining must be distinguished from "effects" bargaining. Even if there is no duty to bargain over the decision to close, the employer must always bargain over the impact of that decision.

20. 379 U.S. at 211.

21. Id. at 214.

22. Id. at 217.

23. See, e.g., ILGWU v. NLRB, 463 F.2d 907 (D.C. Cir. 1972); Weltronic v. NLRB, 419 F.2d 1120 (6th Cir. 1969), cert. denied, 398 U.S. 938 (1970).

24. 582 F.2d 720 (3d Cir. 1978).

25. 452 U.S. 666 (1981).

26. Id. at 686 n.22.

27. Shortly after the ruling came down, General Counsel Lubbers issued an advice memorandum in which he stated his intention to distinguish *First National Maintenance* from removal, subcontracting, automation, or consolidation cases. In these cases, which do not involve a decision to go out of business partially, the General Counsel stated that the Board should apply the balancing test laid out in *First National Maintenance*: weighing the burden on the conduct of business against the benefit to labor-management relations and the collective-bargaining process. Factors to be considered in determining the burden on the employer are the need for speed in meeting a business opportunity, the possible loss of tax or financing advantages based on confidentiality, and any potential negative publicity from the bargaining process itself that might cause economic damage to the business. In assessing the benefits of bargaining, the Board should discover to what extent the employer's decision is based on labor costs or other considerations that are potentially bargainable issues. "Bargaining about Business Changes; What Would Be Beneficial for Labor-Management Relations?" (BNA) Labor Relations Yearbook—1981, at 315; 4 (CCH) Lab. L. Rep. ¶ 9271 (Ad. Mem. of General Counsel, Nov. 30, 1981).

28. 269 N.L.R.B. 891. In *Otis Elevator I*, 255 N.L.R.B. 235 (1981), the Board found an unlawful refusal to bargain on the same facts, on the premise that the relocation was a mandatory subject of bargaining.

29. This presents an interesting problem for union negotiators who will be attempting to determine whether a company's decision to go out of business partially "turned on labor costs." Since this information is clearly relevant, I submit that unions will continue

to press for it notwithstanding *Otis Elevator II*. In a similar situation in 1987, this author pressed for and obtained such information in arbitration by subpoena after being turned down by the Board for the same information.

30. 268 N.L.R.B. 601 (1984).

31. 265 N.L.R.B. 206 (1982).

32. Under *Otis Elevator II* and *Milwaukee Spring II*, which hold that there is no duty to bargain about the decision to close all or part of a business because ''closure'' was not covered under an existing contract, the question arises whether unions should strike in support of a demand for bargaining over this issue. If the Board has held that the contract does not restrict the plant closure, conceivably the matter might be nonarbitrable, and thus no injunction could issue under the rationale of Boys Market v. Retail Clerks, 358 U.S. 235 (1970). Although such a strike could ultimately lead to possible discharge or a lawsuit for damages, it is clearly an option for unions to consider.

33. Such was the case in Brown Co., 278 N.L.R.B. 113 (1986), where the Board found a Section 8(a)(5) violation because the unilateral transfer of work was (1) in the face of a work preservation clause prohibiting such transfer and (2) found to be for the sole purpose of reducing labor costs—thus passing the Board's *Otis II* test. The work preservation clause in that case provided:

> It is the intent of the parties to this Agreement to protect the work performed by employees in the bargaining unit.
>
> The Employer recognizes that it is important and desirable to utilize its own equipment and drivers to the greatest extent possible prior to using sub-haulers and/or non-Company trucks.
>
> Under these conditions, the Employer agrees that sub-haulers and/or non-Company trucks will not be utilized as a subterfuge to defeat the protection of the bargaining unit work.

34. *First National Maintenance*, 452 U.S. at 681.

35. ILGWU v. NLRB, 463 F.2d 907 (D.C. Cir. 1972)

36. NLRB v. R. L. Sweet Lumber, 515 F.2d 758 (10th Cir.), cert. denied, 423 U.S. 986 (1975).

37. Fraser & Johnston Co. v. NLRB, 469 F.2d 1259 (9th Cir. 1972); Universal Security Instruments v. NLRB, 649 F.2d 247 (4th Cir.), cert. denied, 454 U.S. 965 (1981).

38. 672 F.2d 1182 (3d Cir. 1982).

39. 259 N.L.R.B. 102 (1981).

40. 170 N.L.R.B. 389 (1968).

41. Seeburg Corp., 259 N.L.R.B. 819 (1981).

42. A *Boys Market* injunction may be issued if a strike in breach of the collective-bargaining agreement is occurring or is about to occur and if the dispute is over an issue subject to arbitration. Buffalo Forge Co. v. United Steel Workers, 428 U.S. 397 (1976). A reverse *Boys Market* injunction is sought by unions to prevent employers from taking action allegedly in breach of the collective agreement which arbitration will not be able practicably to undo.

43. 554 F.2d 115 (4th Cir. 1976).

44. The appeals court, in upholding the injunction, stated: ''The district court correctly issued the preliminary injunction to preserve the status quo pending the completion of arbitration. Had the district court not preserved the status quo, Lever Bros. would have permanently transferred their plant from Baltimore, Maryland, to Hammond, Indiana. If the union then prevailed in the arbitration, they would have had a double burden to satisfy—first, to convince the company that it should not have moved the plant to Ham-

mond, Indiana—a fait accompli, and then it would have had the burden to convince the company to move the plant back to Baltimore, Maryland. The arbitration in this sense undoubtedly would have been 'but an empty victory' for the union.'' Id. at 122.

45. 668 F.2d 276 (7th Cir. 1981).

46. The *Panoramic* decision is often cited by union lawyers since the court required only that ''the union's position be sufficiently sound to prevent the arbitration from being a futile endeavor.'' It is also interesting to note that the *Panoramic* court found the potential loss of employment sufficient to satisfy the ''irreparable injury'' requirement. 668 F.2d at 284–85. See also Local 590 Meat Cutters v. National Tea, 346 F. Supp. 875 (E.D. Pa. 1972); National Maritime Union v. Commerce Tankers, 325 F. Supp. 360 (S.D.N.Y. 1971); UAW Local 757 v. Budd Co., 345 F. Supp. 42 (E.D. Pa. 1970).

47. There have been an increasing number of situations in which the buying of time was crucial to the eventual salvaging of a plant, in whole or in part. This tactic should not be underestimated. See the text accompanying note 67, infra.

48. 58 L.A. 653 (Lande, 1972).

49. Id. at 655–56.

50. Id.

51. 36 L.A. 871 (Williams, 1961).

52. See also Twin City Milk Producers, 42 L.A. 1121 (Gunderman, 1964); Celanese Corp. of America, 14 L.A. 31 (Wolff, 1950). There are, of course, awards going the other way.

53. 540 F. Supp. 442 (D.N.J. 1982).

54. 60 L.A. 1094 (Sembower, 1973).

55. Id. at 1100.

56. Cox, ''The Legal Nature of Collective Bargaining Agreements,'' 57 Mich. L. Rev. 1 (1958).

57. UAW v. Webster Electric, 299 F.2d 195 (7th Cir. 1962); Martin-Marietta Corp., 46 L.A. 430 (Sembower, 1966).

58. See Olin Mathieson Chemical Corp., 52 L.A. 670 (Bladek, 1969); Stoneware, Inc., 49 L.A. 471 (Stouffer, 1967); Mead Corp., 46 L.A. 459 (Klamon, 1966); Richmond Baking Co., 30 L.A. 493 (Warns, 1957); Waller Bros. Stone Co., 27 L.A. 704 (Dworkin, 1956).

59. UFI Razor Blades v. District 65, 99 L.R.R.M. 2676 (S.D.N.Y. 1978) (enforcing arbitration award), aff'd, 610 F.2d 1018 (2d Cir. 1979).

60. Howard Johnson Co. v. Detroit Joint Executive Board, Hotel & Restaurant Employees, 417 U.S. 249 (1974); NLRB v. Burns Detective Agency, 406 U.S. 272 (1972). However, several arbitrators have held that once an employer has hired a majority of the old work force and does not substantially change the nature of the business, it may be bound to deal with the union and, perhaps, honor the old contract. Cf. Amherst Publishing Corporation, AAA Case No. 1130–1806–78 (Wildebush, 1978); see also, B & K Investments, 71 L.A. 366 (Turkus, 1978).

61. See NLRB v. Fall River Dyeing & Finishing Corp., 107 S. Ct. 2225 (1987); Premium Foods v. NLRB, 709 F.2d 623 (9th Cir. 1983).

62. In situations in which a bankrupt company has sold its assets to another corporation and there is sufficient identity with its prebankruptcy predecessor, the new entity may be held to be bound by the old contract. William B. Allen, 267 N.L.R.B. 700 (1983). Moreover, a successor employer who purportedly buys a failing business in bankruptcy, ''free and clear of all liens,'' is liable for back pay owed by its predecessor resulting

from a prior Board order. International Technical Products Corp., 249 N.L.R.B. 1301 (1980).

63. See B. Bluestone & B. Harrison, The Deindustrialization of America (1982); S. Cobb & S. Kase, Termination: The Consequence of Job Loss (1977).

64. 42 U.S.C. § 2000(e). In Mays v. Motorola, 22 (BNA) FEP Cas, 799 (N.D. Ill. 1979), a violation was premised on the fact that the small number and percentage of minorities at the suburban location could not be explained by geography since other employers in the same area employed significantly more minorities. See also Bell v. Automobile Club, 17 (BNA) FEP Cas. 575 (E.D. Mich. 1978).

65. 29 U.S.C. § 1140.

66. Employees asserting that the employer fired them for the purpose of preventing the vesting of their pension rights have a cause of action under Section 510. See Kross v. Western Electric Co., 701 F.2d 1238 (7th Cir. 1983); Amaro v. Continental Can, 724 F.2d 747 (9th Cir. 1984). Moreover, an employer can violate the Age Discrimination in Employment Act (ADEA), 29 U.S.C. §§ 621–34, by withholding severance pay from employees eligible for retirement. See, e.g. EEOC v. Borden's, Inc., 724 F.2d 1390 (9th Cir. 1984).

67. Unions Today: New Tactics to Tackle Tough Times 17–18 (BNA 1985).

68. The proposed legislation would require the company planning a shutdown of a facility to offer similar or substantially equivalent employment at its other facilities (if such other facilities exist).

69. The Report of the House Subcommittee on Education and Labor of the Committee on Labor-Management Relations, ''Worker Dislocation, Capital Flight & Plant Closings'' 13–20 (Nov. 1985), offers examples of situations in which advance notice of a closing made possible constructive solutions. In some cases, a purchase of the targeted facility was negotiated by local groups, or an outside purchaser was located who agreed to maintain the facility. In other cases, local groups were able to develop cost savings and productivity improvements that were large enough to convince the employer that its prior calculations were wrong and that the facility was too profitable to abandon.

70. ''President Reagan's Statement on his Decision to Let Plant Closing Bill Become Law'' (BNA) Daily Lab. Rep., August 3, 1988, at D1 ff.

71. See Final Report, Lieutenant Governor of New York Task Force on Plant Closings A1–A5 (Mar. 1985).

13

AUTOMATION, TECHNOLOGICAL CHANGE, AND THE LIMITS OF COLLECTIVE BARGAINING: A MANAGEMENT VIEW

William C. Zifchak

Editors' Note. Neither the decentralized, multiunion character of the American labor movement nor the relatively small-bargaining unit focus of the NLRA is conducive, Mr. Zifchak writes, to a constructive labor response to technological advances. On the contrary, federal labor law encourages short-sighted, union job preservation strategies, which may preserve jobs for existing union members but only at the cost of the industry's ability to complete in the marketplace and generate jobs in the future. Mr. Zifchak examines the typical and, in his opinion, counterproductive union reactions to technological change in the longshore and printing industries, and he contrasts them with an encouraging joint management-union effort in the meat-packing industry. The author rejects any approaches that would require bargaining over managerial decision making but favors a government role in assisting and retraining displaced workers. Practical suggestions for management implementation of technological changes are also offered.

The author wishes to dedicate this chapter to his former colleague, the late Frederick R. Livingston, Esq., a pioneer in the search for solutions to labor-management discord, who taught him that helping management and labor to perceive their mutuality of interest was an honorable endeavor. He regrets that Fred could not bring the piercing simplicity of his vision and his near half-century of experience with the subject matter to bear on this work. He also gratefully acknowledges the research assistance of Harlan J. Silverstein, Esq., in the preparation of this chapter.

''Automation conjures up the thought of speed. In collective bargaining, however, automation results in the converse of speed. Automation slows down collective bargaining by introducing new complexities."[1] Labor and management have been battling over technological change since the invention of the wheel. Legend has it that during the French and Indian War, upon the substitution by the British of ox-carts for Indian labor to haul freight, "the displaced Indians retaliated by killing drivers and oxen and burning the carts."[2] And everyone has heard about the Luddites who destroyed labor-saving textile machinery in early nineteenth-century England.

One would have thought that the institution of collective bargaining would afford labor and management the best hope for peacefully accommodating to the mounting stresses of automation and technological change[3]—that resolution of the tension between progress and job security is best accomplished within a consensual framework, refined over decades of use. However, it is this author's perspective that, as we move into the twenty-first century, constraints inherent in the bargaining process and in the sociopolitical climate in which it functions will continue to limit its utility in that endeavor.

My purpose here is, first, to identify the historical origins—social, functional, and legal—of the problem; second, to examine the American industrial experience in dealing with technological change issues in the organized sector; and third, to consider ways in which collective bargaining might be strengthened, including possible alternatives to collective bargaining, if private enterprise is to make the leap successfully into the next century.

ORIGINS

Social Factors

Since the nineteenth century, the American labor movement has viewed its role in industrial relations as that of a worthy adversary to, rather than collaborator with, management. Despite periodic, well-intentioned efforts at labor-management cooperation, American labor generally has viewed management as an arm's-length consumer of its brawn; whereas, management typically has viewed labor as a necessary component of cost and unions as an entirely unnecessary evil.[4] There have been notable exceptions to this rule, of course—the Armour Automation Committee stands out as a leading example of the beneficent results of labor-management collaboration.[5] Nevertheless, labor's instinct has been to shun responsibility for management of the firm, and the industrial entrepreneur has rarely sought to disabuse labor of its studied lack of interest.

Despite their adversarial posture, however, organized labor and management have coexisted largely peacefully because the collective-bargaining process has ensured a dynamic in which, every two or three years in contract negotiations, the parties perceive—and openly acknowledge—their mutuality of interest, the reality that, in the end, each cannot live without the other. But automation and technological change distort or obliterate entirely their perception of common ground because management thereupon discovers that it *can* exist if labor is confined to a much less significant role.

The thrust of labor's reaction to the threat of self-obsolescence brought on by automation has been to fight a rearguard action, raising the stakes of "divorce" and ofttimes coercing management to endure a loveless—and equally costly—"marriage." Put another way, rather than view automation from the broader, long-term perspective as to what might be desirable for working people generally in terms of lower costs and improved services to consumers and the competitive health of the employing firms, the focus of most unions has been a one-dimensional, short-term one—how to survive and protect the jobs of its own members, even though those jobs have been rendered superfluous, in whole or in part. Labor's objective all too frequently has been either to create artificial demand for its services or to hold automation for ransom, and thereby be paid handsomely *in futuro* for *past* services rendered.[6]

Functional Factors

Labor's characteristic resistance[7] to technological change is explainable in part by the fact that unions are organized by industry or craft and, in most cases, by geographic area.[8] This decentralization of the U.S. labor movement into self-governing fiefdoms makes it difficult for individual unions to be statesmanlike in the face of technological change. The impact of automation on job security, in a given industry, is uniquely personal to the union or unions that have organized the affected workers within that industry, whose membership tends to have industry-specific skills and, certainly, loyalties. To illustrate this point, if all American workers were represented by a single union, akin to Israel's Histadrut, the predisposition of the union to react constructively to technological advance in any given industrial sector would be enhanced exponentially. Worker retraining or supplemental income programs would be more prominent, and there would be greater willingness not to obstruct progress in a given sector.

As matters stand, however, unions tend to take an insular view of the economy, and whether the anticipated efficiencies of technological change can be promptly instituted in a given industry has turned fortuitously on the extent of union organization and on the strength of the union at the bargaining table. Put another way, the more mature the industry and the greater the reliance historically on union labor, the more difficult it has been to introduce technological change on a timely and cost-effective basis. It is indeed an ironic quirk of history that profound technological advances have suddenly presented themselves for potential use in labor-intensive industries long dominated by organized labor, such as the shipping, printing, meat-packing, and automotive industries.

Legal Factors

Inevitably, the legal institutions created earlier in this century to foster collective bargaining and the principle of consensual resolution of disputes have spawned a number of legal principles that have contributed to union resistance to technological change. First, Section 9 of the NLRA mandates that unions organize employers for the most part on a unit-by-unit basis.[9] Most legal presumptions point toward bargaining within the smallest appropriate unit,[10] and indeed the parties by law are discouraged from looking beyond the unit at hand in resolving their differences.[11] Although consensual multiemployer unit bargaining, or the looser "coalition" or "pattern" forms of bargaining, can cut across an entire industry,[12] as a rule, bargaining unit parameters do not extend much beyond the single employer or single plant location. At most, in certain industries, such as the meat-packing, garment, and automotive industries, a single employer may bargain with the union of its employees at several locations on a loose, "master" contract basis, reserving uniquely local issues—and ratification—to individual facilities. Thus, the basic procedural unit for collective bargaining under the NLRA reinforces and perpetuates the narrow-minded, parochial instincts of unions. Although the Board's single unit preference may facilitate union organizing,[13] at least with respect to technological innovation, it also fosters union resistance to management's initiatives.

Second, the NLRB requires the parties to bargain only over those subjects that relate directly or indirectly to the cost and trappings of labor,[14] viewed narrowly as the work and workers that comprise the specific bargaining unit at hand.[15] In this manner, unions are discouraged, for example, from acquiring, through bargaining, representation rights in other new, potential bargaining units.[16] Rather, unions are limited by law to exerting economic pressure to preserve those jobs or job functions in the existing unit,[17] or, at most, to reacquire jobs or job functions historically within the unit but lost temporarily.[18] In order for a union to establish a lawful work preservation motive with regard to new technology that threatens to take away union jobs, it must show a functional relationship between the traditional work that the union purports to preserve and the new work created by technological innovation, such that one can fairly conclude that the union's object is not to organize jobs elsewhere.[19]

This may not always be an easy task. Beyond this, unions are left to the uncertainties of traditional organizing techniques. Indeed, under recent case law, unions are confined to job preservation measures—as opposed to aggrandizement of new jobs—as a proper and lawful response to technological innovation. Thus, in *National Labor Relations Board v. International Longshoremen's Association*, the Supreme Court stated that

> in judging the legality of a thoroughly bargained and apparently reasonable accommodation to technological change, the question is not whether the Rules [i.e., the job preservation provision in dispute] represent the most rational or efficient response to innovation, but whether they are a legally permissible effort to preserve jobs.[20]

Psychologically, therefore, unions are conditioned by legal constraints on their organizing objectives and self-help tactics to preserve what they have in the face of automation; this gives them little incentive to consider the bigger picture.

Third, with the exception of its brief foray into social engineering in *Milwaukee Spring (I)*[21] the NLRB, as well as the courts, has been reluctant to enhance union involvement in those fundamental decisions affecting management of the enterprise—principally, organizational structure and the commitment of capital—on the premise that these issues, for the most part, involve considerations of entrepreneurial discretion going well beyond mere labor costs and, therefore, not likely to be appropriately addressed in collective bargaining.[22] The basic decision to automate or to institute technological change is thus not invariably a mandatory bargaining subject (I am not advocating that it clearly ought to be). Whether such an obligation exists may turn on the nature of the automation, on varying factors in management's decision-making process, or on constraints written into collective-bargaining agreements.[23] This laissez faire spirit—faithful to organized labor's self-image as the adversary, not the business partner, of management—gives management largely free rein in running its business. Unions, therefore, are normally relegated to "impact" issues,[24] bargaining over how to deal with the consequences of the automation decision for the bargaining unit, which again casts them in the role of reactive agents and apologists for the status quo.

Furthermore, consistent with this philosophy, certain empirical studies suggest that labor arbitrators generally will condone management's reassignment of bargaining unit work outside of the unit as a result of automation or technological innovation that involves a significant change in the nature of the work of the training necessary to operate the new machinery, without any express contractual language prohibiting it.[25] As with the Board, arbitrators tend to focus on ameliorating the immediate effects of the change on the bargaining unit, for example by requiring training or retraining if the cost is not prohibitive.[26]

These legal forces, therefore, whether mere symptoms or the cause, together operate in such a manner as to virtually preclude unions from advocating broad-based, long-term, ultimately progressive solutions to the work force dysfunctions attendant upon automation and technological change.

EXPERIENCE TO DATE

Experience in the collective-bargaining crucible with accommodation to technological change shows the pervasive influence of the various forces described above.

Focus on Job Security or the Status Quo

Although there have been important exceptions,[27] most union-management "accommodations" to technological innovation have required management to invest heavily in job or financial security as the quid pro quo for the freedom to introduce new technology and to restructure the work force in its discretion.[28] Reports in the newspapers on these accommodations can be seen every day—typically in the automobile, steel, electronics, communications, and other heavy industries.[29] These job security measures have run the gamut from "featherbedding,[30] to restrictive work rules such as minimum manning requirements,[31] to guaranteed income or substantial severance benefits for dislocated employees,[32] to preemptive restrictions on, for example, layoffs, subcontracting, relocation, or reorganization under circumstances other than those condoned by the union.[33] More constructive accommodations, such as worker retraining programs, which stress retooling the work force to function under the new technology or in entirely different trades, have been less prevalent, although they are becoming more common.[34]

The cumulative effect has been to retard or greatly increase the cost of technological innovation in the heavily unionized basic industries, to the ultimate detriment of unionized firms in those industries. In the short run, this lag in productivity gains has kept the price of goods artifically high. In the long run, it has opened the door to the emergence of nonunion and, more recently, foreign competition.

Experience with Income Security Programs: Breakdown of Bargaining

No example better illustrates the inability of traditional collective bargaining to deal rationally with the prospect of automation than the experience in two industries—shipping and printing—with worker income security programs.[35] In each case, the program was the product of crisis bargaining. Although of lasting benefit to immediately affected union members, these programs have each proved to be incapable of adapting to unanticipated changes in competitive conditions. Since union members are paid to sit idly, there is little incentive for employees to be retrained for productive jobs. These programs have become the financial albatross around the collective neck of the organized sector of these respective industries. In retrospect, they are monuments to shortsightedness.

Longshoring. First, in the East Coast shipping industry, in an automation dispute extending back thirty years, the International Longshoremen's Association (ILA) has exacted a heavy price from shippers for the "containerization" revolution, a form of automation whereby ocean going metal shipping containers are loaded and unloaded—"stuffed and stripped"—at locations at a distance from the dock. This process has largely replaced the traditional method of piece-by-piece loading and unloading of vessels at dockside by ILA labor.[36]

In return for the right to ship containerized loads—in accordance, however, with strict "Rules on Containers" governing the overall process, which impose harsh penalties for their breach and essentially call for featherbedding practices[37]—the ILA has enjoyed a Guaranteed Annual Income (GAI) for life for all eligible bargaining unit members.[38]

Guaranteed annual income proved to be the cancer that has undermined the unionized longshoring industry: Whatever gains the employers struggled to achieve in implementing containerization were largely negated by this permanent—and increasingly burdensome—obligation. In less than twenty years' time, the cost of GAI to the steamship companies mushroomed from $ 1.7 million to over $200 million annually.[39] As a result, more and more shippers, in the face of cheaper, non-ILA competition, have lost the ability to compete and thus have gone out of business because of the added burden of GAI, while the burden on the remaining employers has, of course, increased dramatically.[40]

Indeed, much of this time, the shippers and ILA have been preoccupied with legal challenges by nonunion firms to the "Rules on Containers" on a variety of theories under the labor and antitrust laws.[41] In contrast, little time has been spent in retraining the idle, surplus work force for other, more productive pursuits. The union, rather than reinvigorating itself with newly organized members, is a caretaker for its declining, but very comfortable, membership.

Printing. On a comparable scale, the Typographers Union, particularly Local 6 in the New York Metropolitan Area, has cannibalized the unionized commercial printing industry in much the same manner as the ILA has done in shipping.[42] Initially, the union imposed cumbersome work rules on management that rendered noncompetitive those unionized employers who were attempting to introduce new composing room technology. By the mid-1970s, however, the union "acceded" to the introduction of computer technology—"cold type"—into the composing room, but only after extracting guaranteed take-home pay for all regular bargaining unit members then working—approximately 4,000 employees—who would thereafter become unemployed as a result of automation.[43]

Considered a landmark agreement at first, the ten-year master Book and Job Contract negotiated by Local 6 President, Bertram A. Powers, with the Printers League, has proven to be a nightmare for the industry. Almost one-third of the 219 unionized printers existing in 1975 have perished in large part because of their inability under that costly and inflexible agreement to cope with unanticipated nonunion competition.[44] Not only have the employers contributed staggering sums to the union's "Benefit and Productivity" (BAP) Fund—ranging over time up to 16 percent of labor payroll—to pay unemployed union members to sit at home, but inflexible work rules and union propensity to resist change have hamstrung the remaining employers in their efforts to adapt to meet their competition.[45]

Ironically, the 1975 Agreement has proven to be a sufficiently lucrative arrangement for eligible union journeymen that the union has been predictably resistant to any change in basic terms. The concept of retraining obsolete typographers has been given mere lip service. The union's interest in the newer generation of journeymen has also sagged: These workers are not eligible for full BAP Fund benefits, and they might be inclined to depose the current union leadership for propping up the old guard at the expense of lost employment opportunities.[46]

What went wrong? Certain factual parallels in the shipping and commercial printing industries' experience with technological change tellingly illuminate the general problem. First, in each industry, new technology of revolutionary proportions presented itself. Second, since both industries historically have been labor intensive—as well as heavily unionized—their services and products, respectively, were particularly vulnerable to union economic power. Third, in each industry, the unionized employers had joined forces to bargain through multiemployer associations, which was thought to enhance their overall bargaining strength; in fact, it lessened their resolve in the face of outlandish union demands for job security because the absence of effective nonunion competition tended to minimize the perceived real cost of the quid pro quo for effecting technological change, namely, job and income guarantees.[47] Furthermore, bargaining on a multiemployer basis papered over significant differences in the relative ability of large versus small companies to absorb the unanticipated costs of the income guarantee program. It is striking in this latter connection to contrast the Teamsters' Union's acquiescence in the late 1950s to the introduction of "piggybacking"—shipping truck trailers on railroad flat cars—in large part because of a recognition that strong nonunion competitive forces made this innovation both necessary and inevitable. Fourth, both the ILA and the Typographers Union were led by dominant individuals who were extremely powerful and able negotiators, who by sheer force of personality managed to extract programs for their membership that were so advantageous that they weakened the financial underpinnings of their respective industries.

Beyond these common causal factors, there are parallels in consequences as well. In each industry, we have witnessed the steady decline in influence of the first-generation, unionized employers in the face of aggressive, nonunion competition which has been free to innovate without union-imposed restrictions. The ILA and Typographers leadership each have presided over a steadily contracting membership, dominated by first-generation members with a vested personal interest in the guaranteed income funds. Sadly, the seeming preoccupation of entrenched union leadership with preserving the accommodations hammered out at the crossroad of automation has stunted the ability of management and labor in the current era to develop new, more constructive means of accommodating to automation.

The lesson learned from these experiences has been a painful one, and it is doubtful that any employer or group of employers will be so shortsighted as to agree to a guaranteed job or income program in the future.

Alternatives to Bargaining: Automation Study Committees

Contrast the experience of the shipping and printing industries with that of the meat-packing industry. Although the meat-packing industry shared many of the characteristics enumerated above, management laid the groundwork for automation and the closing of outmoded plants with long-range planning programs and, thus, avoided having to confront last-minute union demands for costly income or job maintenance programs. The goal was to remove the volatile issues of automation and worker displacement from the bargaining table by providing instead a vehicle for continuous joint study, by a management-union team, of the problem of automation. Whether fortuitous or clairvoyant, programs such as the Armour Automation Committee enabled meat packers to transform their processing and marketing techniques to meet nonunion competition while salvaging and adapting the skills of workers without, however, mortgaging the company's competitive future.[48]

The Armour Automation Committee comprises an equal number of high-level representatives of management and labor. Distinguished neutrals, such as George Shultz and Clark Kerr, have served as impartial chairmen of the committee. The work of the committee has been funded entirely by the Armour Company. Its mission has been expressly stated in the applicable collective-bargaining agreement[49] to be: first, "*studying* the problems resulting from the modernization program"; second, "*making recommendations* for their solution"; third, "*promoting employment opportunities* within the Company for those employees affected"; fourth, "*training* qualified employees in the knowledge and skill required to perform new and changed jobs so that the present employees may be utilized for this purpose to the greatest extent possible"; fifth, "*providing allowances* towards moving expenses for employees who transfer from one plant to another of the Company's plants"; and sixth, "*continuing to consider other programs* and methods that might be employed to promote continued employment opportunities for those affected."[50] The committee's findings and recommendations are not binding upon the parties, "but shall be made to the Company and to the Union for their further consideration."[51] Notably, the committee from time to time would be charged with recommending contractual provisions for consideration by the traditional bargaining teams or offering interpretations of existing clauses.[52]

The committee has been most active in three areas. First, it has regularly provided retraining and relocation assistance—financial and otherwise—for displaced employees. Second, it has made substantive recommendations for each ensuing round of traditional bargaining. Over the years, the Armour Automation Committee has recommended such benefits as early retirement, transfer rights to new plants, and supplemental benefits for the period of awaiting transfer. Importantly, since these provisions were recommended by a joint committee in advance of bargaining—after intensive, confidential study and debate—their controversial aspects were minimized. Finally, the committee was regularly made privy to the company's long-range business plans and thus was in a position to plan manpower needs on a more rational basis, and did so.[53]

The committee's work has proceeded in tandem with a contractually established minimum six-months' notice of plant closings and a "Technological Adjustment Plan," whereby the separation benefits of eligible employees would be enhanced.[54]

The principal attributes of the study committee concept are that it envisions a consensual and ongoing process. Its purpose is to study possible means by which to minimize the impact of technological innovation upon the company's employees. Since the study committee is consensual in nature, it is, of course, not for every employer; it is suitable only for those who have developed a rapport over time with their workers and their unions and, indeed, those who are prepared to compromise or surrender their management prerogatives.[55] Consent, grounded in mutual respect, is critical to the process: "A study committee can come to grips with the problems of technological change only when the parties have outgrown their preoccupation with rights and prerogatives."[56]

In addition to removing long-range issues from the pressured environment of collective bargaining, study committees can be used to cut across otherwise rigid boundaries. Study committees can function on a company-wide or industry-wide basis, transcending parochial local union interests, and they can accommodate multiple unions, or even multiple employers.

FUTURE PROGNOSIS

Historically, the unions that have resisted automation and technological change have done so largely because of the perception that these advances would erode the number of jobs, and union membership as well, over time.[57] While this might be the case with respect to a given industry, it is apparently not the case with respect to the overall number of jobs in the U.S. economy: A recent Bureau of Labor Statistics study concluded that "changing technology is not incompatible with employment growth."[58] In general, automation, by improving productivity per worker, allows management to remain competitive and to survive. This preserves jobs and, indeed, the new technology creates new and different jobs. Recent studies suggest that the result of automation in many industries, which previously had relied on cheap foreign labor, has been to diminish the economies of manufacturing overseas: Articles produced in this country by machines also require American labor to complete the process, where heretofore foreign labor was used.[59]

My point is that automation and jobs are not mutually exclusive. Lack of jobs is not the problem. The problem has been, and will continue to be, matching existing employee skills to the existing jobs and creating those skills where none exist. How then can this best be accomplished in the context of the industrial relations system described? Collective bargaining has an important role to play in the process, but it can play a critical, or decisive, role only if certain changes in attitude and emphasis prevail.

Attitude of Big Labor

The American labor movement has been floundering for almost twenty years. It has no real vision, it lacks strong leadership, and what leadership it does have is out of touch with the workers of the 1980s. It is understandable that, in this atmosphere, the AFL-CIO has not made finding a way to retool the organized sector to coexist with robots and other machines a top priority. I submit, however, that doing so would be in its ultimate self-interest. Only when organized labor takes a global, constructive perspective of its membership's interests and a more dynamic, functional approach to the manpower needs of business, will it finally enter the new age of technological revolution.

There are signs that labor is beginning to make this change. To mark its fiftieth anniversary in 1985, the AFL-CIO began to implement a number of major organizational changes to reverse its decline in influence.[60] It has begun to rally around legislation that will fund worker retraining and education programs, that provides short-term assistance to workers displaced by automation, and that calls for greater notice of plant closings.[61]

Although my preference would be that these latter programs be negotiated privately between union and employer, it may be that, as noted, in the present bargaining environment, privately bargained solutions may not be feasible. Hopefully, such programs, or ideally their collectively bargained equivalent, will over the long term alleviate much of the pressure on unions to obstruct technological innovations.

Bargaining Arena

Legal Scope. Some commentators have argued that the simple solution to the problem of accommodating to technological and other managerial innovations is to make such decisions clearly mandatory subjects of bargaining.[62] Others suggest that giving unions the power to compel bargaining with regard to jurisdiction over, new, nontraditional tasks created by automation, which would augment their organizational strength, would achieve the same desirable result of injecting labor into management's decision-making process.[63]

I see little merit in either recommendation. In regard to the latter point, the law on work preservation agreements gives unions adequate protection against encroachments on their turf. Mandating bargaining for plainly secondary objectives is anathema to the principle of majority rule and turns the NLRA on its head.

More problematic is the duty to bargain over decision making. My principal problem with this is its utter impracticality in most situations. Managerial decision making often requires speed and secrecy.[64] It usually involves considerations beyond manpower and labor costs. Furthermore, traditional collective bargaining is carried out under artificial pressures of strike deadlines and media scrutiny, which makes it difficult to be constructive. To inject the union into managerial decision making involuntarily through mandatory bargaining would be counterproductive.

But that is not to say that regular dialogue is counterproductive. The proponents of mandatory bargaining feel that this will force the parties to talk to one another and to achieve a consensus. The practical problem is that this kind of talk often comes too late in the day, and it is charged with adversarial posturing and emotion. Where planning of long-range manpower needs is desirable, a voluntary, institutionalized dialogue between management and labor is a viable alternative to impasse bargaining—as demonstrated by the experience with the Armour Automation Committee.[65] The more recent emergence of labor-management cooperation committees may provide another useful vehicle.[66]

Such formats are symbolic of a nascent, broader movement toward labor-management cooperation under conditions stripped of posturing. From the union's perspective, it can in this manner be alerted at the earliest opportunity to management's long-range, new technology plans and to mold its bargaining strategy accordingly.

Practical Observations. Of course, the employer who is suddenly presented with an opportunity to inaugurate technological change, but who has no long-range manpower planning vehicle in place, is likely to face stiff opposition from the affected union. The employer's negotiating talents and imagination will be severely taxed, particularly if the opportunity arises in the middle of the contract term. Without careful planning, creativity, and luck, the employer may not achieve his goal, or the union may exact too great a price. An employer faced with this situation ought to consider proceeding along the following lines:

1. Study applicable labor contract and arbitration awards. Obviously, it is desirable to be dealing with the union from documented strength. The existing contract, arbitral precedent, and past practice set the initial legal parameters for effecting technological change. Only in this light can the employer accurately assess his bargining obligations and options.

2. Consistent with legal constraints, agree internally on the optimal timetable for the introduction of the new technology. It is essential that the planners and the negotiators be on the same wavelength. Too often a company's labor relations specialists are consulted too late or not at all in the course of corporate planning; not only can this result in last-minute, wasteful changes in plans, but the perceived ignorance of an employer's spokespersons to labor can undermine the employer's credibility with the union. Their input on the practicability of a given timetable is invaluable—for example, whether to attempt an innovation now and risk an adverse arbitration award or to wait for contract expiration.

3. Give the union advance notice. Depending on the relationship with the union, give as much advance notice as prudent, even if only to a confidant in the union hierarchy. Any successful change will require that the employer enlist the union's support in selling the plan to the membership. How those plans are first presented is therefore crucial.

4. Be prepared to preempt the union's job security concerns. The union's initial reaction invariably will be how to protect its sphere of influence and the jobs of its members. There is a distinct advantage to thinking this through in advance and presenting these ideas in general concept, rather than waiting to react to the union's inevitable demands. A job security package can range the gamut from ceding to the union jurisdiction over newly created jobs, to employee buy-out options, to retraining programs. It should be tailored as much as possible

to the practical needs of the union, without, however, giving away all of the economic benefits of automation.

5. Don't blink. Unless the contract bars technological change, the employer normally has the upper hand in effecting such change. He must communicate to the union through "body language" his resolve and the inevitability of change.

Government Initiatives

As noted, although the long-range study committee can be an invaluable tool for easing the strain of automation and technological change, it can thrive only in the proper environment of mutual trust. Accordingly, other alternative must also be considered.

Twenty-five years ago, the role of government was seen as limited to "assist(ing) private investment to create a full employment economy in which collective bargaining can function most effectively."[67] Today, however, we live in a world of global economic competition; there are additional things the government can and ought to do to ameliorate those stresses on private collective bargaining that derive from preoccupation with the immediate bargaining unit. For example, there is no reason why government cannot establish in effect the counterpart of a labor-management automation study committee on a comprehensive basis, one that would cut across industry lines and target the nation's future manpower needs on a more rational basis. On the legislative level, such a vehicle could make recommendations—with the bipartisan support of management and labor—about training, retraining, and worker education needs; import and other international trade issues; immediate assistance for employees and employers directly affected by plant closings; and even the structure and substance of traditional collective bargaining, by, for example, urging the restructuring of appropriate bargaining units. Of course, such a committee could ultimately touch on other, related manpower issues, such as the "graying" of our work force.

Short of such an ambitious endeavor, there is no question that the Congress needs to pay immediate attention to stimulating training and retraining programs that are more comprehensive and react in a more timely fashion to the consequences of automation and technological change.[68] This would alleviate many of the natural constraints on collective bargaining, thus permitting it to better accommodate the issues of technological innovation.

CONCLUSION

It is wishful thinking to believe that normal collective bargaining, as currently constituted given the sociopolitical framework in which it functions, can successfully resolve the competing stresses of automation and job security in an efficient and timely manner. The process as now structured makes it too easy for unions to abandon reason and push the panic button. Yet the need to accommodate these competing stresses is greater than ever. We must take these issues out of adversarial bargaining altogether in those circumstances where the parties' relationship permits cooperative dialogue. More generally, the task at hand is to work to reshape or eliminate the legal and practical constraints that inhibit constructive solutions to technological change at the bargaining table.

NOTES

1. My former partner, the late Frederick R. Livingston, composed this apt introduction almost a quarter-century ago in an unpublished address before the Association of the Bar of the city of New York entitled "The Impact of Automation upon Collective Bargaining," on March 25, 1964, at 1 (text available in author's files) [hereinafter cited as Livingston]. Livington's thesis, which appears to have withstood the test of time (and which I have incorporated into my own views) is that "the problems of adjustment to technological change have often proved too complex for the best intentioned parties to handle within the traditional forms of collective bargaining" and, therefore, that "the study committee technique is a device better adapted to rational examination of the problem of automation." Id. at 6. Livingston's view was based principally on his experience with the Armour Automation Committee, the prototype for the study committee he helped create. See discussion infra note 5 and notes 48–54 and accompanying text.

2. R. Beaumont & R. Helfgott, Management, Automation, and People 21 (1964). This is a reference to the "Devil's Hole Massacre."

3. See "High Tech: Blessing or Curse?," U.S. News & World Rep. Jan. 16, 1984, at 38, 43.

4. See St. Antoine, "The Collective Bargaining Process," in American Labor Policy 233 (C. Morris ed. 1987).

5. The Armour Automation Committee was established in 1959 as part of Armour's collective bargaining agreements with the Packinghouse and the Meat Cutters Unions. Its purpose was to cushion employees against the consequences of automation or other operational changes as much as possible without hampering management's flexibility. See infra notes 48–54 and accompanying text. For a historical discussion, see especially Livingston, "Avoidance and Settlement of Strikes and Contract Disputes," N.Y.U. 20th Ann. Conference on Labor 323 et seq. (1968); and G. Shultz & A. Weber, Strategies for the Displaced Worker (1966).

6. Professor Philip Ross has suggested, for example, that the vicious opposition of the International Longshoremen's Association to containerization in the East Coast shipping industry, at a cumulative cost in strikes alone of several billion dollars—particularly when contrasted with the lesser success of its West Coast counterpart, the International Longshoremen's and Warehousemen's Union—was a perfectly laudable reaction, an effort "to buy time in which the human costs of change can be softened and made more tolerable." Ross, "Waterfront Labor Response to Technological Change: A Tale of Two Unions," 21 Lab. L.J. 397, 419 (June 1970).

7. See Note, "Automation and Collective Bargaining," 84 Harv. L. Rev. 1822 (1971) [hereinafter cited as Harvard Note]. Cf. Bamber, "New Technology—The Challenge to Unions: A Comparative View," 37 Lab. L.J. 502 (Apr. 1986), which attempts to dispel the misconception that Western European unions "always oppose new technology," id.

at 502, showing that unions vary in their receptivity to automation depending on, for example, the size and strength of the union and the political security of the union's leadership, the relative unity and strength of the employer, and the economic incentives afforded to the work force by the new technology. Id. at 506–7.

8. See D. Bok & J. Dunlop, Labor and the American Community 207–12 (1970) [hereinafter cited as Bok & Dunlop].

9. See NLRA § 9(a), 29 U.S.C. § 159(a) (1986). Section 9(a) requires that exclusive union representation rights be accorded within "a unit appropriate for such purposes." Section 9(b) states that the "employer unit, craft unit, plant unit, or sub-division thereof" may be appropriate for bargaining.

10. The NLRB, which is granted substantial discretion under the statute, NLRA § 9(b), in defining an appropriate unit in a given case, applies a rebuttable presumption as to the appropriateness of single location units, particularly in the manufacturing section. See Temco Aircraft Corp., 121 N.L.R.B. 1085 (1958).

11. This alludes to the implication in Justice White's plurality opinion in United Mine Workers v. Pennington, 381 U.S. 657 (1965), that a given employer and union must resist, on pain of breaching the antitrust laws, the entirely natural temptation to bargain with reference to, and in light of, developments at neighboring competitor employers. *Pennington* held that a union's agreement with one set of employers to impose ruinous wage standards on competitors, thus restraining the union's bargaining freedom, loses its antitrust exemption. 381 U.S. at 665–66. Under the NLRA, for example, it is an unfair labor practice for a union to condition the signing of an agreement on the employer's capitulating to its demands in other bargaining units. Lone Star Steel Co. v. NLRB, 639 F.2d 545 (10th Cir. 1980), cert. denied, 450 U.S. 911 (1981). See generally Handler & Zifchak, "Collective Bargaining and the Antitrust Laws: The Emasculation of the Labor Exemption," 81 Colum. L. Rev. 459 (1981).

12. See generally The Developing Labor Law 473–87 (C. Morris ed. 1983) (multiemployer bargaining); id. at 666–71 (coalition bargaining); Livingston, "Changing Relations between Union and Management," in Trade Union Government and Collective Bargaining 285–92 (J. Seidman ed. 1970).

13. See F. Bartosic & R. Hartley, Labor Relations Law in the Private Sector 158–59 (2d ed. 1986).

14. The duty to bargain under NLRA § 8(d) is limited to "*wages, hours*, and other *terms and conditions of* employment" (emphasis added); beyond this, the parties are permitted, but not required, to bargain over any topics of their mutual choosing that are not otherwise unlawful. NLRB v. Wooster Div. of Borg-Warner Corp., 356 U.S. 342 (1958). See generally Harper, "Leveling the Road from *Borg-Warner* to *First National Maintenance*: The Scope of Mandatory Bargaining," 68 Va. L. Rev. 1447 (1982).

15. See supra note 11. A matter involving issues or individuals outside the immediate employment relationship will be a mandatory bargaining subject only if it vitally affects the terms and conditions of employment within the bargaining unit. See Allied Chemical and Alkal. Workers Local No. 1 v. Pittsburgh Plate Glass Co., 404 U.S. 157, 179 (1971).

16. It is an unfair labor practice for a union to condition agreement on securing bargaining rights for nonbargaining unit personnel, Sperry Sys. Management Div., Sperry Rand Corp. v. NLRB, 492 F.2d 63 (2d Cir. 1974); and an agreement awarding bargaining rights would constitute unlawful assistance to a minority union. See, e.g., Meijer, Inc., 222 N.L.R.B. 18 (1976), enf'd, 564 F.2d 737 (6th Cir. 1977). See also Connell Construction Co., Inc. v. Plumbers and Steamfitters Local 100, 421 U.S. 616 (1975), which

prohibited top-down organizing agreements in the construction industry as violative of Section 8(e) of the Taft-Hartley Act, 29 U.S.C. § 158(e), and as falling outside of labor's antitrust exemption. Work "acquisition" agreements, which are secondary in their object and are by design organizational, are also banned by Section 8(e). See, e.g., Culinary Alliance Local 402 (Bob's Enterprises, Inc.), 175 N.L.R.B. 161 (1969).

17. National Woodwork Mfrs. Ass'n v. NLRB, 386 U.S. 612, 644–45 (1967), held that a "hot cargo" agreement may be lawful when the union's objective is the primary one of preserving work for current bargaining unit numbers. The employer must have, however, the "right of control" over the work in question. NLRB v. International Longshoremen's Ass'n, 447 U.S. 490, 504–05 (1980) [hereinafter cited as *ILA I*].

18. United Brotherhood of Carpenters Local 433 (Bauer Constr. Co.) v. NLRB, 509 F.2d 447 (D.C. Cir. 1975) (work recapture agreement held lawful). See U.S. Dept. of Labor, Bureau of Labor Statistics, Current Wage Developments, Feb. 1987, at 2 (reporting on a recent accord between the National Electrical Contractors Association and the IBEW aimed at recapturing outside utility construction work lost to nonunion contractors in recent years).

19. *ILA I*, 447 U.S. at 505–11. See also NLRB v. International Longshoremen's Ass'n, 473 U.S. 61 (1985) [hereinafter cited as ILA II]. See F. Bartosic & R. Hartley, supra note 13, at 264–66.

20. *ILA I* 447 U.S. at 511.

21. Milwaukee Spring Division of Illinois Coil Spring Co., 265 N.L.R.B. 206 (1982), remanded, 718 F.2d 1102 (7th Cir. 1983) (*Milwaukee Spring I*). There, the Board held that a company decision to relocate bargaining unit work for economic reasons during the term of a current collective-bargaining agreement was an unfair labor practice, absent an express reservation in the contract of management's right to transfer operations during the life of the contract. This would have turned collective bargaining on its head by requiring management to secure in advance the union's affirmative consent to management's basic operational rights. On review, the case was remanded by the Seventh Circuit at the Board's request and was reversed by the Reagan Board. 268 N.L.R.B. 601 (1984).

22. Compare First National Maintenance Corp. v. NLRB, 452 U.S. 666 (1981) (partial plant closing not a mandatory bargaining subject) with Fiberboard Paper Products Corp., 379 U.S. 203 (1964) (subcontracting decision that replaces bargaining unit employees with those of an independent contractor is a mandatory subject). See generally Comment, "Automation and the Work Preservation Doctrine: Accommodating Productivity and Job Security Interests," 32 U.C.L.A. L. Rev. 135 (1984) (advocating that automation be designated a mandatory bargaining subject)[hereinafter cited as UCLA Comment]; P. Miscimarra, The NLRB and Managerial Discretion: Plant Closings, Relocation, Subcontracting and Automation (1983); Harper, supra note 14.

23. In *First National Maintenance*, the U.S. Supreme Court declined to rule that automation was per se a mandatory bargaining subject, commenting that this and other types of management decisions "are to be considered on their particular facts." 452 U.S. at 686 n.22. The Court obliquely suggested, however, that where labor costs are "an important factor" in the management decision in question, bargaining with the union might be required. 452 U.S. at 682. See generally Harvard Note, supra note 7, at 1826–42.

24. *First National Maintenance*, 452 U.S. at 681–82.

25. M. Hill, Jr. & A. Sinicropi, Management Rights—A Legal and Arbitral Analysis 400–4 (1986); Ornati, "Rights Arbitration and Technological Change," in Proceedings

of the Thirty-Eighth Annual Meeting, National Academy of [Labor] Arbitrators 225, 233 (1985)[hereinafter cited as Ornati]. Ornati, a labor arbitrator, surveyed published arbitration decisions between 1980 and 1984 dealing with contractual disputes arising from the introduction of new technology. Significantly, he concluded that his assumption that arbitration would tend to preserve the status quo and seek to ameliorate the negative impact of technological change on bargaining unit employment opportunities, id. at 225, was erroneous. Rather, consistent with the dominant practice identified by the Elkouris prior to 1973, he found that: ''in situations involving automation or technological change, absent language specifically constraining it, management is generally given the right to assign bargaining unit work to employees outside the unit (usually more skilled and salaried personnel). Management does not win, however, when transferred work is very similar in nature to that done before and if the work does not involve changes in procedure, level of training required, and so on'' Id. at 233.

26. For example, Ornati, supra note 25, at 233–34, and the arbitration awards cited therein. See also Bell Tel. Co. (Case 14–30–1000–72) (unpublished) (Hill, Arb.), quoted in Bell Tel. Co., 75 L.A. 750, 755 (Garrett, 1980).

27. For example, the unionized coal industry, where the United Mine Workers exchanged higher wages, rather than job security, for cooperation in automating the mines. Taylor, ''Collective Bargaining,'' in Automation and Technological Change 84, 90 (J. Dunlop ed. 1962).

28. See Harvard Note, supra note 7, at 1854–55. Many academics have studied the manner in which collective bargaining accommodates to technological change. Those read by this author have concluded that job security in some form is almost always the quid pro quo for management's freedom to automate without union interference. See, e.g., Employment Security in a Free Economy 20–26 (J. Rosow & R. Zager eds. 1984) (noting that employees afforded employment security cooperate with technological change, but that job guarantees are not cost effective because they reduce the availability of capital for technological modifications that increase productivity); Ornati, supra note 25, at 228–29 (identifying an increase since 1980 in the frequency with which job security measures appear in collective-bargaining agreements, notably provisions for advance notice, retraining, and severance).

29. See ''U.A.W. Proposed Ford Guarantee Jobs in New Pact,'' N.Y. Times, Sept. 9, 1987, at A16, col. 3.

30. At the same time that the Board and courts have equivocated over the right of unions to compel bargaining over decision making on technological change, they have largely condoned restrictive union actions, such as featherbedding practices, that negate change and help perpetuate the status quo. See, e.g., American Newspaper Publishers Ass'n v. NLRB, 345 U.S. 100 (1953) (upholding ''bogus'' type featherbedding practice in the printing industry); United States v. American Federation of Musicians, 47 F. Supp. 304 (N.D. Ill. 1942), aff'd per curiam, 318 U.S. 741 (1943) (union requirement that broadcasting companies hire unnecessary musicians). See Featherbedding and Technological Change (P. Weinstein, ed. 1965); Bok & Dunlop, supra note 8, at 268–80.

31. See R. Beaumont & R. Helfgott, supra note 2, at 96–99.

32. Severance programs range from the modest general variety—e.g., one week's pay for each year of service, applicable to any permanent layoff—to major programs providing extended benefits, sometimes for life, for employees specifically displaced by automation. See 2 BNA Collective Bargaining Negotiations and Contracts, at 53:51–82 (1987); T. Kennedy, Automation Funds and Displaced Workers (1962).

33. See 2 BNA Collective Bargaining Negotiations and Contracts at 65:1 et seq. (1987) (sample clauses).

34. In The Continuous Learning/Employment Security Connection (J. Rosow & R. Zager eds. 1987), the Work in America Institute analyzes several case studies of worker retraining programs in place at Xerox Corporation, General Electric, and Pacific Bell. See also "Helping Workers to Work Smarter," Time, June 8, 1987, at 86. The Communications Workers of America has designated training and retraining programs to aid employees displaced by technological change as one of its long-term bargaining objectives. See "CWA's Bargaining Strategy for the Future," in 1 BNA Collective Bargaining Negotiations and Contracts, at 14:751–53 (1983).

35. See 2 BNA Collective Bargaining Negotiations and Contracts, at 53:51 et seq. (1987), for an extensive review of the many forms of income maintenance programs. A nonpartisan history of these and other worker displacement funds in the mining, music, and garment industries is set out in depth by Professor Thomas Kennedy of the Harvard Business School in his book, Automation Funds and Displaced Workers (1962). The recording industry has been saddled with perhaps the longest running income security plan, the "Music Performance Trust Fund," established after the devastating two-year ban on recording by the Musicians Union during World War II. The fund was created to offset the move from live to prerecorded music. Its financial impact on the industry has not been as pronounced as initially feared, however, since there is little nonunion competition, the program is funded out of retail record sales, and it does not guarantee full take-home pay. See "Musicians Ratify Master Contract with Nation's Recording Companies," (BNA) Daily Lab. Rep., Feb. 27, 1987, at A5.

36. The containerization process, as well as the protracted history of the attendant labor-management controversy, is described in detail in many Board and court decisions and journal articles. See Consolidated Express, Inc. v. N.Y. Shipping Ass'n, Inc. [hereinafter cited as *Conex*], 602 F.2d 494 (3d Cir. 1979), vacated and remanded, 448 U.S. 902 (1980) (per curiam); International Longshoremen's Ass'n (N.Y. Shipping Ass'n), 266 N.L.R.B. 230, 242–46 (1983), enf'd in part, American Trucking Ass'n v. NLRB, 734 F. 2d 966 (4th Cir. 1984), aff'd sub nom. NLRB v. International Longshoremen's Ass'n (*ILA IIR*), 473 U.S. at 61. See also Ross, supra note 6, at 397.

37. Beginning in 1959, the shipping employers—led by the New York Shipping Association, the principal employer bargaining group—agreed to pay a royalty into the union welfare fund for the use of containers loaded or unloaded by non-ILA labor. The dramatic increase in container usage thereafter, however, led to a series of lengthy strikes, which culminated in 1969 with the adoption of the comprehensive "Rules on Containers." These rules were intended to discourage the proliferation of "consolidators," companies that gathered odd-lot shipments into single containers at off-pier sites using non-ILA labor. Such containers, if consolidated at off-pier facilities within a fifty-mile radius of the port in question, would have to be "stuffed and stripped" a second time at dockside by ILA labor. Other containers remained subject to the royalty payments. *Conex* 602 F.2d at 498–99.

38. "GAI" was first granted by the shipping employers during the contract negotiations in the mid-1960s. *International Longshoremen's Ass'n*, 266 N.L.R.B. at 245; "Rising Labor Costs Threaten New York Port," N.Y. Times, June 22, 1983, at A1, col. 2 [hereinafter cited as "Rising Labor Costs"].

39. "Rising Labor Costs," supra note 38.

40. For example, the average daily total ILA crew in the port of New York declined

from 27,000 active workers in 1968 to 7,500 in 1980. 266 N.L.R.B. at 247. At the same time, as of 1983, 1,300 longshoremen in the port of New York were drawing GAI for all or most of the year, at a total cost of over $70 million. ''Rising Labor Costs,'' supra note 38.

41. The rules have been unsuccessfully challenged both as an unlawful work acquisition agreement under NLRA Section 8(e) and as an illegal boycott arrangement violative of the Sherman Act. See *ILA I*, 447 U.S. at 490, and *Conex*, 602 F.2d at 494. For a review of this litigation history through 1980, see Handler & Zifchak, supra note 11, at 464–67 nn. 27–43. The current rules have been upheld by the NLRB in substantial respect as a valid work preservation agreement in *International Longshoremen's Association*, 266 N.L.R.B. 230 (1983); supra note 36. However, the Federal Maritime Commission subsequently struck the rules down as ''facially discriminatory and burdensome'' under the Shipping Act of 1916. See ''Containerized Shipping Rules Are Illegal, Maritime Commission Says,'' (BNA) Daily Lab. Rep., Aug. 5, 1987, at A-10.

42. See ''Rising Labor Costs,'' supra note 38; ''Guaranteed Wage Is Crux of Pier Economics,'' N.Y. Times, June 23, 1983, at B1, col. 1.

43. Prior to 1975, the union not only had secured jurisdiction over every new machine or process that would displace traditional typesetting, but also could veto its introduction into the workplace. In the fall of 1975, the financial printing industry—at that point in time, 95 percent unionized—in order to overcome the fierce resistance of Local 6 to the introduction of automation into the composing room, agreed in exchange for the freedom to automate to guarantee 100 percent take-home pay for some 4,000 eligible journeymen. The program—termed the ''Benefit and Productivity Fund''—was to be funded by a fixed percentage of each employee's labor payroll. The contract, initially rejected by the Printers League membership, had an unprecedented ten-year term, ostensibly to provide an extended period during which the parties were to monitor developing automation issues. The guaranteed take-home commitment purported to be for life and to survive the expiration of the agreement. For an excellent account of this aspect of printing industry labor-management relations, see J. Hornig, The Commercial Printing Industry 1975 Automation Agreement: Its Origins and Its Impacts on the Labor-Management Relationship (1982) (unpublished Columbia Business School term paper in author's files.)

44. Hornig, supra note 43, at 49–51 and exhibit VI. Since 1975, the Printers League has lost over 50 percent of its union shop members, and the majority of shops in the industry are now nonunion. Id. at 49–50.

45. Id. at 46–48.

46. Id. at 52–57.

47. See Ross, ''The Teamsters' Response to Technological Change: The Example of Piggybacking,'' 21 Lab. L.J. 283 (Apr. 1970).

48. Interestingly, the automation committee concept was proposed by Armour management in response to union bargaining–table demands for guaranteed employment and other stiff limitations on plant closings. The proposal defused a dangerous bargaining impasse while at the same time sidestepping those extraordinarily expensive and burdensome proposals. See Livingston, ''An Approach to Automation,'' N.Y.U. 14th Ann. Conference of Labor 301, 302–03 (1961). Regarding the genesis of the Armour Automation Committee, see generally G. Shultz & A. Weber, Strategies for the Displaced Worker (1966).

49. Master Agreement by and between Armour and Company and Amalgamated Meat

Cutters and Butcher Workmen of North America, AFL-CIO, 1973–76 (text available in author's files) [hereinafter cited as 1973 Armour Contract].

50. 1973 Armour Contract, supra note 49, Appendix H: Automation Fund, at 70.

51. Id. at 70–71.

52. Id. at 71.

53. Livingston, supra note 1, at 8–13.

54. 1973 Armour Contract, supra note 49, Article XXV: Nature of Plant Closing and Technological Adjustment Plan, at 52–54.

55. Livingston, supra note 1, at 15–17.

56. Id. at 16–17.

57. Harvard Note, supra note 7, at 1822–23 and nn.7–10.

58. Mark, ''Technological Change and Employment: Some Results from BLS Research,'' 110 Monthly Lab. Rev. 26, 29 (Apr. 1987).

59. Feder, ''Production Returning to U.S.,'' N.Y. Times, Feb. 19, 1987, at D1, col. 3.

60. ''AFL-CIO Rejuvenation Program,'' 109 Monthly Lab. Rev. 14–15 (Jan. 1986).

61. For example, the Economic Dislocation and Worker Adj. Assistance Act (H.R. 3), 3/27/87.

62. See, e.g., Harvard Note, supra note 7, at 1824.

63. See, e.g., UCLA Comment, supra note 22, at 176.

64. See *First National Maintenance*, 452 U.S. at 682.

65. J. Dunlop, Dispute Resolution: Negotiation and Consensus Building 227–39 (1984). See generally Teamwork: Joint Labor-Management Programs in America (J. Rosow ed. 1986).

66. See ''Analysis of U.S. Labor Law and Future of Labor-Management Cooperation,'' Report of Duty Undersecretary of Labor for Labor-Management Relations, reprinted in (BNA) Daily Lab. Rep., June 17, 1986, at D1–13; R. Beaumont & R. Helfgott, supra note 2, at 126.

67. Livingston, supra note 1, at 16.

68. The Reagan Administration in 1987 proposed the establishment of a $980 million Worker Adjustment Assistance Program for workers dislocated by technological change and international competition. ''Extensive Displaced Worker Program Called For in DOL Fiscal 1988 Budget,'' (BNA) Daily Lab. Rep., Jan. 6, 1987, at A7–A9.

14

AUTOMATION AND TECHNOLOGICAL CHANGE: A UNION VIEW

Judith P. Broach and Ann F. Hoffman

Editors' Note. Recognizing that unions do not now have the power they once did to obtain job guarantees in the event of technological change, Mss. Broach and Hoffman nevertheless believe that unions have an important role to play in protecting employee and consumer interests against the adverse effects of new technology. The authors discuss present bargaining strategies in regard to technological change: securing advance notice, information sharing, and consultative rights; expanding jurisdiction to cover substituted technology and jobs, including homework; ensuring employees' safety and health, with requirements for employee record keeping; and obtaining higher rates for more skilled work and responsibility. The authors also consider ways in which unions can appeal to and identify with common concerns of the public in relation to the impact of new technology. Finally, the authors recognize that unions must improve their technological expertise.

The authors gratefully acknowledge the assistance of the Coalition of Labor Union Women (CLUW) Center for Education and Research, Washington, D.C.

It is an old story for unions and their counsel, but the pace is quickening. Employers are attempting to automate, with the intention of increasing productivity and profits, without regard to worker-related concerns. Unions are resisting the negative impact of technological change, utilizing every weapon in their standard arsenal. To date, however, the results of union efforts to protect their members from the adverse effects of new technology have been discouraging.

In the telephone industry alone, the impact of technology on workers has been enormous and negative. Automation of call placement and computerization of telephone directories has eliminated 100,000 operator jobs in ten years.[1]

Many craft jobs related to the installation and repair of telephone and central office equipment are gone, replaced by computer chips or performed by customers or clerical workers.[2] Clerical work involved in customer billing, record maintenance, and processing of service orders has been taken over by computers. "The general downgrading of skill and lack of systemwide knowledge in what is a more and more complex technology has made the entire system more authoritarian."[3] The melding of the telephone industry with other segments of the information industry has placed "telephone workers, who had [previously] organized most of their industry, . . . in a predominantly non-union sector,"[4] drastically curtailing their control over technology, job security, and other aspects of their work lives. The combination of computers and advanced telecommunications equipment has made it possible for telephone operators to work from their homes.[5]

The changes observed in the telephone industry can be found in industry after industry. Technology often makes it easier to do more work with fewer workers.[6] Technology can decrease the skill level of jobs, making the jobs more routine and the workers less essential to the employer.[7] Technology permits close management monitoring of worker activity.[8] Technology may reduce the freedom of thought and action of the workers.[9] Technology makes it easier to move jobs to areas that are more difficult for unions to organize: a worker's home, suburban areas, the South, or low-wage foreign countries.[10] Technology may produce health and safety hazards, including increased stress.[11]

The technological revolution of the 1970s and 1980s is not the first such event. In the early stages of the industrial revolution in England, the introduction of power-driven machinery and the factory system caused similar disruption. A group of skilled craft workers, who became known as Luddites, made a number of proposals to the employer community to deal with the technological change of the 1800s, including:

A gradual introduction of machinery with an alternative employment fund for displaced workers.

A tax on cloth with the proceeds to be used for the unemployed.

A minimum wage.

Control over the quality of the goods produced.

Wage arbitration.

Restrictions on work by juveniles.

Obligation of employers to find work for skilled workers who lost their jobs to the new machinery.

Right to free and open trade unions.

Reduction of work to a ten-hour day.[12]

When their proposals were ignored, the Luddites turned to sabotage of the new equipment—the only "platform" for which they are remembered.

The approach of the unions in the 1980s is quite similar to that of the Luddites while there was still hope for a constructive response. Some unions are using all of their traditional weapons; others are trying to craft new ones, aware that machine-smashing is as ineffective today as it was for the Luddites. The thesis of unions today is the same as that of the early Luddites: "Employees should not have to bear all the costs of implementation and adjustment to the new ways of doing work."[13]

UNION REACTIONS TO TECHNOLOGY

When technology first impinged on unionized industries, unions were at the peak of their power. They also had less awareness of the forces that technology would unleash in the future, and fewer sophisticated weapons were at their disposal. Their responses were accordingly tougher, more direct, and less geared to future generations than unions try to be in the 1980s.

The introduction of containerization of cargo permitted a drastic reduction in the number of longshore workers needed to load and unload ships. The longshore unions were powerful enough to negotiate work preservation clauses in their national and regional agreements to prevent the total elimination of their members' jobs.[14] They were also able to negotiate a guaranteed annual income, a full year's pay for unemployed longshore workers.[15] Locals of the International Typographical Union permitted newspaper employers to use automated typesetting equipment only in return for lifetime employment guarantees for all composing room employees. Similar measures were adopted in other industries.

In the intervening years, high unemployment, decreased union solidarity, deregulation of many industries, recession, the increased import of goods and export of jobs, and a host of other factors have drastically curtailed the power of unions to maintain job security in the face of technology.

Labor unions and their lawyers often find themselves in a defensive posture on issues involving technological change for several reasons: The relative strength of labor and management at the bargaining table has shifted; the management rights clause in many collective-bargaining agreements is broadly written and construed; and the law has not generally recognized the right of unions to be involved in the decision-making process prior to the introduction of new technology. Today, in most instances, the union is first notified that the employer intends to introduce new technology immediately before its installation. By that time, the employer usually has spent a significant amount of time and money examining his options and has reached a firm decision that such technology will be economically beneficial. The employer probably also has decided how much he is willing to spend to alleviate the impact of the new technology, including severance pay, job retraining, and other similar "labor costs." At that point, the role of the union can only be one of minimizing the damage—bargaining over how many employees will be laid off, whether retraining will be available, whether severance pay will be provided and in what amount, and so on.

Unions have had mixed results, at best, in grieving and arbitrating job loss, job restructuring, and other adverse effects of new technology. "In the absence of specific and restrictive contract language, arbitrators, the National Labor Relations Board and the courts all permit employers to introduce technological innovation, combine or eliminate jobs, assign work, set rates of pay and determine crew size as demanded by business needs or objectives."[16]

The fact that unions have been placed in the position of having to react to technological change late in the decision-making process has had a serious, detrimental impact upon the public's view of the labor movement. A union struggling to react to imminent technological change inevitably appears resistant to progress and unrealistic about economic issues, concerned only about saving jobs without regard to the economic consequences for the employer. Since unions usually are not able to accomplish much at that point, the results also tend to reinforce in the minds of the public and of union members the impression that unions are weak and ineffective.

Unions need to find new strategies for dealing with technological change in the work place. What follows are some ideas which union lawyers may want to explore with their clients, even though they extend beyond the realm of customary "legal advice." Many have been put into place in one form or another by some union somewhere.

BARGAINING OVER THE EFFECTS OF TECHNOLOGY

Unions have been bargaining over the effects of new technology for more than a decade. The Manual of Collective Bargaining Clauses,[17] prepared for the field staff of the Machinists Union fourteen years ago, proposed eight separate clauses dealing with technological change, capturing the fundamental ideas expressed by every union since then trying to grapple with workplace innovation. The Machinists advised their staff to seek a minimum of six months' advance notice prior to the introduction of "any change in equipment, material and/or methods" which may have an impact on the bargaining unit; the establishment of a joint union-management committee on technological change; agreement on new wages for affected workers, equal to or higher than their previous wages, prior to the introduction of new technology; no layoffs or pay reductions because of technology; necessary training of potentially displaced workers during work time at employer expense; and transfer rights for employees forced to give way to new technology.

In practice, some unions have been able to negotiate a variety of clauses limiting technology or its impact. For example, the Service Employees International Union (SEIU), Local 925 and Cambridge and Somerville Legal Services negotiated a clause prohibiting assignment of clerical workers to new equipment except "through mutual agreement between the Employer and the affected employee,'' following consultation and negotiations with the union.[18] The Graphic Arts International Union negotiated a provision with the Chicago Newspaper Publishers Association preserving the union's jurisdiction over ''any process, machinery or equipment which functions as a substitute for or evolution of current composing room work (processes, machinery, or equipment).''[19] Several unions have secured job guarantees for workers whose jobs are diminished or eliminated by technological change, either by training them to use the new technology or by transferring them to comparable jobs.[20] At the General Motors Guide Lamp plant in Anderson, Indiana, members of the United Automobile, Aerospace and Agricultural Implement Workers of America (UAW) install, repair, and reprogram the robots that do the spray painting the workers used to do.[21]

The advent of video display terminals (VDTs) has brought about drastic changes in clerical work. District Council 37 of the American Federation of State, County and Municipal Employees (AFSCME) took advantage of a ''window of opportunity,'' when VDTs were first introduced and few workers knew how to use them.[22] The union negotiated a new ''word processor'' title at a higher rate than clerical workers had received for typing, contending that VDTs required the exercise of greater discretion and would make workers more productive. The new title provided a promotional opportunity for existing workers willing to undergo the necessary training.

VDTs have probably produced more demands for contractual safeguards than any other single technological innovation. The Newspaper Guild's VDT Collective Bargaining Program calls for a variety of safeguards:

- Periodic inspection of all VDTs for conformity to governmental standards and testing for radiation emissions, with the results available to the Guild.
- Comprehensive eye examinations before a worker begins VDT work and periodically during use, with the costs of examinations and corrective glasses to be paid by the employer.
- Rest breaks of fifteen minutes after one hour or thirty minutes after two hours of continuous VDT work and one-half hour of adjustment time at the end of the day; Guild involvement in setting proper lighting levels and in designing machines, chairs, and work stations for worker comfort and health, including metal shielding to guard against very-low-frequency radiation.
- Transfer rights with no loss of pay at the request of pregnant employees.
- The right to grieve and arbitrate problems related to VDT use.[23]

SEIU Locals 390 and 400 negotiated with the city and county of San Francisco that the employer will ''keep records on each employee for the duration of his/her employment plus twenty–five (25) years'' on health conditions including eye examinations, with access to the records limited to the employee, the union, and bona fide health researchers.[24] SEIU District 925 negotiated with the University of New Haven for a ten-minute break away from the VDT after fifty minutes of work on it and ten minutes away from the VDT at the end of the day.[25]

AFSCME negotiated a prohibition on the use of "[m]easures of employee performance obtained through electronic or 'line count' monitoring" as "the sole criterion applied in evaluating performance."[26]

District Council 24 of AFSCME tackled what may be the most serious technological threat—computer homework or telecommuting—through a carefully controlled bargaining experiment. The University of Wisconsin Hospital Medical Records Department employed AFSCME–represented medical transcriptionists who used word processors to prepare patient records. Overflow work was subcontracted to an outside vendor. When the hospital had no space to expand its staff and three members of the bargaining unit expressed interest in working from their homes, the union negotiated a detailed addition to the contract for them, mandating a separate work area in the home with proper lighting, ventilation, and a smoke detector, all to be reviewed by a joint union–hospital committee; a word processor, chair, desk, extra telephone line, and locked storage space to be provided and maintained by the employer; set hours of work; and regular contact with supervision. The homeworkers received the same wages and fringe benefits as did their hospital–based counterparts. The one–year experiment has become a permanent arrangement, with additional workers operating from home and new employees added in the original unit as well.[27]

THE UNION DIRECTION FOR THE FUTURE

Unions should recognize that collective bargaining must shift from bargaining over the effects of technology to bargaining for a greater role in the decision–making process regarding what kind of new technology, if any, will be introduced. In our view, unions should seek provisions in their collective-bargaining agreements permitting them to become involved at the time the employer decides to explore the possibility of introducing new technology. As the Communications Workers of America (CWA) states in the opening paragraphs of its manual on the subject:

> Historically, American unions have left the choice [of the type and pace of technology] to management. We traded control of technology for better wages. Today this trade–off is no longer in our best interest. Choices about the type of technology to be used are too important to leave solely to management. Left in their hands, new technology can be a potent weapon used to destroy union jobs and union security.[28]

Collective-bargaining agreements should contain provisions requiring the employer to notify the union if it intends to begin investigating the introduction of new technology; to permit the union to have access to all information in the employer's possession regarding such new technology; to permit the union to provide the employer with information in its possession regarding such new technology, including alternatives to the technology of which the employer may be unaware; and to permit the union to provide the employer with any information it can obtain regarding the actual economic benefit or detriment of introducing new technology. Contracts should also state that, to the extent the technology has to be adapted to the needs of the particular employer, the union will be consulted about the design.[29]

Ideally, the collective-bargaining agreement should also contain a provision stating that, in the event the parties cannot agree on the design or the introduction of new technology, the matter should be submitted to final and binding arbitration. No change should be permitted until the arbitrator's decision has been issued.

While this may sound utopian, we are not the only people who advocate such an approach. The National Research Council (NRC), the research arm of the National Academy of Sciences, has recently advocated increased worker involvement in decisions traditionally reserved to management. According to the NRC report entitled *Computer Chips and Paper Clips*: "Worker participation enhances the effectiveness of new technology, helps ensure that technology is not used in ways that decrease the quality of jobs, and leads to increased commitment to the decisions that employees have helped reach."[30] But these advantages follow only if the employer is willing to guarantee job security for affected workers.

Implementing ambitious bargaining programs, of course, requires more than good ideas. Union representatives, shop stewards, and rank-and-file members must be trained to be alert to, and concerned about technological change and to be equipped with techniques for dealing with such change. CWA Local 4309 in Cleveland, Ohio has trained all of its stewards on technological change, including the history of automation, recent developments, and case studies. Workers have received written advice on fighting production standards, including not speeding up just because a time study is done and documenting the roadblocks to meeting standards. The local has been able to grieve successfully in some cases and to organize to strike in others because of its educational campaign among stewards and members.[31] The Machinists include technology training in all of their training programs for staff and stewards.

Unions must become more adept at using methods outside the scope of traditional collective bargaining to obtain their ends. For example, unions should think creatively about inducing legislative or administrative action as a means of accomplishing goals which have customarily been obtained through collective bargaining. The CWA encourages members to raise the technology consciousness of potential legislators through use of a candidate questionnaire on employment policy and technology.[32] Unions which have had little success in bargaining for improvements in the working conditions of VDT operators have turned to state legislatures and OSHA and have assisted in drafting laws and regulations governing working conditions of VDT operators.[33]

Similarly, unions representing employees of public utilities have had some success in limiting the introduction or the manner of introduction of new technology where the union could demonstrate to the state public utilities commission that the implementation or design of such new technology was not cost effective or was otherwise detrimental to the public interest.

If the technology that the employer intends to introduce will have an impact upon consumers as well as the company's employees, unions may wish to consider the use of advertising to sway public opinion against the introduction of the technology or toward implementation of the technology in a way which will benefit the union's membership. In developing an advertising campaign, it should be kept in mind that public opinion is not likely to be affected by appeals to abstract notions of justice, nor even by stressing the negative effect of such technology on the employees involved. Instead, the unions should stress the negative effects of the technology on the consumer. This kind of appeal to the self-interest of the public has not been used, to any great extent, by American labor unions. It has been used with some success in other countries, notably in Australia, where a railway union was able to thwart the employer's intention to replace ticket takers with machines which would perform the same function.[34] One American labor union also has been successful: The CWA helped move a ban on remote monitoring of telephone workers through the West Virginia legislature by pointing out that the privacy of consumers was violated if the customers' conversations were overheard when the telephone companies spied on workers.[35] Similar cooperation with nonlabor groups in a community should be possible when a plant is being closed or large numbers of jobs are being transferred to another location.

The formation and effective use of coalitions must be an integral part of union organizing in the age of technology. SEIU President John Sweeney told the 1986 DPE Conference on Technological Change that, in organizing, unions "must raise issues of broad public concern in order to garner community support. . . . [We] have to talk about the quality of patient care, the quality of education, the quality of services, the quality of the product."[36]

Sometimes unions must make common cause with employers in the effort to save their jobs. The Amalgamated Clothing and Textile Workers Union (ACTWU) has spearheaded a joint labor-industry-government coalition called the Textile-Clothing Technology Corporation (TC^2), which has developed an automated machine to sew sleeves into men's suits. The machine will replace union-represented sleeve sewers, but the union hopes that, by reducing overall costs, it will make possible the survival of a domestic men's clothing industry and thousands of jobs. "The technology is going to move on, with us or without us," stated Jack Sheinkman, president of ACTWU. "By getting involved, we hope to be able to provide a greater measure of security to our people."[37]

Direct involvement in technology is indeed another way in which unions can be better fitted to survive the new age. Each union's research staff ideally should include an individual whose responsibility is the identification and analysis of emerging technology in the industry or industries in which the union represents employees. Thus, a union could identify areas in which technological change is likely to be implemented in the foreseeable future and anticipate the impact of such technology upon its membership. The research department could develop information on such matters as whether the technology will produce real cost savings for the employer and whether there are means of instituting the technology in ways that improve the quality of work life for the union's members.[38] Australian telephone unions, for example, resisted the telephone company's plan to introduce electronic switching and centralized repair bureaus by coming up with an alternative plan. After a public relations campaign and minor job actions, the company adopted a compromise plan.[39]

If unions do not yet have their own experts or employers will not accept the conclusions of a union expert, unions can and do commission outside experts to help them develop their research and arguments. The Newspaper Guild, the International Typographical Union, and the Office and Professional Employees International Union arranged for the National Institute for Occupational Safety and Health to investigate health hazards of VDTs used by three large employers in the San Francisco Bay area.[40] The Newspaper Guild has since participated in other VDT studies. Seven locals of the CWA in North Carolina and the North Carolina Occupational Safety and Health Project surveyed 2,500 VDT workers in 1983 and 1984 and concluded that VDT use was linked with angina symptoms, stress, and other health problems.[41] American unions have been tracking studies performed in Sweden measuring the effects of VDT radiation on reproduction.[42] The Coalition of Labor Union Women (CLUW) conducted a similar survey of its members, who come from dozens of unions and a host of different occupations, about the impact on them of technological change.[43]

William Lucy, secretary-treasurer of AFSCME, described well what the technology-conscious labor union must do:

> To begin with, we have to modernize our labor organizations right up to the hilt. We have to take every advantage that technology offers—for record keeping, education, public relations, research, communications, organizing. We have to be every bit as capable of calling up information or communicating as the people we're up against.[44]

CONCLUSION

The American labor movement has had a late start in the technological revolution of the late twentieth century. Unions can catch up, because they must. The consequences of failure are too great. As Thomas Donahue, secretary-treasurer of the AFL-CIO, stated in his opening remarks at the 1986 Conference on Technological Change of the Federation's Department for Professional Employees:

> Without serious consideration of our future by people like us, and without government involvement, the evolving system of work in the United States will produce desperate consequences for huge numbers of workers with the consequent threatening of the entire structure of our economy and of society.

Left unattended and unchanged, the trends now firmly in place will seriously erode the employment prospects and the earnings of our workforce and effectively prevent our maintaining—much less improving—the standard of living to which we've grown accustomed.[45]

Harley Shaiken, one of the nation's leading experts on automation, insists that "the real choice is not new technology or no technology but the development of technology with social responsibility, the development of technology in such a way that workers, the community, and the entire society benefit."[46]

NOTES

1. Grumhaus, "What's New in Telephone Services, Taking the Joy out of an Old Job," N.Y. Times, Nov. 16, 1986, at F19.

2. "The Telephone System—Changing Technology—Changing Jobs," CWA News, Oct. 1982, at 9.

3. Id.

4. Kohl, "Changing Competitive and Technology Environments in Telecommunications," in D. Kennedy, C. Craypo & M. Lehman, Labor and Technology: Union Response to Changing Environments 53, 64 (1981), reprinted in CWA Training Department, Technological Change: Challenges and Choices 116 (1985) [hereinafter cited as Technological Change].

5. "U.S. West Brings TOPS Home," Communications Week, May 19, 1986, at 37.

6. For example, UAW estimates that technology will eliminate 120,000 jobs in the domestic automobile industry in the next five years, regardless of the effects of imports. Feder, "GM's Cuts Reflect a Long-Term Trend,"N.Y. Times, Nov. 10, 1986, at D1, col. 3.

7. Morton Bahr, President, Communications Workers of America, AFL-CIO (CWA), "High Noon in the Information Age," address to Conference on Technological Change and Professional, Technical and Office Employment of AFL-CIO Department for Professional Employees, Apr. 11–12, 1986 [hereinafter cited as DPE Technological Change Conference], reprinted in Interface, Summer, 1986, at 6.

8. Id. William Lucy, International Secretary-Treasurer, American Federation of State, County and Municipal Employees, AFL-CIO, told the same conference of "preposterous schemes afoot . . . to use brain wave monitoring to measure the concentration of workers on the job." Interface, Summer, 1986, at 11.

9. "World Workers Warned to Factor in Computers," Chi. Tribune, Apr. 20, 1986, at 1, 6.

10. During a 1979 strike in San Francisco, Blue Cross/Blue Shield transferred 500 jobs to remote terminals. Harley Shaiken, "Technological Change around the World," reprinted in Technological Change, supra note 4, at 241, 245. CWA President Bahr advised the DPE Technological Change Conference, supra note 7, that American Airlines tickets are now keypunched in Barbados, and the data are returned to Tulsa by satellite. The Trammel Crow Company, a Dallas-based real estate developer, has a data entry shop in the People's Republic of China. See Interface, Summer, 1986, at 6.

11. See Bahr, supra note 7; North Carolina Occupational Safety and Health Project

and North Carolina CWA Joint Study, Office Workers Stress Survey Results [hereinafter cited as Joint CWA–NCOSH Study], Mar. 1985.

12. See Technological Change, supra note 4, at 107.

13. American Federation of State, County and Municipal Employees, Facing the Future—AFSCME's Approach to Technology 26, 1986 [hereinafter cited as AFSCME, Facing the Future].

14. "New Technology: What's at Stake For Management . . . and for Workers," 13 Am. Lab. 2 (1981). Litigation over clauses in contracts between the ILA and employer associations giving ILA members the right to strip and repack certain types of containers entailed a ten-year odyssey through the NLRB and the courts. NLRB v. ILA, 473 U.S. 61 (1985).

15. "ILA, Shippers Agree on Contract Cutting Benefits," Star-Ledger, Nov. 1, 1986, at 9.

16. "You Can't Win . . . without Contract Clauses," 13 Am. Lab. 6 (1981). The CWA has, with mixed results, arbitrated a number of technology issues under contract language not specifically designed for such issues. Some twenty cases are summarized in Technological Change, supra note 4, at 212, 260–74.

17. International Association of Machinists and Aerospace Workers, AFL-CIO, Manual of Collective Bargaining Clauses, Summer, 1972, Article 51. Similar model language is recommended by the Service Employees International Union, AFL-CIO, in an appendix to its manual, Technological Change: Contract Provisions. Many of the same principles were incorporated into the 1980 collective-bargaining agreement between the CWA and the Bell System.

18. Service Employees International Union, AFL-CIO, supra note 17, at 4.

19. K. Murphy, Technological Change Clauses in Collective Bargaining Agreements 11 (1981).

20. Marc Stepp, International Vice President, UAW, AFL-CIO, in Interface, Summer, 1986, at 16; AFSCME, Facing the Future, supra note 13, at 37–38.

21. "New Technology: The Tug of War Begins at the Bargaining Table," 13 Am. Lab. 3, 5 (1981).

22. Interview with Deborah Bell, Director of Negotiations and Research, District Council 37, AFSCME.

23. The Newspaper Guild and International Typographical Union, Humanizing the VDT Workplace 35–36 (1985) [hereinafter cited as Humanizing the VDT Workplace]. Similar suggestions are made by the UAW in a 1983 publication called VDT Contract Language and by the CWA in an Occupational Safety and Health Fact Sheet.

24. Service Employees International Union, Office Automation Series, Bargaining, at 5.

25. Id. at 6.

26. AFSCME, Facing the Future, supra note 13, at 45.

27. Allen Highman, DPE Technological Change Conference, supra note 7, quoted in (BNA) White Collar Report, Apr. 23, 1986, at 398, and in written materials provided to the authors.

28. Technological Change, supra note 4, at 102.

29. SEIU has drafted model contract language along these lines. SEIU Office Automation Series, Bargaining, at 2.

30. This characterization of the NRC report is taken from ''Technology Not Expected to Decrease Clerical Jobs,'' (BNA) Daily Lab. Rep. Oct. 1, 1986, at 1–2.

31. Perception, July 1985 and Aug.-Sept. 1985.

32. Technological Change, supra note 4, at 251–52.

33. CWA, SEIU, and The Newspaper Guild have drafted model state laws on VDTs, encompassing many of the operator protections which unions have tried to obtain through collective bargaining.

34. Hull, ''Telephones, Ticket Machines and Toilets: Case Studies in Technology Change and Worker's Control,'' unpublished paper presented at Interuniversity Center, Dubrovnik (Jan. 1983) at 10–12.

35. Technological Change, supra note 4, at 252–57. The statute, W. Va. Code § 61–3–24c (1981), was enacted after a two-year fight, which also included a successful multiunion effort to defeat the reelection bid of the State Senate President.

36. Interface, Summer, 1986, at 9.

37. Interview with Mr. Sheinkman.

38. European unions have developed this kind of expertise and, as a result, have far more control than do their American counterparts over the introduction of new technology. Philip J. Jennings, International Federation of Commercial, Clerical, Professional and Technical Employees, in Interface, Summer, 1986, at 12–13.

39. Technological Change, supra note 4, at 209.

40. Humanizing the VDT Workplace, supra note 23, at 3, 37–42.

41. Joint CWA–NCOSH Study, supra note 11, at 3–4.

42. ''Debate Surrounds Swedes' Report on VDT's, Pregnancies,'' Guild Rep., Apr. 11, 1986, at 1.

43. CLUW, Automation in the Workplace, Oct. 11, 1984, at 1–3.

44. Interface, Summer, 1986, at 11.

45. Interface, Summer, 1986, at 3.

46. ''Technological Change around the World,'' reprinted in Technological Change, supra note 4, at 245.

15

EMPLOYEE OWNERSHIP: A UNION VIEW

Stephen L. Hester

Editors' Note. Mr. Hester views the reasons for unions' historic skepticism about employee stock ownership plans (ESOPs) as a key to understanding their bargaining goals when employers seek wage and benefit concessions in return for according employees equity interests. For example, in response to an employer's effort to recover pension plan "overfunding," unions will seek ways to ensure that federally guaranteed, defined pension benefit plans will not be replaced by unguaranteed, defined contribution ESOP plans. The author notes that unions will insist in an ESOP that they have meaningful ownership, including stock voting rights, and that there be carefully crafted provisions for subsequent stock distribution to the employees. He cautions that mere stock ownership, in contrast to actual participation in decision making, has no demonstrated positive effect on productivity. Mr. Hester also notes that ESOP bargaining requires that unions, no less than managements, have expert investment counsel and access to all relevant corporate financial information.

In recent years, employee ownership has become an increasingly important issue for labor unions. A recent issue of the *IUD Digest*, published by the Industrial Union Department of the AFL-CIO, reports as follows:

> Employee ownership has become a significant issue in the American Labor relations system. Workers have been asked to assume some or all of the ownership in the firms for which they work—sometimes in exchange for wage and benefit concessions. In a few cases, workers themselves have proposed employee ownership as an alternative to a plant

closing. In some other cases, employees are buying small businesses from employers who are retiring. In almost every unionized situation in which it has surfaced, the employee ownership question has become a topic of collective bargaining.[1]

Despite labor's recognition that employee ownership is an important issue, employee stock ownership plans (ESOPs) generally have been viewed by the labor movement with a high degree of skepticism. The principal reasons for this skeptical view of ESOPs, which are listed below, will explain the basis for the guarantees and protections which unions seek in collectively bargained employee ownership plans.

1. Most labor unions are rightfully proud of the pension plans they have negotiated to provide retirement income to their members. They support the laws that guarantee the integrity and solvency of pension plans, including ERISA's vesting and funding rules, fiduciary requirements, and the guarantee of pension benefits by the PBGC. An ESOP plan can also provide retirement income (if an employee's stock is distributed to him at retirement age), but ESOP benefits are not guaranteed by the PBGC. Labor unions are therefore dubious of proposals under which employee stock ownership would serve as a total or partial substitute for a soundly funded, government-guaranteed pension fund.

2. Many union officials believe that employee ownership is generally proposed for companies with severe financial difficulties, whose stock is of dubious value. This point of view is represented in a well-known cartoon which pictures the "Boss" telling a worker that there is good news and bad news. The good news is that the worker now owns stock in the company. The bad news is that the company is broke, and workers have to take a 20 percent pay cut.[2]

3. Labor union leaders are familiar with cases in which ESOP programs have been oversold to employees, leading to initial high expectations followed by disillusionment. In many cases, this disillusionment is attributable to the fact that ESOPs (1) have not produced any changes in authoritarian management styles and (2) have been designed to prevent workers from exercising voting control over the stock nominally owned by them.

4. In dealing with stocks and securities, union officials sometimes feel that they are outside of their field of expertise and are playing on management's home turf. In order to address prudently such issues as the valuation of securities, unions may need to retain expensive experts. The feeling of uneasiness is accentuated by well-known cases in which stock contributed to employee ownership plans has been valued unfairly. Indeed, this was identified by the Comptroller General of the United States as a significant problem in a 1980 report to the United States Senate.[3]

5. Some union officials have been concerned that employee ownership might be used by management to undermine union solidarity and persuade workers that, as owners, they no longer need union representation. However, the unions that have carefully considered this issue have concluded that the needs that cause

workers to join together in a labor union are basically unaffected by the institution of an employee stock ownership plan.

Each of the above concerns is discussed in greater detail below, together with possible approaches to address these legitimate union concerns.

EMPLOYEE OWNERSHIP SHOULD NOT BE SUBSTITUTED FOR SOUNDLY FUNDED, GOVERNMENT-GUARANTEED PENSION PLANS

To some extent, the implementation of employee ownership plans has been correlated with the curtailment or elimination of defined benefit pension plans which provide assured and government-guaranteed pensions to retired workers. In recent years, interest rates have greatly exceeded the rates assumed by actuaries in calculating the funding required for pension funds. As a result, some pension funds have become "overfunded," so that, by purchasing annuities which lock in high interest rates, it is possible to terminate a pension plan and return substantial sums to the employer. At the same time, in other industries, unanticipated large numbers of early retirements together with a declining active work force have greatly increased the underfunding of pension plans and the cost per hour of meeting the continuing funding obligations imposed by ERISA.

Both overfunding and underfunding have presented corporate management with reasons to seek the termination of standard, defined benefit pension plans. In cases of overfunding, corporations have wished to recapture the amount of overfunding in order to provide additional liquidity, reduce bank borrowings, or facilitate a leveraged buy-out. In cases of severe underfunding, management has regarded pension plans as an uncontrollable cost and has looked for substitute mechanisms to prevent a repetition in the future of the runaway costs attributable to defined benefit pension plans.

Despite the temptation to address short-run problems by eliminating or curtailing pension plans, unions generally have opposed the substitution of employee stock ownership plans or other forms of defined contribution plans for a traditional, defined benefit pension plan. Pension benefits provided by a defined benefit plan are guaranteed by the PBGC, so that in the event of the employer's insolvency, the payment of pension benefits is not threatened. No similar guarantee is extended to benefits provided by defined contribution plans, including ESOPs. ESOP benefits are sometimes considered particularly vulnerable since contributions to ESOP plans are not diversified but are invested entirely or primarily in the stock of a single employer. The result of substituting an ESOP plan for a pension plan is therefore to put workers in a position where they are using their retirement income to play the market with a single stock. As stated in a speech given by Steve Newman on behalf of United Steelworkers' President Lynn Williams:

> The stock ownership plans which our union has negotiated have not involved and will not involve the sacrifice of pension benefits. It is our view that workers should not be

dependent solely upon the business success of their employer for the provision of an adequate retirement income. This is particularly important because the benefits provided through an employee stock ownership plan are not guaranteed by the Pension Benefit Guaranty Corporation. We therefore will continue to insist that stock ownership plans should be in addition to, and not a substitute for, an adequately funded pension program. We have long since accepted the opinion uniformly expressed by pension advisers that pension funds should be invested broadly rather than being concentrated in a single business.[4]

The United Steelworkers of America has been a leader in the creative use of employee stock ownership plans as a partial solution to the severe financial problems confronting the metals industries where most of its members are employed. The ESOPs negotiated by the Steelworkers have frequently taken place in the context of contracts which reduced wages and benefits and invested the reductions in stock of the employer through an ESOP program. However, as indicated in the above speech, the Steelworkers have preferred to adjust wages and nonpension benefits rather than to curtail or eliminate the pension plans established to provide retirement income to their members.

The Industrial Union Department of the AFL-CIO has also, in the April 1986 *IUD Digest*, warned employers against trading pension benefits for an ESOP plan. According to the IUD, such a trade would put employees ''in the position of having their current *and* future security dependent solely on the survival and health of a single firm.''

Until recently, some companies have used ESOPs to reduce the cost of their pension program while maintaining the benefit of a government-guaranteed pension. Programs of this sort utilize a so-called floor plan under which pension benefits are reduced by the value of the benefit provided under an ESOP. The value of the ESOP benefit is measured when it is cashed out, at the time of retirement, so that if the ESOP stock proves to be of little ultimate value to a worker, his pension benefit will be proportionately increased. Conversely, if the ESOP stock is very valuable when it is received by an employee, his pension benefit will be reduced and may even be eliminated entirely. Similarly, the funding requirements for the pension plan will be greatly reduced as long as the ESOP stock holds its value.

However, a plan of this type subjects the governmental pension guarantee system to greater risk because it undermines the requirement that pension plan assets must be diversified. Under Section 407(a)(3)(A) of ERISA,[5] no more than 10 percent of the assets of a pension plan may be invested in the stock of an employer. If ESOP benefits are used to offset the benefits payable under a pension plan, the two plans combined may be no more than 10 percent invested in employer stock. For this reason, Section 9345 of the Omnibus Budget Reconciliation Act of 1987 (Public Law 100–203) outlaws the establishment of any so-called floor plan after December 17, 1987.

UNION VERIFICATION OF FINANCIAL PROBLEMS

Among major companies (including Eastern Air Lines, TWA, Chrysler, Bethlehem Steel, LTV Steel, and Kaiser Aluminum & Chemical), the greatest use of collectively bargained ESOPs has occurred in the context of troubled industries. In many cases, the pattern has been one in which management seeks reductions in labor costs which are alleged to be necessary to avoid insolvency or to promote funds for vital modernization expenses. In many cases, demands for reduced labor costs have been backed up by the threat of taking the company into bankruptcy and rejecting the outstanding collective-bargaining contract unless concessions were granted.[6]

Companies that wish to negotiate employee stock ownership financing because of severe financial problems should anticipate that their claims will be met with understandable skepticism on the part of labor representatives. Labor representatives are used to hearing about economic problems every time collective-bargaining negotiations are commenced. Furthermore, even where financial problems are real and serious, they often coexist with wasteful management practices and astronomical salaries paid to major executives. Under these circumstances, unions have sought access to company records in order to verify claims that a stock investment program is necessary in order to avoid financial catastrophe.

Prior to agreeing to the 1984 Wage Investment Program, District 100 of the International Association of Machinists (IAM) had its own experts study Eastern Air Lines' financial situation and prepare a report to measure the extent of Eastern's financial difficulties. Similarly, it has been the practice of the United Steelworkers of America to require an employer to open its books to union investment bankers or accountants prior to negotiating a plan which would substitute a stock investment for wages and benefits which the company would otherwise pay in cash. As might be expected, the union's accountants and investment bankers do not always agree with company experts concerning the extent of the company's problems or the amount of money that is needed to be invested in stock by employees. Nevertheless, unions have recognized that it is in the common interest of both management and labor to ensure the continued existence of the corporation, and they have been willing to enter into stock programs when they were convinced such programs were necessary to preserve the jobs of their members. This approach has been explained by United Steelworkers' President Lynn Williams as follows:

In the metals industries, the involvement of our union in employee stock ownership plans has been a matter of necessity. In a number of cases, we have been approached by companies whose long-term viability was threatened by depressed conditions in the industry. In such cases, we have been willing to recommend, and have gained the approval of our members, for programs of wage and benefit investments under an employee stock ownership plan. In essence, we have agreed to increase the employer's cash flow and earnings by substituting an employee stock ownership program for some portion of wages and benefits which would otherwise be paid in cash.[7]

A further safeguard adopted by the Steelworkers Union to meet the skepticism with which their members traditionally view claims of employer poverty has been to require ratification by the membership of any contracts that provide for the substitution of stock ownership in place of wages and benefits otherwise paid in cash.

UNION BELIEF THAT STOCK OWNERSHIP PROGRAMS SHOULD BE ACCOMPANIED BY MEANINGFUL VOTING RIGHTS AND PARTICIPATIVE MANAGEMENT

Voting Rights

A principal difference between collectively bargained ESOP programs and those established by management for nonorganized employees relates to the voting rights in the stock held in trust under the ESOP program. The 1980 comptroller general's study of ESOPs established in closely held companies found that:

Participants generally were not permitted to vote or direct the voting of company stock allocated to their Plan accounts. Rather, a Plan committee, usually appointed by the employer, voted the Plan company stock without formal direction from the participants.[8]

In the context of leveraged ESOPs, this problem is addressed to some extent by Internal Revenue Code Section 409(e),[9] which requires "pass-through" voting of stock which is allocated to employees under the ESOP plan of a company having a class of securities registered with the Securities and Exchange Commission (SEC). For closely held companies, pass-through voting (for "allocated" stock only) is required only upon "major" corporate matters including merger or consolidation, recapitalization, reclassification, liquidation, dissolution, or sale. Since very few issues fall into the major category, the requirement is meaningful only in unusual circumstances. Furthermore, even in the context of SEC-registered companies, the voting protection of Section 409(e) extends only to "allocated" shares.[10] At the beginning of an ESOP program, this often represents a small fraction of the ESOP shares because stock is generally released from a security interest and allocated to accounts over a period of years as the ESOP loan is paid.

In many cases, the voting rights which have been negotiated by major unions are substantially more extensive than those that would be required under Section 409(e). Voting programs negotiated by unions have generally extended to all of the stock held in the ESOP program whether or not allocated or vested. The Eastern Air Lines IAM ESOP provides that voting control over all of the shares in the ESOP would be concentrated and cast by a trustee named by the union, rather than dispersed among the 13,000 participants of the stock trust.[11] The Kaiser Aluminum ESOP negotiated by the United Steelworkers of America passes through voting rights to individual participants, but requires shares to be voted by the ESOP trustee even if participants fail to return their proxies. This is an important consideration since the experience under some ESOP plans has been that fewer than 50 percent of plan participants may return proxies in the initial years of the ESOP program. The Kaiser Aluminum ESOP provides that all of the stock in the ESOP is to be voted in a proportion based on the proxies received from those ESOP participants who return proxies.

Participative Management

Guided by the Japanese experience, both business schools and managements have recently begun to emphasize the need for greater cooperation between labor and management and for the involvement of workers in any management decisions that directly affect their jobs. Successful programs of participative management have been instituted at many companies where there is no employee ownership program. Conversely, some companies which have adopted employee stock ownership plans have not changed traditional authoritarian management styles. Although there is no necessary connection between employee ownership programs and participative management approaches, the two concepts have a natural affinity. A study by the National Center of Employee Ownership (NCEO) found that ''companies which combine ownership with employee participation in job level decision-making have much higher growth rates than companies that do not.''[12] The *NCEO Newsletter* further explains this finding as follows:

> Previous NCEO research had found that employee attitudes about employee ownership were most strongly related to the financial benefits of ownership; that is the more stock a company contributes to its ESOP, the more satisfied and committed are the employees. Based on this study we now believe that if companies want to translate that employee enthusiasm and commitment into more creative and productive employee behaviors, they must create a mechanism for allowing greater employee involvement. The most successful companies do this in a variety of ways. Our measures of employee participation emphasized employee involvement in many of the day-to-day decisions of how companies operate: quality control; work methods; purchasing supplies and equipment; budget control; and labor/management relations. Although many of the participative companies also involve employees in ''control'' of the firms through voting rights and board representation, these factors were not independently related to superior performance.[13]

President Williams of the Steelworkers has also underscored the importance of combining employee ownership with participative management:

> As shown by numerous studies, effective labor management participation can increase productivity by raising morale, preventing waste, improving the design and engineering

of tools and equipment, and bringing about improved coordination of work efforts. In addition, the role of labor management participation teams can be supplemented and made more effective by union representation on the board of directors. In several cases where we have negotiated ESOPs, we have also agreed to nominate union representatives to serve on corporate boards as another means to improve communications and increase productivity.[14]

As a union representative nominated by the United Steelworkers to serve on two corporate boards of directors, I am personally convinced that a labor nominee can play an important role in facilitating communication between labor and management and in sensitizing board members to employee relations issues.

ISSUES INVOLVED IN THE DESIGN OF THE ESOP STOCK AND THE ESOP PLAN

Designing the ESOP Stock

In negotiating an employee stock ownership plan, union officials need to become familiar with corporate and securities issues affecting the design and valuation of the stock to be issued under the employee stock ownership plan. For this purpose, the options available depend to a significant extent on the type of plan involved. In the case of a "leveraged ESOP," where the stock will be bought with the proceeds of a loan, Section 409(1) of the Internal Revenue Code[15] requires the use of common stock or preferred stock which is convertible at any time into common stock at a reasonable price. A plan of this type also qualifies for some additional tax advantages such as the deduction by the company of cash dividends passed through to employees. On the other hand, if a "stock bonus plan" is used, under which the employer contributes a certain amount of stock each year for the benefit of employees, any type of common or preferred stock is permissible.

Under a leveraged ESOP, an employee must be given the right to sell his shares on an established market or to the employer.[16] However, prior to enactment of the 1986 Tax Reform Act, it was legally possible to adopt a stock bonus plan which did not provide employees an assured means of selling the stock. Plans of this type have sometimes caused bitterness when employees learned that the stock they receive produces a tax bill but no cash income. For this reason, unions have generally tried to ensure that there would be a guaranteed means of selling stock that had been distributed to workers from an ESOP. Under the 1986 Tax Reform Act, stock bonus plans (as well as other types of ESOPs) must provide a guaranteed means for an employee to sell stock distributed to him from the plan. This new rule applies to all stock contributed to a stock bonus plan after 1986. The law still permits some flexibility with respect to the terms of sale. For example, the statute permits payment of the purchase price over a period of not more than five years in the case of a total distribution.[17] More rapid payment is also permissible.

Many of the collectively bargained ESOP plans have been established through concessionary bargaining where employees agree to accept stock in exchange for reductions in the level of wages and other benefits. When an ESOP is established in this way, the principal concern of the employees may be to obtain eventual repayment of their sacrifices. For example, if wages and benefits are reduced $2.00 an hour for a one-year period and the average employee works 2,000 hours a year, the worker may consider that he has made a $4,000 investment in the employer. The stock contributed on behalf of this worker may be worth less than $4,000 in current dollars, and employees may therefore seek some assurance that their stock will eventually be worth $4,000. This approach would indicate the use of a preferred stock designed to secure the eventual return of a specific dollar amount to each employee. The value of common stock is to a greater extent more uncertain and subject to market risks. On the other hand, the owners of common stock are the ultimate owners of the company, and an increasing number of collectively bargained ESOPs are designed to hold common stock as a means of maximizing the voice of the employees in corporate affairs.

When a preferred stock ESOP is established through collective bargaining, a special class or series of preferred stock will usually be created expressly for the purposes of the ESOP program. Since no market will exist for this newly designed class of preferred stock, the ultimate redemption of this stock will depend upon the right of retiring employees (statutorily required for stock contributed after 1986) to sell their stock directly to the employer for the stock's fair market value. This right to employer redemption will draw cash out of the employer, possibly depriving the employer of needed liquidity.

In the case of a publicly held company, an alternative is the use of publicly traded stock (usually common stock) which allows the ESOP stock to be cashed out through a market mechanism rather than imposing an additional cash drain upon the employer. For example, if retiring employees receive ESOP stock with a value of $1 million, they must be given some mechanism to convert their stock into cash. In the case of preferred stock, this mechanism is usually provided by a sale to the employer, thereby reducing the liquid assets of the employer by $1 million. On the other hand, if common stock is used and the company is publicly traded, the retiring employees can cash out their stock by asking a stockbroker to sell it for them. A possible accommodation between the two points of view is the use of a special preferred stock which is convertible into publicly traded common under circumstances specified in the negotiations between the parties.

In 1986, ESOPs were created at LTV Steel and Bethlehem Steel as a result of negotiations with the United Steelworkers of America. Both these ESOPs utilize a preferred stock, freely convertible into a publicly traded common stock. However, if a retiring employee does not receive full payment of his wage investment through the conversion mechanism, both companies established a separate profit-sharing program designed to provide eventual full repayment of the investment.

When a preferred stock is created for the purposes of an ESOP, it is necessary for unions to become familiar with a number of issues they may not have previously encountered. The type of stock which is available will be determined by the provisions of the corporation's articles of incorporation, the laws of the state of incorporation, and any restrictions which may exist under the terms of financing agreements or indentures.

The terms of the preferred stock will be governed by a certificate of designation, adopted by the employer's board of directors, which will define the attributes of the stock and the protections available in the event of unusual corporate transactions such as merger, bankruptcy, or liquidation. The issues governed by the certificate of designation will include such issues as (1) the liquidation preference of the preferred stock in the event of bankruptcy; (2) the dividend rights of the preferred stock, including the rate of dividends, whether dividends are cumulative, and whether the dividends are payable in cash or with additional stock; (3) the circumstances under which new preferred stock can be issued in the future with a priority superior or equal to the ESOP stock in the payment of dividends or in liquidation; (4) the treatment of the preferred stock in the event of a merger or sale of assets; (5) any rights of conversion of the preferred into common stock and the ratio at which the conversion is to take place; (6) provisions for redemption of the stock and whether or not a sinking fund is to be established for purposes of redemption; and (7) any voting rights of the preferred, as well as a number of other issues. Typically, some of these issues will be resolved in the collective-bargaining agreement, and others will be left to later agreement between the parties in the event lawyers for the two sides are unable to agree on appropriate terms for the certificate of designation.

Designing the ESOP Plan

Because of the flexibility permitted under the ESOP laws, two employee stock ownership plans will rarely be identical. Employees should participate in the design of their plan; their choices will be shaped by their individual preferences as well as by the economic circumstances of their employer. Some of the principal issues that should be considered by workers and their unions are listed below.

Timing of Stock Distribution. Prior to enactment of the 1986 Tax Reform Act, ESOP stock was required to be distributed to employees at the time of their retirement age or, if later, ten years after the commencement of the ESOP program. This rule still applies to stock held by a leveraged ESOP prior to complete repayment of the ESOP loan. For other ESOP plans, Section 409(o)[18] of the Internal Revenue Code, as added by the 1986 Act, requires distribution not later than one year after death, disability, or normal retirement, nor later than five years after termination of employment for other reasons. Earlier distribution is permitted, in the event of termination of employment, after a fixed period of years (at least two years) or in the event of financial hardship.

The issue of when stock will be distributed from an ESOP program will interact with issues involving the employer's financial condition and its loan agreements.

If the employer is in severe economic difficulties, it may be necessary to delay the distribution of ESOP stock in order to minimize the financial drain on the employer. Unless the stock distributed is publicly traded, Section 409(h) of the Internal Revenue Code may require that the employee be given the right, once the stock is received from the ESOP, to sell the stock to the employer for a fair price. Covenants in the employer's loan agreements may prevent the employer from redeeming stock from its stockholders, including employee stockholders. If so, one option is to renegotiate the loan. If this is impossible, the only alternative may be to delay distribution of stock from the plan as long as legally permitted in order to prevent the employer from paying out cash to its employee stockholders prior to repayment of the loan. The union's interest in obtaining earlier benefits for its members would ordinarily suggest bargaining for earlier distribution of stock. On the other hand, in some cases, one objective of an ESOP program is to give employees a greater voice in corporate affairs through the ownership of a block of common stock. Earlier distribution of the stock may undermine employee influence by reducing the amount of stock owned by the ESOP. Furthermore, the union's interest in ensuring adequate corporate funds for capital improvements or other purposes may lead to a program in which distribution of stock is delayed for a specified period of years.

Division of Stock among Employees. The law permits a number of different approaches to the division of stock among the employees. Any method of division is proper so long as it does not result in (1) discrimination in favor of stockholders or highly paid employees or (2) benefits for any employees in excess of the limits established by law.[19] The most common form of allocation formula generally divides the stock based upon the compensation of employees. However, when an ESOP is established in the context of concessionary bargaining with reductions in wages and benefits, it is sometimes preferable to divide the stock among employees on the basis of the sacrifices imposed on them under the collective-bargaining agreement. In addition to allocating stock based upon financial sacrifices of the worker or compensation, stock may be divided on the basis of hours worked. Where stock is allocated on the basis of compensation, a limit is sometimes imposed on the amount of compensation taken into account in order to prevent higher paid workers from obtaining a disproportionate share of the stock. For example, in the ESOP program negotiated by the United Steelworkers for the White Pine Copper Mine, stock is allocated to employees based upon their compensation, but any compensation in excess of $19,000 per year is disregarded for this purpose.

Stock Retention and Redemption. As explained above, the time of distribution may be affected by economic factors bearing upon the employer, including covenants in outstanding or newly negotiated loan agreements. Once the stock is distributed (whether after a fixed period of years or by reason of hardship, termination of employment, or retirement), employees may be given the right to keep the stock and receive dividends, and they should be guaranteed also the right to sell their stock for a fair price. If the stock is publicly traded, the sale can be made through a stockbroker. If not publicly traded, the law requires, under certain types of ESOPs, that employees be given the right to sell their stock to the company. The statutory right of an employee to sell his or her stock to the company must be available at least twice: once for a sixty-day period following distribution of the stock and a second time for a sixty-day period following the next annual valuation of the (untraded) stock.[20] If employees do not exercise their right to sell the stock on either of these two occasions, they need not be guaranteed any further right. If the right to sell shares to the employer expires at any point and the ESOP stock is not publicly traded, one would expect most employees to sell their stock to the employer. In order to encourage employees to retain the stock rather than to sell it to the employer immediately or in the following year, some plans offer employees the right to sell their stock to the employer at any subsequent time. If such a right is offered, however, it may be restricted as a result of financial or legal constraints. It is therefore desirable to specify a priority list for redemption. This can be either on a first come, first served basis or on the basis of priority determined by the year or month in which the stock is distributed.

Voting of Stock. Various voting schemes are available, including one person–one vote, pass-through vote to employees based upon the shares in each employee's account (i.e., one share–one vote) and trustee voting. As explained above, unions will want some democratic voting mechanism to be part of the ESOP program.

One issue that may arise is the method for voting ESOP stock for which no proxies are returned. In this case, some plans require such stock to be voted on the basis of the proportion of votes received from employees returning proxies. Other plans require unallocated stock to be cast on the basis of a majority of the votes returned. The Labor Department has expressed doubts about the validity of these approaches in the contexts of tendering shares, based on the view that the fiduciaries under the plan are required to take responsibility for all decisions not validly passed through to individual employees.[21]

Amendment of the Plan. Although ESOP plans are usually amendable by their sponsor (the employer), this principle is rarely applied to employee benefit plans created through collective bargaining. If the terms of the plan are established through collective bargaining by the agreement of the two parties, any amendment or termination of the plan should similarly require the agreement of the parties. Sometimes an exception is made for amendments which are necessary because of changes of the law in order to ensure the continued legality of the ESOP plan. Even in these circumstances, unions will usually want to retain the right to approve amendments since a legal problem with the plan can usually be remedied in several ways. The particular remedy selected should be the subject of agreement between the parties whose actions created the plan.

Power of the Board of Directors to Issue Additional Stock. When employees have a significant ownership in the stock of their employer through an ESOP program, they may object to the dilution of their interest through the issuance of additional shares or to the elimination of employee stock ownership through a merger or sale of assets. Protection of these arrangements can be written into a preferred stock certificate of designation or the articles of incorporation of the employer if bargained for at the time the ESOP program is initiated. For example, in the Copper Range ESOP negotiated by the United Steelworkers of America, 70 percent of the common stock is owned by employees under an ESOP program. In order to preserve ESOP ownership, the plan requires any stock redeemed from retiring employees to be recontributed to the ESOP. In addition, restrictions are placed upon the issuance of additional stock (or convertible securities) by the board of directors in order to ensure the continuation of at least 51 percent employee ownership through the ESOP program. However, this restriction can be waived by vote of the employee shareholders themselves.

EFFECT OF AN ESOP PROGRAM ON THE ROLE OF THE UNION

In discussions of employee stock ownership plans, workers sometimes ask what function a union will serve in the context of an employee-owned company. President Williams of the Steelworkers has addressed this issue as follows:

> In essence then we must recognize that the worker-owner has two sets of interest arising out of his separate roles of worker and investor. Business managers, even if the worker helps select them through stock voting processes, cannot effectively represent workers' interest *as workers*. The need for unions will therefore continue, and unions will continue because workers will continue to perceive the need for them. I certainly would not fear for the future of the USWA if every employer in the United States became an ESOP company.[22]

The validity of this point of view is recognized in the ESOP laws themselves which require ESOP trustees to act solely in the interest of the participants *as stockholders* and forbid those fiduciaries to act based on the interests of the employees *as workers*.[23]

CONCLUSION

This chapter has discussed some of the reasons for the labor movement's skeptical view of employee stock ownership programs. However, despite such skepticism, unions have recognized the new technique of ESOP financing as an important tool which can sometimes be of substantial benefit to workers.

The continuing surge of mergers, acquisitions, and leveraged buy-outs has undermined the financial stability of many companies and has contributed to a growing sense of insecurity on the part of workers. Employee ownership is one way in which employees can seek greater control over their own destiny and obtain some protection from corporate raiders and unsound financing techniques.

This author expects continuing growth in labor's interest in employee ownership and in the willingness of union leaders and their members to evaluate employee ownership as a means of increasing job security and improving their standard of living.

NOTES

1. IUD Digest, Apr. 1986.
2. 6 Lab. Research Rev. 61 (Spring 1985).
3. Comptroller General, General Accounting Office, Report to the Committee on Finance, United States Senate, HRD-80–88, Employee Stock Ownership Plans: Who Benefits Most in Closely Held Companies? (1980) [hereinafter cited as GAO Report].
4. Address by Steve Newman on behalf of United Steelworkers of America President Lynn Williams, "Labor Unions and Employee Ownership," delivered to the Employee Stock Ownership Association, May 15, 1985 [hereinafter cited as Williams Speech].
5. 29 U.S.C. § 1107 (a)(2) (1982).
6. In 1984 the Supreme Court held in NLRB v. Bildisco & Bildisco, 465 U.S. 513 (1984), that a company undergoing a Chapter 11 reorganization and bankruptcy may reject its collective-bargaining agreements. This device has been successfully used in a number of cases to restructure wage costs in a manner disadvantageous to employees. The *Bildisco* decision was later modified by Congress so as to allow the rejection of collective-bargaining contracts in bankruptcy but only after certain strict procedural requirements were met. 11 U.S.C. § 1113. See Wheeling-Pittsburgh Steel Corporation v. United Steelworkers of America, 791 F.2d 1074 (3d Cir. 1986).
7. Williams Speech, supra note 4.
8. GAO Report, supra note 3, at ii.
9. 26 U.S.C.A. § 409(e), as amended by Tax Reform Act of 1986, Pub. L. No. 99–514, § 1854(f).
10. In a leveraged ESOP, the stock purchased by the employee trust fund is initially pledged to secure a loan obtained to acquire the shares. Shares are released from the pledge and assigned (or "allocated") to employee accounts on an annual basis as payments are made on the ESOP loan.
11. The Eastern Air Lines ESOPs are governed by the Railway Labor Act and are therefore not subject to the provisions of the Taft-Hartley Act prohibiting union control over an employee benefit trust fund.
12. "Employee Ownership," National Center for Employee Ownership Newsletter, Employee Ownership, vol. 6, no. 3 (May-June 1986), at 1.
13. Id. at 12.
14. Williams Speech, supra note 4.
15. 26 U.S.C.A. § 409(1), as amended by Tax Reform Act of 1986, Pub. L. No. 99–514 § 1176(h).
16. I.R.C. § 409(h), 26 U.S.C.A. § 409(h), as amended by Tax Reform Act of 1986, Pub. L. No. 99–514, § 1174(c), 1854(f)(3)(c); I.R.C. § 401(a)(23), 26 U.S.C.A. § 401(a)(23), as amended by Tax Reform Act of 1986, Pub. L. No. 99–54, § 1174(c)(2).
17. I.R.C. § 409(h), 26 U.S.C.A. § 409(h), as amended by Tax Reform Act of 1986, Pub. L. No. 99–514, §§ 1174(c), 1854(f)(3)(c).

18. 26 U.S.C.A. § 409(o), as added by Tax Reform Act of 1986, Pub. L. No. 99–514, §§ 1874(b)(1), 1854(a)(3)(A).

19. See, e.g., I.R.C. § 401(a)(4), 26 U.S.C.A. § 401(a)(4), as amended by Tax Reform Act of 1986, Pub. L. No. 99–514, § 1114(b)(7); I.R.C. §§ 404(a)(3),(7) and (9), 26 U.S.C.A. §§ 404(a)(3),(7) and (9), as amended by Tax Reform Act of 1986, Pub. L. No. 99–514, §§ 1131(a) and (b); I.R.C. § 415, 26 U.S.C.A. § 415, as amended by Tax Reform Act of 1986, Pub. L. No. 99–514.

20. I.R.C. § 409(h), 26 U.S.C.A. § 409(h), as amended by Tax Reform Act of 1986, Pub. L. No. 99–514, §§ 1174(c), 1854(f)(3)(c).

21. See Labor Department Advisory Opinion, Apr. 30, 1984 (Carter Hawley Hale Stores, Inc., unnumbered), 11 Pens. Rep. (BNA), no. 19, at 633 (1984).

22. Williams Speech, supra note 4.

23. 29 U.S.C. § 1104(a)(1982).

16

BANKRUPTCY REORGANIZATION AND REJECTION OF COLLECTIVE-BARGAINING AGREEMENTS—AN ALTERNATIVE TO OPPRESSIVE LABOR CONTRACTS?

Harvey R. Miller and Debra A. Dandeneau

Editors' Note. Mr. Miller and Ms. Dandeneau observe that Continental Airlines' successful use of corporate reorganization to reject its collective-bargaining agreements generated immense interest in standards for utilizing this procedure—which were clarified in the *Bildisco* case and then redefined in the 1984 Bankruptcy Act Amendments. Now the debtor must, before seeking to reject an agreement, make a "necessary modification" proposal, that is "fair and equitable" to the unions and share with them all relevant information. Ultimately, if bargaining is unsuccessful, rejection may occur if the bankruptcy court finds that "the balance of equities clearly favors rejection." The authors discuss the cases that have applied these standards, and they conclude that the controversial *Wheeling-Pittsburgh* ruling of the Third Circuit has misinterpreted them. The authors also caution that not only may the reorganization process be long and laborious, but also a union may strike over rejection of a collective-bargaining agreement.

The public acceptance of the use of the bankruptcy process as a means of rehabilitating financially and operationally distressed business entities has made available to management an important option for dealing with some of the causes of the distress. Thus, when management of a distressed entity is confronted with high costs of operations and lack of competitiveness—both of which are traceable in large measure to the costs and other expenses imposed by collective-bargaining agreements and are compounded by union resistance to their modification—should it seek reorganization under Chapter 11 of the bankruptcy law? In evaluating the strategic value of the Chapter 11 option, management and its attorneys must understand the purpose of the bankruptcy reorganization process, particularly in light of the recent enactment of Section 1113 of the Bankruptcy Code and the decisions construing that section.

The underlying philosophy of business reorganization pursuant to the federal bankruptcy law is that distressed businesses should be afforded a reasonable opportunity to restructure their operations and finances in order to preserve going concern values and jobs. This reorganization philosophy—an alternative to the draconian option of liquidation—has its roots in the equity receivership proceedings in the railroad industry during the latter nineteenth century and early twentieth century and in the emergency legislation enacted during the so-called Great Depression of the early 1930s to aid the rehabilitation of financially troubled companies. The rehabilitation philosophy has been refined in successor legislation[1] and confirmed by the Supreme Court of the United States.[2] The bankruptcy law implements the national policy in favor of reorganization by providing a debtor with respite from the payment of debt obligations, creditor pressures, and litigation while allowing for the use of the statutory mechanism of reorganization to permit the debtor's business to return to economic viability.

The commencement of a reorganization case under the Code creates an immediate distinction between the obligations incurred prior to the filing of the Chapter 11 petition and those arising after the petition date. All obligations arising before petition, even if unmatured, unliquidated, or contingent, are, in effect, frozen and subject to treatment and discharge under a plan of reorganization in accordance with the provisions of the bankruptcy law.[3]

In contrast, debts and liabilities incurred subsequent to the filing of a Chapter 11 petition enjoy administrative expense status. Such administrative expense obligations should be paid in the ordinary course of the debtor's postpetition business. The terms of administrative expense obligations cannot be changed unilaterally, and they are entitled to payment or satisfaction before all pre–Chapter 11 unsecured debts and liabilities. Assuming that the debtor's property is substantially unencumbered, persons doing business with a debtor after the filing of the petition (the debtor sometimes is referred to for administrative purposes as a "debtor-in-possession") may do so with a higher degree of confidence that they will be paid than if there were no reorganization.

The date of cleavage created by the filing of the reorganization petition thus serves two purposes. First, it suspends payment of prepetition debts and liabilities so that all holders of that debt will be treated equally in accordance with applicable legal principles. Second, it gives reasonable assurance to postpetition creditors that they will be paid, thereby encouraging such persons to do business with the debtor and enhancing the possibility of the debtor's successful reorganization.

LABOR-BANKRUPTCY LAW PRIOR TO THE 1984 AMENDMENTS

Collective Bargaining Agreements as Executory Contracts

Traditionally, federal bankruptcy statutes have authorized rejection or breach of those contracts that a trustee or debtor deems in its business judgment to be onerous and burdensome or not in the best interests of the debtor's estate or the reorganization effort.[4] Section 365 of the Code generally permits a debtor, subject to approval of the bankruptcy court, to "assume or reject any executory contract or unexpired lease of the debtor.[5] Although the Code does not provide a definition of "executory contract," the legislative history suggests, and most courts have adopted, a definition that "includes contracts on which performance remains due to some extent on both sides."[6]

Even though bankruptcy law authorizes this form of contractual breach, it does not deprive the nondebtor party of its damages claim for breach. Instead, the effect of rejection under Section 365 is to treat the damages claim as if it were a prepetition liability.[7] This treatment is consistent with the underlying principle that all obligations of the debtor existing as of the filing of a petition are deemed accelerated for the purposes of treatment and discharge as a part of the bankruptcy reorganization case. The objective of reorganization is to give the debtor a fresh start.

A collective-bargaining agreement is an executory contract,[8] subject to rejection under the Code.[9] Although the ability to reject a collective-bargaining agreement in bankruptcy has existed as long as the law has provided for the rejection of executory contracts, debtors did not often attempt to exercise this power. Prior to the early 1970s, most reorganization cases involved closely held companies located in major industrial centers. Because of union solidarity and public support for organized labor in those regions, debtors did not have a nonunionized labor pool as an alternative source of workers. Consequently, motions to reject collective-bargaining agreements were relatively rare.

Since then, however, union membership has been on the decline.[10] Further, as more reorganization bankruptcies occur, particularly in nonunionized geographic areas and businesses, debtors have more often invoked the power to reject collective-bargaining agreements as executory contracts under the bankruptcy law. The use of the bankruptcy law to deal with labor problems has highlighted the tension between the policies underlying the federal bankruptcy and labor laws. Consequently, public and congressional attention has increasingly focused on the propriety of using bankruptcy law to deal with the continued enforceability of labor contracts.

The labor-bankruptcy controversy rose to the fore in 1984 as a result of the confluence of three events: the Chapter 11 cases involving Continental Airlines, the Supreme Court's decision in *Bildisco*, and the passage of the Bankruptcy Amendments and Federal Judgeship Act of 1984.

The Continental Airlines Reorganization

In September 1983, Continental Airlines Corporation and certain of its subsidiaries (Continental) each commenced a petition under Chapter 11. Continental announced that a primary cause of the filings was the high labor costs imposed by its collective-bargaining agreements covering pilots, mechanics, and flight attendants. Immediately after filing, Continental, consistent with the bankruptcy law principles generally applicable to executory contracts, modified the terms of employment and employee work rules for unionized and nonunionized employees without regard to the provisions of the pre–Chapter 11 collective-bargaining agreements and employment policies. Continental then filed motions with the bankruptcy court for approval of its rejection of collective agreements covering pilots, flight attendants, and mechanics in accordance with Section 365 of the Code. Over the vigorous opposition of the organized labor groups, which had unsuccessfully struck Continental, the bankruptcy court granted the motions and approved the rejection.

The *Bildisco* Case

In March 1984, the Supreme Court issued its decision in the *Bildisco* case, addressing two issues also raised by the Continental cases: (1) what is the proper standard for permitting rejection of collective-bargaining agreements and (2) may a trustee or debtor-in-possession, prior to court approval of rejection, unilaterally modify the terms and conditions of employment of unionized employees without regard to prepetition collective-bargaining agreements, thereby disregarding provisions of other federal laws governing labor relations, including the requirement of good faith bargaining and restrictions on midterm modification of such agreements?

Concerning the first issue, *Bildisco* resolved a dispute among the circuits as to the proper standard for approval of rejection of a collective-bargaining agreement. In 1975, the Second Circuit in the *REA Express* case had held that rejection should not be approved unless, in its absence, the debtor "will collapse and the employees will no longer have their jobs."[11] The Third and Eleventh Circuits disputed this "forced liquidation" standard and held that rejection was proper if (1) the agreement was onerous and burdensome and (2) the competing equities favored rejection of the collective-bargaining agreement.[12]

In unanimously rejecting the Second Circuit's standard for rejection, the Supreme Court noted that, although there was "no indication" in the Bankruptcy Code that "rejection of collective-bargaining agreements should be governed by a standard different from that governing other executory contracts," every court of appeals that had previously considered the issue found that such agreements were entitled to special treatment.[13] The Court agreed that the "special nature" of such agreements required a "somewhat stricter standard" for approval of their rejection.[14] As between the "forced liquidation" test of *REA Express* and the "onerous and burdensome" test adopted by the Third and Eleventh Circuits, the *Bildisco* Court chose the latter: the bankruptcy court must find that the collective-bargaining agreement is a burden to the reorganization effort and that the balance of the equities favors rejection. The Court explained that the *REA Express* test unjustifiably subordinated the "multiple, competing considerations underlying a Chapter 11 reorganization" to parochial consideration of the collective-bargaining agreement.[15]

As to balancing the equities, the Court directed the lower courts to consider the interests of all affected parties—the debtors, creditors, and employees—with the focus of the inquiry to remain directed to the "ultimate goal of Chapter 11," the rehabilitation of the debtor.[16] The Supreme Court noted that the Bankruptcy Code did "not authorize free-wheeling consideration of every conceivable equity, but rather only how the equities relate to the success of the reorganization."[17] It also emphasized that a debtor's use of the power to reject under the bankruptcy law should occur only after bilateral negotiations have proven unsuccessful. The Court admonished that bankruptcy court intervention was proper only after the debtor made "reasonable efforts" to negotiate a modification, and such efforts were "not likely" to yield "prompt and satisfactory results."[18]

The second issue presented to the Supreme Court in *Bildisco* was whether the debtor-in-possession committed an unfair labor practice under the NLRA by rejecting or modifying a collective-bargaining agreement before approval of rejection by the bankruptcy court. By a five-to-four vote, the Court held that, since the agreement was "no longer immediately enforceable, and may never be enforceable again," the trustee or debtor-in-possession was not bound by the bargaining or modification procedures of the NLRA.[19] Thus, under *Bildisco*, upon commencement of a Chapter 11 case, any existing collective-bargaining agreement is suspended, and the debtor employer is empowered unilaterally to change compensation levels and work rules despite the NLRA and other labor laws.

THE BANKRUPTCY AMENDMENTS AND FEDERAL JUDGESHIP ACT OF 1984

The third event which caused increased awareness of the tension between the bankruptcy law and the labor laws was the constitutional crisis in the bankruptcy court system created by the decision of the United States Supreme Court in *Northern Pipeline Construction Co. v. Marathon Pipe Line Co.*[20] Organized labor recognized that the bankruptcy court crisis represented an opportunity to obtain congressional concessions on labor issues in exchange for its support of legislation curing the constitutional defects of the bankruptcy court system. They concentrated their efforts initially in the House of Representatives. As a result, on March 21, 1984, within twenty-four hours of the *Bildisco* decision, the House passed a bill which would have negated *Bildisco* in both of its holdings, reinstating the *REA Express* forced liquidation standard for rejection and prohibiting interim modifications of collective-bargaining agreements, and would have applied retroactively to all pending cases.[21] However, the Senate did not accede to the extreme position adopted by the House. Ultimately, a compromise package to cure the constitutional crisis was agreed to by both houses.

Section 1113 was added to the Code as part of the Bankruptcy Amendments and Federal Judgeship Act of 1984[22] (1984 Amendments). Section 1113 substantially adopted the *Bildisco* standard for rejection of a collective-bargaining agreement, but it overruled the Supreme Court's determination that a debtor may unilaterally modify the terms of employment of unionized employees.[23] The 1984 Amendments also strengthened the theme of good faith bargaining that was articulated in *Bildisco* by shifting the focus of the bankruptcy court inquiry away from the existing agreement to the promotion of consensual modifications as a result of mandatory bargaining and consideration of at least the debtor's proposal of modifications. Unfortunately, however, Section 1113 is in many respects a poorly drafted, ambiguous statutory provision which reflects the pressures of time and the perils of compromise.[24]

Section 1113—An Overview

Section 1113 contemplates a series of discrete steps that are prerequisites to court approval. The statute emphasizes negotiation and builds on the point stressed in *Bildisco* that "[t]he Bankruptcy Court need step into this [collective-bargaining] process only if the parties' inability to reach an agreement threatens to impede the success of the debtor's reorganization."[25] The first step is that, prior to filing a formal motion to reject a labor agreement, the debtor must make a proposal to the union based on the "most complete and reliable information available at the time of such proposal," and the union must be provided with "such relevant information as is necessary to evaluate the proposal."[26] The proposal has to satisfy a vague statutory standard that it must "provide for those necessary modifications in the employees[sic] benefits and protections that are necessary to permit the reorganization of the debtor and assure that all creditors, the debtor and all affected parties are treated fairly and equitably."[27]

Thus, Section 1113 focuses on the new proposal rather than on the existing agreement. The statute, however, does not specify how extensive this proposal must be, or whether it should address the long-term relationship between the debtor and its unionized employees or simply cover this relationship over the course of the debtor's reorganization case.[28]

Following the literal strictures of Section 1113, once the new proposal has been transmitted to the authorized representative of the unionized employees, the debtor may file its motion to reject the labor agreement. During the period before the hearing on the motion, the debtor must meet "at reasonable times, with the authorized representative [of the bargaining unit] to confer in good faith in attempting to reach mutually satisfactory modifications of such agreement.''[29] If the parties are still unable to reach an accommodation, the court should approve rejection if (1) the debtor has, prior to the hearing on the motion to reject, made a proposal consistent with Section 1113(b)(1), (2) the employees' authorized representative has refused to accept management's proposal ''without good cause,'' and (3) ''the balance of the equities clearly favors rejection of such agreement.''[30]

Although Section 1113 prohibits unilateral modifications, it attempts to ameliorate the potentially negative effects of delayed modification by providing for an expedited hearing within fourteen days of filing an application to reject a collective-bargaining agreement.[31] Unless the debtor and the authorized representative otherwise agree, in no event may the hearing commence later than twenty-one days after the motion is filed.[32] Furthermore, the court must rule on the motion for approval of rejection within thirty days of the commencement of the hearing or such additional time as agreed to by the parties.[33] Absent a ruling within thirty days, the debtor may terminate or otherwise alter the terms of employment of union members despite an existing collective-bargaining agreement.[34] Nonetheless, a subsequent court ruling disapproving rejection may retroactively reinstate suspended employment terms and work rules. Such a reinstatement probably would create substantial administrative expense claims.

Although Section 1113 prohibits a debtor from unilaterally modifying a collective-bargaining agreement pending consideration of a rejection motion in the manner permitted by *Bildisco*, immediate relief may be available in extreme circumstances under Section 1113(e). The standard for obtaining such relief is more rigid than that for rejection: The relief must be ''essential to the continuation of the debtor's business, or in order to avoid irreparable damage to the estate.'' The court may grant this interim relief only after a hearing that ''shall be scheduled in accordance with the needs'' of the debtor. Even if the court grants the debtor interim relief, the debtor must pursue its motion to reject the collective-bargaining agreement.[35]

The Debtor's Proposal—Are the Proposed Modifications "Necessary" and "Fair and Equitable"?

The critical burden on the debtor in the rejection process is the development of a proposal that can pass the ''necessary modifications'' and ''fair and equitable'' tests in Section 1113(b)(1)(A). As stated above, Section 1113 is silent as to the meaning of ''necessary.'' Thus, it is unclear whether the modifications must be necessary to the success of the debtor after the reorganization process is completed, or whether they must be necessary for the debtor's continued viability during the administration of the reorganization case.

That ambiguity aside, two points are readily apparent from the statute. First, any evaluation of the new proposal is fact-specific and requires a detailed examination of the debtor's entire financial and operational structure. Second, the courts wield extremely broad discretion since the Code gives no specific guidance as to the critical elements of the review process. This absence of objective criteria presents the danger that the court's analysis will be subjective, driven by the judge's personal views of labor-management relations and the economic realities of the situation.[36]

As a general proposition, Section 1113 presents the courts with a difficult task because its application requires the courts to predict the outcome of the debtor's reorganization effort. On a more specific level, if one compares this prerequisite for approval of rejection to the prerequisite for granting interim relief under Section 1113(e) (which must be "essential to the continuation of the debtor's business"), one must conclude that Congress understood that "necessary" was something less than "essential."

In *Wheeling-Pittsburgh*, the litigation centered on the question of Congress' intent in requiring that the proposed modifications be "necessary" to permit the reorganization of the debtor. The district court in that case ruled that the modifications proposed by the debtor were necessary[37] for the reorganization of the debtor because they would enhance the prospects of a successful reorganization.[38] Although Wheeling-Pittsburgh was operating at a loss, it had sufficient cash resources to continue to pay employees at existing contract rates as a result of unanticipated cash produced by the suspension of payment of all prepetition debts and liabilities. The union urged that these facts argued against the necessity for the requested modification. The trial court, however, focused the inquiry on the long-range reorganization of the debtor rather than on its short-term survival, stating that, "in order for the debtor to successfully reorganize, it will be necessary to do more than just emerge from the current labor contract with enough cash on hand to meet current operating expenses."[39]

On appeal, the Third Circuit reversed.[40] In the absence of a congressional conference committee report, the court of appeals placed substantial reliance upon comments by certain legislators for its construction of Section 1113. The court ignored the ambiguity of the legislators' comments[41] and the context in which many of the statements were made, holding that "[t]he substantive standard of *Bildisco* had been overturned and that the *REA Express* standard, or something close to it, had been reinstated [by Section 1113]."[42] The appeals panel explicitly rejected what it characterized as the "hypertechnical argument that 'necessary' and 'essential' have different meanings because they are in different subsections. The words are synonymous."[43] Accordingly, the Third Circuit focused the "necessary modifications" inquiry upon "the somewhat shorter term goal of preventing the debtor's liquidation" rather than the longer term reorganization of the debtor.[44] However, it did emphasize that a debtor's cash position is "not the only relevant factor in determining whether any modifications are necessary." Cash availability, as in Wheeling-Pittsburgh's case, may only be the result of the suspension of payments as to pre–Chapter 11 debts and liabilities because of the commencement of the reorganization case. As stated by the court of appeals, "Congress cannot have intended the bankruptcy court to hold all other parties at bay, while pointing to the resulting cash as the reason why no modifications to the labor contract are needed."[45]

In *Carey Transportation*, however, the Second Circuit rejected the Third Circuit's interpretation of "necessary modifications" and shifted the analysis to those "changes that will enable the debtor to complete the reorganization process successfully."[46] Furthermore, the modifications suggested by the debtor do not have to represent the bare minimum changes with which the debtor can survive, but can leave the debtor ample room to negotiate about the terms.[47]

In so holding, the Second Circuit questioned the Third Circuit's interpretation of the legislative history, reasoning instead that Congress' failure to accept Senator Packwood's labor-oriented language in the final version of Section 1113 "suggests that [Congress] was uncomfortable with language suggesting that a debtor must prove its initial post-petition proposal contained only bare-minimum changes essential to survival."[48] The Second Circuit also noted the distinction between interim relief under Section 1113(e)—which warrants application of a stricter standard—and the postpetition modifications allowed under Section 1113(b).[49]

The difficulty represented by the lack of definition as to what is a "necessary" modification is further illustrated by the decisions of lower courts in other jurisdictions. The bankruptcy court for the Northern District of Ohio has posed the issue as whether "the adoption of the modifications would result in a significantly greater probability of the debtor's successfully reorganizing than would result if the debtor were required to continue under the collective bargaining agreement sought to be rejected."[50] One court concluded that a debtor's proposal failed the statutory test because it included, in addition to "necessary modifications," certain modifications to which the debtor attributed no savings.[51] Another bankruptcy court has recognized that a "necessary" modification does not rise to the level of an "essential" modification, but it has not attempted to establish a precise standard.[52]

Whatever verbal standards the courts adopt, the analysis of a request for approval of rejection requires a detailed factual examination in each instance. As the bankruptcy court in *Carey Transportation* recognized,

> [t]here can be no pat formula. Any analysis must be undertaken on a case by case basis with due consideration given to the nature of the business and industry patterns . . . [T]he § 1113 process is designed to encourage selective, necessary contract modification rather than a total elimination of all provisions in the collective bargaining agreement.[53]

Under Section 1113, not only must the modifications be "necessary to permit the reorganization," but such modifications must also "assure that all creditors, the debtor and all of the affected parties are treated fairly and equitably."[54] Section 1113 provides no explanation of the critical phrase "fair and equitable."[55] In *Bildisco*, the Supreme Court had ruled that the bankruptcy court must consider the interests of "all affected parties."[56] Although this consideration was to occur somewhat later in the context of the "balancing of the equities," the cases construing this provision in Section 1113 focus on whether the burdens of the Chapter 11 reorganization are shared by the debtor, creditors, unionized employees, nonunionized employees, and equity interest holders alike.[57] One court has stated that the "fair and equitable" test "is not different from the standard articulated by the Supreme Court in *Bildisco*."[58]

The dual requirements of Section 1113(b)(1)(A)—the "necessary modifications" and "fair and equitable" tests—require concurrent analysis. The fair and equitable test is intended to ensure an equal sharing of the financial sacrifices required in a reorganization, a standard difficult to evaluate and implement in the initial stages of a reorganization case. During that period, it is often not clear that the debtor will be reorganized. Further, it is difficult to determine the extent to which creditors and equity interest holders will be impaired. Nonetheless, cost and pain are immediately inflicted upon such parties as debt payments are suspended and the value of equity, if any, is diluted. In that context, required maintenance of noncompetitive labor cost after a request for approval of rejection would give the unionized employees better and, perhaps, non-painful treatment. Continued labor operations with mandated noncompetitive labor costs would, in effect, be subsidized by the use of cash freed from the need to satisfy accounts payable because of the intervention of the reorganization petition. The erosion of the cash by continued adherence to the labor contract inures to the prejudice of the other parties in interest and may limit recoveries by such parties.

Allied Delivery System[59] is another case which demonstrates the interplay between these requirements. In this case, the debtor's union labor costs constituted 87 percent of its $5 million of gross revenues. Adding current pension, health, and welfare benefits to other labor costs increased that figure as a percent of gross revenues to *greater* than 100 percent. The debtor had losses of $287,000 in 1983 and anticipated a 20-percent decline in revenues in 1985. Projected savings from the proposed concessions by both unionized and nonunionized employees were between $296,000 and $388,000. The court found that such cost reductions were "absolutely required" if the debtor was to reorganize.

Although the debtor's proposed modifications required a greater percentage reduction for unionized employees than nonunionized employees, the court nevertheless found the proposal fair and equitable because the earnings and benefits of nonunionized employees were less than those of the unionized employees, and the wages of the nonunionized employees would be reduced on a graduated scale based on such earnings. In the court's view, "fair and equitable" did not mean "identical" or "equal."[60]

Several courts have found that the debtor's proposed modifications have failed on one or both of the "necessary modifications" and "fair and equitable" tests. For example, in *American Provision*,[61] only two employees (out of seventeen) were subject to the collective-bargaining agreement, which would have expired eight months after the debtor's request for rejection. The court found that the proposed savings of $1,185 a month (2% of the debtor's monthly operating expenses) for eight months were not necessary to permit reorganization. In *Cook United*,[62] the court questioned how the anticipated savings of $4.3 million from labor contract modifications could be necessary since the debtor's operating plan for 1985 showed a positive cash flow of over $1 million without such savings. Even if such modifications were necessary, they fell disproportionately on senior, full-time employees who would be replaced by younger, part-time employees. In addition, the court credited the allegation of union members that ''top management was not doing its fair share in taking cuts.''[63]

Similarly, in *K&B Mounting*,[64] the debtor failed to provide any information, other than the usual schedule of debts required to be filed with the bankruptcy court, to support the necessity of its proposed modifications. The *K&B Mounting* court also held that, because the only major debt obligation of the debtor was for employee benefits under the labor contract, the proposal required sacrifice only from unionized workers and was therefore not fair and equitable. The court faulted the proposal for not requiring a sharing of cost and pain from other constituencies such as management, nonunion employees, and suppliers.[65] The court failed to explain, however, why such constituencies should be required to share the cost and pain if they are not the cause of the debtor's distress.

Relevant Information

In connection with the debtor's proposal to the union, the debtor must also provide the union with the ''relevant information . . . necessary to evaluate the proposal.''[66] The information should include ''detailed projections and recommendations, perhaps made by a management consultant, preferably one who is an independent one of the interested parties. The debtor should present full and detailed disclosure of its difficulties and its proposed short run and long run solutions.''[67]

The union will be charged with knowledge of the information it received from the debtor prior to the filing of a Chapter 11 petition.[68] Relevant information would include the anticipated possibility that one-third of the union work force would be laid off,[69] but would not include the facts necessary for the union to evaluate its own counterproposals.[70]

"Good Faith" Negotiations

Section 1113(b)(2) of the Code requires that the debtor ''meet at reasonable times'' and ''confer in good faith'' with the union after the new proposal is made and before the *hearing* on the rejection motion takes place. The statute does not specify, and the courts have not required, any mandatory waiting period between the time the proposal is made and the filing of the rejection motion.[71] However, in view of the expedited hearing schedule provided in Section 1113(d)(1), it is incumbent upon a debtor to meet immediately with the collective-bargaining agent if the debtor files its rejection motion promptly after submitting its new proposal.

The courts have interpreted the good faith requirement consistently with the mandate from the Supreme Court in *Bildisco* that a court must be convinced that "reasonable efforts to negotiate a voluntary modification have been made [by the debtor] and are not likely to produce a prompt and satisfactory solution."[72] The "number of meetings and the reasonableness of the time spent in negotiation depends upon the complexity and detail of the proposal and of the data given to the union for its evaluation."[73] In *Carey Transportation* and in *Salt Creek II*, nine meetings and four meetings, respectively, between the debtor and the collective-bargaining agent satisfied the requirement of meeting "at reasonable times."[74] In contrast, the one meeting attended by the debtor in *American Provision* was held to be insufficient.[75]

Union's Refusal to Accept Proposal "Without Good Cause"

Congress included in Section 1113 the requirement that, before rejection is permitted, the authorized union representative must refuse to accept the debtor's proposal "without good cause."[76] The statute provides no guidance for construing "good cause." The case law and commentary generally concur that, if the debtor complies with all the other requirements of Section 1113, a refusal by the union representative to accept the proposed modifications would per se be without good cause.[77] Thus, an authorized labor representative may not refuse to bargain in good faith or to respond to the debtor's proposal with unrealistic or unattainable demands. Such conduct may be found by the court to demonstrate a lack of good cause.

Equities Must Favor Rejection

The draftsmen of Section 1113 again borrowed from *Bildisco* in adopting a balancing of equities test. Section 1113 requires that the court find that "the balance of the equities *clearly* favors rejection." The modifier "clearly" reflects congressional intent that rejection is appropriate only where the equities tip decidedly in favor of rejection.[78] In *Bildisco* the Supreme Court outlined the following equitable considerations: "the likelihood and consequences of liquidation for the debtor absent rejection, the reduced value of the creditors' claims that would follow from affirmance and the hardship that would impose on them, and the impact of rejection on the employees."[79]

Courts have considered additional equities (which may also be included in other elements of Section 1113), such as (1) whether the union has asserted that the debtor's sole reason for filing the bankruptcy case was to terminate the collective-bargaining agreement, (2) whether the policy of reorganization will be furthered by rejection of the collective-bargaining agreement, (3) whether claims arising from rejection would be given priority treatment under the Bankruptcy Code, and (4) the potential consequences of a strike for the debtor.[80]

Interim or Prerejection Modifications

Section 1113(e) requires court approval of any interim modification, and it employs a standard adopted from *REA Express*, i.e., interim modifications are permissible only if collapse of the business or irreparable harm to the debtor is imminent. The debtor must present a strong case to satisfy its "heavy burden."[81] In view of the emergency nature of Section 1113(e) and the relative absence of statutory guidance, the courts have applied this provision with considerable flexibility. One court authorized an interim reduction in an amount 10 percent less than that requested by the debtor.[82] Another court granted relief under Section 1113(e), but also required a temporary reduction for nonunionized employees.[83]

On its face, Section 1113(e) appears to be a harsh rebuke of *Bildisco*'s sanction of a debtor's unilateral modification of a collective-bargaining agreement. However, in certain respects, Section 1113(e) is a favorable development for debtors. First, the expedited hearing schedule for the debtor's rejection application under Section 1113(d) eliminates much of the need for interim or unilateral modifications. Second, under *Bildisco*, a debtor which unilaterally modified its collective-bargaining agreements risked ultimate disapproval by the court of its application to reject the agreements. Unilateral modification followed by forced reassumption of the collective-bargaining agreement would probably create an administrative expense claim for the difference between the contractual wages and the modified wages. Depending upon the number of employees, the amount of the reduction, and the time lag between unilateral modification and the ruling of the court on the rejection motion, the damages claim could be significant. The possibility of such a large aggregate administrative expense claim could thwart attempts by the debtor to establish postpetition lines of credit and could possibly jeopardize the reorganization effort.

Accordingly, if the court grants relief under the more rigorous standards of Section 1113(e), it is more probable that the court will grant the debtor's rejection application as well. This potential reduction of uncertainty on the part of prospective postpetition vendors and customers may make a critical difference in the early days of a Chapter 11 case.

WHEELING-PITTSBURGH AND THE APPLICATION OF SECTION 1113

The *Wheeling-Pittsburgh* case represents the classic dilemma that may confront management of a labor-intensive, highly unionized, mature business. In that case, the bankruptcy court noted that the debtor had experienced "significant" losses over the prior three years, production was at 50 to 60 percent of capacity, and labor costs constituted from 35 to 40 percent of total costs. Outstanding obligations consisted of (1) $50–65 million for the prior year's pension fund liabilities, (2) $125 million to unsecured creditors, (3) $547 million to secured creditors (with collateral values of perhaps $100 million), and (4) $121–363 million of unfunded liabilities to pension plans. The existing collective-bargaining agreement, which had thirteen months to run, provided for a $21.40 hourly labor cost. Pursuant to Section 1113, the debtor proposed a five-year contract with a $15.20 hourly labor cost. Wheeling-Pittsburgh estimated that, with this hourly labor cost, it would be able to break even and then achieve profitability in five years. The debtor's proposal also provided that its creditors would recover only 50 percent of their claims paid over a ten-year period. Creditors had neither agreed to any plan of reorganization nor expressed approval of the debtor's proposed treatment of their claims.

The bankruptcy court found, and the district court affirmed, that the $15.20 five-year proposal was necessary to ensure the long-term survival of the debtor. The lower courts also agreed that the proposal was fair and equitable because under it creditors would lose over 50 percent of their claims, and salaried employees previously had taken wage cuts.[84] The court of appeals was properly skeptical, however, of the lower courts' acceptance of the debtor's offer of "an unusually long five-year term at markedly reduced labor costs based on a pessimistic five-year projection without at least also providing for some 'snap back' to compensate for worker concessions."[85] The absence of such a snapback provision compelled the appeals panel to conclude that the debtor's proposal satisfied neither the "necessary modifications" nor the "fair and equitable" requirements of Section 1113. Thus, it may be concluded that the absence in the debtor's proposal of a snapback or other means for unionized employees to share in any enhanced future of Wheeling-Pittsburgh was a fatal flaw. The proposal, as accepted by the lower courts, was based upon projections that simply did not take into account the possibility of improved performance.[86]

The paradox of the three decisions in the *Wheeling Pittsburgh* case is that the lower courts articulated the proper legal standard but came to a highly questionable result, whereas the court of appeals may have articulated an incorrect legal standard but came to a proper result. The lower courts went beyond the precepts of Section 1113 in attempting to bind the debtor and the union to a five-year contract based on virtually worst case economic assumptions at the very onset of the reorganization case. Rejection should provide a basis for commencing the negotiation of the labor provisions of the plan of reorganization, but not necessarily establish such provisions at the onset of the reorganization process.

The disturbing aspect of the Third Circuit's ruling in *Wheeling-Pittsburgh* is not its effect on that particular case, but the potentially precedential influence of its erroneous legal standard. The court of appeals may have misconstrued the purpose of Section 1113 in its zeal to protect the interests of unionized employees in sharing in the future prospects of the debtor. To protect those interests, it was unnecessary to reach the unfounded conclusion that Section 1113 represents a codification of the *REA Express* standard for approving a rejection of collective-bargaining agreements.[87] The approach and rationale expressed by the Second Circuit in *Carey Transportation* presents a more balanced construction of Section 1113 based upon the pertinent legislative history.

REJECTION AS A MANAGEMENT TOOL

The Supreme Court's decision in *Bildisco*, as noted, unleashed a large-scale public relations effort on the part of organized labor designed to convince Congress and the public at large that businesses would, as if they were lemmings, rush into Chapter 11 in order to reject collective-bargaining agreements.[88] This reaction was greatly exaggerated. It is highly doubtful that viable firms would resort to the bankruptcy courts to solve their labor disputes even without the enactment of Section 1113.

Debtors who seek the protection of the bankruptcy courts and attempt to reject collective-bargaining agreements generally are financially distressed businesses unable to survive in the existing competitive marketplace. For example, prior to the time it filed for relief under Chapter 11, Continental Airlines Corporation operated the nation's eighth largest passenger airline with approximately $1.5 billion in annual revenues and employed over 12,000 people. In the five-year period commencing with Congress' deregulation of the airline industry in 1978, Continental's cumulative losses were approximately $520 million. These losses were caused primarily by Continental's inability to compete with the airline industry's new entrants, whose lower labor costs provided a significant operating advantage. Faced with a severe cash crisis, the exhaustion of its free assets and credit, and the failure to achieve additional and necessary concessions from its unions, Continental filed under Chapter 11.

While Continental was reeling under deregulation of the airline industry, Wheeling-Pittsburgh fell victim to a shrinking steel market, increased competition from abroad, and continuing high labor costs. During the three years prior to its Chapter 11 filing, Wheeling-Pittsburgh produced steel at only 50 to 60 percent of capacity. Labor costs alone made up from 35 to 40 percent of the company's total costs. At the commencement of its Chapter 11 case, Wheeling-Pittsburgh expected to propose a plan under which its unsecured creditors would receive a payout of only 50 percent of their $500 million of claims over ten years. From an operational standpoint, even assuming implementation of the unionized employee wage cuts proposed by Wheeling-Pittsburgh, the company estimated that it would still need five years to begin making some profits.

Although bankruptcy may no longer carry the stigma once attached to debtors, the Chapter 11 alternative is still a drastic action and often one of last resort. The debtor choosing the Chapter 11 alternative must be prepared for a long, expensive, and sometimes acrimonious adversarial process with its various creditor, equity, and labor constituencies. Particularly in labor-management relations, the debtor seeking to reject a collective-bargaining agreement faces not only the legal obstacles presented by Section 1113, but also the very real obstacle of a hostile unionized group that may be indispensable to the rehabilitation of the debtor's business. Nonetheless, and despite the rigidity of the basic holding of the Third Circuit in *Wheeling-Pittsburgh*, Section 1113 does present a mechanism for modification of labor contracts when the union insists upon a contract that will not permit the debtor to be viable in its marketplace; however, successful use of Section 1113 depends in large part on the existence of an alternative source of labor as well as acceptance by the debtor's customers, clients, suppliers, and vendors of its resort to Section 1113.

Wheeling-Pittsburgh, Continental Airlines, and a nonbankruptcy situation involving Geo. A. Hormel & Company illustrate the varying degrees of strength of an organized labor group's opposition to the proposed modification of collective-bargaining agreements, whether under applicable labor laws or via the Chapter 11 process. Although Wheeling-Pittsburgh obtained authority from the bankruptcy court to reject its agreements that provided for hourly labor costs of $21.40, unionized employees struck the debtor for ninety-eight days and almost destroyed the company when, after rejection, the debtor determined that it would offer employment to unionized employees at an effective rate of $17.50 an hour despite the bankruptcy court's finding that an effective rate of $15.20 an hour was necessary for Wheeling-Pittsburgh's reorganization.[89] Settlement of the strike required a raise in effective hourly compensation to $18 an hour and institution of a "cooperation plan" with the union employees.[90]

In the Continental Airlines example, after the commencement of the Chapter 11 cases and the changes effected by Continental in compensation and working conditions, the unions struck the airline for almost two years in an attempt to defeat Continental's use of the bankruptcy law to become cost effective. After drastically shrinking its operations immediately after the commencement of the Chapter 11 cases, Continental gradually restored itself to its approximate prefiling size and to profitability. The pilots' union and other unions eventually ended their strikes as Continental prospered despite the efforts of the unions. Continental has emerged from Chapter 11 after almost three years as a larger, more consumer- and cost-oriented airline than the entity that initiated the reorganization case.

Finally, in the Hormel situation, several hundred workers began a bitter strike in August 1985 to resist reductions in wages and benefits and changes in work rules imposed by Hormel.[91] The local union had been waging an intense battle not only with the company, but with the parent union and the AFL-CIO officials who denounced the strike.[92] Despite attempts by the local union to keep the Hormel plant shut, the plant reopened in January 1986 with "crossover" strikers and new hires.[93] The reopening was made possible by the existence of a viable business entity, as well as the availability of an alternative labor source and the support of the parent union and AFL-CIO officials, notwithstanding a militant local union chapter.

CONCLUSIONS

Bildisco and Section 1113 were designed fundamentally to encourage negotiations so that the debtor never reaches the formal rejection stage. As the bankruptcy court in the *Wheeling-Pittsburgh* case recognized,

> this court, as a place for resolving a collective bargaining dispute, is not the proper forum. The real decisions must be made at the bargaining table . . . This court cannot compel, but it can and does encourage the parties to continue negotiations to reach a solution, without which the likelihood of liquidation is very real.[94]

When the district court affirmed the *Wheeling-Pittsburgh* bankruptcy court's approval of the rejection motion, it echoed the same sentiment in more dramatic terms:

> A word to the wise has not yet been sufficient . . . The inability or unwillingness to [negotiate a fair accord] will not produce a winner and a loser but the premature fall of proud warriors whose last struggle will be overshadowed by a failure to sense their need for each other.[95]

Debtors and organized labor alike must recognize that no party can be spared the cost and pain of reorganization. Such cost and pain may be the price of the debtor's continued existence in a competitive marketplace. Although not the desired route, bankruptcy reorganization may be the only means left to a financially and operationally distressed debtor to deal with unwillingness on the part of organized labor to face reality and participate with other parties in interest in meaningful remedial actions to preserve a business.[96] The recent Chapter 11 reorganizations of companies such as AM International, Inc., The Wickes Companies, Inc., and Revere Copper and Brass Incorporated, as well as Continental Airlines Corporation, demonstrate the utility and potential of Chapter 11. Section 1113 is one of the tools provided by Congress to enable the reorganization process to be successful. Properly used, it provides management with an alternative to succumbing to oppressive demands and conditions of existing labor agreements that preclude the attaining of economic viability.

NOTES

1. See Act of Mar. 3, 1933, ch. 204, 47 Stat. 1467 (adding provisions regarding general compositions and extensions, agricultural compositions, and reorganization of interstate railroads); Act of June 7, 1934, ch. 424, 48 Stat. 911–12 (adding section 77B regarding corporate reorganizations generally); Chandler Act, ch. 575, 52 Stat. 840 (1938) (adding chapters X, XI, and XII regarding business reorganizations and chapter XIII regarding individual payment plans); Bankruptcy Act of 1898, ch. 541, 30 Stat. 544; Bankruptcy Reform Act of 1978, 11 U.S.C. §§ 101 et seq. (1982).

2. See NLRB v. Bildisco & Bildisco, 465 U.S. 513, 527–28 (1984); United States v. Whiting Pools, Inc., 462 U.S. 192, 203 (1984).

3. H.R. Rep. No. 595, 95th Cong., 1st Sess. 353 (1977); S. Rep. No. 989, 95th Cong., 2d Sess. 63 (1978).

4. See Group of Institutional Investors v. Chicago, Mil., St. P. & Pac. R.R., 318 U.S. 523, 549–50 (1943); 2 Collier on Bankruptcy paragraph 365.03 (15th ed. 1985); see also Chandler Act, ch. 575, § 70(b), 52 Stat. 840 (1938) [superseded by 11 U.S.C. § 365 (1982)].

5. Section 365(a) of the Bankruptcy Code provides that, with certain exceptions regarding commodity broker liquidations, "the trustee, subject to the court's approval, may assume or reject any executory contract or unexpired lease of the debtor." Appointment of a trustee in a Chapter 11 case is discretionary and is appropriate only under specific circumstances. A collective-bargaining agent or a union cannot compel the appointment of a trustee. See Bankruptcy Code § 1104(a). A debtor-in-possession exercises the rights of a trustee if no trustee is appointed. Bankruptcy Code § 1107(a).

6. H.R. Rep. No. 595, 95th Cong., 1st Sess. 347 (1977); S. Rep. No. 989, 95th Cong., 2d Sess. 58 (1978). See generally Countryman, "Executory Contracts in Bankruptcy, Part I," 57 Minn. L. Rev. 439 (1973); "Executory Contracts in Bankruptcy, Part II," 58 Minn. L. Rev. 479 (1974).

7. Bankruptcy Code § 502(g).

8. *Bildisco*, 465 U.S. at 522; see also Code § 1113.

9. Id.

10. See, e.g., Raskin, "Big Labor Tries to End Its Nightmare," N.Y. Times, May 4, 1986, § 1, at 1, col. 2; Kotlowitz, "Labor's Ultimate Weapon, the Strike, Is Mostly Failing," Wall St. J., Oct. 13, 1986, § 1, at 6, col. 1.

11. Brotherhood of Railway, Airline and Steamship Clerks v. REA Express, Inc., 523 F.2d 164, 172 (2d Cir.), cert. denied, 423 U.S. 1017 (1975).

12. See In re Brada Miller Freight System, Inc., 702 F.2d 890, 899 (11th Cir. 1983); In re *Bildisco*, 682 F.2d 72, 81 (3rd Cir. 1982), aff'd sub nom. *Bildisco*, 465 U.S. at 513.

13. *Bildisco*, 465 U.S. at 523. At that time, the Bankruptcy Code's only explicit treatment of collective-bargaining agreements was found in Bankruptcy Code § 1167, which states that rejection or modification of collective-bargaining agreements involving railroad workers is specifically subject to the Railway Labor Act, 45 U.S.C. § 151. Bankruptcy Code §§ 1167, 103(g).

14. *Bildisco*, 465 U.S. at 524.

15. Id. at 525.

16. Id. at 527.

17. Id.

18. Id. at 526.

19. Id. at 534.

20. 458 U.S. 50 (1982) (holding unconstitutional the provisions of 28 U.S.C. § 1421, which delegated certain decision-making powers to bankruptcy judges as Article I judges).

21. H.R. 5174, 98th Cong., 2d Sess. (1984).

22. Bankruptcy Amendments and Federal Judgeship Act of 1984, Pub. L. No. 98–353, Title III, § 541(a), 98 Stat. 390 (July 10, 1984).

23. See Statement by the Hon. Orrin G. Hatch on H.R. 5174, 98th Cong., 2d Sess. (June 29, 1984), reprinted in 1984 U.S. Code. Cong. Ad. News 576, 592.

24. No Congressional reports were ever issued in connection with the 1984 Amendments; therefore, no "legislative history" as such accompanies Section 1113. Certain commentators and courts have cited statements read into the Congressional Record by various members of Congress in connection with Section 1113 as support for a construction of the statute. See, e.g., Gibson, "The New Law on Rejection of Collective Bargaining Agreements in Chapter 11," 58 Am. Bankr. L.J. 325 (1984); Wheeling-Pittsburgh Steel Corp. v. United Steelworkers, 791 F.2d 1074 (3d Cir. 1986); In re Royal Composing Room, Inc., 62 Bankr. 403 (Bankr. S.D.N.Y. 1986); In re Salt Creek Freightways, 46 Bankr. 347 (Bankr. D. Wyo. 1985) (*Salt Creek I*).

25. *Bildisco*, 465 U.S. at 526.

26. The court may protect against further disclosure of such information by a confidentiality order. Bankruptcy Code § 1113(d)(3).

27. Bankruptcy Code § 1113(b)(1)(A).

28. The proper construction should be the latter. Allowing the Section 1113 proposal to govern only the period of the debtor's transition to a reorganized entity would leave to plan negotiations the terms of any new postreorganization collective-bargaining agreement. Such a construction would permit the parties and the court to evaluate the proposed new collective-bargaining agreement in the context of the proposed reorganization plan and the impact of that plan on all impaired classes of creditors, employees, and equity interest holders.

29. Bankruptcy Code § 1113(b)(2).

30. The courts construing Section 1113 generally have analyzed the statute in terms of nine discrete elements that must be satisfied before approval of rejection:

1. The debtor-in-possession must make a proposal to the union to modify the collective-bargaining agreement.
2. The proposal must be based on the most complete and reliable information available at the time of the proposal.
3. The proposal modifications must be necessary to permit the reorganization of the debtor.
4. The proposed modifications must assure that all creditors, the debtor, and all of the affected parties are treated fairly and equitably.
5. The debtor must provide to the union such relevant information as is necessary to evaluate the proposal.
6. Between the time of the making of the proposal and the time of the hearing on approval of the rejection of the existing collective-bargaining agreement, the debtor must meet at reasonable times with the union.
7. At the meetings, the debtor must confer in good faith in attempting to reach mutually satisfactory modifications of the collective-bargaining agreement.
8. The union must have refused to accept the proposal without good cause.
9. The balance of the equities must clearly favor rejection of the collective-bargaining agreement.

See *Wheeling-Pittsburgh*, 791 F.2d 1074; In re Salt Creek Freightways, 47 Bankr. 835 (Bankr. D. Wyo. 1985) (*Salt Creek II*); In re Cook United, Inc., 50 Bankr. 561 (Bankr. N.D. Ohio 1985); Carey Transportation Inc., 50 Bankr. 203 (Bankr. S.D.N.Y. 1985); In re K&B Mounting, Inc., 50 Bankr. 460 (Bankr. N.D. Ind. 1985); In re Century Brass Products Inc., 55 Bankr. 712 (Bankr. D. Conn. 1985), rev'd on other grounds, 795 F.2d

265 (2d Cir. 1986); In re Kentucky Truck Sales, Inc., 52 Bankr. 797 (Bankr. W.D. Ky. 1985); In re American Provision Co., 44 Bankr. 907 (Bankr. D. Minn. 1984).

The debtor must prove by a "preponderance of the evidence" that each of the nine elements has been satisfied. However, once the debtor has established prima facie compliance, the union has the burden to produce evidence to contradict one or more of the nine elements. *American Provision*, 44 Bankr. at 909; *Salt Creek II*, 47 Bankr. at 838. But see *Royal Composing Room*, 62 Bankr. at 406, which rejects the nine-step analysis as essentially tautological and focuses instead upon Section 1113(c) and, in particular, the facts of the case as they relate to subparagraphs (2) and (3) of that section.

31. Bankruptcy Code § 1113(d)(1).

32. Id.

33. Id. § 1113(d)(2).

34. Id.

35. See id. § 1113(e).

36. Section 1113 requires that the element of "necessity" be evaluated in the context of a specific proposal of modifications. Under *Wheeling-Pittsburgh*, 791 F.2d at 1085, in the absence of a specific set of proposals, a bankruptcy court may not determine the abstract question of whether modifications, in general, are necessary.

37. The standard of review of factual determinations made by the bankruptcy court is the "clearly erroneous" test. See Bankruptcy Rule 8013; *Wheeling-Pittsburgh* 52 Bankr. at 999; Truck Drivers Local 807 v. Carey Transportation, Inc., 816 F.2d 82, 88 (2d Cir. 1987). The Third Circuit has held, however, that the finding as to whether modifications are necessary should be reviewed more intensively as a mixed question of law and fact. *Wheeling-Pittsburgh*, 791 F.2d at 1091. In contrast, the Second Circuit has held that, so long as the lower court has interpreted the legal standard correctly, its conclusions as to compliance with the standard should be reversed only if clearly erroneous. *Carey Transportation*, 816 F.2d at 88.

38. Since the Bankruptcy Code's overriding goal is to prevent the debtor from going into liquidation, which would ensure the loss of jobs, the necessary standard should be satisfied by considerations of feasibility for reorganization. *Wheeling-Pittsburgh* 52 Bankr. at 1003.

39. Id. at 1001–2. See also *Carey Transportation*, 816 F.2d at 90; *Royal Composing Room*, 62 Bankr. 403; *Century Brass*, 55 Bankr. 712; In re Allied Delivery System Co., 49 Bankr. 700 (Bankr. N.D. Ohio 1985).

40. For all practical purposes, the rejection issue was moot by the time the appeal reached the Third Circuit. The debtor and its union had agreed on the terms of a new contract and had settled all outstanding issues except the priority status of $146,000 of claims by plant guards for work during a three-month period postpetition. The Court of Appeals seized upon the existence of this unresolved $146,000 claim to address the entire rejection issue. See *Wheeling-Pittsburgh*, 791 F.2d at 1079–80.

41. For instance, the court just as easily could have relied upon the statement of Sen. Hatch that Section 1113 "adheres to the spirit of [the] unanimous Supreme Court opinion" in *Bildisco*. Statement by the Hon. Orrin G. Hatch, supra note 23.

42. *Wheeling-Pittsburgh*, 791 F.2d at 1088.

43. Id.

44. Id.

45. Id. at 1089.

46. *Carey Transportation*, 816 F.2d at 90.

47. Id. at 89–90.

48. Id. at 89.

49. Id.

50. *Cook United*, 50 Bankr. 563.

51. In re Valley Kitchens, Inc., 52 Bankr. 493, amend. denied 51 Bankr. 113 (Bankr. S.D. Ohio 1985).

52. See *American Provision*, 44 Bankr. at 910.

53. *Carey Transportation*, 50 Bankr. at 209. See also International Brotherhood of Teamsters v. IML Freight, Inc., 789 F.2d 1460 (10th Cir. 1986) (reversing approval of rejection of labor contracts under Section 365 based on inadequacy of fact finding by the bankruptcy judge). Although governed by Section 365, *IML Freight* interprets the legislative history of Section 1113 differently than the Third Circuit did in *Wheeling-Pittsburgh*. The Tenth Circuit cited Senator Hatch's statement that Section 1113 ''adheres to the spirit of [the] unanimous Supreme Court opinion'' and went on to state that while ''new procedural requirements have been imposed [by Section 1113], the approach to the required balancing of the equities should not be different from the instruction provided in *Bildisco*.'' *IML Freight*, 789 F.2d at 1461.

54. Bankruptcy Code § 1113(b)(1)(A).

55. One would expect that this phrase would have a meaning similar to the same phrase in Section 1129(b)(1) of the Bankruptcy Code. Section 1129 sets forth the standards that must be satisfied for the confirmation of a plan of reorganization. It permits the confirmation of a plan of reorganization over the objection of a class of claims or shareholder interests under certain circumstances. However, the ''fair and equitable'' term in Section 1129(b)(1) refers to the ''absolute priority rule'' that requires a dissenting class to be paid in full before a junior class may share under the plan. With its focus on payments under a plan, the absolute priority rule has no apparent relevance to Section 1113. See *Wheeling-Pittsburgh*, 791 F.2d at 1091 n.3. Section 1113 does not deal with or establish a hierarchy of priorities for the distribution of assets from the debtor's estate or set the prerequisites for the confirmation of a plan of reorganization. Thus, Section 1129's judicial gloss, which has resulted in the establishment of the fair and equitable rule, is not applicable to the purposes of Section 1113. See Consolidated Rock Products Co. v. Du Bois, 312 U.S. 510 (1941); Case v. Los Angeles Lumber Products Co., 308 U.S. 106 (1939).

56. *Bildisco*, 465 U.S. at 527.

57. See, e.g., *Carey Transportation*, 816 F.2d at 90; *Wheeling-Pittsburgh*, 791 F.2d 1074; *Wheeling-Pittsburgh*, 52 Bankr. 997; *Allied Delivery System*, 49 Bankr. 700; *Carey Transportation*, 50 Bankr. 203; *K&B Mounting*, 50 Bankr. 460.

58. *Valley Kitchens*, 52 Bankr. at 497.

59. *Allied Delivery System*, 49 Bankr. 700.

60. Id. at 703. In *Carey Transportation*, 50 Bankr. 203, and *Salt Creek II*, 47 Bankr. 835, the bankruptcy courts also held that the debtor's proposals satisfied the ''necessary modification'' and ''fair and equitable'' tests. However, these holdings in favor of the debtor appear in large part to be the result of weak factual presentations by the unions. For example, in *Carey Transportation*, the court stated that ''[t]he Union argued to the contrary [that the proposed modifications were unnecessary] without developing any factual contradiction.'' 50 Bankr. at 209. In *Salt Creek II*, the court stated that ''the Union has not invited the court's attention to any of the specific modifications contained in the proposal to allege in what manner, if any, they may be considered unnecessary to

the planned reorganization.'' 47 Bankr. at 338. As unions become increasingly sophisticated in this area of the law (witness *Wheeling-Pittsburgh*), debtors can expect a much more difficult fight.

61. *American Provision*, 44 Bankr. at 907.

62. *Cook United*, 50 Bankr. at 561. The debtor sought interim relief under Section 1113(e). Interestingly, the court used the nine-step analysis (see supra note 30) usually applicable to the ultimate question of approval or disapproval of rejection to determine whether such relief was essential.

63. Id. at 467.

64. Id.

65. Id. at 468.

66. Bankruptcy Code § 1113(b)(1)(B).

67. *K&B Mounting*, 50 Bankr. at 467.

68. *Wheeling-Pittsburgh*, 50 Bankr. at 981.

69. In re Fiber Glass *Industries*, 49 Bankr. 202 (Bankr. N.D.N.Y. 1985).

70. *Salt Creek II*, 47 Bankr. at 839.

71. *Century Brass*, 55 Bankr. at 716; *Wheeling-Pittsburgh*, 52 Bankr. at 1006.

72. *Bildisco*, 465 U.S. at 526; see, e.g., *Wheeling-Pittsburgh*, 50 Bankr. at 976.

73. *K&B Mounting*, 50 Bankr. at 465; See also *Royal Composing Room*, 62 Bankr. at 403.

74. *Carey Transportation*, 50 Bankr. at 211; *Salt Creek II*, 47 Bankr. at 839.

75. *American Provision*, 44 Bankr. at 911.

76. Bankruptcy Code § 1113(c)(2). The Second Circuit has held that a union is not the authorized representative of retired employees. Consequently, the debtor in *Century Brass* could not negotiate with the union regarding modifications of retired employees' benefits. 795 F.2d at 275.

77. See *Royal Composing Room*, 62 Bankr. 403; *Allied Delivery System*, 49 Bankr. 700; *Wheeling-Pittsburgh*, 50 Bankr. 969; *Salt Creek II*, 47 Bankr. 835; Gibson, ''The New Law on Rejection of Collective Bargaining Agreements in Chapter 11,'' 58 Am. Bankr. L.J. 325, 341 (1984). In *Carey Transportation*, the Second Circuit stated that this standard is proper where the union has neither participated meaningfully in postpetition negotiations nor offered any reason for rejecting the proposal other than its view that the proposed modifications were excessive. 816 F.2d at 92.

78. *Salt Creek II*, 47 Bankr. at 841.

79. *Bildisco*, 465 U.S. at 527.

80. *Salt Creek II*, 47 Bankr. at 841; *IML Freight*, 789 F.2d at 1460; *Brada Miller Freight*, 702 F.2d at 899–900; In re Braniff Airways, Inc., 25 Bankr. 216, 218–19 (Bankr. N.D. Tex. 1982). The *Salt Creek II* court apparently considered one of the equities to be whether ''the debtor has filed this bankruptcy solely for the purpose of ridding itself of its collective bargaining agreement.'' 47 Bankr. at 841. The bankruptcy court in *Carey Transportation* thought that this issue was ''more appropriate fodder'' in connection with a motion to dismiss the bankruptcy case under Section 1112(b) or for the appointment of a trustee or for the appointment of an examiner under Section 1104 of the Bankruptcy Code—and not an issue to be determined under Section 1113. The Second Circuit disagreed, however, stating that ''equity would preclude a court from approving rejection if the debtor were misusing the entire Chapter 11 process.'' 816 F.2d at 93.

81. See In re Wright Airlines, Inc., 44 Bankr. 744 (Bankr. N.D. Ohio 1984) (denying

relief); In re Russell Transfer, Inc., 48 Bankr. 241 (Bankr. W.D. Va. 1985) (granting relief); *Salt Creek I*, 46 Bankr. 347 (granting relief). Cf. *Wheeling-Pittsburgh*, 791 F.2d 1074 (concluding, in effect, that the Section 1113(e) standard is same as that for court-approved rejection).

82. In re Evans Products Co., 55 Bankr. 231 (Bankr. S.D. Fla. 1985).

83. *Russell Transfer*, 48 Bankr. at 244.

84. *Wheeling-Pittsburgh*, 50 Bankr. at 980.

85. *Wheeling-Pittsburgh*, 791 F.2d at 1090.

86. Id. at 1090–91. The Third Circuit's conclusion may also have been influenced by the fact that subsequent to the bankruptcy court's finding that the $15.20 five-year proposal was "necessary," Wheeling-Pittsburgh offered to increase the hourly wage cost to $17.50. See Serrin, "Early Signs of Promise in Union Partnership at Steel Company," N.Y. Times, Apr. 7, 1986, at A8, col. 2. The Second Circuit, in *Carey Transportation*, specifically stated that it was not addressing the issue of a "snapback" provision since the argument had not been raised in the bankruptcy court. 816 F.2d at 90.

87. See In re William P. Brocna and Co., Inc., 64 Bankr. 390, 393 (Bankr. E.D. Pa. 1986), in which the court, applying the Third Circuit's standard, refused to approve the debtor's rejection of its collective-bargaining motion.

88. See e.g., Barbash, "Inside: The Federal Judiciary," Wash. Post, Nov. 25, 1983, at A2, col. 1.

89. *Wheeling-Pittsburgh*, 50 Bankr. at 978; see e.g., Serrin, supra note 86.

90. Id.

91. See Serrin, "Hormel Plant Shut As Troops Arrive and Strikers Thin Ranks," N.Y. Times, Jan. 22, 1986, at A12, col. 1; Serrin, "The Hormel Strike: A Union Divided," N.Y. Times, Apr. 21, 1986, at A12, col. 3.

92. Id.; Raskin, "Big Labor Tries to End Its Nightmare," N.Y. Times, May 4, 1986, § 3, at 1, col. 2. 93. Id.

94. *Wheeling-Pittsburgh*, 50 Bankr. at 984. Even if the debtor successfully rejects the collective-bargaining agreement, the debtor nevertheless has a continuing obligation to bargain collectively with the union. *Bildisco*, 465 U.S. at 534; *Salt Creek II*, 47 Bankr. at 842.

95. *Wheeling-Pittsburgh*, 52 Bankr. at 1007; see also Kentucky Truck Sales, 52 Bankr. at 806.

96. *Royal Composing Room*, 62 Bankr. at 403.

17
PROTECTING UNION INTERESTS IN EMPLOYER BANKRUPTCY

Michael E. Abram and Babette Ceccotti

Editors' Note. Mr. Abram and Ms. Ceccotti postulate a comprehensive union approach when an employer initiates the process of corporate reorganization in bankruptcy. They pose a series of union responses to an employer's demand for prebankruptcy concessions on wages and work rules—for example, insistence on separate accounts for and prompt payment of payroll items such as retirement plan contributions to be transmitted to third parties. The authors also discuss union strategies in dealing with an employer's filing of a Chapter 11 petition, the formation of the creditors' committee, and debtors' efforts to achieve postpetition financing. The authors deal in detail with the processes and standards applicable to employer attempts, in the bankruptcy court, to obtain interim or permanent relief from collective-bargaining agreements.

Employer bankruptcy generates for unions and their members the usual hazards of ordinary business change, such as loss of jobs and contract rights, but it also creates opportunities to participate in fundamental business decisions not available under the labor laws. In bankruptcy proceedings, a union may have a voice in restructuring the direction of the business, its management, debt, and ownership, in addition to the normal range of collective-bargaining activities designed to protect the employees and their contract.

This chapter focuses on a filing under Chapter 11 of the Bankruptcy Reform Act of 1978, as amended, 11 U.S.C. § 1101 et seq. (the Code), which deals with business reorganizations as distinct from liquidations under Chapter 7 of the Code. The discussion presupposes a debtor-in-possession, that is, a company remaining in possession of its property and continuing to operate.[1]

The purpose of a Chapter 11 filing is to rehabilitate the business and establish an orderly means of paying the company's debt. This is accomplished through a plan of reorganization, which determines whether and in what form the business will continue and how creditors will be paid. The Bankruptcy Code requirements for acceptance and court approval of the plan[2] include voting by creditors and thus contemplate negotiation of the plan among the debtor and the various creditor groups.[3] A plan may provide for change in the direction or management of the business, sale or transfer of assets to other entities, merger or consolidation of the debtor with other entities, or liquidation of assets and termination of the business.[4]

PREBANKRUPTCY PREPARATION

When an employer is faced with poor cash flow or a burdensome debt load, the union will probably be approached for wage and work rule concessions. The union should seize this opportunity to begin planning for a possible bankruptcy filing by the employer. For example, the union may attempt to condition its concessions on commitments from a parent or holding company to assume the cost of the contract if the employer subsidiary successfully rejects the contract.[5] A concessionary agreement could also contain a termination provision or, if concessions are exchanged for stock ownership, a stock redemption provision triggered by nonperformance of "snapback" or repayment conditions.[6] Moreover, because the position of the company's secured lenders at the prebankruptcy stage is likely to dictate the terms of any lending arrangement during bankruptcy, the union should seek contact with the lenders and access to existing lending agreements at the earliest opportunity. The union can also try to obtain a commitment not to collateralize unencumbered assets in the event of further financing[7] or, if possible, to obtain its own security interest in assets of the employer for wage concessions in the form of loans, which would mature if the contract is not performed.

As part of any concession package, the union should also insist on a separate account for payroll items transmitted by the employer to third parties (e.g., employee contributions to retirement plans, credit union payments, or union dues) so that these monies may be paid immediately after a bankruptcy filing on the ground that they are not part of the debtor's estate.[8] The union should also seek an agreement for a short turnover (e.g., having this done over weekly rather than monthly installments) in the payment of these items, as well as employer pension and welfare contributions, to avoid having them "caught" in the general revenue funds in the event of a bankruptcy.

ESTABLISHING THE UNION'S PRESENCE

The filing of a Chapter 11 petition initiates a new set of ground rules for the employer, the union, secured lenders, and the company's other creditors. It is not unusual for the Chapter 11 petition to be filed in an incomplete state, along with a flurry of preliminary motions involving the retention of counsel, compensation of key employees, and postpetition financing. From the outset of the case, the union should establish its presence and begin to exercise its leverage to protect employee interests.

If the union is in the midst of litigation or arbitrations against the company, these proceedings will be affected by a statutory automatic stay of all actions against the debtor, which takes effect upon the filing of the bankruptcy petition.[9] However, the debtor-in-possession may still be sued for actions after the bankruptcy filing without reference to the automatic stay.[10] In the labor context, this might include unfair labor practices and enforcement of the collective-bargaining agreement prior to any rejection of the agreement.

Upon learning of a Chapter 11 filing, the union should immediately obtain a copy of the bankruptcy petition and file a notice of appearance and request for service of all pleadings and notice of all proceedings.[11] Informal contact with debtor's counsel establishes the union's presence; it should include a request for notice of any expedited hearings.

FILING A CLAIM AND SEEKING APPOINTMENT TO THE CREDITORS' COMMITTEE

The petition is typically accompanied by a list of the debtor's largest unsecured creditors.[12] If the union or a related pension or welfare fund is not listed among those creditors, the union should estimate all monies owed to the union, the employees, and the funds as of the petition date and promptly file a claim.[13]

The union's right to enforce its collective-bargaining agreement establishes its status as a creditor.[14] A pension or welfare fund would also be a creditor for unpaid contributions. Based upon their status as creditors, the union and funds should seek immediate appointment to the official committee of unsecured creditors—the statutorily authorized body that represents the debtor's unsecured creditors and acts as the creditors' negotiating body for the formulation of a plan of reorganization and supervision of the debtor.[15] The creditors' committee, which "ordinarily" consists of those entities, willing to serve, that hold the seven largest claims,[16] is usually appointed by the court or the United States Trustee early in the case based upon the debtor's list of its unsecured creditors. However, additional committees may be appointed in order to ensure "adequate representation of creditors. . . ."[17] Thus, an early assessment of the union's claims allows it to seek appointment to the creditors' committee, either as the holder of one of the largest unsecured claims or as the representative of the employee interests in the case.[18]

In a Chapter 11 case, any "party in interest," including a creditor, may appear and be heard on any issue in the case.[19] This affords the union standing to be heard on any matter. Nonetheless, it is advisable to seek appointment to the creditors' committee because of the committee's broad powers under the Code. Committees may conduct investigations of the debtor's financial condition and operations, participate in the formulation of a plan of reorganization, seek the replacement of the debtor's managers with a trustee or examiner, and "perform such other services as are in the interest of those represented."[20] They may retain counsel, accountants, or other consultants at the debtor's expense.[21] The creditors' committee may also pursue debtors' remedies, such as voidable preference actions, where the debtor fails to act.[22] The committee may file its own plan of reorganization if the debtor does not do so within the time provided when only the debtor may file a plan.[23] In short, the creditors' committee can control the direction of the case. Membership on the committee thus affords the union an important opportunity to participate in the case at each step of the proceedings.

DEBTOR'S MOTION FOR POSTPETITION FINANCING

Another typical aspect of the early stages of the case is the debtor's motion for authority to enter into a postpetition financing arrangement in order to secure operating cash. This is often filed simultaneously with the Chapter 11 petition. Postpetition financing motions provide for the use of "cash collateral" (cash or cash equivalents such as accounts receivable) "in which the estate and an entity other than the estate have an interest."[24] Typically, the application provides that the use of cash collateral is subject to restrictive provisions insisted upon by the secured lender. The most common provision is for "cross-collateralization" of the debtor's assets, that is, granting a new security interest on property already collateralized under prefiling lending arrangements as well as assets still unencumbered or to be acquired postpetition.[25] A lender providing such financing, in addition to obtaining cross-collateralization, is permitted a "superpriority," or payment over all other claims afforded "priority" under the Code.[26]

Lenders often threaten that, unless cross-collateralization and other onerous terms[27] are approved, they will walk away from the arrangement, leaving the debtor with no source of financing. For the interested union, this can be a compelling threat because it places jobs in jeopardy. However, the postpetition financing arrangement may be so burdensome that no assets are left unencumbered, and therefore no significant recovery for unsecured creditors is possible. The financing arrangement may even jeopardize payment of important administration expenses.[28]

Although some courts have refused to approve onerous provisions contained in financing arrangements,[29] successful attacks upon lending arrangements are difficult to achieve.[30] Nonetheless, some safeguards may be sought to monitor the arrangement and avoid unnecessary turnover of assets to the lenders. For example, the union may seek a provision for adequate notice where the lenders attempt to pursue default remedies under the agreement. The financing order should also provide that any sale of collateral by the lenders be accomplished through the bankruptcy court so that the Bankruptcy Code notice and sale procedures apply. Enumeration of the permitted uses of the funds in the court's order approving the financing could also commit the debtor to use the funds for wages and benefits.

INTERIM RELIEF FROM COLLECTIVE-BARGAINING AGREEMENTS

Another possible early tactic by the debtor could be an attempt to secure a preliminary reduction of its labor costs. Section 1113 of the Bankruptcy Code, which governs a debtor's efforts to modify a collective-bargaining agreement, expressly provides that a debtor may not unilaterally alter or terminate any provision of a collective-bargaining agreement prior to compliance with the strict prerequisites for rejection or temporary modification of a collective-bargaining agreement.[31] Nonetheless, under certain circumstances, a debtor may secure interim relief from contractual wages or work rules by invoking the provisions of Section 1113(e). While this provision requires that the court grant an application for interim relief only "after notice and a hearing,"[32] these procedures are subject to the exigencies of the circumstances.[33] However, although two courts have granted interim relief before the debtor actually filed a motion to reject the contract,[34] an application for interim relief should be made only "in conjunction with" an application to reject a collective-bargaining agreement,[35] that is, after the debtor has made a postpetition proposal to the union for modification of the contract. This requirement may preclude a surprise motion for interim relief.

Moreover, interim relief should not be granted unless continuation of the contract will lead to immediate collapse of the business.[36] If granted, the period of interim relief may not extend beyond the period during which the application to reject the contract is pending, and, if the motion to reject is subsequently denied, the employees are entitled to an administrative claim for wages and benefits under the contract for the interim relief period.[37] Although no case has yet discussed the issue, the union is also free to strike if interim relief is granted.[38]

REJECTION OF COLLECTIVE-BARGAINING AGREEMENTS

A Chapter 11 filing "for the sole purpose of escaping a union contract" is an "abuse of the bankruptcy and labor laws and will not be tolerated under any circumstances."[39] One court has found that it is not "bad faith" for a debtor in poor financial condition to file a bankruptcy petition intending, among other things, to reject a collective-bargaining agreement.[40] However, underlying the drafting of Section 1113 (enacted in 1984 after the Supreme Court's decision in *NLRB v. Bildisco & Bildisco*[41]) was the ''understanding that a Chapter 11 reorganization case that is brought for the sole purpose [of] repudiating or modifying a collective bargaining agreement is a case brought in bad faith.''[42]

The right to reject a collective-bargaining agreement is governed solely by Section 1113 and not by Code Section 365(a), which authorizes rejection of other executory contracts of the debtor.[43]

Although Section 1113(a) provides that a debtor ''may assume or reject'' a collective-bargaining agreement, a debtor may no longer unilaterally abrogate an agreement prior to rejection under Section 1113.[44] Thus, unlike the pre–Section 1113 situation, under the 1984 amendments the collective-bargaining agreement remains in effect postfiling.[45] The sole recourse for a debtor seeking unilateral modification of a labor contract is the interim relief permitted by Section 1113(e) or rejection through court action under Section 1113(b).

Section 1113 emphasizes the collective-bargaining process rather than the bankruptcy court as the primary means of modifying an agreement.[46] Thus, under Section 1113(b), the debtor may not file a motion to reject a collective-bargaining agreement unless it first proposes modifications to the union. The debtor's proposal must be based upon ''the most complete and reliable information'' then available, and this and all other relevant information must be provided to the union.[47] Moreover, the proposal must be limited to ''those necessary modifications . . . that are necessary to permit the reorganization of the debtor.''[48] The Third Circuit has held that the term ''necessary,'' twice used in Section 1113(b)(1)(A), means ''essential,'' and it refers to the short-term goal of preventing liquidation, i.e., ''permit[ting] reorganization, rather than the longer term issue of the debtor's ultimate future.''[49] In addition, proposals not related to the debtor's financial condition are not ''necessary'' modifications.[50] The proposal must also contemplate, if not a detailed reorganization plan, at least a general scheme for dealing with the debtor's liabilities in order to meet the requirement that the proposed modifications be ''necessary to permit the reorganization of the debtor.''[51]

The debtor's proposal must also ''assure that all creditors, the debtor and all of the affected parties are treated fairly and equitably.''[52] Thus, the employees covered by the contract must not be requested to bear a disproportionate share of the economic sacrifice in relation to other employees, management, and creditors.[53] For example, a debtor's proposal for a five-year contract with no snapback provision was seen as disproportionately burdensome to the unionized employees because these features foreclosed any future benefit to them should the company's condition improve.[54]

In comparing the economic sacrifices of unionized and nonunionized employees, greater weight should be given to the former precisely because they are the product of collective bargaining under the labor laws.[55] Furthermore, a dollar or percentage comparison between employee concessions and other creditors' sacrifices should also be weighted in the employees' favor because a trade creditor draws revenue from many customers whereas an employee normally relies exclusively on the employer for income.[56]

After presenting its proposal, the debtor must meet and ''confer in good faith'' with the union up to the time of the rejection hearing.[57] The ''good faith'' requirement in practice has been assessed in virtually the same manner as a determination under the bargaining obligation of the labor laws even though the courts claim to be using a more general approach.[58] A showing by the debtor that it met with the union has been considered sufficient to shift the burden to the union to produce evidence of lack of bad faith.[59] However, the debtor may not avoid a duty to negotiate by claiming a need for speedy action on its proposed modifications. Section 1113(e) is available to the debtor should the need for interim relief arise.[60]

Even if the debtor has made a proposal which meets the stringent standards discussed above and has negotiated in good faith with the union, the court may not approve rejection of the contract if the union has ''good cause'' for its position.[61] Most courts have subordinated this potent requirement by ruling that the union's good cause depends upon whether the debtor has made a proposal and has negotiated in accordance with the requirements of Section 1113(b).[62] However, the legislative history suggests that the court address the good cause requirement in terms of the burden of proof analysis set forth by Bordewieck and Countryman,[63] who argued that ''considerable weight'' should be given to a ''considered union view that rejection is not necessary,'' since almost any debtor can be expected to argue that rejection is essential for reorganization strictly on the basis of the debtor's competitive position, while the union and its members have a great deal to lose if rejection is denied and the debtor is then forced into liquidation.[64] This weighting of the evidence would shift against the union, however, if it were motivated primarily by the desire to protect union standards in other bargaining units.[65]

Finally, in order to grant rejection, the court must find that ''the balance of the equities clearly favors rejection'' of the agreement.[66] This provision has been generally described as a codification of the *Bildisco* standard.[67] The test is ''a broad equitable one, lacking rigidity.''[68] In *Bildisco*, the Supreme Court ruled that the bankruptcy court must consider the likelihood and consequences of liquidation for the debtor absent rejection, the reduced value of the creditors' claims if the contract is affirmed, and the impact of rejection on the employees.[69]

One impact of rejection that should be considered under the ''balance of the equities'' test is the effect of a possible strike if rejection is granted because of the impact of a strike on the interests of creditors and employees. There is no dispute that the right to strike exists when the contract has been rejected.[70] Although the union may be circumspect in exercising this right if it threatens the survival of the business, the strike may cost the employer more than it would save by implementing its proposal to the union. The court may face great difficulty in assessing the likelihood or possible impact of a strike, but it should make the effort if the rejection decision is to be fully informed.

Effect of Rejection

If the court approves rejection of the collective-bargaining agreement,[71] the debtor may not implement wage reductions or work rule changes inconsistent with the proposal presented to the court in the rejection hearing.[72] Moreover, as previously indicated, the union has a right to strike in response to rejection.

If the union does not have the economic strength to force the debtor to improve the wages or work rules implemented after rejection, the union might consider proceeding with the rejection hearing rather than accepting a new reduced contract pre-rejection. This option stems from the effect of rejection on the union's and employees' positions as creditors of the estate. Rejection constitutes a breach of the agreement[73] and gives rise to an unsecured damages claim "the same as if such claim had arisen before the date of the filing of the petition."[74] The claim for rejection damages for the remaining term of the contract could significantly enhance the union's and employees' positions in negotiations over a plan of reorganization, because of the right of creditors whose claims are not fully paid under the plan to vote on acceptance of the plan.[75] The claim for rejection damages and the leverage thereby provided could be lost if the union agreed upon reduced wages or working conditions in a new collective-bargaining agreement prior to the rejection of its old agreement.[76] However, any delay in the effective date of a new agreement could leave the employees without a collective-bargaining agreement or reduce their bargaining leverage—a position which may not be offset by the value of the rejection damages.

The rejection damages claim can include "all losses attributable to the non-performance of the contracts."[77] Claims arising from the breach of collective-bargaining agreements are not subject to the Bankruptcy Code's limitation on claims arising from the breach of other employment contracts.[78] The union should endeavor to liquidate its claim for rejection damages and avoid having the claim vulnerable to the bankruptcy court's power to "estimate" both "contingent" and "unliquidated" claims.[79]

PENSION CLAIMS

Unpaid pension and welfare contributions share the statutory priority for employee wages.[80] A union may assert these claims if it is entitled to enforce an obligation to contribute to a plan pursuant to a collective-bargaining agreement,[81] or to the extent that the union is a fiduciary with respect to the plan.[82]

Pension plan termination may also give rise to a claim against the debtor, where the company has not met its funding or benefits requirements under the terms of the plan or a collective-bargaining agreement. Payment of the statutory liability to the PBGC as a result of the PBGC's payment to retirees of guaranteed benefits does not extinguish the employer's liability for payments above the PBGC guarantee.[83]

Claims for withdrawal liability under ERISA,[84] like rejection damage claims, may also provide a significant degree of leverage. Withdrawal liability claims are most likely to be treated as general unsecured claims and not first priority administrative claims.[85] Consequently, such claims enhance the union's role in the negotiation of a plan of reorganization. Moreover, in a reorganization case, an employer is not entitled to the reduction in liability permitted a liquidating employer.[86]

REMEDIES UNDER THE LABOR LAWS

Notwithstanding the threat of a court-imposed contract rejection, the union's arsenal of rights and remedies remains substantially intact during an employer's bankruptcy.

Rejection of a collective-bargaining agreement does not affect the union's status as collective-bargaining representative or the employer's obligation to bargain with the union.[87] As noted earlier, rejection is also subject to the employees' right to strike. The Bankruptcy Code does not override the restrictions on injunctive relief imposed by the Norris-LaGuardia Act.[88]

Unfair labor practice charges, lawsuits, or arbitrations which were pending prepetition are affected by the automatic stay imposed under the Bankruptcy Code, but, as noted above, relief from the stay may be sought from the bankruptcy court. The NLRB is not subject to the automatic stay by virtue of a statutory exception for government enforcement agencies or regulatory entities, although the exception does not apply to collection of a money judgment.[89] However, because debts are generally not paid outside of the bankruptcy proceedings, any resolution of prebankruptcy proceedings in the union's favor gives rise to a claim in the bankruptcy subject to the Code's priority scheme.[90]

Postpetition acts of the debtor are subject to the usual remedies, without regard to the automatic stay. Thus, if a grievance arises postpetition, the arbitration should proceed as dictated by the contract. Expiration or rejection of a collective-bargaining agreement does not alter the employer's duty to arbitrate with respect to matters that arose during the term of the agreement.[91]

While the debtor may attempt to avoid arbitration or litigation before the NLRB or elsewhere and centralize all proceedings in the bankruptcy court, the courts have recognized the limited expertise of the bankruptcy court in matters of labor relations.[92] Particularly when NLRB proceedings and arbitrations are at issue, the bankruptcy court should defer to those specialized forums for resolution of the dispute.[93]

In sum, a bankruptcy filing by an employer forces the union and employees to adapt to a legal forum that places strong emphasis on the debtor's reorganization. This bias often results in a reinterpretation and "accommodation" of labor law principles.[94] However, a union alert to the possibilities may succeed in making effective use of both labor law remedies and its unique status in a bankruptcy case to protect the employees' interests.

EPILOGUE

Since this chapter was first prepared, there have been several important developments in the interpretation of Section 1113. In addition, a new Bankruptcy Code section patterned on Section 1113 has been enacted to prohibit unilateral termination of retiree benefits.

Recent case law interpreting Section 1113(f) makes clear that the debtor must adhere to the terms of a collective bargaining agreement after a bankruptcy filing, including the payment of health benefits to retired workers and recognition of vacation and severance benefits accrued pre and post-petition by active employees. *In re Unimet*[95] clarified the post-bankruptcy status of collectively bargained retiree benefits. In *Unimet*, the Sixth Circuit held that the clear language of Section 1113(f) prohibiting the unilateral modification of ''any'' provision of a collective bargaining agreement absent compliance with Section 1113 forecloses any argument that retiree benefits are not covered by Section 1113, or that the payment must qualify as an ''administration expense'' in order to be paid. The court held that the debtor must continue to pay retiree insurance premiums as required by the collective bargaining agreement regardless of whether the premiums qualify as administration expenses under 11 U.S.C. § 503. In *In re St. Louis Globe-Democrat, Inc.*,[96] the bankruptcy court held that Section 1113(f) effects an assumption of the collective bargaining agreement by operation of law, with the result that all vacation pay and severance pay due upon termination of employment under the terms of the collective bargaining agreement, and not merely that portion earned during the post-petition period, are entitled to payment as an administration expense.

The rejection standard in Section 1113 has been further interpreted by the Second Circuit in *In re Royal Composing Room, Inc.*[97] In that case, the court, over the strong dissent of Judge Feinberg, held that where the union ''refuses to negotiate'' over aspects of the proposal, it may not challenge the proposal, or any element of the proposal, as failing to meet the ''necessary modifications'' requirement as long as the total savings are ''necessary.''[98] This conclusion erroneously considers the union's negotiating posture as an element of the ''necessary'' standard.[99] The court also reiterated its earlier holding in *Carey Transportation* that the ''necessary modifications'' standard did not mean ''absolutely minimal.''[100]

The status of retiree benefits and representation of retirees in bankruptcy has been resolved by the Retiree Benefits Bankruptcy Protection Act of 1988,[101] enacted as Section 1114 of the Bankruptcy Code. Section 1114 prohibits an employer from modifying retiree health, life or disability insurance benefits absent compliance with stringent procedural and substantive requirements similar to those in effect under Section 1113. Under Section 1114, the union is the ''authorized representative'' of the retirees unless the union elects not to serve or the court finds that a conflict of interest prevents the union from acting as the retirees' representative.[102] In that event, the court will appoint a retiree committee, which will have the status of an official creditors' committee under the Code,[103] to negotiate with the debtor over proposed benefit modifications.

Where the debtor seeks to modify retiree benefits, it must make a proposal to the retirees' representative limited to those modifications necessary to permit reorganization,[104] and that is fair and equitable to all parties. If there is no agreement on modifications, the debtor may seek court approval to impose the modifications and must demonstrate that the proposal meets the substantive ''necessary'' and ''fair and equitable'' requirements, that the retirees refused to accept the proposal ''without good cause,'' and that modification is ''clearly favored by the balance of the equities.''[105] Section 1114 protections are intended to augment, and not replace, the protections for collectively bargained retiree benefits already provided under Section 1113.[106]

Section 1114 deems retiree benefits paid during the reorganization to be administration expenses.[107] The statute further requires that the debtor's plan of reorganization provide for the continuation of retiree benefits ''for the duration of the period the debtor has obligated itself to provide such benefits'' or the plan cannot be confirmed by the bankruptcy court.[108]

NOTES

1. See 11 U.S.C. §§ 1107, 1108. Unlike a Chapter 7 liquidation, Chapter 11 does not require the appointment of a trustee, thus permitting management to remain in control of the debtor's property and operations.

2. See 11 U.S.C. §§ 1121–1129.

3. H.R. Rep. No. 95–595, 95th Cong., 1st Sess. 220–21 (1977) reprinted in 2 Collier on Bankruptcy (Appendix) (15th ed. 1987).

4. 11 U.S.C. § 1123.

5. See Texas Air Corp. v. Air Line Pilots Ass'n, 118 L.R.R.M 2493 (S.D. Tex. 1985) (describing side letter between union and parent of debtor, under which the parent company agreed to honor the collective-bargaining agreement of a debtor subsidiary).

6. Termination provisions should not be activated solely by the event of bankruptcy or insolvency because bankruptcy law invalidates such clauses in executory contracts. 11 U.S.C. § 365(e).

7. See Wheeling-Pittsburgh Steel Corp. v. United Steelworkers, 791 F.2d 1074, 1076–77 (3d Cir. 1986) (describing concessionary bargaining proposals by the union and the company which included agreement not to pledge current assets for past debts).

8. See In re Columbia Packing Co., 35 Bankr. 447, 448–49 (Bankr. D. Mass. 1983) (payroll deduction items were placed in company's general cash account and funds were therefore considered property of the estate).

9. 11 U.S.C. § 362(a). The purpose of the automatic stay is to stop all collection action against the debtor. See National Mediation Board v. Continental Airlines Corp., 50 Bankr. 342, 352–53 (S.D. Tex. 1985), aff'd per curiam, 790 F.2d 35 (5th Cir. 1986).

Application may be made to lift the automatic stay so that a proceeding may go forward. 11 U.S.C. § 362(d).

10. See 11 U.S.C. § 323(b); 28 U.S.C. § 959.

11. Bankruptcy Rule (Bankr. Rule) 2002.

12. Bankr. Rule 1007(b), (c).

13. The union should list all amounts owed to covered employees pursuant to its collective-bargaining agreement with the employer, including aggregate estimates for unpaid prepetition payroll, vacation and other fringe benefits, outstanding grievances, pension and welfare contributions, dues checkoff, and any other miscellaneous items. Wages and benefits earned within ninety days of either the bankruptcy filing or the cessation of operations are entitled to distribution priority under 11 U.S.C. § 507(a)(3) and (a)(4), up to a maximum of $2,000 per employee. Wages and benefits earned on or after the filing are entitled to payment as first priority "administration" claims. 11 U.S.C. § 503(b)(1)(A).

14. In re Altair Airlines, Inc., 727 F.2d 88 (3d Cir. 1984). See also *Continental Airlines Corp.*, 50 Bankr. at 353; In re Enduro Stainless, Inc., 59 Bankr. 603 (Bankr. N.D. Ohio 1986); 11 U.S.C. § 101(4), (9).

15. See H.R. Rep. No. 95–595, supra note 3, at 401.

16. 11 U.S.C. § 1102(b)(1).

17. 11 U.S.C. § 1102(a)(2). While the statute states only that "the court may order the appointment of additional committees," the trustee can increase the size of a single committee in order to obtain a representative committee "of adequate size to meet the need of the case." L. King, Collier Handbook for Creditors' Committees ¶6.03 (1988). See also In re Beker Industries, 55 Bankr. 945 (Bankr. S.D.N.Y. 1985) (court authorized separate official committee of debenture holders to ensure adequate representation).

18. To guard against the possibility that the debtor may challenge the union's standing to assert and pursue its claims later in the proceedings, the union might wish to encourage individual members to file their own claims for monies owed individually as well. Individual claims also facilitate the determination of amounts owed to each employee and comparison with the debtor's payroll records. In any event, claim filing deadlines should be ascertained immediately because late claims may be disallowed. See, e.g., In re Solvation, Inc., 48 Bankr. 670 (Bankr. D. Mass. 1985) (court disallowed late claim despite claimant's confusion about filing deadline). The failure to file a timely claim may bar payment of the claim because a creditor who does not file a claim that must be filed under the rules is not entitled to distribution. Bankr. Rule 3002(a), 3003(c). In a Chapter 11 case, a creditor must file a claim if the claim is not listed, or is incorrectly listed, by the debtor on its schedule of assets and liabilities, or it is listed by the debtor as "disputed, contingent or unliquidated."

19. 11 U.S.C. § 1109(b).

20. 11 U.S.C. § 1103(c).

21. 11 U.S.C. § 1103(a).

22. In re Joyanna Holitogs, Inc., 21 Bankr. 323 (Bankr. S.D.N.Y. 1982).

23. 11 U.S.C. § 1121(c).

24. 11 U.S.C. § 363(a).

25. See 11 U.S.C. § 363(e); 11 U.S.C. § 364(c), (d).

26. U.S.C. § 364(c)(1).

27. See, e.g., In re FCX, Inc., 54 Bankr. 833, 837 (Bankr. E.D.N.Y. 1985) (post-petition financing agreement contained provisions for cross-collateralization, automatic

lifting of stay in the event of default, concession that prepetition loan balance was correct and all liens were perfected, and a waiver of all defenses).

28. See In re Flagstaff Foodservice Corp., 739 F.2d 73 (2d Cir. 1984), opinion adhered to, 762 F.2d 10 (2d Cir. 1985) (court disallowed payment of creditors' committee fees as an impermissible encroachment upon the superpriority obtained by the secured lender).

29. See In re Roblin Industries, 52 Bankr. 241 (Bankr. W.D.N.Y. 1985); *FCX, Inc.*, 54 Bankr. at 833 (disallowance of provisions for waiver of notice and other rights by the debtor).

30. See, e.g., In re W.T. Grant & Co., 699 F.2d 599 (2d Cir.), cert. denied, 464 U.S. 822 (1983) (court rejected the claim that secured lenders engaged in domination and control of the debtor's management resulting in inequitable improvement of the banks' position as creditors).

31. 11 U.S.C. § 1113(f).

32. 11 U.S.C. § 1113(e).

33. 11 U.S.C. § 102(1).

34. See In re Salt Creek Freightways, 46 Bankr. 347 (Bankr. D. Wy. 1985); In re Evans Products Co., 55 Bankr. 231 (Bankr. S.D. Fla. 1985).

35. 130 Cong. Rec. H7496 (daily ed. June 29, 1984) (statement of Rep. Morrison) [hereinafter cited as 130 Cong. Rec.——(statement of——)].

36. *Salt Creek Freightways*, 46 Bankr. at 349–50; 130 Cong. Rec. H7496 (statement of Rep. Morrison). See also In re Russell Transfer, Inc., 48 Bankr. 241 (Bankr. W.D. Va. 1985); In re Wright Air Lines, Inc., 44 Bankr. 744 (Bankr. N.D. Ohio 1984) (relief granted only if it is essential to continued operations and if failure to obtain relief will cause irreparable harm).

37. 130 Cong. Rec. H7496 (statement of Rep. Morrison).

38. Cf. Briggs Transportation Co. v. International Brotherhood of Teamsters, 116 L.R.R.M 2241 (D. Minn.), aff'd, 739 F.2d 341 (8th Cir.), cert. denied, 469 U.S. 917 (1984) (court denied the debtor's application for an injunction against a strike following rejection of a collective-bargaining agreement, concluding that the strike is a labor dispute protected by the Norris–LaGuardia Act).

39. In re Brada Miller Freight System, Inc., 702 F.2d 890, 891 (11th Cir. 1983). See also In re Mamie Conti Gowns, Inc., 12 F. Supp. 478, 480 (S.D.N.Y. 1935); In re Tinti Construction Co., 29 Bankr. 971 (Bankr. E.D. Wisc. 1983) (applications to set aside labor agreements denied where court found that the purpose of the bankruptcy was not to reorganize but to obtain rejection of the agreements).

40. In re Continental Airlines Corp., 38 Bankr. 67, 71 (Bankr. S.D. Tex. 1984).

41. NLRB v. Bildisco & Bildisco, 465 U.S. 513 (1984).

42. 130 Cong. Rec. H7496 (statement of Rep. Morrison). No committee reports accompanied the 1984 legislation enacted as Section 1113. In determining the legislative intent, guidance may be sought from the statements of the House and Senate members involved in drafting and managing the bill. See *Wheeling-Pittsburgh*, 791 F.2d at 1086.

43. 11 U.S.C. § 365(a). Section 1113 applies to a Chapter 11 debtor. A Chapter 7 trustee may use Section 365 to reject a collective-bargaining agreement. Railroads under Title I of the Railway Labor Act (RLA) 45 U.S.C. §§ 151, et seq., are subject to 11 U.S.C. § 1167, which prohibits modifications of a collective-bargaining agreement subject to the RLA except in accordance with the procedures set forth in that statute.

44. See 11 U.S.C. § 1113(e), (f). See *Wheeling-Pittsburgh*, 791 F.2d at 1085; 130

Cong. Rec. H7495 (statement of Rep. Lungren); 130 Cong. Rec. S8898 (statement of Sen. Packwood).

45. Cf. *Bildisco*, 465 U.S. at 513.

46. In re Mile Hi Metal Systems, Inc., 51 Bankr. 509, 510 (Bankr. D. Col. 1985), rev'd on other grounds, 67 B. R. 114 (D. Col. 1986); In re K&B Mounting, Inc., 50 Bankr. 460 (Bankr. N.D. Ind. 1985).

47. 11 U.S.C. § 1113(b)(1). This has been construed to require sufficient information to justify each proposed modification, including "detailed projections and recommendations," a "full and detailed disclosure of [the company's] difficulties and its proposed short-run and long-run solutions." In re K&B Mounting, Inc., 50 Bankr. at 467; see also In re Valley Kitchens, 52 Bankr. 493 (Bankr. S.D. Ohio 1985); 130 Cong. Rec. S8898 (statement of Sen. Packwood).

48. 11 U.S.C. § 1113(b)(1)(A). Where the proposal includes a modification of retiree insurance benefits, the debtor must meet a "threshold" burden that it has negotiated with the proper representative of the company's retirees. In re Century Brass Products, Inc., 795 F.2d 265, 276 (2d Cir.), cert. denied, 107 S. Ct. 433 (1986).

49. *Wheeling-Pittsburgh*, 791 F.2d at 1088–89. Based upon its analysis of the legislative history, the Third Circuit determined that Congress intended by this standard a return to the strict rejection standard set forth in Brotherhood of Railway Clerks v. REA Express, 523 F.2d 164 (2d Cir.), cert. denied, 423 U.S. 1017 (1975), or "something close to it." 791 F.2d at 1088. See also In re K&B Mounting, Inc., 50 Bankr. at 467 ("liquidation would follow"); In re Kentucky Truck Sales, 52 Bankr. 797, 802, 806 (Bankr. W.D. Ky. 1985) (changes must be critical to survival). But see In re Carey Transportation Inc., 816 F.2d 82, 89 (2d. Cir. 1987); In re Cook United, Inc., 50 Bankr. 561 (Bankr. N.D. Ohio 1985) ("necessary" modifications means something less than "essential").

50. *Wheeling-Pittsburgh*, 791 F.2d at 1088. See also, Mile Hi Metal Systems, 67 B. R. at 117–8 (proposal that included illegal provisions did not meet the requirement that modifications be limited to "necessary modifications").

51. In re Fiber Glass Industries, 49 Bankr. 202 (Bankr. N.D.N.Y. 1985); 130 Cong. Rec. S8898 (statement of Sen. Packwood).

52. 11 U.S.C. § 1113(b)(1)(A).

53. 130 Cong. Rec. H7496, S8898 (statements of Rep. Morrison, Sen. Packwood). *Carey Transportation*, 816 F.2d at 90; *Cook United*, 50 Bankr. at 564–65; Mile Hi Metal Systems, 67 B. R. at 117 (nonwage provisions of the proposals, e.g., that the debtor could hire nonunion employees and pay them less than contract wages, were not "necessary" or "fair and equitable").

54. *Wheeling-Pittsburgh*, 791 F.2d at 1093.

55. See Fiber Glass Industries, 49 Bankr. at 207 (court gave greater weight to proposed concessions by unionized employees because noncovered employees were not protected by a collective-bargaining agreement, and the debtor was "largely free to dictate new employment terms").

56. See Bordewieck & Countryman, "The Rejection of Collective Bargaining Agreements by Chapter 11 Debtors," 57 Am. Bankr. L.J. 293, 312–13 (1983).

57. 11 U.S.C. § 1113(b)(2). *Wheeling-Pittsburgh*, 791 F.2d at 1093.

58. See e.g., *Kentucky Truck Sales*, 52 Bankr. 797, 801 (Bankr. W.D. Ky. 1985) (whether the debtor "seriously attempted to negotiate reasonable modifications" to the collective-bargaining agreement prior to the rejection hearing); *K&B Mounting, Inc.*, 50

Bankr. at 465 (''good faith'' determined in terms of the number of meetings, the reasonableness of the time spent negotiating, the ''complexity and detail'' of the proposal, and the information given to the union).

59. In re American Provision Co., 44 Bankr. 907 (Bankr. D. Minn. 1984).

60. See *Wheeling-Pittsburgh*, 791 F.2d at 1093–94.

61. 11 U.S.C. § 1113(c)(2).

62. See, e.g., *K&B Mounting*, 50 Bankr. at 468; In re Allied Delivery System Co., 49 Bankr. 700, 703–04 (Bankr. N.D. Ohio 1985). See also *Carey Transportation*, 816 F.2d at 92 (where the proposed modifications were necessary, fair, and equitable and the union has given no reason for its refusal to accept the proposal, such refusal is without good cause).

63. 130 Cong. Rec. H7496 (statement of Rep. Morrison): ''The phrase 'without good cause' embod[ies] the standard set out in 'The Rejection of Collective Bargaining Agreements by Chapter 11 Debtors,' 57 Am. Bankr. L.J. at 299–300, 319.''

64. Bordewieck & Countryman, supra note 56, at 299–300, 319.

65. Id.

66. 11 U.S.C. § 1113(C)(3).

67. *Carey Transportation*, 816 F.2d at 92; Cook United, Inc., 50 Bankr. at 564, In re Salt Creek Freightways, 47 Bankr. 835, 841 (Bankr. D. Ky. 1985); In re Kentucky Truck Sales, 52 Bankr. at 805; *K&B Mounting Inc.*, 50 Bankr. at 466; 130 Cong. Rec. S8890, S8892 (statements of Sen. Dole and Sen. Hatch).

68. K&B Mounting Inc., 50 Bankr. at 466.

69. *Bildisco*, 465 U.S. at 527.

70. See *Briggs Transportation*, 116 L.R.R.M. at 2244; In re Sullivan Motor Delivery, Inc., 56 Bankr. 28, 30 (Bankr. E.D. Wisc. 1985); Kentucky Truck Sales, 52 Bankr. at 806.

71. Section 1113 provides that where a court fails to rule on a motion to reject within thirty days, or within such extension of time as the parties have agreed upon, the debtor may unilaterally alter or terminate the agreement pending the court's decision. 11 U.S.C. § 1113(d)(2).

72. Mile Hi Metal Systems, Inc., 51 Bankr. at 510; Sullivan Motor Delivery Inc., 56 Bankr at 30.

73. 11 U.S.C. § 365(g).

74. 11 U.S.C. § 502(g).

75. 11 U.S.C. § 1126(a), (c), (e). However, the debtor could successfully classify the rejection claims separately under the plan, thereby diffusing the voting leverage of the claims. See Teamsters National Freight Industry Negotiating Committee v. U.S. Truck Co., 800 F.2d 581, 586 (6th Cir. 1986) (union opposed classification of rejection damages claim as a separate class of unsecured claims). Arguably, a classification of this type would not be justified because of the Bankruptcy Code's requirement that a creditor class contain ''substantially similar'' claims. 11 U.S.C. § 1123(a). However, this requirement has not been extended to require that all claims of the same type, e.g., all general unsecured claims, be classified together. *Teamsters v. U.S. Truck*, 800 F.2d at 585; see also Barnes v. Whalen, 689 F.2d 193 (D.C. Cir. 1982). But see Granada Wines, Inc. v. New England Teamsters and Trucking Industry Pension Fund, 748 F.2d 42 (1st Cir. 1984).

76. Cf. In re U.S. Truck Co., Inc., 74 B.R. 515, 528–530 Bankr. E.D. Mich. 1987 (new agreement effective after courtordered rejection of collective-bargaining agreement

did not eliminate a rejection claim because new agreement was not a voluntary modification of the prior agreement).

77. Teamsters v. IML Freight, 789 F.2d 1460, 1463 (10th Cir. 1986).

78. In re Gee & Missler Services, Inc. 62 Bankr. 841, 843 (Bankr. E.D. Mich. 1986) (legislative history demonstrates that the limitation described in 11 U.S.C. § 502(b)(7) applies to contracts of key employees and not employees subject to a collective-bargaining agreement).

79. 11 U.S.C. § 502(c). Under this section, "there shall be estimated for purpose of allowance . . . any contingent or unliquidated claim" where liquidation "would unduly delay the administration of the case." Practically, estimation by the court results in a preliminary ruling on allowance of the claim, with potentially adverse results. See, e.g., Bittner v. Borne Chemical, 691 F.2d 134 (3d Cir. 1982) (court estimated value of stockholders' state law tort claims at zero for voting purpose); see also In re Continental Airlines Corp., 64 Bankr. 865, 868, 874 (Bankr. S.D. Tex. 1986) (Bankruptcy court estimated rejection damages at zero).

80. 11 U.S.C. § 507(a)(4).

81. See In re Schatz Federal Bearings Co., 5 Bankr. 543 (Bankr. S.D.N.Y. 1980) (court found that employer's pension plan obligations were incorporated in the collective-bargaining agreement, giving rise to the union's "claim" for unpaid contributions).

82. See 29 U.S.C. §§ 1002(21); 1132(a)(3).

83. See Murphy v. Heppenstall Co., 635 F.2d 233 (3d Cir. 1980), cert. denied, 454 U.S. 1142 (1982); In re M&M Transportation Co., 3 Bankr. 722 (S.D.N.Y. 1980).

84. 29 U.S.C. § 1381 et seq.

85. See Trustees of Amalgamated Ins. Fund v. McFarlin's Inc., 789 F.2d 98 (2d Cir. 1986).

86. 29 U.S.C. § 1405(b); *Granada Wines*, 748 F.2d at 42.

87. *Bildisco*, 465 U.S at 534; Kentucky Truck Sales, 52 Bankr. at 806.

88. *Briggs Transportation*, 116 L.R.R.M. at 2241; In re Crowe & Associates, 713 F.2d 211 (6th Cir. 1983); In re Petrusch, 667 F.2d 297 (2d Cir.), cert. denied, 456 U.S. 974 (1981). See also 130 Cong. Rec. S8898 (statement of Sen. Packwood).

89. 11 U.S.C. § 362(b)(4), (5). NLRB v. Evans Plumbing Co., 639 F.2d 291 (5th Cir. 1981); Nicholas, Inc. v. NLRB, 55 Bankr. 212 (Bankr. D.N.J. 1985); 11 U.S.C. § 362(b)(4), (5).

90. See Nathanson v. NLRB, 344 U.S. 25 (1952) (back-pay award was a claim in bankruptcy subject to the priority scheme of the Bankruptcy Act).

91. Nolde Brothers, Inc. v. Local 358, Bakery Workers, 430 U.S. 243 (1977); Truck Drivers Local Union No. 807 v. Bohack Corp., 567 F.2 237 (2d Cir. 1976), cert. denied, 439 U.S. 825 (1978).

92. See, e.g., *Bildisco*, 465 U.S. at 534.

93. *Nathanson*, 344 U.S. at 30; Garland Coal & Mining v. United Mine Workers, 778 F.2d 1297 (8th Cir. 1985).

94. See, e.g., *Century Brass Products*, 795 F.2d 265.

95. United Steelworkers v. Unimet Corp., 842 F. 2d 879 (6th Cir. 1988).

96. 17 Bankr. Ct. Dec. (CRR) 926 (Bankr. E.D. Mo. 1988).

97. New York Typographical Union v. Royal Composing Room Inc., 848 F. 2d 345 (2d Cir. 1988).

98. Id. at 349.

99. Id. at 354–55 (Feinberg, J. dissenting).

100. Id. at 348–49. The dissent argued that the majority's holding does not actually follow *Carey* because antiunion or other modifications that create no savings would be permitted as part of the proposal as long as the focus is on whether the proposal as a whole is necessary. Such modifications could not be said to significantly aid the reorganization, yet would still be permitted under the majority's interpretation of the ''necessary'' standard. Id. at 354–55.

101. H.R. 2659, 100th Cong. 2d. Sess.

102. 11 U.S.C. § 1114(c).

103. 11 U.S.C. § 1114(b)(2).

104. 11 U.S.C. § 1114(f)(1)(a). Legislative statements at the time of enactment make clear that the ''necessary modifications'' standard is a stringent one, intended to permit only modifications that are necessary to prevent liquidation of the debtor. 134 Cong. Rec. H3488 (daily ed. May 23, 1988) (statement of Rep. Edwards); 134 Cong. Rec. S6825 (daily ed. May 26, 1988) (statement of Sen. Metzenbaum). Senator Metzenbaum cited the *Wheeling-Pittsburgh* standard as the applicable rule and rejected the less stringent *Carey Transportation* standard as not affording the full protection intended by the statute.

105. 11 U.S.C. § 1114(g).

106. 134 Cong. Rec. S6825 (daily ed. May 26, 1988) (statement of Sen. Metzenbaum).

107. 11 U.S.C. § 1114(e)(2).

108. 11 U.S.C. § 1129(a)(13).

BIBLIOGRAPHY

BOOKS

American Law Institute, Restatement (Second) of Contracts (1979).
S. Anderman, Unfair Dismissal (3d ed. 1985).
F. Baldwin, Conflicting Interests (1984).
E. Batstone, I. Boraston & S. Frenkel, Shop Stewards in Action (1977).
F. Bartosic & R. Hartley, Labor Relations Law in the Private Sector (2d ed. 1986).
R. Beaumont & R. Helfgott, Management, Automation and the People (1964).
R. Blanpain, F. Blanquet, F. Herman & A. Mouty. The Vredeling Proposal: Information and Consultation of Employees in Multinational Enterprises (1983).
B. Bluestone & B. Harrison, The Deindustrialization of America (1982).
D. Bok & J. Dunlop, Labor and the American Community (1970).
S. Cobb & S. Kase, Termination: The Consequence of Job Loss (1977).
R. Cole, Work Mobility and Participation (1979).
1(BNA) Collective Bargaining Negotiations and Contracts (1983).
2(BNA) Collective Bargaining Negotiations and Contracts (BNA 1987).
2 Collier on Bankruptcy (15th ed. 1987).
The Continuous Learning/Employment Security Connection (J. Rosow & R. Zager eds. 1987).
W. Daniels & N. Millward, Workplace Industrial Relations in Britain (1983).
P. Davies & M. Freedland, Labour Law: Text and Materials (2d ed. 1984).
The Developing Labor Law (C. Morris ed. 1983 plus supplements).
J. Dunlop, Dispute Resolution: Negotiation and Consensus Building (1984).
F. Elkouri & E. Elkouri, How Arbitration Works 304-10 (4th ed. 1985).
Employment Security in a Free Economy (J. Rosow & R. Zager eds. 1984).
O. Fairweather, Practice and Procedure in Labor Arbitration (2d ed. 1983).
Featherbedding and Technological Change (P. Weinstein ed. 1965).
R. Freeman & J. Medoff, What Do Unions Do? (1984).

S. Gompers, Seventy Years of Life and Labor: An Autobiography (N. Salvatore ed. 1984).
T. Hanami, Labour Law and Industrial Relations in Japan (1979).
M. Hill, Jr. & A. Sinicropi, Management Rights—A Legal and Arbitral Analysis (1986).
M. Josephson, The Robber Barons (1962).
T. Kennedy, Automation Funds and Displaced Workers (1962).
L. King, Collier Handbook for Creditors' Committees (1988).
T. Kochan, H. Katz & R. McKersie, The Transformation of American Industrial Relations (1986).
T. Kochan, H. Katz & N. Mower, Worker Participation and American Unions: Threat or Opportunity? (1984).
W. Kolvenbach, Employee Councils in European Companies (1978).
R. Marshall, Unheard Voices: Labor and Economic Policy in a Competitive World (1987)
R. Meidner, Employee Investment Funds (1978).
P. Miscimarra, The NLRB and Managerial Discretion: Plant Closings, Relocation, Subcontracting and Automation (1983).
K. Murphy, Technological Change Clauses in Collective Bargaining Agreements (1981).
R. Nader, M. Green & J. Seligman, Taming the Giant Corporation (1976).
J. O'Reilly, Unions' Right to Company Information (1981).
S. Perlman, A Theory of the Labor Movement (1928).
Plant Closing Legislation (A. Aboud ed. 1984).
F. Schmidt, Law and Industrial Relations in Sweden (1977).
P. Selznik, Law, Society and Industrial Justice (1969).
G. Shultz & A. Weber, Strategies for the Displaced Worker (1966).
J. Slain, C. Thompson & F. Bein, Agency , Partnership and Employment: A Transactional Approach (1980).
Teamwork: Joint Labor-Management Programs in America (J. Rosow, ed. 1986).
B. Townley, Labor Law Reform in U.S. Industrial Relations (1986).
Unions Today: New Tactics to Tackle Tough Times (BNA 1985).
U.S. Dept. of Commerce, Statistical Abstract of the United States (1987).
L. Wedderburn, The Worker and the Law (1986).
H. Wellington, Labor and the Legal Process (1968).
A. Whitehill & S. Takezawa, The Other Worker (1968).

ARTICLES, CHAPTERS, AND REPORTS

Aaron, "Plant Closings: American and Comparative Perspectives," 59 Chi.-Kent L. Rev. 941 (1984).
Abramowitz, "Broadening the Board: Labor Participation in Corporate Governance," 34 Sw. L.J. 963 (1980).
Adams, "Changing Employment Patterns of Organized Workers," 108 Monthly Lab. Rev., Feb. 1985, at 25.
"AFL-CIO Rejuvenation Program," 109 Monthly Lab. Rev. 14–15 (Jan. 1986).
Alchian & Demsetz, "Production, Information Costs and Economic Organization," 62 Amer. Econ. Rev. 777 (1972).
American Federation of State, Country and Municipal Employees, AFL-CIO, Facing the Future—AFSCME's Approach to Technology, 1986.
"Analysis of U.S. Labor Law and Future of Labor-Management Cooperation," Report

of Deputy Undersecretary of Labor for Labor-Management Relations, reprinted in (BNA) Daily Lab. Rep., June 17, 1986, at D1.

Anderman, "Unfair Dismissals and Redundancies," in Labour Law in Britain 439 (R. Lewis ed. 1986).

Anthony, "Japan," in Managing Workforce Reduction: An International Survey 92 (M. Cross ed. 1981).

Baer, "Duty to Provide Information during Collective Bargaining," N.Y.L.J., Mar. 2, 1984, at 3, col. 1.

Bamber, "New Technology—The Challenge to Unions: A Comparative View," 37 Lab. L.J. 502 (Apr. 1986).

Barbash, "Do We Really Want Labor on the Ropes?," Harv. Bus. Rev., July-Aug. 1985, at 10ff.

"Bargaining about Business Changes; What Would Be Beneficial for Labor-Management Relations?" (BNA) Labor Relations Yearbook—1981 at 315; 4(CCH) Lab. L. Rep. ¶ 9271 (Ad. Mem. of General Counsel, Nov. 30, 1981).

Bellace, "Disclosure of Information to Unions in the United States and Britain," in Proceedings of the Fiftieth Anglo-American Conference on Law, in London, England (1982).

Bellace & Gospel, "Disclosure of Information to Trade Unions: A Comparative Perspective," 122 Int'l. Lab. Rev. 57 (1983).

Berle, "For Whom Corporate Managers *Are* Trustees: A Note," 45 Harv. L. Rev. 1365 (1932).

Berquist, "Worker Participation in Decisions within Undertakings in Sweden," 5 Comp. Lab. L. 65 (1982).

Blades, "Employment at Will v. Individual Freedom: On Limiting the Abusive Exercise of Employer Power," 67 Colum. L. Rev. 1404 (1967).

Blanpain, "Belgium," in International Encyclopedia of Labor Law and Industrial Relations 116 (R. Blanpain ed. 1985).

Blanpain, "Structural Adjustment in Industrial Relations: Labour Law Aspects," 10 Lab. & Soc'y 175 (1985).

Block & Miller, "The Responsibilities and Obligations of Corporate Directors in Takeover Contests," 11 Sec. Reg. L.J. 44 (1983).

Bok, "Reflections on the Distinctive Character of American Labor Law," 84 Harv. L. Rev. 1394 (1971).

Bordewieck & Countryman, "The Rejection of Collective Bargaining Agreements by Chapter 11 Debtors," 57 Am. Bankr. L.J. 293 (1983).

Bosch, "West Germany," in Managing Workforce Reduction: An International Survey 164 (M. Cross ed. 1985).

Brudney, "Corporate Governance, Agency Costs, and the Rhetoric of Contract," 85 Colum. L. Rev. 1403 (1985).

Cantor, "*Buffalo Forge* and Injunctions against Employer Breaches of Collective Bargaining Agreements," 1980 Wis. L. Rev. 247.

Cohen, "How Congress Disposed of What Carter Proposed," 10 Nat'l J. 1689 (Oct. 21, 1978).

Comment, "Automation and the Work Preservation Doctrine: Accommodating Productivity and Job Security Interests," 32 U.C.L.A. L. Rev. 135 (1984).

Comment, "Union Busters and Front Line Supervisors: Restricting and Regulating the

Use of Supervisory Employees by Management Consultants during Union Representation Campaigns,'' 135 U. Pa. L. Rev. 453 (1987).
Comment, ''Wrongful Termination of Employees at Will: The California Trend,'' 78 Nw. U.L. Rev. 259 (1983).
Communications Workers of America (CWA) Training Department, Technological Change: Challenges and Choices (1985).
Comptroller General, General Accounting Office, Report to the Committee on Finance of the United States Senate, HRD-80-88, ''Employee Stock Ownership Plans: Who Benefits Most in Closely Held Companies?'' (1980).
Cordova, ''Collective Bargaining,'' in Comparative Labour Law and Industrial Relations 307 (R. Blanpain ed. 1986).
Countryman, ''Executory Contracts in Bankruptcy, Part I,'' 57 Minn. L. Rev. 439 (1973); ''Part II,'' 58 Minn. L. Rev. 479 (1974).
Cox, ''Labor Decisions of the Supreme Court at the October Term, 1957,'' 44 Va. L. Rev. 1057 (1958).
Cox, ''The Legal Nature of Collective Bargaining Agreements,'' 57 Mich. L. Rev. 1 (1958).
Cox, ''Rights under a Labor Agreement,'' 69 Harv. L. Rev. 601 (1956).
Dahiem, ''The Practice of Codetermination on the Management Level of German Enterprises,'' in Participation in Management: Industrial Democracy in Three West European Countries (W. Albeda ed. 1977).
Daniel, ''The United Kingdom,'' in Managing Workforce Reductions: An International Survey 67 (M. Cross ed. 1985).
Davies, ''Employee Representation on Company Boards and Participation in Corporate Planning,'' 38 Mod. L. Rev. 254 (1975).
Dickens & Bain, ''A Duty to Bargain? Union Recognition and Information Disclosures,'' in Labour Law in Britain, ch. 3 (R. Lewis ed. 1986).
Docksey, ''Employee Information and Consultation Rights in Member States of the European Communities,'' 7 Comp. Lab. L.J. 32 (1985).
Dodd, ''For Whom Are Corporate Managers Trustees?,'' 45 Harv. L. Rev. 1145 (1932).
Dose-Digenopoulos & Holand, ''Dismissal of Employees in the Federal Republic of Germany,'' 48 Mod. L. Rev. 539 (1985).
Easterbrook & Fischel, ''The Proper Role of Target's Management in Responding to a Tender Offer,'' 94 Harv. L. Rev. 1161 (1981).
Eklund, ''A Look at Labour Law in the Context of Transfers of Undertakings,'' 7 Comp. Lab. L.J. 71 (1985).
''Employee Ownership,'' National Center for Employee Ownership Newsletter, vol. 6, no. 3, May-June 1986, at 1.
Epstein, ''A Common Law for Labor Relations: A Critique of the New Deal Labor Legislation,'' 92 Yale L.J. 1357 (1983).
Estreicher, ''Strikers and Replacements,'' 3 Lab. Lawy. 897 (1987).
Estreicher, ''Unjust Dismissal Laws: Some Cautionary Notes,'' 33 Am. J. Comp. L. 310 (1985).
Estreicher & Wolff, Report of Committee on Labor and Employment Law, ''At-Will Employment and the Problem of Unjust Dismissal,'' 36 Record of the Assn. of the Bar of the City of N.Y. 170 (April 1981).
Fahlbeck, ''The Swedish Act on Joint Regulation of Working Life,'' in Law and the Weaker Party 145 (A. Neal ed. 1981).

Feller, ''A General Theory of the Collective Bargaining Agreement,'' 61 Calif. L. Rev. 663 (1973).

Ferguson & Gaal, ''Codetermination: A Fact or a Future in America?,'' 2 Employee Rel. L.J. 176, 191 (1984).

Final Report, Lieutenant Governor of New York Task Force on Plant Closings (Mar. 1985).

Frankel, ''Fiduciary Law,'' 71 Calif. L. Rev. 795 (1983).

Fraser, ''Worker Participation in Corporate Government: The U.A.W.–Chrysler Experience,'' 58 Chi.-Kent L. Rev. 949 (1981).

Fried, ''Individual and Collective Rights in Work Relations: Reflections on the Current State of Labor Law and Its Prospects,'' U. Chi. L. Rev. 1012 (1984).

Gennard, ''Great Britain,'' in Workforce Reductions in Undertakings 107 (E. Yemin ed. 1982).

Gibson, ''The New Law on Rejection of Collective Bargaining Agreements in Chapter 11,'' 58 Am. Bankr. L.J. 325 (1984).

Glendon, ''French Labor Law Reform 1982–3: The Struggle for Collective Bargaining,'' 32 Am. J. Comp. L. 449 (1984).

Gospel, ''Trade Unions and the Obligation to Bargain: An American, Swedish and British Comparison,'' 21 Brit. J. of Indus. Rel. 343 (1983).

Gould, ''On Labor Injunctions Pending Arbitration: Recasting *Buffalo Forge*,'' 30 Stan. L. Rev. 533 (1978).

Hagizawa, ''Procedures and Structures for Collective Bargaining at the Enterprise and Plant Levels in Japan,'' 7 Comp. Lab. L.J. 277 (1986).

Hamer, ''Serving Two Masters: Union Representation on Corporate Boards of Directors,'' 81 Colum. L. Rev. 639 (1981).

Hanami, ''Japan,'' in Workforce Reductions in Undertakings 173 (E. Yemin ed. 1982).

Hanami, ''Employee Participation in the Workshop and the Enterprise,'' in Comparative Labour Law and Industrial Relations, ch. 143 (R. Blanpain & F. Millard eds. 1982).

Handler & Zifchak, ''Collective Bargaining and the Antitrust Laws: The Emasculation of the Labor Exemption,'' 81 Colum. L. Rev. 459 (1981).

Harper, ''Leveling the Road from *Borg-Warner* to *First National Maintenance*: The Scope of Mandatory Bargaining,'' 68 Va. L. Rev. 1447 (1982).

Harper, ''Union Waiver of Employee Rights under the NLRA,'' pts. 1&2, 4 Indus. Rel. L.J. 335 (1981).

Hetzler & Schienstock, ''Federal Republic of Germany,'' in Toward Industrial Democracy 40 (B. Roberts ed. 1979).

Hepple, ''Great Britain,'' in International Encyclopedia of Labor Law and Industrial Relations 176 (R. Blanpain ed. 1980).

Hepple, ''Security of Employment,'' in Comparative Labour Law and Industrial Relations, ch. 20 (R. Blanpain & F. Millard eds. 1986).

Hepple, ''Transfer of Undertakings (Protection of Employment) Regulations,'' 11 Indus. L.J. 29 (1982).

Hopt, ''New Ways in Corporate Governance: European Experiments with Labor Representation on Corporate Boards,'' 82 Mich. L. Rev. 1338 (1984).

Hornig, ''The Commercial Printing Industry 1975 Automation Agreement: Its Origins and Its Impacts on the Labor-Management Relationship'' (1982) (unpublished manuscript).

H.R. Rep. 595, 95th Cong., 1st Sess. 347 (1977).

"How Representative Are Published Decisions?" in Proc. of 37th Ann. Meeting of the National Academy of [Labor] Arbitrators 170 (1984).

Hull, "Telephones, Ticket Machines and Toilets: Case Studies in Technology Change and Workers' Control," unpublished paper presented at Interuniversity Center, Dubrovnik (Jan. 1983), at 10–12.

Inagami, "Employment Adjustments in Japan," 23 Japan Lab. Bull., No. 7 (1984).

"Interlocking Directorates–Union Representation," 5 (CCH) Trade Reg. Rep., para 50, 425 (Feb. 26, 1981).

Jensen & Meckling, "Agency Costs and the Theory of the Firm," 3 J. Fin. Econ. 305 (1976).

Jensen & Ruback, "The Market for Corporate Control," 11 J. Fin. Econ. 5 (1983).

Joint Committee on Taxation, "General Explanation of the Tax Reform Act of 1986," 99th Cong., 2d Sess. (1987).

Klare, "Judicial Deradicalization of the Wagner Act and the Origins of Modern Legal Consciousness, 1937–1941," 62 Minn. L. Rev. 265 (1978).

Klee, "Worker Participation in Japan: The Employee and Enterprise Unionism," 7 Comp. Lab. L.J. 365 (1986).

Kohl, "Changing Competitive and Technology Environments in Telecommunications," in D. Kennedy, C. Craypo, & M. Lehman, Labor and Technology: Union Response to Changing Environments 53 (1981), reprinted in CWA Training Department, Technological Change: Challenges and Choices 116 (1985).

Kohler, "Dictinctions without Differences: Effects Bargaining in Light of *First National Maintenance*," 5 Indus. Rel. L.J. 402 (1983).

Koike, "Internal Labor Markets: Workers in Large Firms," in Contemporary Industrial Relations in Japan 46 (T. Shirai ed. 1983).

Kuttner, "Austerity or Collaboration," unpublished paper given at Industrial Cooperation Council Symposium on the Future of Business, Labor and Government Relations, New York City (Nov. 18–19, 1987).

Levmore, "Monitors and Freeriders in Commercial and Corporate Settings," 92 Yale L.J. 49 (1982).

Lewis, "The Role of the Law in Employment Relations," in Labour Law in Britain 20 (R. Lewis ed. 1986).

Linzer, "The Decline of Assent: At-Will Employment as a Case Study of the Breakdown of Private Law Theory," 20 Ga. L. Rev. 323 (1986).

Livingston, "An Approach to Automation," N.Y.U. 14th Ann. Conf. on Lab. 301 (1961).

Livingston, "The Impact of Automation Upon Collective Bargaining," Unpub. Address to the Association of the Bar of the City of New York, March 25, 1965.

Livingston, "Avoidance and Settlement of Strikes and Contract Disputes," N.Y.U. 20th Ann. Conf. on Lab. 323 (1968).

Livingston, "Changing Relations between Union and Management," in Trade Union Government and Collective Bargaining 285 (J. Seidman ed. 1970).

McCormick, "Union Representatives as Corporate Directors: The Challenge to the Adversarial Model of Labor Relations," 15 U. Mich. J.L. Ref. 219 (1982).

McKersie, "Union Involvement in Entrepreneurial Decisions of Business," in Challenges and Choices Facing American Labor 149–66 (T. Kochan ed. 1985).

Majerus, "Workers Have a Right to a Share of Profits," Harv. Bus. Rev., Sept.–Oct. 1984, at 42ff.

Mark, ''Technological Change and Employment: Some Results from BLS Research, 110 Monthly Lab. Rev. 26 (Apr. 1987).

Merrifield, ''Worker Participation in Decisions within Undertakings,'' 5 Comp. Lab. L. 1 (1982).

National Academy of Arbitrators, American Arbitration Association & Federal Mediation and Conciliation Service, Code of Professional Responsibility for Arbitrators in Labor-Management Disputes (1974 rev. ed.).

46th NLRB Ann. Rep. (1981).

''New Technology: The Tug of War Begins at the Bargaining Table,'' 13 Am. Lab. 3, 5 (1981).

''New Technology: What's at Stake for Management and for Workers,'' 13 Am. Lab. 2 (1981).

North Carolina Occupational Safety and Health Project and North Carolina CWA Joint Study, Office Workers Stress Survey Results, Mar. 1985.

Note, ''Automation and Collective Bargaining,'' 84 Harv. L. Rev. 1822 (1971).

Note, ''Collective Authority and Technical Expertise: Reexamining the Managerial Employee Exclusion,'' 56 N.Y.U. L. Rev. 694 (1981).

Note, ''Collective Bargaining as an Industrial System: An Argument against Judicial Revision of Section 8(a) (2) of the National Labor Relations Act,'' 96 Harv. L. Rev. 1662 (1983).

Note, ''An Economic and Legal Analysis of Union Representation on Corporate Boards of Directors,'' 130 U. Pa. L. Rev. 919 (1982).

Note, ''Implied Contract Rights to Job Security,'' 26 Stan. L. Rev. 335 (1974).

Note, ''Labor Unions in the Boardroom: An Antitrust Dilemma,'' 92 Yale L.J. 106 (1982).

Note, ''Severance Pay Claims after a Sale of Assets: ERISA Sweeps the Field,'' 60 St. John's L. Rev. 300 (1986).

Okamoto, ''Japan,'' in Toward Industrial Democracy 197 (B. Roberts ed. 1979).

Oldham, ''Organized Labor, the Environment and the Taft-Hartley Act,'' 71 Mich. L. Rev. 935 (1973).

Olson, ''Union Experiences with Worker Ownership: Legal and Practical Issues Raised by ESOPs, TRASOPs, Stock Purchases and Co-operatives,'' 1982 Wis. L. Rev. 729.

Ornati, ''Rights Arbitration and Technological Change,'' in Proceedings of the Thirty-Eighth Annual Meeting, National Academy of [Labor] Arbitrators 225 (1985).

Pelissier, ''France,'' in Workforce Reductions in Undertakings 64 (E. Yemin ed. 1982).

Plett & Gessner, ''Insolvency and the Worker: The Case of the Federal Republic of Germany,'' 12 Int'l J. Sociol. L. 307 (1984).

''President Reagan's Statement on his Decision to Let Plant Closing Bill Become Law'' (BNA) Daily Lab. Rep., Aug. 3, 1988, at D1ff.

Rabin, ''The Decline and Fall of *Fibreboard*,'' N.Y.U. 24th Ann. Conf. on Lab. 237 (1972).

Ramm, ''Federal Republic of Germany,'' in International Encyclopedia of Labor Law and Industrial Relations 177 (R. Blanpain ed. 1979).

Reisman & Campa, ''The Case for Adversarial Unions,'' Harv. Bus. Rev., May-June 1985, at 22.

Report, Committee on Inquiry on Industrial Democracy, cmnd. 6706 (London HMSO, 1977).

Report of the Biedenkopf Commission, "Codetermination in the Enterprise" (1970).
Report of the House Subcommittee on Education and Labor of the Committee on Labor-Management Relations, "Worker Dislocation, Capital Flight & Plant Closings" (Nov. 1985).
Report of the Secretary of Labor's Task Force on Economic Adjustment and Worker Dislocation, Dec. 31, 1986, reprinted in (BNA) Daily Lab. Rep., Jan. 13, 1987, at D1ff.
Reports of the 10th International Congress of International Society of Labor Law and Social Security, "Termination of Employment on Initiative of the Employer," 5 Comp. Lab. L.J. 221 (1982).
Ricardi, "Worker Participation in Decisions within Undertakings in the Federal Republic of Germany," 5 Comp. Lab. L. 23 (1982).
Roberts, "Introduction," in Toward Industrial Democracy 19 (B. Roberts ed. 1979).
Ross, "The Teamsters' Response to Technological Change: The Example of Piggybacking," 21 Lab. L.J. 283 (Apr. 1970).
Ross, "Waterfront Labor Response to Technological Change: A Tale of Two Unions," 21 Lab. L.J. 397 (June 1970).
S. Rep. 989, 95th Cong., 2d Sess. 58 (1978).
St. Antoine, "The Collective Bargaining Process," in American Labor Policy 233 (C. Morris ed. 1987).
St. Antoine, "Legal Barriers to Worker Participation in Management Decision Making," 58 Tul. L. Rev. 1301 (1984).
Schmidt, "Conflict and Community in Decision-Making within the Undertaking," 5 Comp. Lab. J.L. 197 (1982).
Schmidt & Neal, "Collective Agreements and Collective Bargaining," in 15 International Encyclopedia of Comparative Law, Labour Law, ch. 12 (R. Hepple ed. 1984).
Schwartz, "A Case for Federal Chartering of Corporations," 31 Bus. Law. 1125 (1976).
Schwartz, "Governmentally Appointed Directors in a Private Corporation—The Communications Satellite Act of 1962," 79 Harv. L. Rev. 350 (1965).
Sengenberger, "Federal Republic of Germany," in Workforce Reductions in Undertakings 88-89 (E. Yemin ed. 1982).
Service Employee International Union, Office Automation Series, Bargaining.
Shirai, "Characteristics of Japanese Management," in Contemporary Industrial Relations in Japan 369 (T. Shirai ed. 1983).
Shirai, "A Theory of Enterprise Unionism," in Contemporary Industrial Relations in Japan 135 (T. Shirai ed. 1983).
Small, "The Evolving Role of the Director in Corporate Governance," 30 Hastings L.J. 1353 (1979).
"Special Interest Directors," Report of the Committee on Corporation Law, 35 Record of the Assn. of the Bar of the City of N.Y. 26 (Jan.–Feb. 1980).
Statement by the Hon. Orrin G. Hatch on H.R., 5174, 9th Cong. 2d Sess. (June 29, 1984), reprinted in 1984 U.S. Code Cong. & Ad. News 576.
"Statement Examining Question 'Has Labor Law Failed?' before House Labor Subcommittee on Labor-Management Relations," (BNA) Daily Lab. Rep., June 22, 1984, at F6.
"Statements before House Labor Subcommittee on Labor-Management Relations Hearing on Labor Law, June 25, 1984," (BNA) Daily Lab. Rep., June 26, 1984, at F9.
Stone, "The Post-War Paradigm in American Labor Law," 90 Yale L.J. 1509 (1981).

Sugeno, "The Coexistence of Rival Unions at Undertakings and Unfair Labor Practices," 23 Japan Lab. Bull. No. 10 (1984).
Sugeno, "Collective Bargaining with Rival Unions—The Supreme Court's More Significant Second Ruling," 24 Japan Lab. Bull. No. 10 (1985).
Summers, "Individual Protection against Unjust Dismissal: Time for a Statute," 62 Va. L. Rev. 481 (1976).
Summers, "The Usefulness of Unions in a Modern Industrial Society—A Comparative Sketch," 58 Tul. L. Rev. 1409 (1984).
Summers, "Worker Participation in Sweden and the United States: Some Comparisons from an American Perspective," 133 U. Pa. L. Rev. 175 (1984).
Summers, "Worker Participation in the U.S. and West Germany: A Comparative Study from an American Perspective," 28 Amer. J. Comp. L. 367 (1980).
Suna, "Recent Trends in Collective Bargaining Agreements in Japan," 18 Japan Lab. Bull. No. 7 (1979).
"Sweden: Employee Funds Law Enacted," Eur. Ind. Rel. Rev. 120 (Jan. 1984).
Taylor, "Collective Bargaining," in Automation and Technological Change (J. Dunlop ed. 1962).
The Newspaper Guild and International Typographical Union, Humanizing the VDT Workplace (1985).
Unger, "The Critical Legal Studies Movement," 96 Harv. L. Rev. 563 (1983).
U.S. Dept. of Labor, Bureau of Labor Statistics, Current Wage Developments (Feb. 1987).
Vagts, "Reforming the 'Modern' Corporation: Perspectives from the German," 80 Harv. L. Rev. 23 (1966).
Victorin, "Co-Determination in Sweden: The Union Way," 2 J. Comp. Corp. L. & Sec. Reg. 111 (1979).
Weiler, "Promises to Keep: Securing Workers' Rights to Self-Organization under the NLRA," 96 Harv. L. Rev. 1769 (1983).
Weiler, "Striking a New Balance: Freedom of Contract and the Prospects for Union Representation," 98 Harv. L. Rev. 351 (1984).
Weiss, "Germany," in Encyclopedia for Labor Law and Industrial Relations (R. Blanpain ed. 1987).
Williamson, "Corporate Governance," 93 Yale L.J. 1197 (1984).
Worker Adjustment and Retraining Notification Act of 1988, reprinted in (BNA) Daily Lab. Rep., July 15, 1988, at E1ff.
Yemin, "Comparative Survey" in Workforce Reductions in Undertakings 26 (E. Yemin ed. 1982).
"You Can't Win . . . without Contract Clauses," 13 Am. Lab., No. 6 (1981).

NEWSPAPER ARTICLES

"AFL-CIO Rejuvenation Program," 109 Monthly Lab. Rev. (Jan. 1986).
Bahr, "High Noon in the Information Age," Interface, Summer, 1986, at 6.
Barbash, "Inside: The Federal Judiciary," Wash. Post, Nov. 25, 1983, at A2, col. 1.
Beazely & Russell, "Steel Union Is Balking at Further Givebacks, Terming Them Futile," Wall St. J., July 29, 1986, at 12.
Brown, "American Air's Flight-Attendant Accord Will End 2-Tier Wage Carrier Pioneered," Wall St. J., Dec. 24, 1987, at 2, col. 1.

"Chrysler Is Likely to Name UAW's Bieber to Board; Union Seen Controlling Seat," Wall St. J., Oct. 4, 1984, at 5, col. 1.

"Containerized Shipping Rules Are Illegal, Maritime Commission Says," (BNA) Daily Lab. Rep., Aug. 5, 1987, at A10.

Cowes, "Pension Funds Weather the Market Collapse," N.Y. Times, Nov. 1, 1987, § 3, at 12, col. 1.

"Debate Surrounds Swedes' Report on VDTs, Pregnancies," Guild Repr., Apr. 11, 1986, at 1.

"A Demanding Year for Labor: In Most Industries, It Faces Fierce Fights to Win Job Security," Bus. Week, Jan. 11, 1988, at 34.

"Detroit Strikes Back," N.Y. Times, Sept. 14, 1980, § 6, at 28, col. 1.

"Eastern Air Union Head Is Nominated a Director," Wall St. J., Mar. 2, 1984, at 35, col. 5.

"Eastern Air's Borman Badly Underestimated Obduracy of Old Foe," Wall St. J., Feb. 25, 1986, at 1, col. 1.

"ESOPs: Revolution or Ripoff?," Bus. Week, Apr. 15, 1985, at 94.

"Extensive Displaced Worker Program Called For in DOL Fiscal 1988 Budget," (BNA) Daily Lab. Rep., Jan. 6, 1987, at A7–9.

Feder, "GM's Cuts Reflect a Long-Term Trend," N.Y. Times, Nov. 10, 1986, at D1, col. 3.

Feder, "Production Returning to U.S.," N.Y. Times, Feb. 19, 1987, at D1, col. 3.

"Focus on Corporate Boards, Directors Feel the Legal Heat," N.Y. Times, Dec. 15, 1985, § 3, at 12, col. 3.

"GM's Cuts Reflect a Long-term Trend," N.Y. Times, Nov. 10, 1986, at D1.

"GM Chief Hits Chrysler's Plan to Seat Fraser," Wall St. J., Nov. 8, 1979, at 4, col. 1.

Gould, "Watch for a Historic Auto Pact," N.Y. Times, July 27, 1987, at A19, col. 1.

Greenhouse, "LTV Problems Stir Concerns on Survival of Steel Industry," N.Y. Times, July 28, 1986, at A1, col. 2.

Grumhaus, "What's New in Telephone Services, Taking the Joy out of an Old Job," N.Y. Times, Nov. 16, 1986, at F19.

"Guaranteed Wage Is Crux of Pier Economics," N.Y. Times, June 23, 1983, at B1, col. 1.

"Helping Workers to Work Smarter," Time, June 8, 1987, at 86.

Hicks, "Who Has to Keep a Troubled Company's Pension Promises?," N.Y. Times, Oct. 11, 1987, § 4, at 5, col. 1.

Highman, DPE Technological Change Conference, quoted in (BNA) White Collar Report, Apr. 23, 1986, at 398.

"High Tech: Blessing or Curse?," U.S. News & World Rep., Jan. 16, 1984, at 38, 43.

Holusha, "Auto Job Guarantees Sought," N.Y. Times, July 7, 1987, at D1, col. 3.

Holusha, "A New Spirit at U.S. Auto Plants," N.Y. Times, Dec. 29, 1987, at D1, col. 1.

Holusha, "The Strains of Fraser's Dual Role: Chrysler and the Auto Union Disagree over the Meaning of his Seat on the Board," N.Y. Times, May 1, 1983, at F1.

"Hometown Fights for Phillips," N.Y. Times, Feb. 11, 1985, at D1, col. 3.

"How Citizens and Businesses Rally Round When a Takeover Threat Strides into Town," Christian Sci. Monitor, Apr. 22, 1985 at 13, col. 2.

''House Subcommittee Plans Oversight Hearing on Changes at Enforcement Division of NLRB,'' (BNA) Daily Lab. Rep., June 7, 1983, at A8.

''ILA, Shippers Agree on Contract Cutting Benefits,'' Star-Ledger, Nov. 1, 1986, at 9.

Kotlowitz, ''Labor's Ultimate Weapon, the Strike Is Mostly Failing,'' Wall St. J., Oct. 13, 1986, § 1, at 6.

''Labor's New Role inside Eastern Airlines Seems to Be Succeeding,'' Wall St. J., Oct. 31, 1984, at 1, col. 6.

Lewin, ''Workers Rights in a Closing Contested,'' N.Y. Times, July 19, 1984, at D1.

''Musicians Ratify Master Contract with Nations' Recording Companies,'' (BNA) Daily Lab. Rep., Feb. 27, 1987, at A5.

''New Era for Eastern's Unions,'' N.Y. Times, Apr. 20, 1984, at D1, col. 3.

Noble, ''Labor Takes a Chair in the Board Room,'' N.Y. Times, Mar. 9, 1986, § 4, at 4, col. 3.

Noble, ''Steel Union Locals Back USX Pact,'' N.Y. Times, Jan. 19, 1987, at D1, col. 3.

Novack, ''Hidden Taxes,'' Forbes, Sept. 21, 1987, at 37.

''Power-Sharing between Management and Labor: It's Slow Going,'' Bus. Week, Feb. 17, 1986, at 37.

Raskin, ''Big Labor Tries to End Its Nightmare,'' N.Y. Times, May 4, 1986, § 3, at 1, col. 2.

Raskin, ''The Steelworkers: Limping at 50,'' N.Y. Times, June 15, 1986, § 3, at 1, col. 2.

''Retirees' Health Care Could Shock Firms; Study Says Planned Regulations Could Cause Big Economic Woes,'' L.A. Times, Nov. 12, 1987, pt. 1, at 1, col. 4.

''Rising Labor Costs Threaten New York Port,'' N.Y. Times, June 22, 1983, at A1, col. 2.

''The Risk of Putting a Union Chief on the Board,'' Bus. Week, May 19, 1980, at 149.

Salpukas, ''Labor Pact Could Foil United Bids,'' N.Y. Times, Nov. 24, 1987, at 1, col. 6.

Salpukas, ''The Maneuvering at Eastern Air,'' N.Y. Times, Dec. 24, 1987, at D2, col. 1.

Salpukas, ''New Era for Eastern's Unions: Stock Pact Changes Role,'' N.Y. Times, April 20, 1984, at D1, col. 3.

Salpukas, ''Pan Am, in a Union Deal, Ousts 2 Top Executives,'' N.Y. Times, Jan. 22, 1988, at A1, col. 2.

Salpukas, ''Pan Am Pilots at the Controls,'' N.Y. Times, Dec. 3, 1987, at D2, col. 1.

Salpukas, ''Pan Am's Unions Offer Wage Cuts for Security,'' N.Y. Times, Feb. 2, 1987, § D1, col. 1.

Salpukas, ''People Express Sale Talks Reported,'' N.Y. Times, July 3, 1986, at D1, col. 3.

Salpukas, ''Western to Be Sold by Allegis,'' N.Y. Times, Oct. 28, 1987, at D1, col. 6.

Serrin, ''Early Signs of Promise in Union 'Partnership' at Steel Company,'' N.Y. Times, Apr. 7, 1986, at A8, col. 2.

Serrin, ''Hormel Plant Shut As Troops Arrive and Strikers Thin Ranks,'' N.Y. Times, Jan. 22, 1986, at A12, col. 1.

Serrin, ''The Hormel Strike: A Union Divided,'' N.Y. Times, Apr. 21, 1986, at A12, col. 3.

Skrzychi, "Investment Fund for Steelworkers' Pension Proposed," Wash. Post, Oct. 23, 1987, at D3.

Stevenson, "Henley Lifts Stake in Santa Fe to 14%," N.Y. Times, Oct. 29, 1987, at D5, col. 1.

Stevenson, "United's Pilots Pick Acquisition Chief," N.Y. Times, Aug. 14, 1987, at D1, col. 4.

"Strains of Fraser's Dual Role," New York Times, May 1, 1983, § 3, at 1, col. 1.

"Technology Not Expected to Decrease Clerical Jobs," (BNA) Daily Lab. Rep., Oct. 1, 1986, at 1.

"The Telephone System—Changing Technology—Changing Jobs," CWA News, Oct. 1982, at 9.

"U.A.W. Proposed Ford Guarantee Jobs in New Pact," N.Y. Times, Sept. 9, 1987, at A16, col. 3.

"UAW's Fraser to Speak Out for Labor, Public in Role as Director at Chrysler," Wall St. J., Oct. 29, 1979, at 6, col. 2.

"U.S. West Brings TOPS Home," Communications Week, May 19, 1986, at 37.

Vartan, "Market Place: More Airline Mergers Seen," N.Y. Times, Sept. 11, 1986, at D8, col. 3.

Wessel, "Split Personality: Two-Tier Pay Spreads, but the Pioneer Firms Encounter Problems," Wall St. J., Oct. 14, 1985, at 1, col. 1.

"Will the Labor-Management Revolution Survive at Eastern?," Bus. Week, Jan. 20, 1986, at 64.

"World Workers Warned to Factor in Computers," Chi. Tribune, Apr. 20, 1986, at 1.

INDEX

ABOUT THE CONTRIBUTORS

MICHAEL E. ABRAM is a partner in the firm of Cohen, Weiss and Simon in New York City specializing in the representation of labor organizations under the labor laws, ERISA, and Bankruptcy Code. Mr. Abram received his bachelor of arts degree, magna cum laude, from Harvard College in 1966 and his juris doctor from Harvard Law School in 1971.

BROOKES D. BILLMAN is Professor of Law and former Director of the Graduate Tax Program at the New York University School of Law. He received his bachelor of arts degree from Princeton University in 1971, his juris doctor from the University of Cincinnati in 1974, and his LL.M. (in taxation) from New York University in 1975. In addition to teaching a full range of tax courses (including courses on qualified retirement plans), he has served as Editor-in-Chief of the *Tax Law Review*, and he has been associated with Hughes Hubbard & Reed, Paul Weiss Rifkind Wharton & Garrison, Hogan & Hartson, and Howrey & Simon.

JUDITH P. BROACH is a partner in the New York City law firm of Broach & Stulberg, representing unions, multiemployer Taft-Hartley benefit funds, and plaintiffs in employment discrimination litigation. Ms. Broach is an honors graduate of Vassar College and received her juris doctor degree in 1975 from the University of San Francisco School of Law, where she was Senior Editor of the Moot Court Board. She is a member of the New York and California bars. Ms. Broach has taught and lectured on a wide variety of topics in the labor/employment and employee benefits field under the auspices of Cornell University, the American Arbitration Association, and other entities.

BABETTE CECCOTTI is an associate in the firm of Cohen, Weiss and Simon. Ms. Ceccotti received her juris doctor from New York Law School in 1983 and a bachelor of arts degree, cum laude, from Clark University in 1977.

DANIEL G. COLLINS has been a Professor of Law at New York University School of Law since 1961, teaching contracts, labor law and labor arbitration. Previously, he was associated with the law firm of Cravath, Swaine and Moore. He is a 1951 graduate of Hofstra College, and he received his bachelor of laws from New York University in 1954, where he was Editor-in-Chief of the *Law Review*. Since 1980, he has served as an Impartial Member of the New York City Office of Collective Bargaining. He is a former Governor of the National Academy of Arbitrators and currently serves as a national arbitrator for the United States Postal Service and American Postal Workers Union and as impartial chairman for the League of American Theatres and Producers and Actor's Equity Association, and the National Basketball Association and National Basketball Players Association.

DEBRA A. DANDENEAU is an associate at Weil, Gotshal & Manges, specializing in business reorganizations. She received her bachelor of arts degree from the University of Miami in 1983 and her juris doctor from Columbia University in 1986, where she was a Harlan Fiske Stone scholar.

WILBUR DANIELS started his career with the International Ladies' Garment Workers Union in 1943. He retired as its executive vice-president in 1987. He is presently the executive director of the S.H. & Helen R. Scheuer Family Foundation. Mr. Daniels is a 1942 graduate of City College of New York; he received his law degree in 1950 from New York University.

MARVIN DICKER is a member of Proskauer Rose Goetz & Mendelsohn. He graduated from Brooklyn College in 1954 and received his law degree from Columbia University in 1957, where he was a Kent and Stone Scholar and an editor of the *Law Review*. After graduating from Columbia, he served as a law clerk to the Hon. William B. Herlands in the Southern District of New York. Mr. Dicker has been active as a member of the Labor Practice Committee of the American Arbitration Association, a speaker at the International Foundation of Employee Benefit Plans, a member of the Association of the Bar of the City of New York committees on Labor and Social Security and Arbitration, and an active member of the New York State Bar Association Labor Committee. He has recently been appointed chairman of a task force to investigate and make recommendations on changes in the Workers' Compensation Board procedures. From time to time, he has served as a faculty member at the New School for Social Research, Adelphi University, and the Practicing Law Institute. He is also chairman of the Personnel and Labor Relations Committee of the UJA-Federation in New York City.

EUGENE G. EISNER is a partner in the law firm of Eisner & Levy, P.C. with offices in Manhattan. The firm is general counsel to several large labor organizations including Local 1199, RWDSU, AFL-CIO and District 65, United Auto Workers, AFL-CIO. Mr. Eisner is a graduate of the New York University School of Law and the Cornell University School of Industrial and Labor Relations. He is an Adjunct Professor of Law at Hofstra University where he teaches courses in labor law and arbitration. He has lectured and written on numerous subjects concerning employees' rights.

SAMUEL ESTREICHER is a Professor of Law at New York University, where he teaches labor law, employment discrimination law, labor law theory, civil procedure, administrative law, and federal courts. A 1970 graduate of Columbia College, he earned his master of science degree in Labor Relations from Cornell University in 1974 and received his juris doctor degree in 1975 from Columbia University, where he was Editor-in-Chief of the *Law Review*. Upon graduating from law school, he served as law clerk to the late Harold Leventhal of the U.S. Court of Appeals for the D.C. Circuit, was an associate at Cohn, Glickstein Lurie, Ostrin & Lubell, and law clerk to Justice Lewis F. Powell, Jr., of the U.S. Supreme Court. Since 1984, he has also been Counsel to Cahill, Gordon and Reindel, specializing in labor and employment law. From 1984 to 1987, he was chair of the Committee on Labor and Employment Law of the Association of the Bar of the City of New York. He is also a member of the labor panel of the American Arbitration Association. In addition to extensive writings in the labor and employment law area, he is coauthor of *Rethinking the Supreme Court's Role* (1986) (with J. Sexton) and *The Law Regulating the Employment Relationship: Cases and Materials* (forthcoming in 1989) (with M. Harper).

JOHN D. FEERICK has served as Dean of Fordham Law School since 1982. From 1968 to 1982, he was a member of Skadden, Arps, Slate, Meagher & Flom, concentrating in the field of labor and employment law. Mr. Feerick has taught and written in this field. He currently serves as impartial chairman of labor disputes at the Jacob K. Javits Convention Center, and he is a former member of the New York City Office of Collective Bargaining. He received his bachelor of arts degree in 1958 and his bachelor of laws in 1961 from Fordham University, where he was Editor-in-Chief of the *Law Review*. He is a former vice-president of the Association of the Bar of the City of New York. Among his extensive writings, he is the author of *From Failing Hands: The Story of Presidential Succession* (1965), *The First Book of Vice-Presidents of the United States* (1967) (with E. Feerick), *The Twenty-Fifth Amendment* (1976), and *NLRB Representation Elections: Law, Practice & Procedure* (1979–80) (with H. Baer & J. Arfa).

MICHAEL C. HARPER is Professor of Law at Boston University. He is the author of numerous articles on labor, administrative and constitutional law topics, which has been published in journals both of general circulation, such as those of Harvard and Yale, and of specialized employment law interest. Professor Harper is a 1973 graduate of Harvard Law School, where he served as Supreme Court Note Editor of the *Law Review*, and a 1970 graduate of Harvard College, where he earned Phi Beta Kappa honors. A professor at Boston University since 1978, he has served as a law clerk to the late J. Skelly Wright of the Court of Appeals for the D.C. Circuit, and as an attorney in both private and public interest practice. He engages in labor arbitration, and he has delivered numerous lectures in a variety of continuing legal education forums. Among numerous writings in the labor law field, he is the coauthor of the forthcoming casebook: *The Law Regulating the Employment Relationship: Cases and Materials* (forthcoming in 1989) (with S. Estreicher).

STEPHEN L. HESTER is a partner in the Washington, D.C., law firm of Arnold & Porter. He graduated from Duke University in 1958 and from Harvard Law School, magna cum laude, in 1965. Mr. Hester specializes in legal matters related to employee ownership and the establishment of employee-owned businesses through collective bargaining. He has represented the United Steelworkers of America in connection with a number of employee stock ownership plans, including the stock plans established by such major industrial corporations as LTV Steel, Bethlehem Steel, and Kaiser Aluminum and Chemical Corporation. He has also represented the IAM Eastern Airlines Stock Plan, which was established to hold the common and preferred stock in Eastern acquired by IAM-represented employees. Mr. Hester recently represented the USWA in connection with establishment of the 70-percent employee-owned copper mine in White Pine, Michigan; this transaction was highlighted in a series of articles in the May 1987 Michigan Bar Journal as a unique example of cooperation between government, labor, and business. Mr. Hester has been a Visiting Professor at Duke University Law School and an Adjunct Professor at Georgetown University Law Center. In the past several years, he has been a speaker on employee ownership at various conferences including forums sponsored by the Harvard Business School, the Kennedy School of Government at Harvard, the AFL-CIO Lawyers Conference, and the Industrial Union Department (AFL-CIO). He is currently an employee-nominated director of Copper Range Company, and he has also served as an employee-nominated director of Continental Steel Corporation.

ANN F. HOFFMAN was a 1972 honors graduate of the University of Maryland School of Law, where she was Editor-in-Chief of the *Law Review*. Ms. Hoffman was an associate of Edelman, Levy and Rubenstein in Baltimore, Maryland, and then became Associate General Counsel of the International Ladies' Garment Workers' Union and Counsel to District One of the Communications Workers of America from 1981 to 1984. From 1979 to 1981, she served as Executive Assistant to United States Attorney General Benjamin R. Civiletti. In 1984, Ms.

Hoffman was named Administrative Assistant to the Vice President of District One of CWA. Since June 1987, Ms. Hoffman has been Director of PACE, Professional and Clerical Employees of the International Ladies' Garment Workers' Union, and Assistant Director of the ILGWU's Department of Organization and Field Services. Ms. Hoffman is the coauthor of *Bargaining for Child Care: Contract Language for Union Parents*, published in 1985 by the Coalition of Labor Union Women (CLUW) and "Comparable Worth: A Trade Union Issue," published in the Winter 1984 issue of the Women's Rights Law Reporter.

LEWIS B. KADEN is a member of Davis Polk & Wardwell, where he specializes in litigation and labor and employment law. A 1963 graduate of Harvard College, he received his LL.B. from Harvard University in 1967. He was previously Professor of Law at Columbia University and remains on its adjunct faculty. Mr. Kaden also serves as chairman of the New York Industrial Cooperation Council.

SETH KUPFERBERG is assistant general counsel of the International Ladies' Garment Workers' Union. He is a 1975 graduate of Harvard College, and he received his J.D. from Harvard University in 1979. He is the author of "Political Strikes, Labor Law and Democratic Rights" published in 1985 in the *Virginia Law Review*.

HARVEY R. MILLER is a member of Weil, Gotshal & Manges, specializing in debtors' and creditors' rights and cases under the Bankruptcy Code. He has represented Continental Airlines Corporation and its affiliates in their reorganization cases under Chapter 11; Texaco Inc. and certain of its affiliates in their Chapter 11 cases; the trustee in bankruptcy of W.T. Grant Company; and major institutional creditors or creditors' committees in reorganization cases of Braniff Airlines Corp., Storage Technology Corporation, Itel Corporation, Johns-Manville Inc., Wheeling-Pittsburgh Steel Corporation, Food Fair (Pantry Pride), Lionel Corporation, White Motor Corporation, et al., United States Lines, Inc. He has also served as special counsel to the New York Stock Exchange in connection with the financial distress of member organizations and their liquidation or sale during the early 1970s, including Goodbody & Co., Hayden Stone & Co., McDonnell & Co.; served as special counsel to the City of New York in connection with the financial crisis of the mid-1970s; and assisted in the financial restructurings of Grolier Corporation, Tosco Corporation, Ideal Basic Industries, and numerous real estate investment trusts. In addition, Mr. Miller has been Adjunct Professor of Law at New York University from 1976 to the present, visiting lecturer at Yale Law School from 1983 to 1984, a participant in many continuing legal education programs and seminars, a contributing editor to *Collier on Bankruptcy* and coauthor of *A Practical Guide to the Bankruptcy Reform Act* (1979). Mr. Miller is a 1954 graduate of Brooklyn College; he received his LL.B. from Columbia University in 1959.

PETER G. NASH is a senior partner in the firm of Ogletree, Deakins, Nash, Smoak and Stewart, specializing in management labor law. He is a magna cum laude, Phi Beta Kappa graduate of Colgate University, and a cum laude, Order of the Coif graduate of New York University Law School. He practiced labor law in Rochester, New York, from 1963 through 1969, when he commenced his federal government service as Associate Solicitor for Labor Relations and Civil Rights of the U.S. Department of Labor. In 1970 he became Solicitor of the U.S. Department of Labor, and in 1971, General Counsel of the National Labor Relations Board. In 1975 he returned to private practice in Washington, D.C. Mr. Nash is the author of over thirty publications on labor law.

SCOTT W. SCHATTENFIELD is a recent graduate of George Washington University in Washington, D.C. He has worked for the law firm of Ogeltree, Deakins, Nash, Smoak and Stewart, and he has acquired a varied background in management labor law.

HELEN SCOTT is currently Professor of Law at the New York University School of Law. Her fields of specialty are corporations and federal regulation of securities. Before joining the NYU faculty, Professor Scott was associated with the firm of Shearman & Sterling in New York, where she represented clients in a variety of public and private business transactions. Immediately after graduation from Columbia University Law School in 1977, where she was a Kent Scholar, she was an Attorney-Advisor to the Chairman of the Federal Trade Commission, working on consumer protection and trade regulation matters.

CLYDE W. SUMMERS is Fordham Professor of Law at the University of Pennsylvania; previously he taught for nineteen years at the Yale Law School. A 1939 graduate of the University of Illinois, he received his J.D. from that institution in 1942 and his LL.M. in 1946 and J.S.D. in 1952 from Columbia University. Perhaps the country's leading scholar in the field of individual employee rights, he has lectured widely here and abroad. A member of the American Association's labor panel and the National Academy of Arbitrators, he was chair of the New York Governor's Commission on Improper Union and Management Practices from 1957 to 1959; chair of the Connecticut Advisory Council on Unemployment Insurance from 1961 to 1967; an alternate member of the Connecticut Board of Mediation and Arbitration from 1965 to 1968 and of the Connecticut State Labor Relations Board from 1968 to 1971; and consultant to other federal and state governmental bodies. Among his many extensive writings, Professor Summers is coauthor of *Cases and Materials on Labor Law* (1982) (with A. Hyde and H. Wellington), *Rights of Union Members* (1979) (with R. Rabin), and of the article which helped spark the emerging American common law of unjust dismissal, entitled "Individual Protection against Unjust Dismissal: Time for a Statute," published in 1976 in the *Virginia Law Review*.

WILLIAM C. ZIFCHAK is a partner in the law firm of Kaye, Scholer, Fierman, Hays & Handler, where he has been cochair of its labor department since 1984. Mr. Zifchak specializes in the representation of management in all aspects of labor relations and employment law. He has lectured and written extensively in the field, including a work coauthored with Professor Milton Handler, "Collective Bargaining and the Antitrust Laws: The Emasculation of the Labor Exemption," published in 1981 in the *Columbia Law Review*. Mr. Zifchak served from 1984 to 1987 as secretary of the Labor Employment Law Committee in the Association of the Bar of the City of New York. He received his B.A., cum laude, from Harvard College in 1970 and his J.D. from the Columbia University School of Law in 1973.